Miami, Real and IMAGINED

Dedication

To my loving wife, Lisa Sloat, for her dedication, patience, and contribution to my recovery and my art, and for lending her excellent editing and writing skills to this project.

To my speech therapist, Ann Marie Ojeda, without whose help, persistence, and professional skill my recovery and this book would not have become a reality.

To Books & Books owner Mitchell Kaplan, for his friendship and encouragement, for introducing me to Schiffer Publishing, and for his unwavering support as my mentor and partner in this first-time venture.

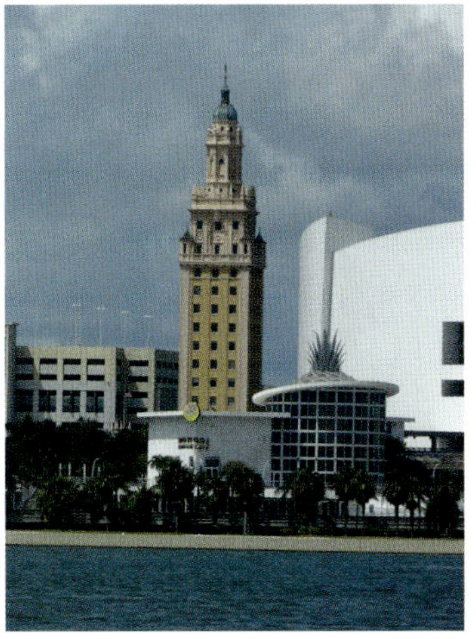

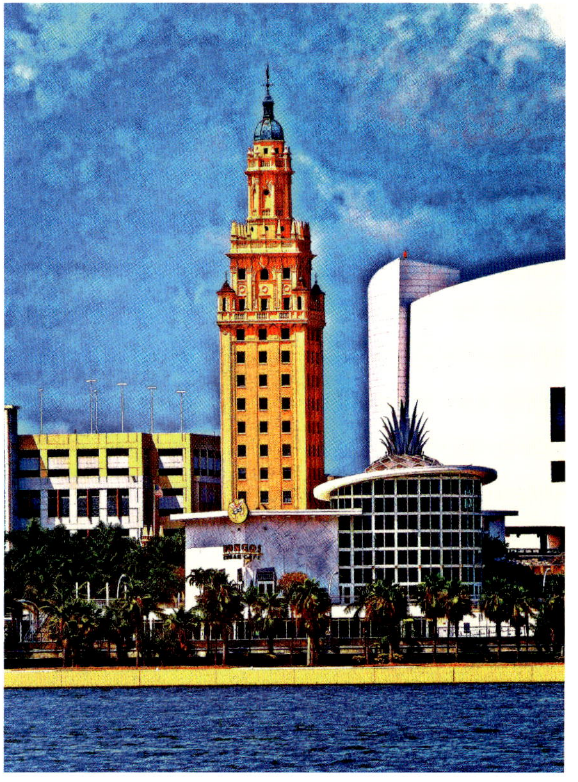

Miami, Real and IMAGINED

THE PHOTOGRAPHY OF HANK KLEIN

Schiffer Publishing Ltd®

4880 Lower Valley Road • Atglen, PA 19310

Other Schiffer Books on Related Subjects:

Miami Graffiti Art, H. Love, ISBN 978-0-7643-4564-7

Miami at Night, Bill Brothers, ISBN 978-0-7643-5028-3

Miami Contemporary Artists, Paul Clemence and Julie Davidow, ISBN 978-0-7643-2647-9

Library of Congress Control Number: 2016942872

Type set in ITC Avant Garde

ISBN: 978-0-7643-5175-4
Printed in China

Published by Schiffer Publishing, Ltd.
4880 Lower Valley Road
Atglen, PA 19310
Phone: (610) 593-1777; Fax: (610) 593-2002
E-mail: Info@schifferbooks.com
Web: www.schifferbooks.com

For our complete selection of fine books on this and related subjects, please visit our website at www.schifferbooks.com. You may also write for a free catalog.

Schiffer Publishing's titles are available at special discounts for bulk purchases for sales promotions or premiums. Special editions, including personalized covers, corporate imprints, and excerpts, can be created in large quantities for special needs. For more information, contact the publisher.

We are always looking for people to write books on new and related subjects. If you have an idea for a book, please contact us at proposals@schifferbooks.com.

Contents

Foreword

For many years I have known and admired Hank Klein, a business and community leader who has left a positive mark on his favorite city. Recently, following a stroke, he found a new passion as a photographer and what he calls a "re-imaginer." Using his knowledge of the community and his artistic eye, he has taken a series of photos and then re-envisioned the historical and traditional views with color and other enhancements. The results are amazing.

This book highlights some of his work, which he describes as being shot with his eye, his brain, and his heart. As a native Miamian and historian who knows and loves Miami, I was absolutely enchanted with his work and connected with his singular views of the Magic City. I am also impressed with his refusal to yield to health setbacks and his determination to continue his community work while discovering a new area of expertise. I highly recommend this book to anyone who wants to see Miami in a new artistic light.—Arva Moore Parks, historian and author

Preface

I have been fascinated by photography for more than fifty years. At age nineteen, after a short stint as a copy boy, I was hired as a staff photographer for the *Miami News*, a widely read, though now defunct, afternoon newspaper. While much of what I photographed had to do with local events, I had the opportunity to photograph the Beatles when they arrived in Miami Beach to appear on the Ed Sullivan show, President Truman at his Key West "White House," and Mohammed Ali when he was still known as Cassius Clay and trained in Miami Beach.

In my thirties I entered the business world, and photography was relegated to the hobby shelf. I established a successful career in commercial real estate and took a leadership role in civic activities. During those years I took very few photos. I often said that business "suppressed" my creativity.

On June 29, 2012, my life changed dramatically. I had a life-threatening stroke that left me unable to communicate verbally or in writing, unable to read the nonfiction books I so loved, unable to comprehend television or a movie. My world narrowed to therapy sessions, naps, and doctor appointments. When not in therapy, I spent hours sitting under a tree, listening to music and staring at the sky. I became so bored that one day I picked up my iPhone and took a photo of the palm tree above me. I taught myself to use a phone app and began to manipulate photos to make my own unique designs. And there a love affair began!

Since that fateful day, I have become what I call "a great manipulator." I am always searching for new apps and finding new ways to enhance my photos. I let my imagination take over as I change colors and textures and re-crop my photos to create unique pieces of art. Today, I am nearly 100 percent recovered, and I owe much of my recovery to rediscovering my love of photography.

I have lived in Miami since 1957. I love this city—its vibrancy, mix of cultures, and complexity. I am thrilled that my first book features Miami, filtered through a combination of my vision, imagination, and heart. In this book, you will see my original photos and then my re-imagined work.

And the captions are re-imagined, too. From the concept of haiku, a form of Japanese poetry, I have created what I call with a wink, "Hank-ku."

I hope you enjoy my art as much as I enjoy having the opportunity to share it with you.

Acknowledgments

A very special thank you to Arva Moore Parks. She is an exceptional person who truly loves Miami, and it means a great deal to have the support of such an important author and historian.

Chapter One

BUILDINGS

The buildings in this chapter represent the colorful and culturally eclectic past, present, and future of Miami. While many are considered iconic, others are little known. By historical standards, Miami is considered a "young" city. The effects of real estate booms and busts can be seen in the architectural landscape. Most of Miami's oldest structures were built during the real estate boom of the 1920s. Each has a story to tell. For example, the Freedom Tower, on the front cover of this book, was built in 1925 to house the now-defunct *Miami News*. Abandoned for many years, the tower got its name in the early 1960s, when it became the "Ellis Island" of Miami welcoming Cubans fleeing the communist Castro regime. Today, the Freedom Tower is owned by Miami Dade College, the nation's largest community college. The last photo in this chapter shows one of Miami's newest icons—the Perez Art Museum, representing the city's future as a growing presence in the world art scene. This collection of buildings offers a glimpse of the unique and colorful world of Miami's ever-changing communities.

FREEDOM TOWER

Freedom Tower is our Ellis Island
Beginning in 1959
It welcomed hundreds of thousands of Cuban refugees
Originally built in 1925, it changed our community
Forever

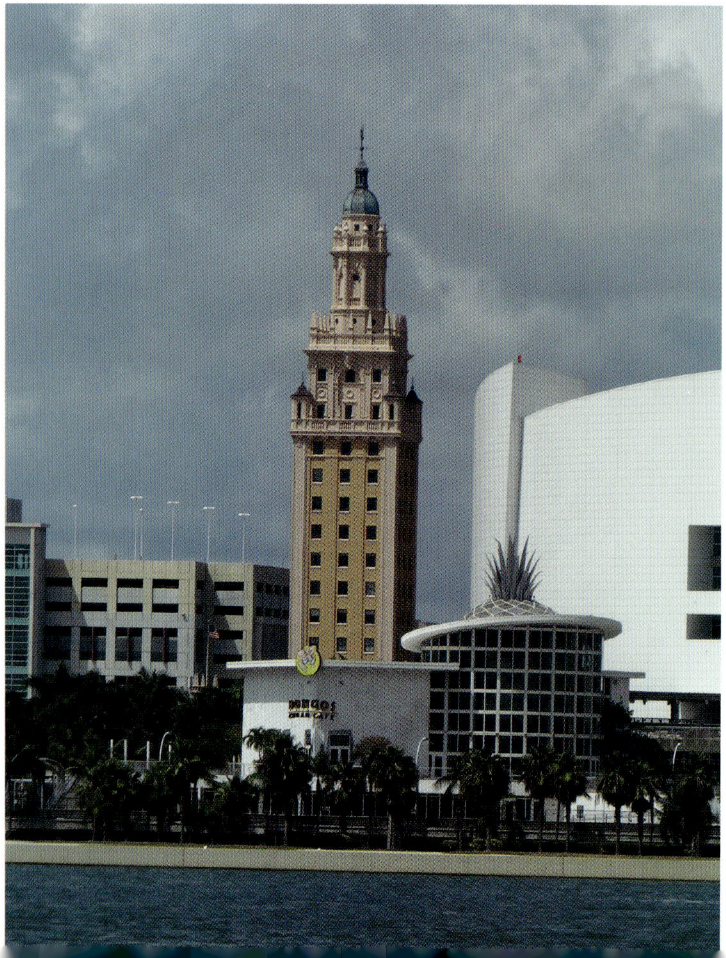

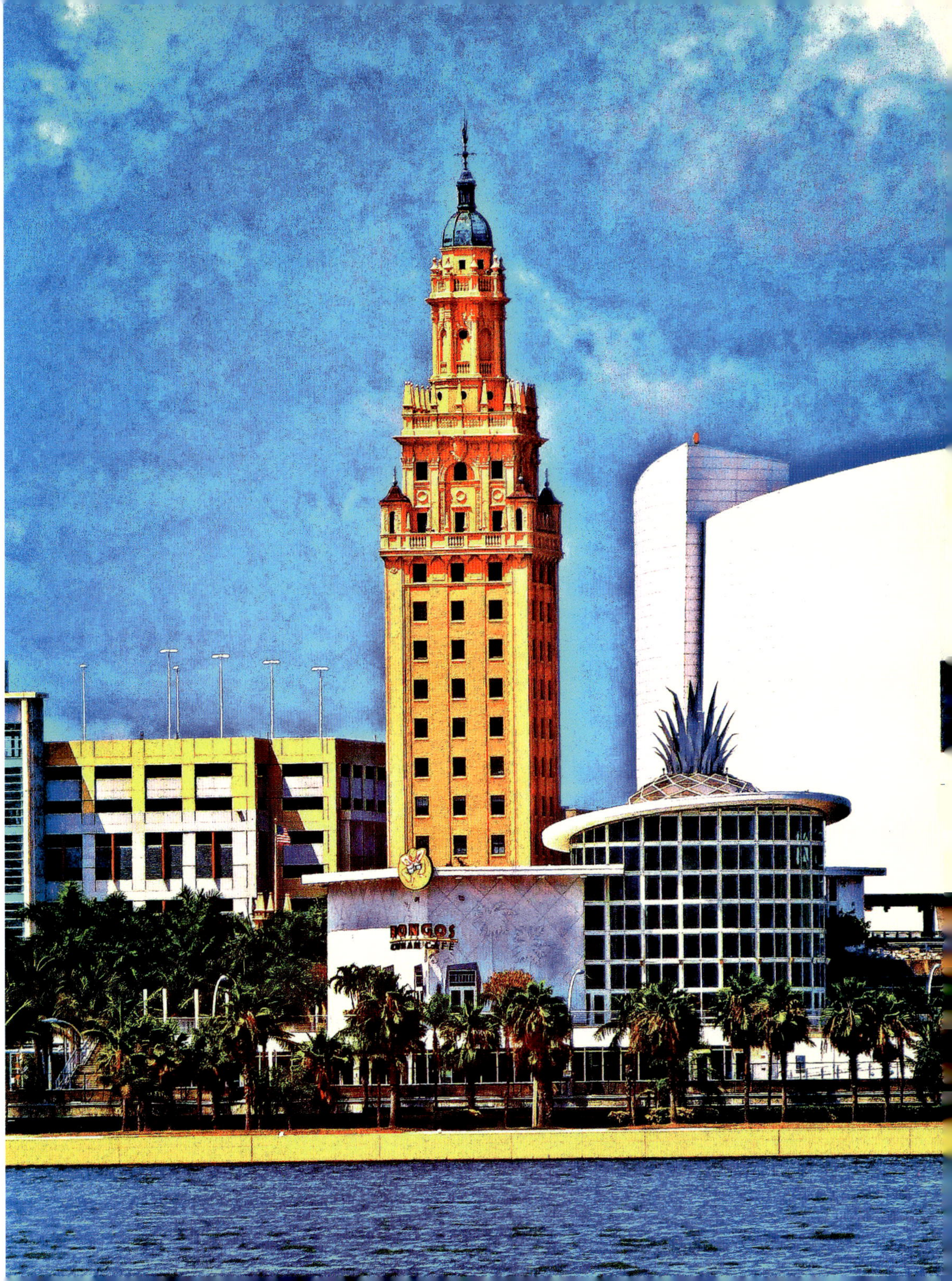
BONGOS

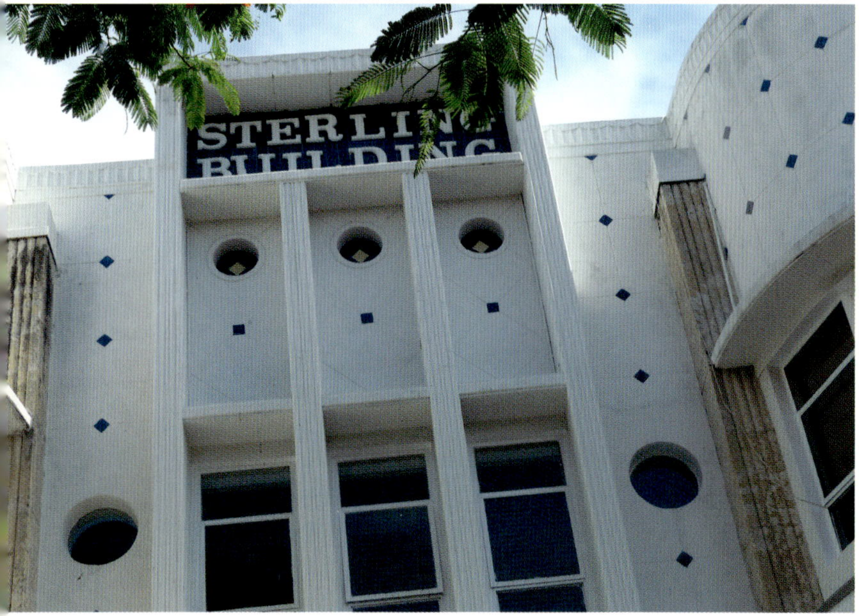

STERLING BUILDING

An example of art deco 1930s architecture
It began as a positive image
Transformed into a photographic negative image
South Beach beauty

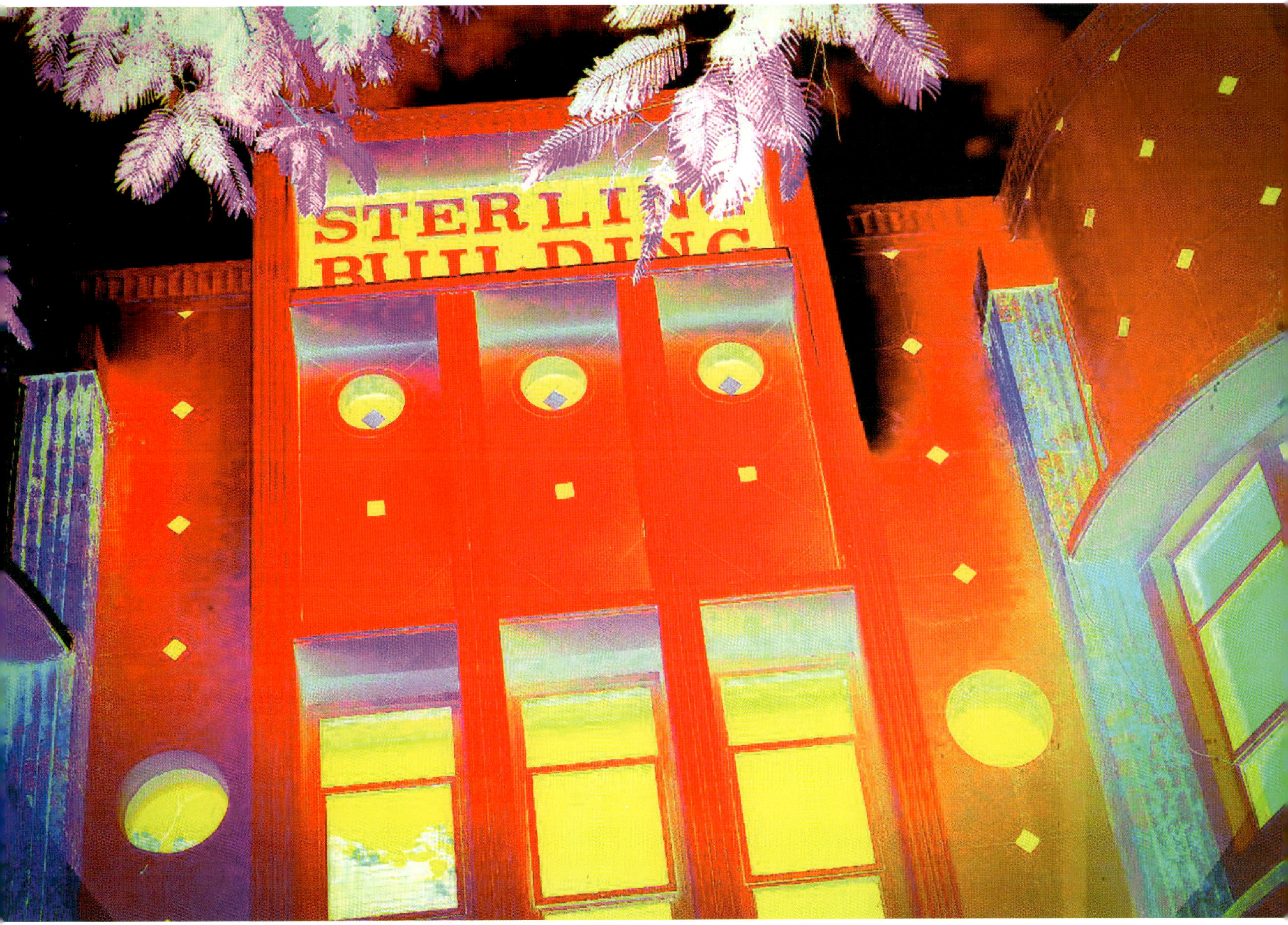

WATER TOWER

Coral Gables water tower
Built in 1924
It was abandoned and then revived in 1993
I gave it two views
An ooh and an aah

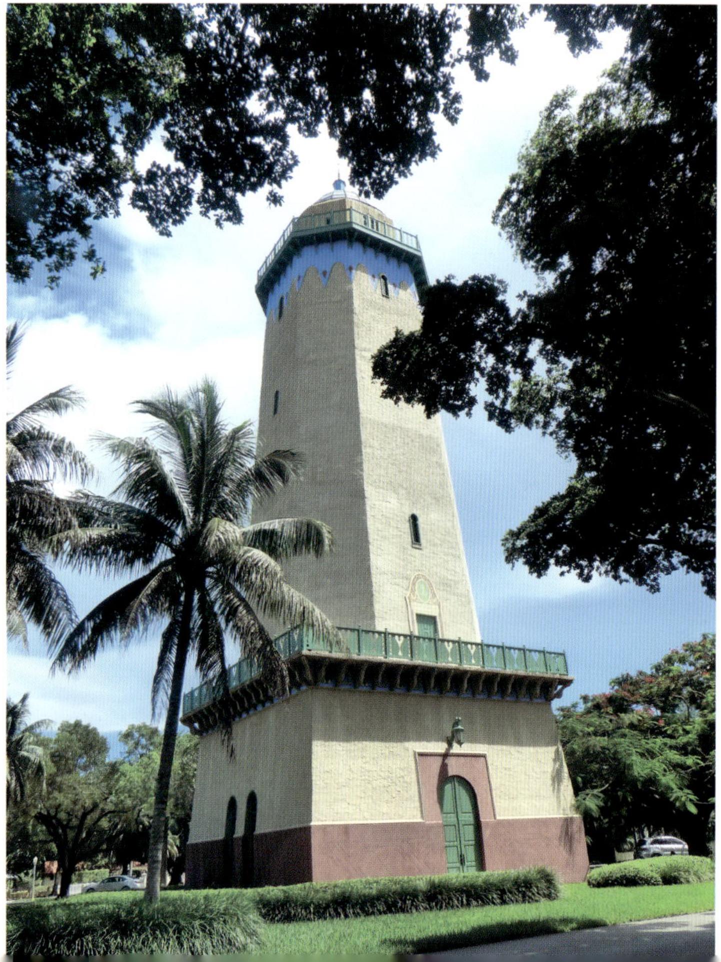

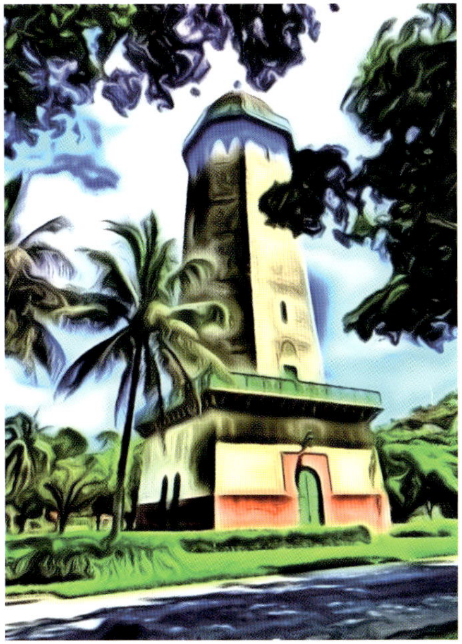

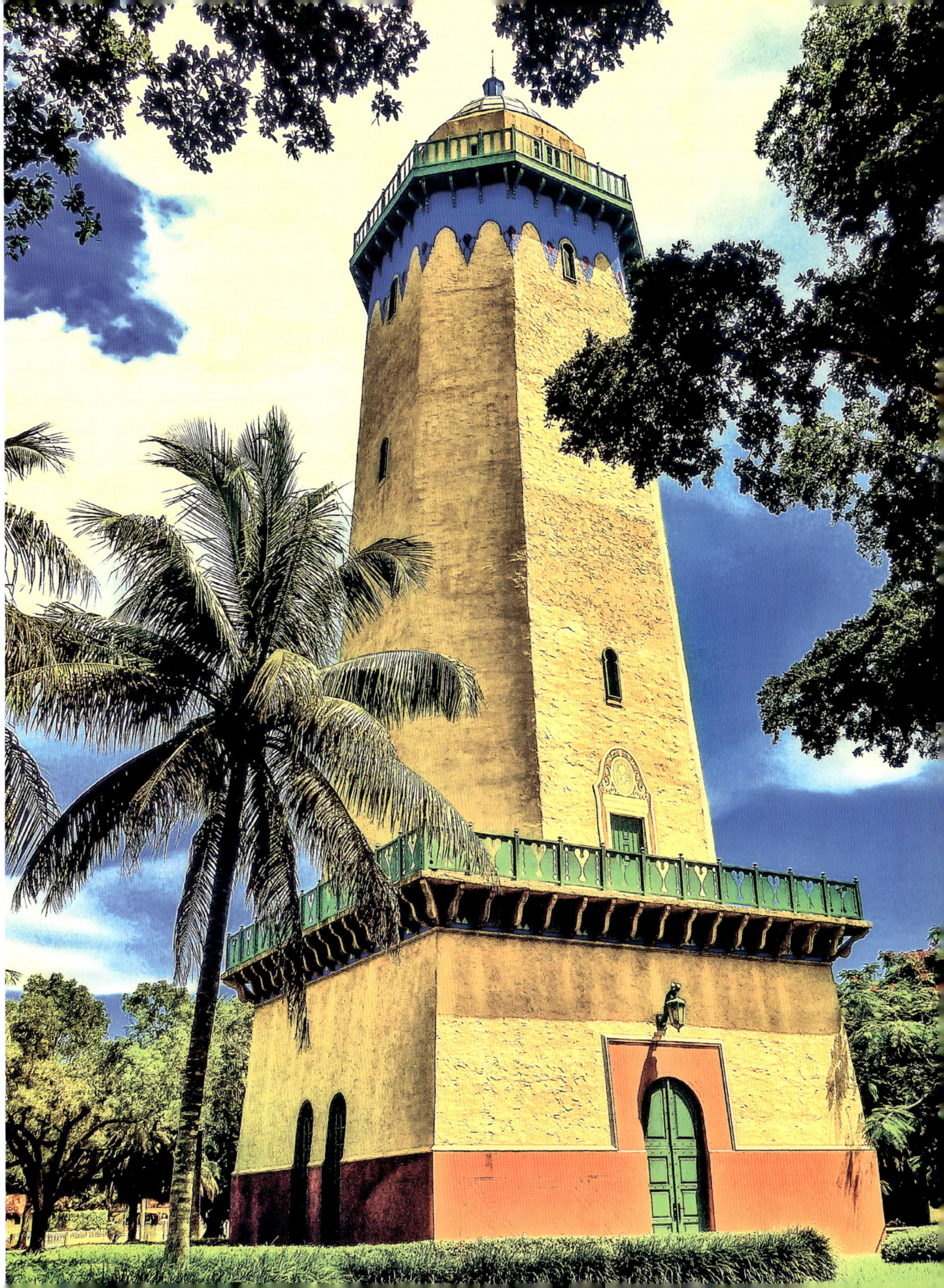

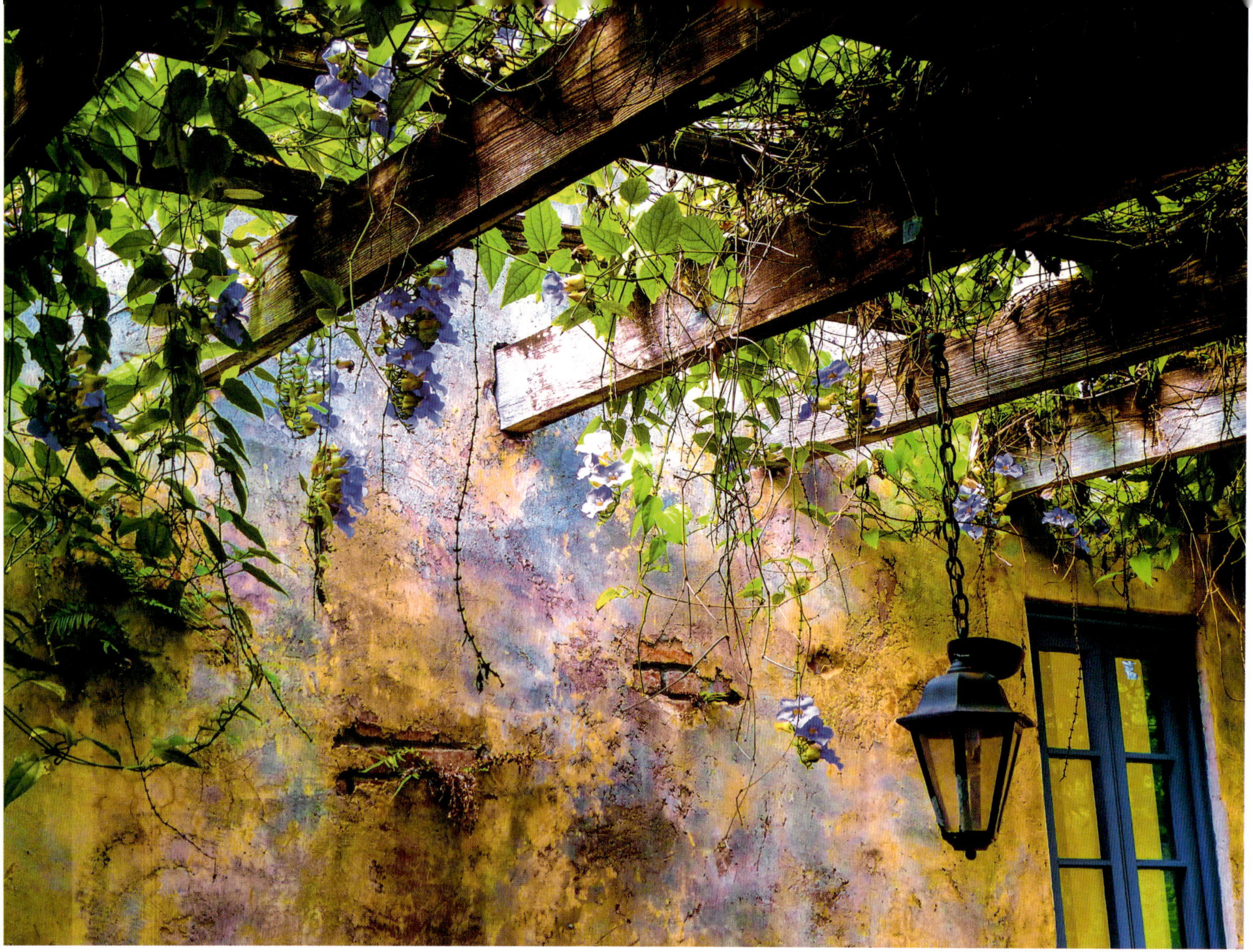

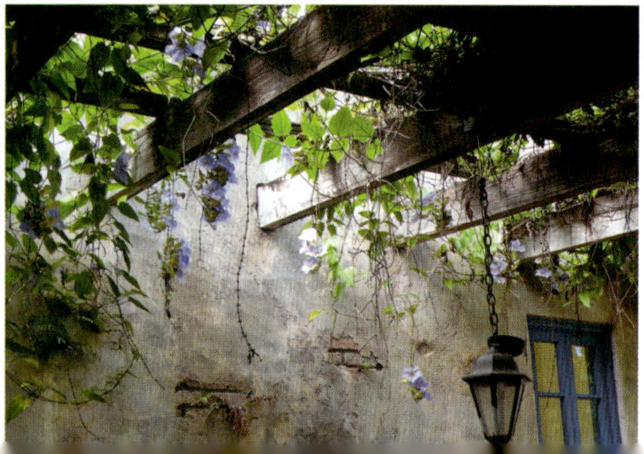

VENETIAN POOL

Entrance to a public pool
In Coral Gables
This pool is peaceful
Quiet

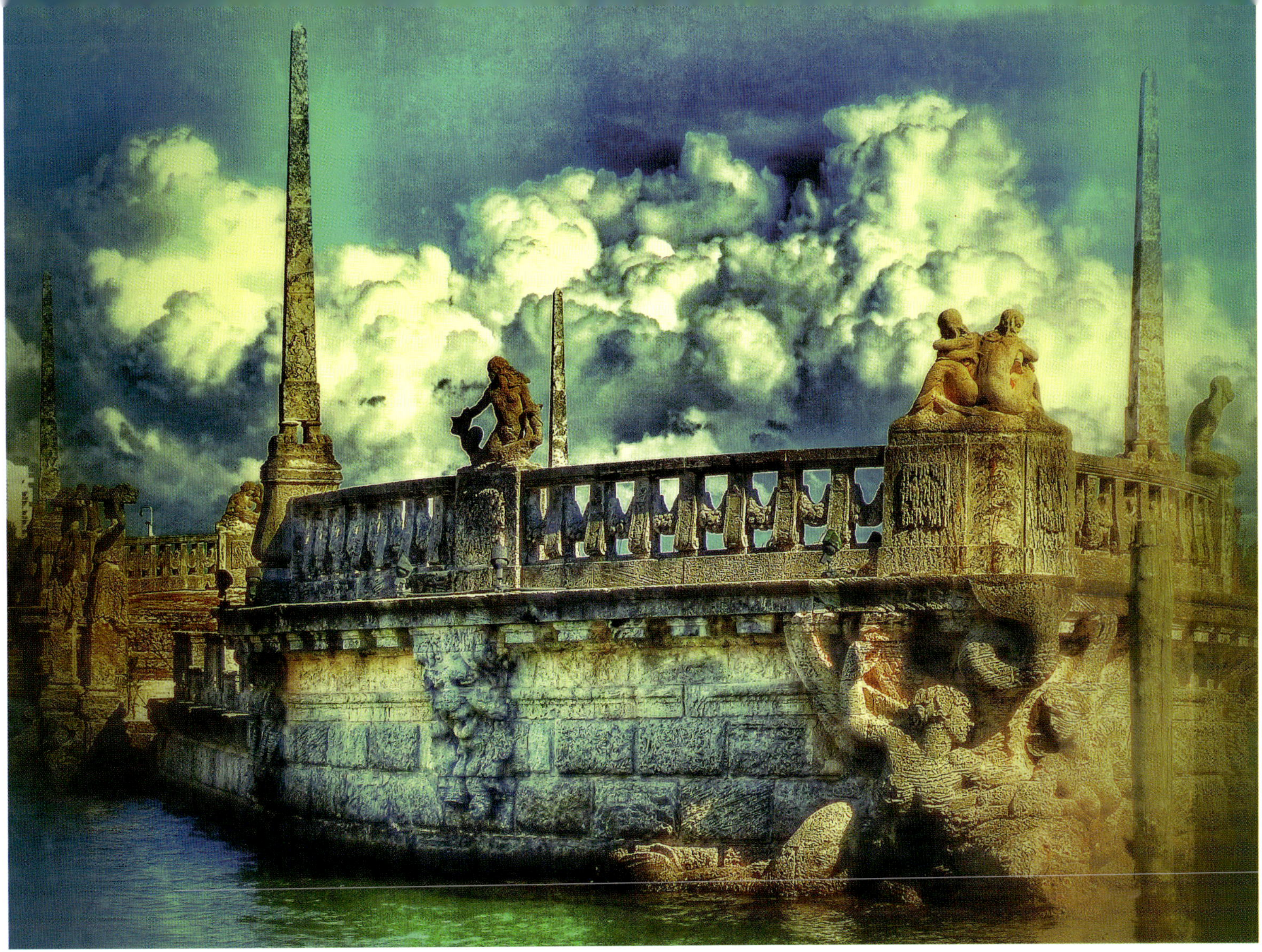

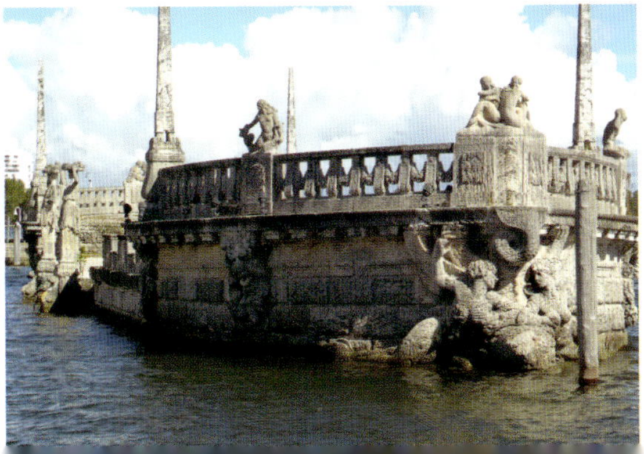

VIZCAYA

A concrete boat at Vizcaya
A historic Miami Dade County p
An ordinary view
Grows moody and temperamental
Columns of clouds

VIZCAYA AFTERNOON

A view of Vizcaya
The slanting afternoon light created a perfect mood
For a stroll through the park
Golden sun on stairs

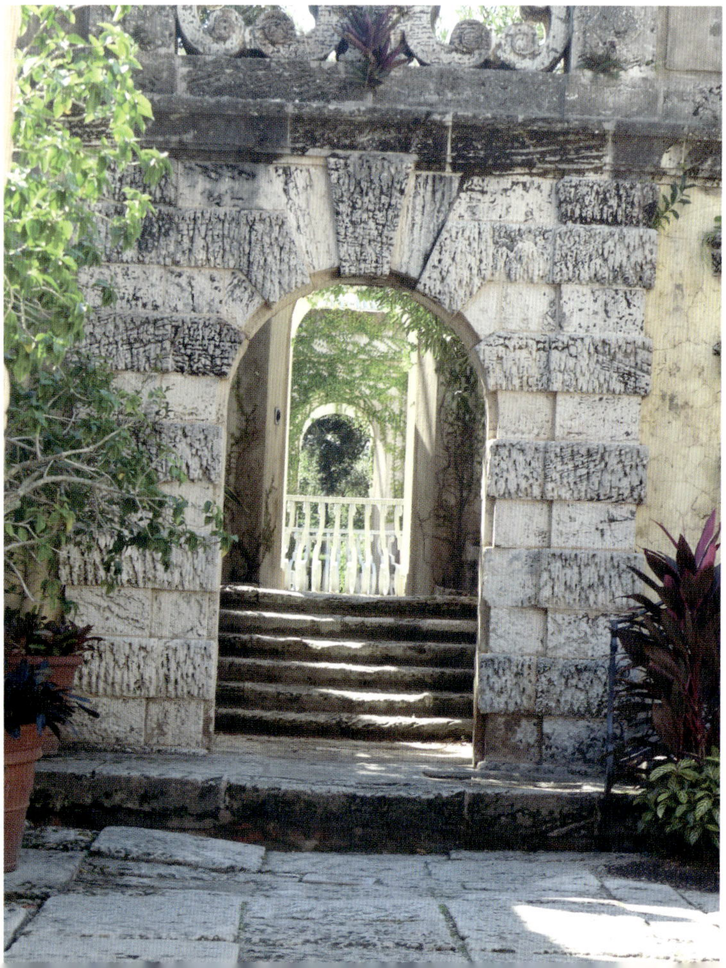

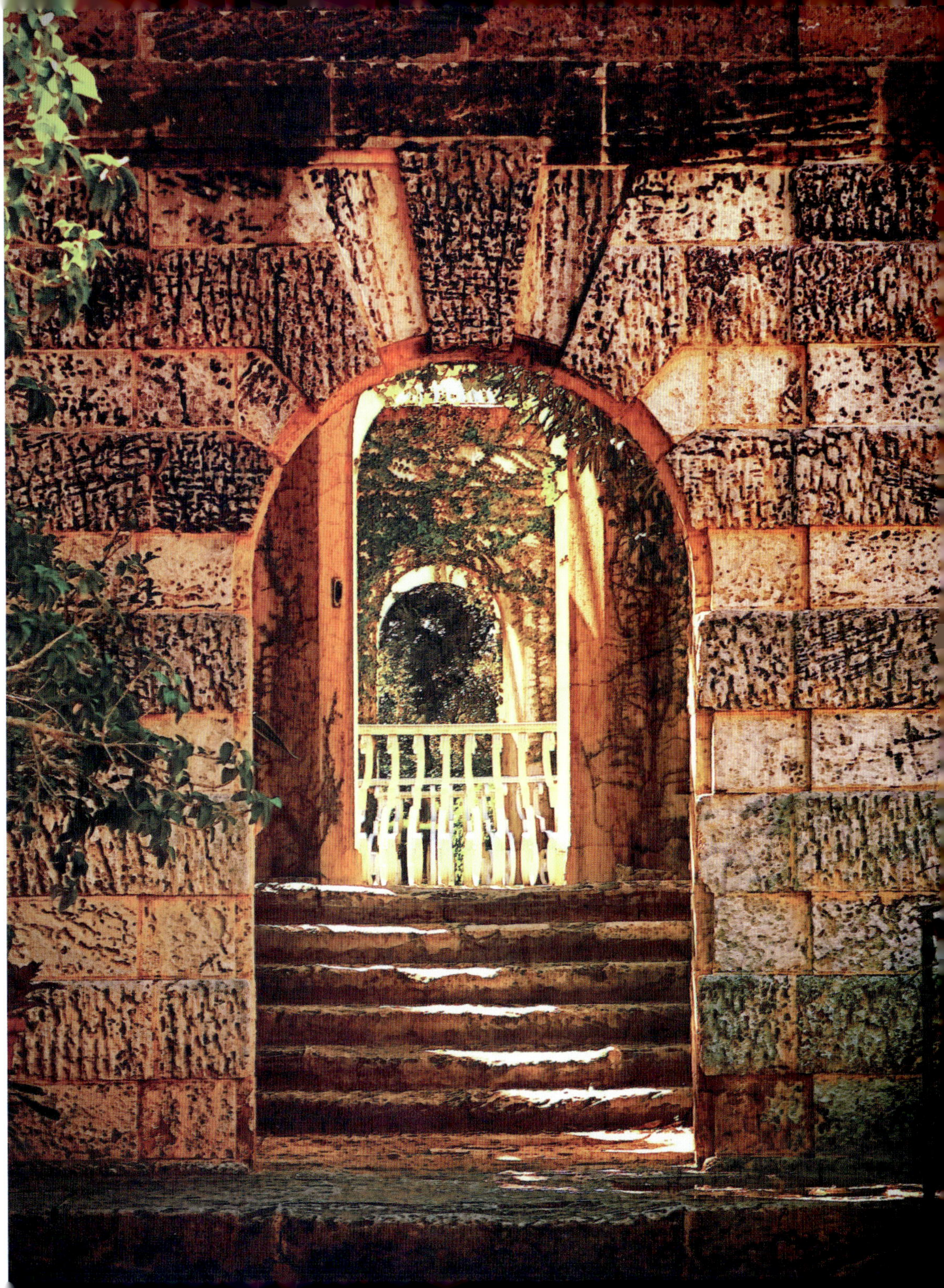

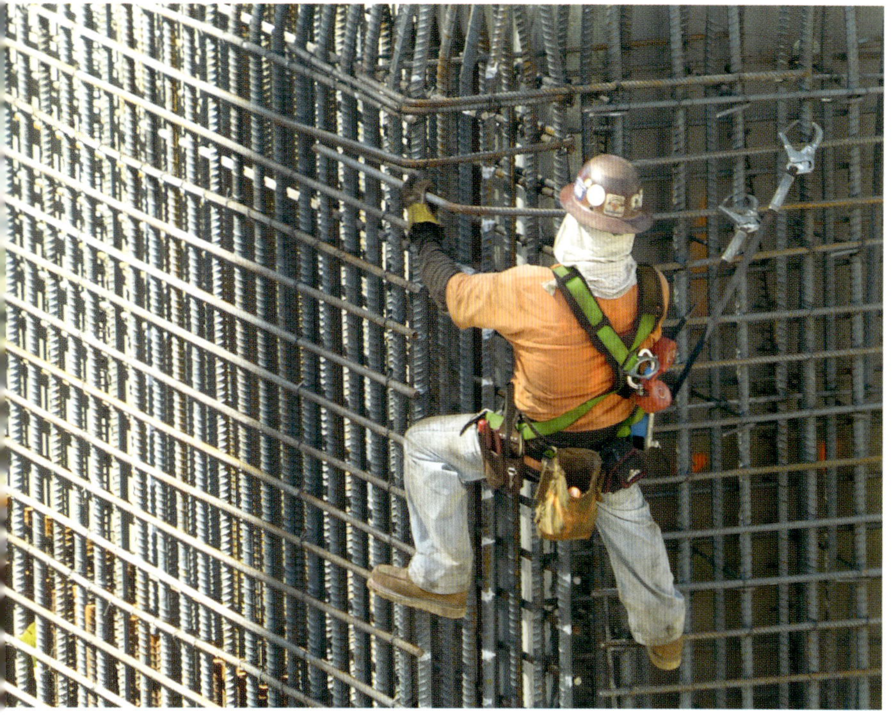

IRON WORKER

Brickell City Center under construction
A $1 billion-plus project
Changing downtown forever
An iron worker places rebar
He's hanging on

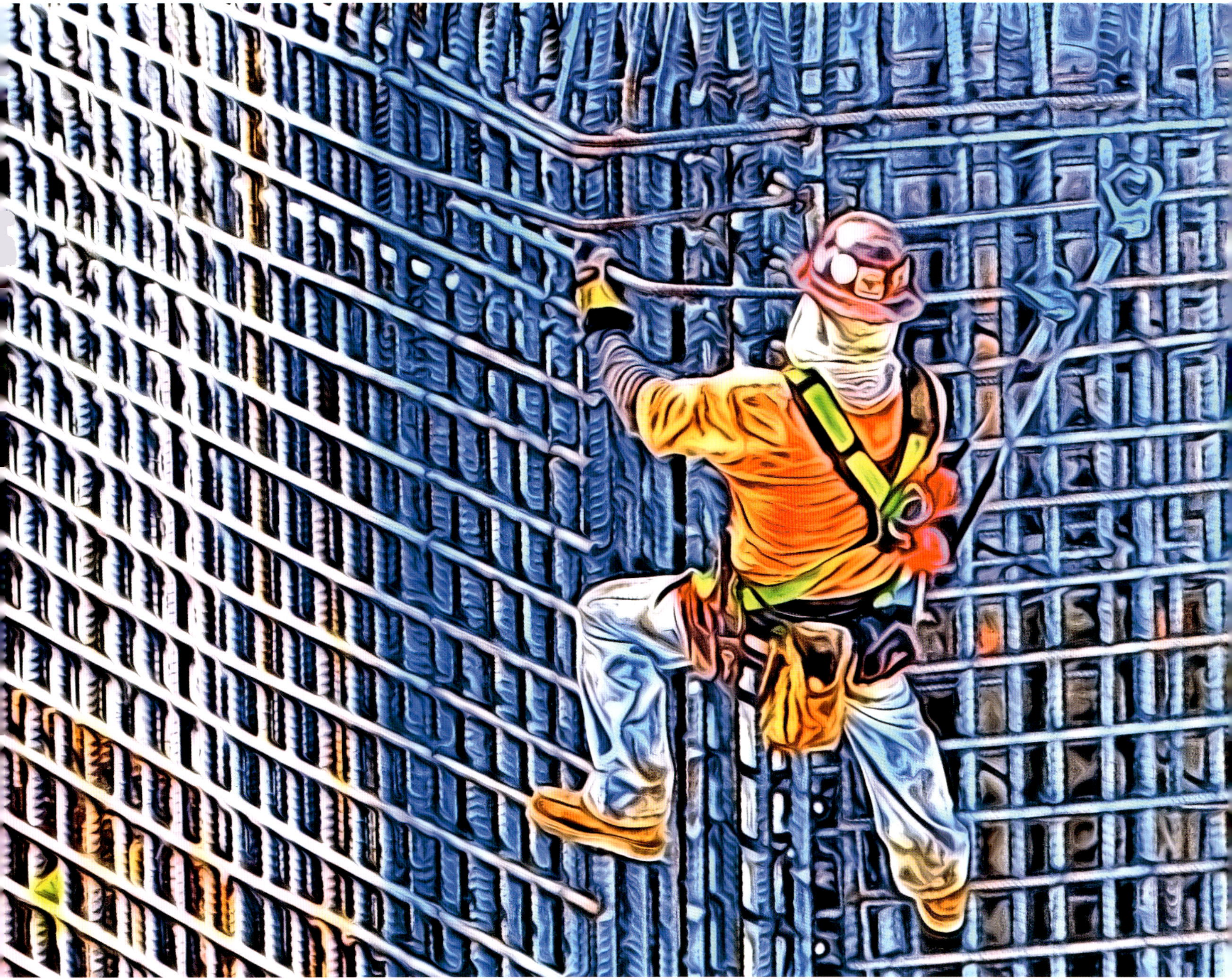

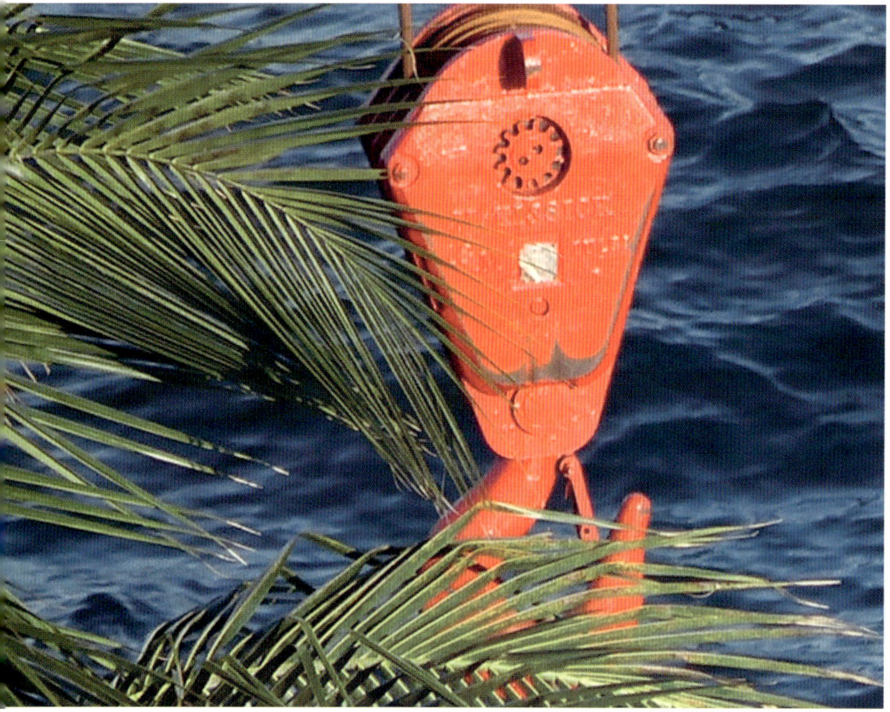

CONSTRUCTION HOOK

Behind my home
On Biscayne Bay
Working on the sea wall
A crane

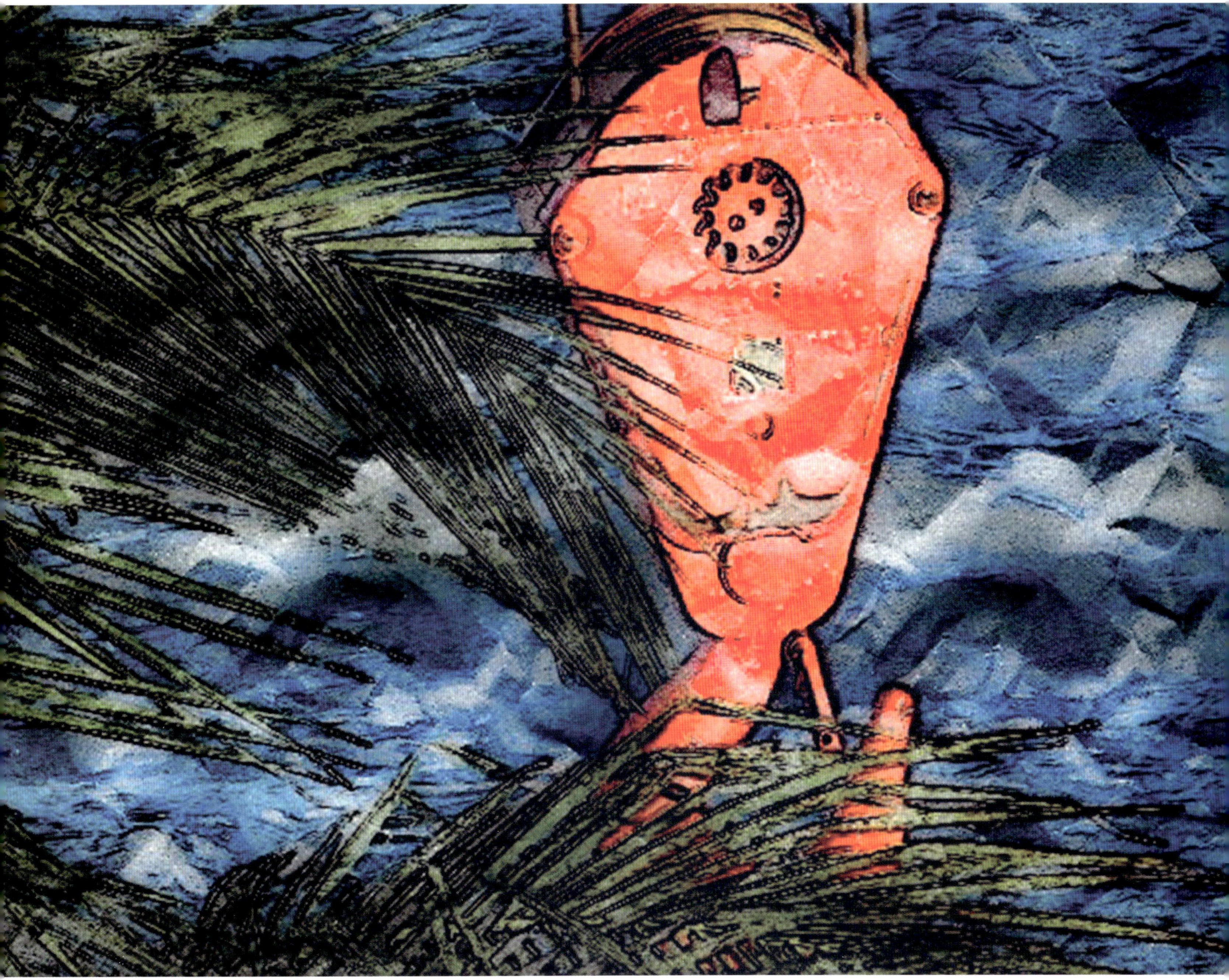

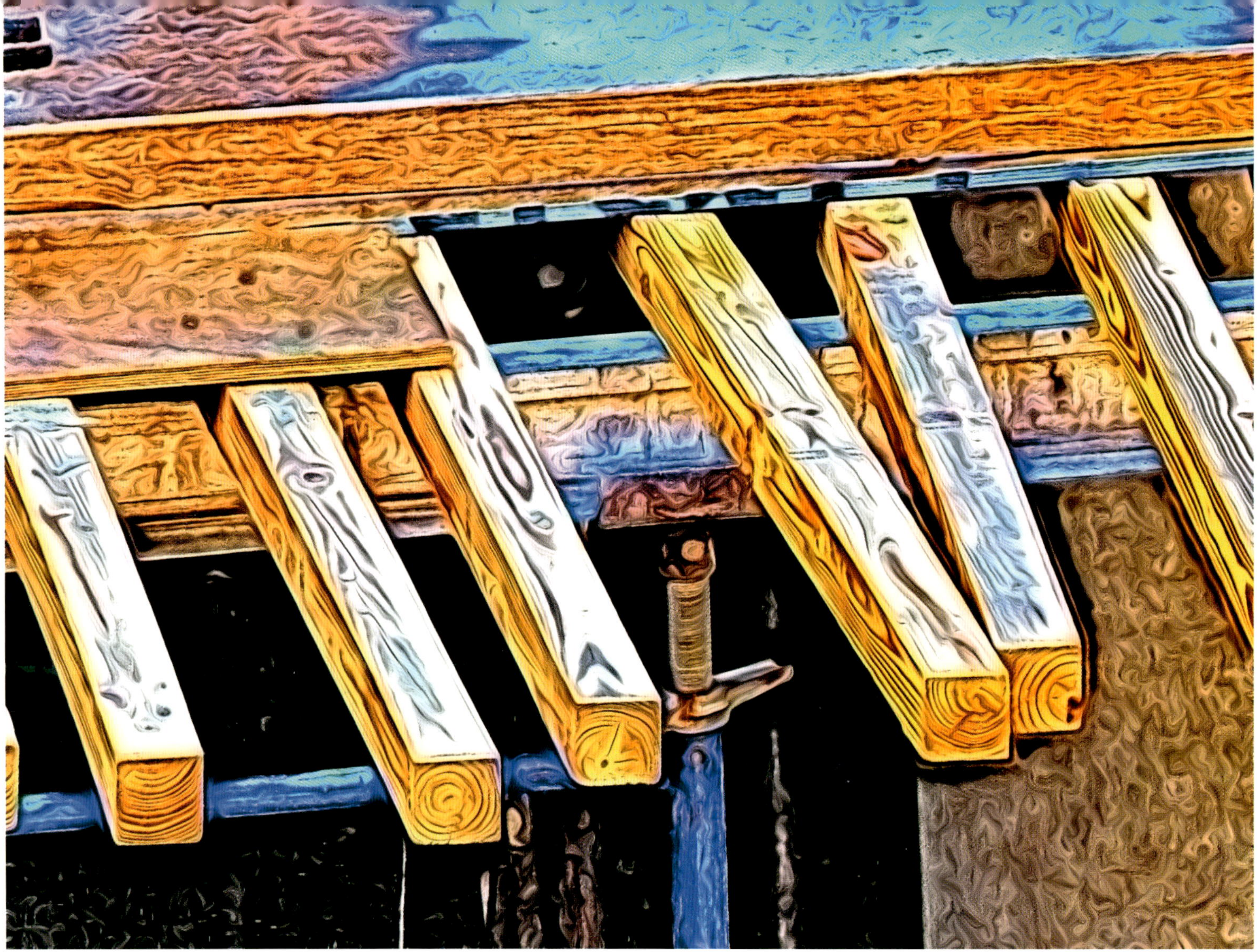

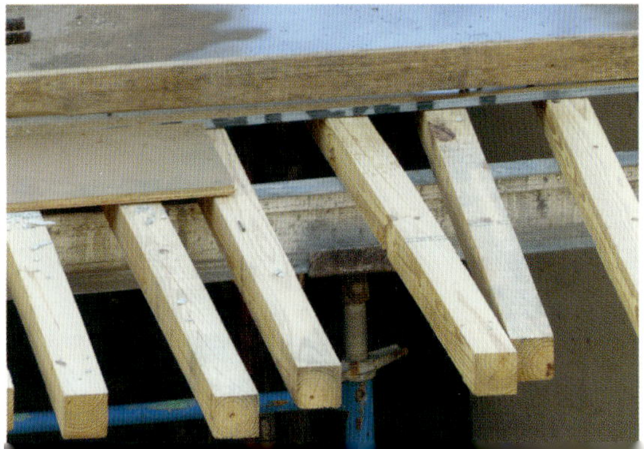

FLOOR FOUNDATION

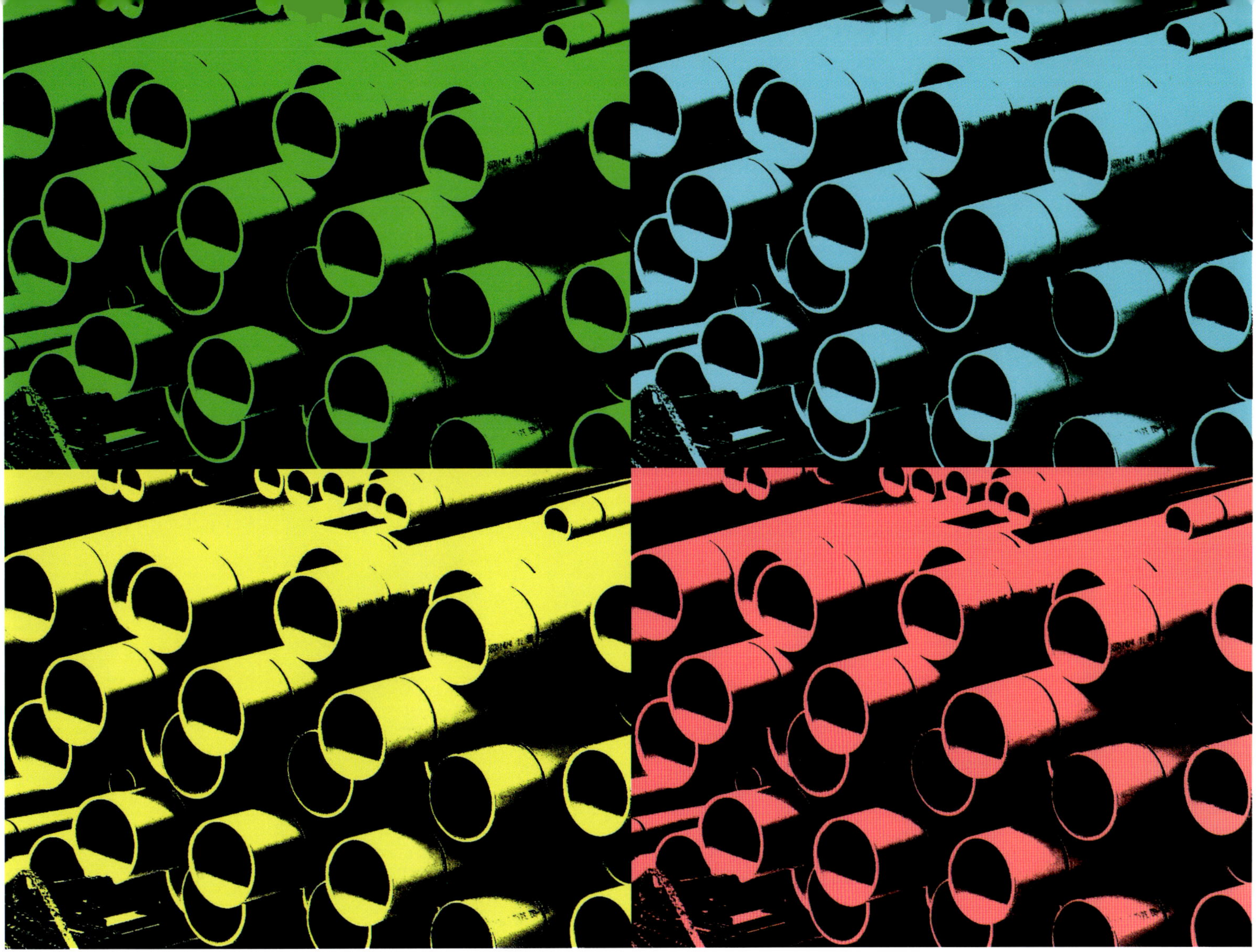

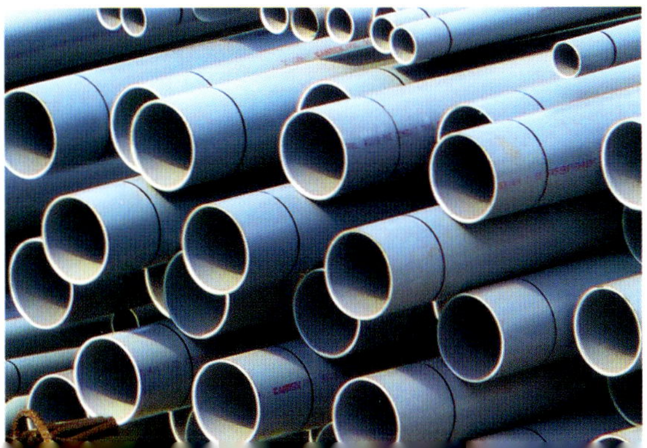

CONSTRUCTION PIPES

A MASONIC TEMPLE

The Scottish Rite is a Masonic temple
Built in the 1920s and reconditioned in 1992
The gargoyles are in charge
They're watching

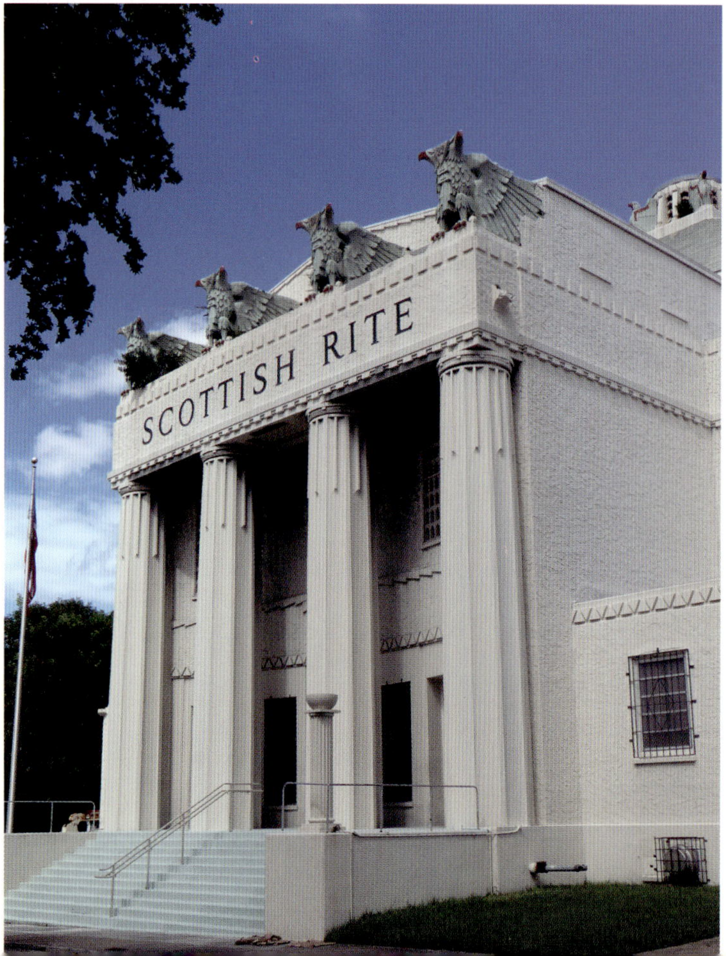

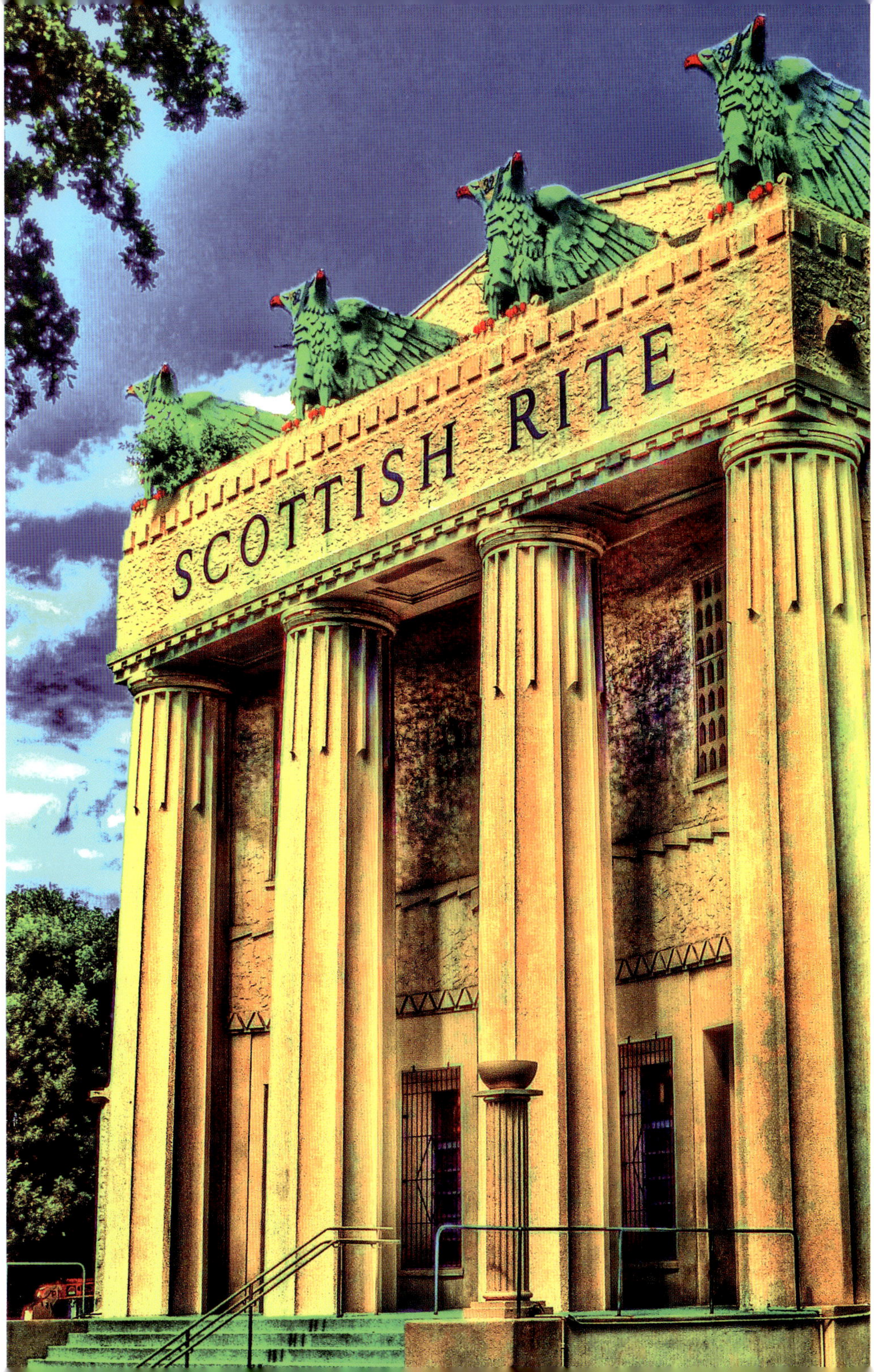
SCOTTISH RITE

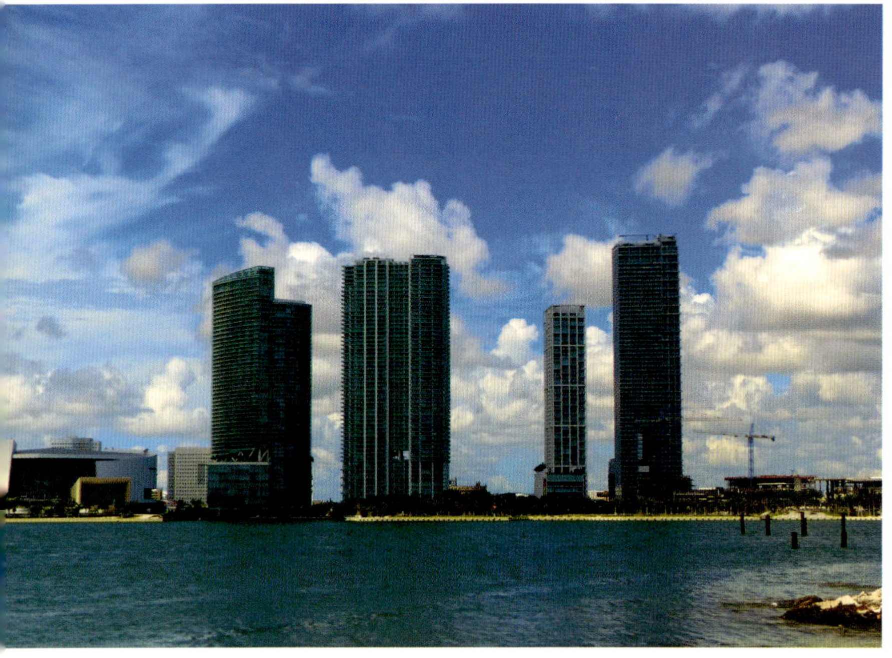

CONDOS

Gazing across Biscayne Bay at new condos
Now people are living downtown
Dreamy views

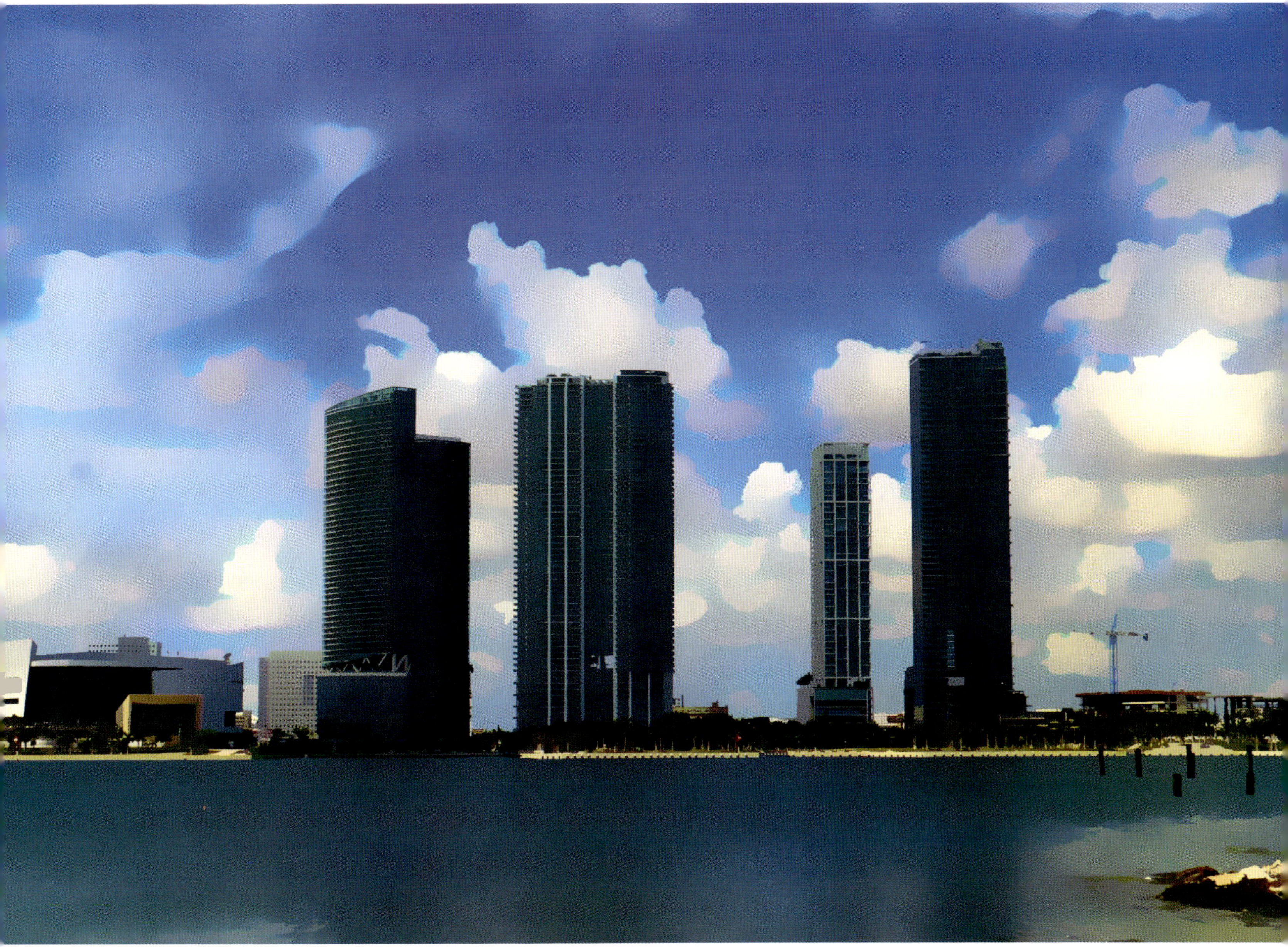

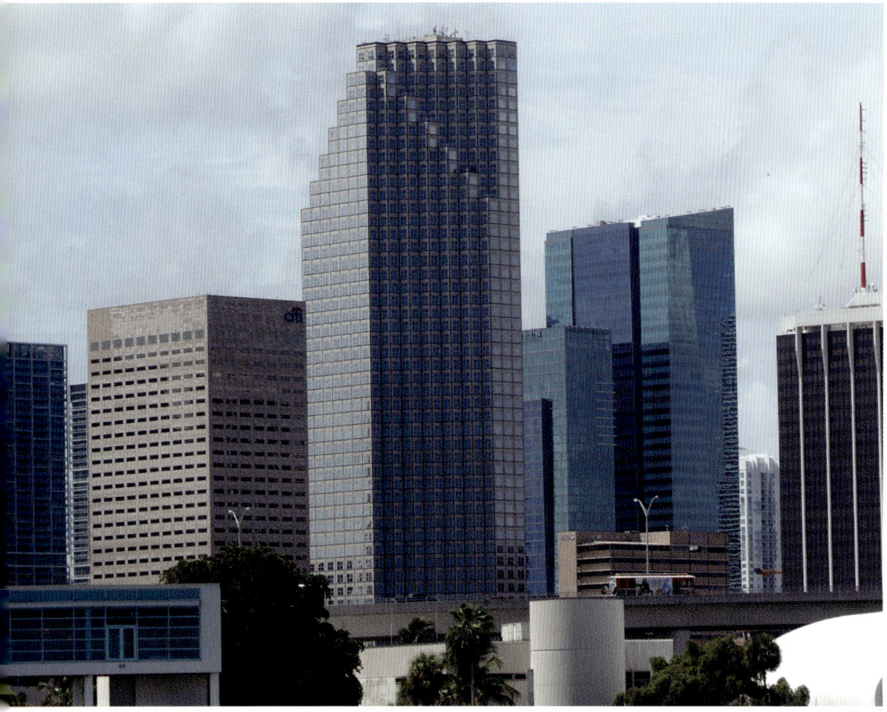

OFFICES

Have a look at the downtown office market
Twentieth and twenty-first-century buildings
Take on new colors
Bold personalities

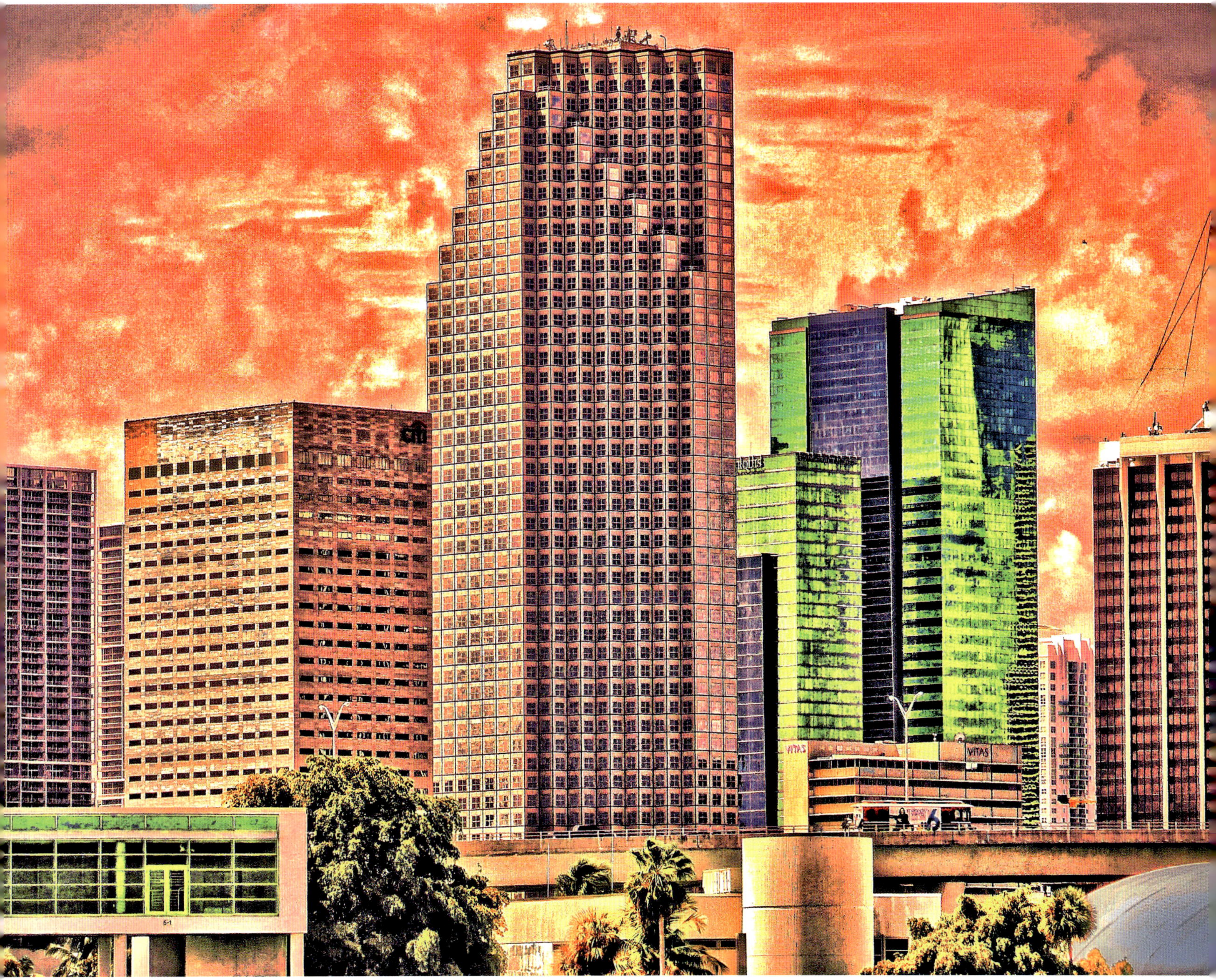
citi
VITAS
VITAS

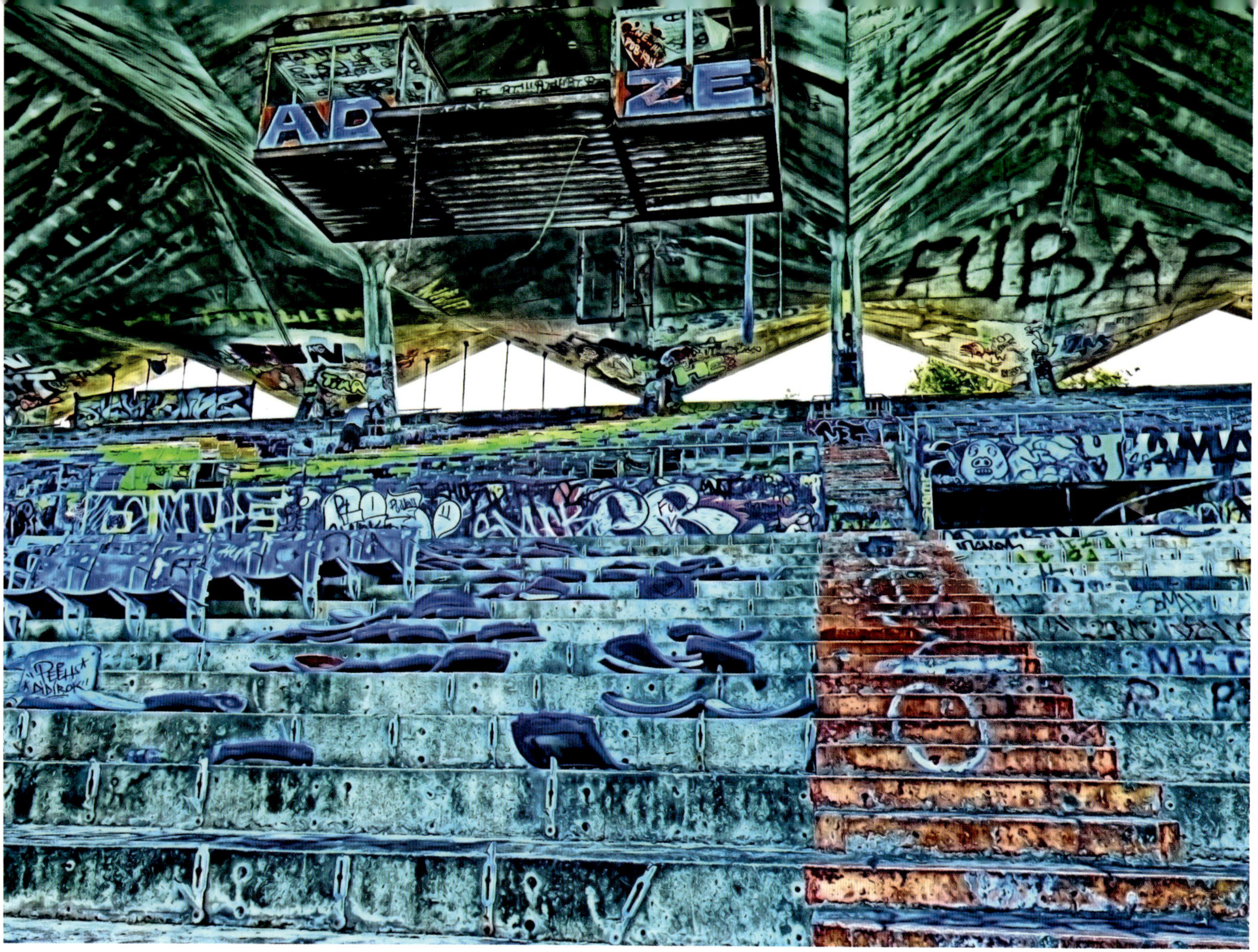

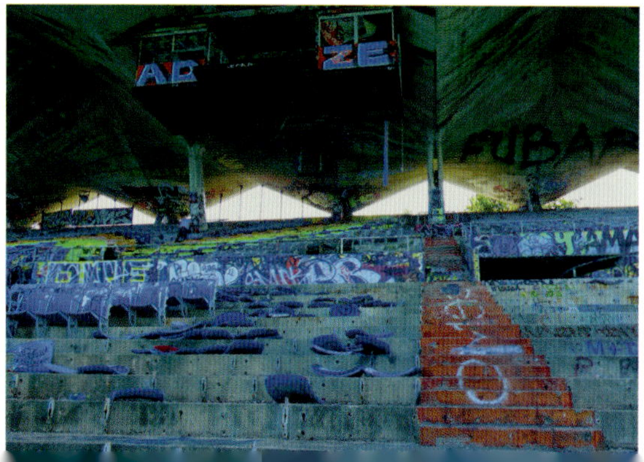

MARINE STADIUM

6,000-seat stadium on the water

Built in 1963

Badly damaged by Hurricane Andrew in 1992

Beauty in abandonment

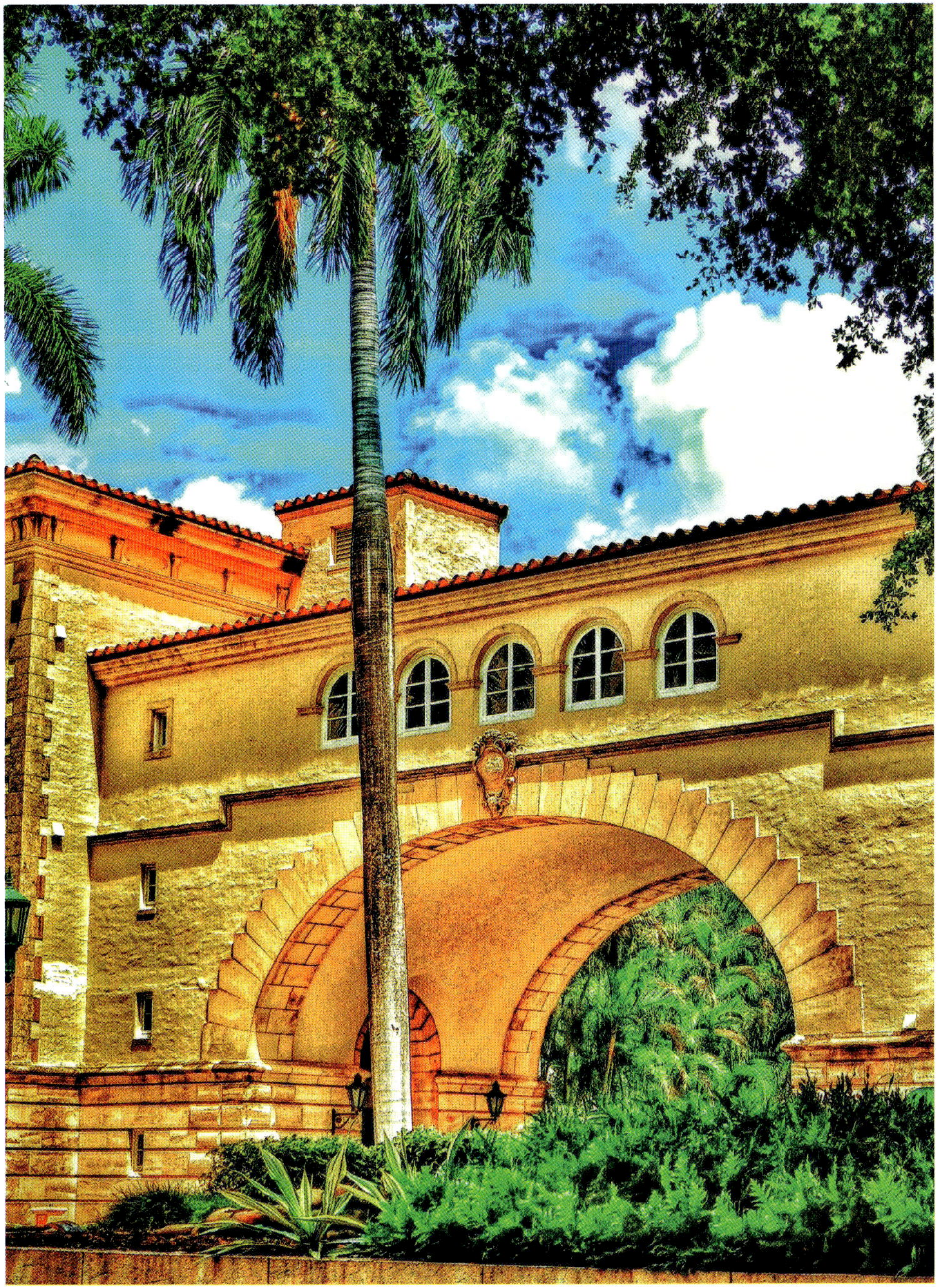

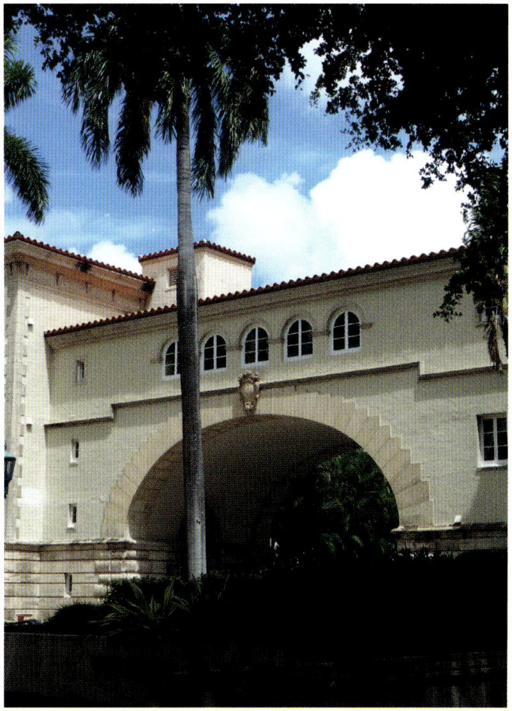

DOUGLAS ENTRANCE I

Historic entrance to Coral Gables
Completed in 1924
Also known as La Puerta Sol
Designed by Phineas Paist
Delightful

DOUGLAS ENTRANCE II

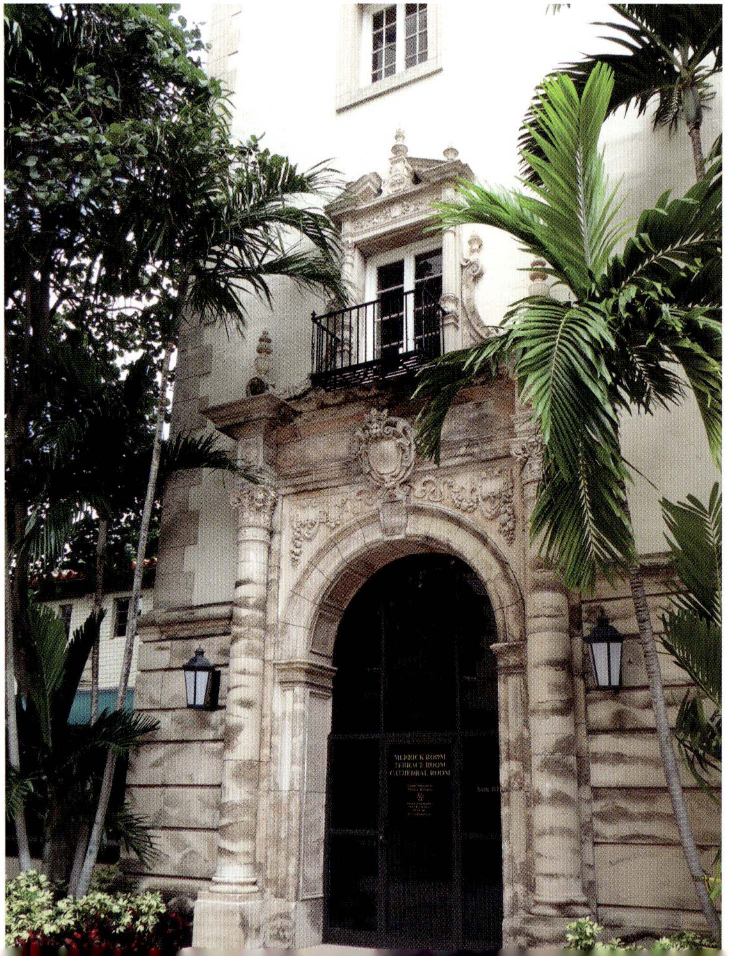

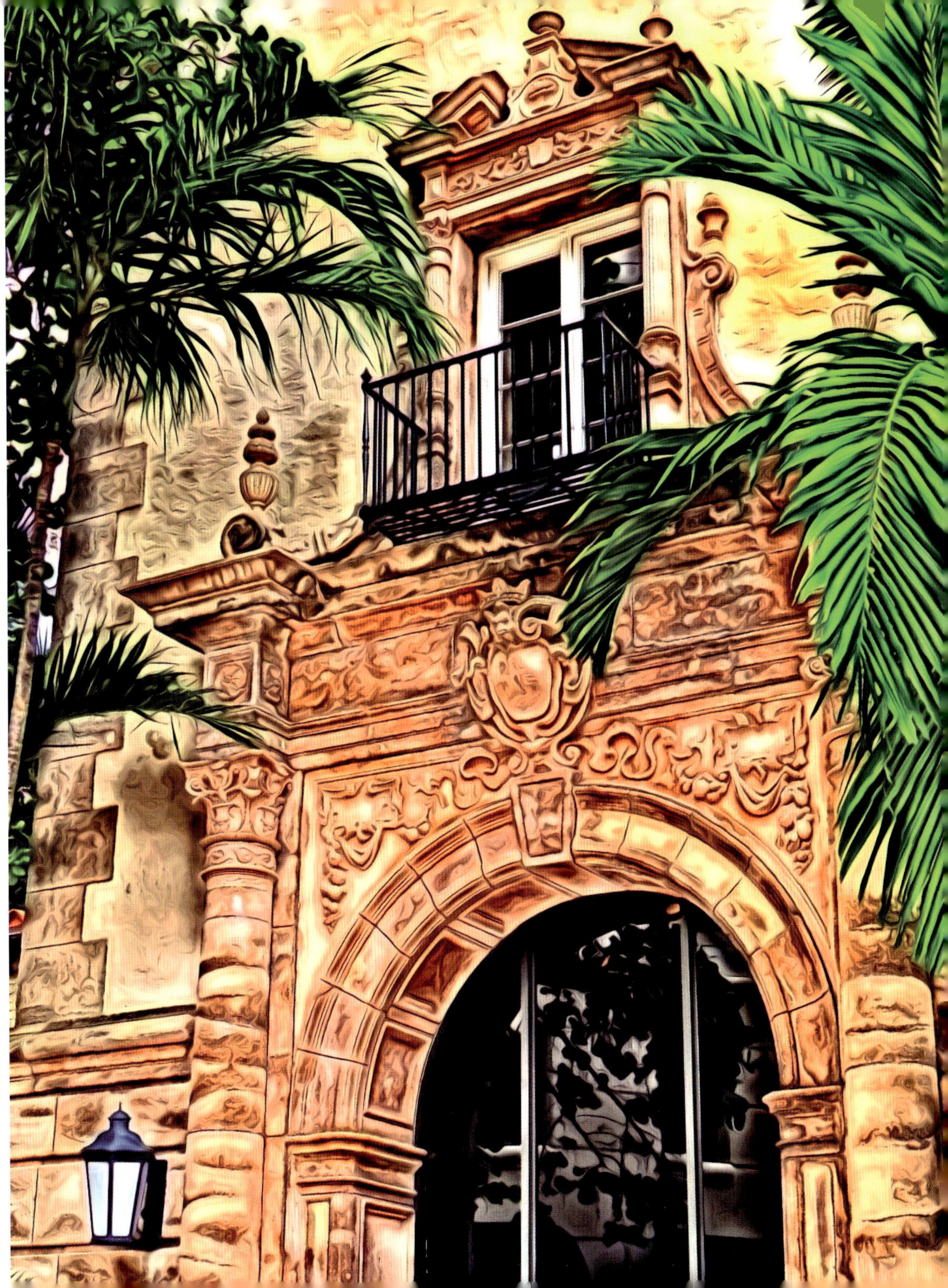

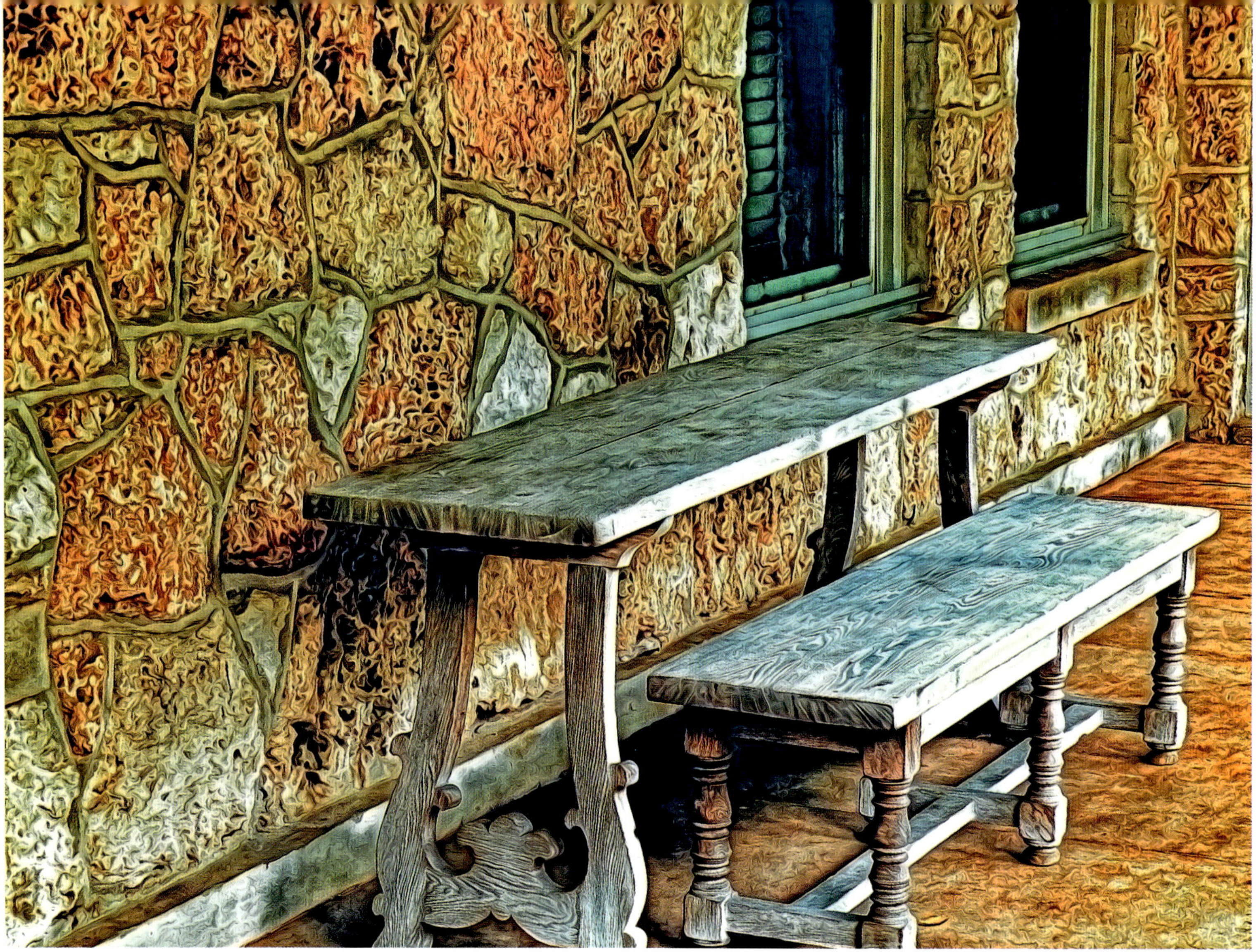

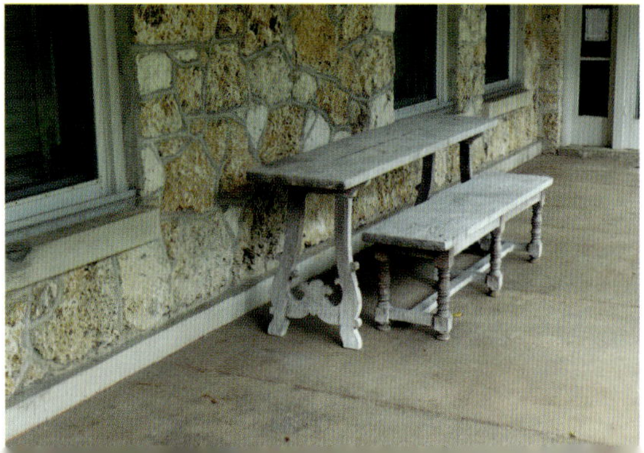

MERRICK HOUSE

George Merrick founded Coral Gables
His home is historic
The porch is large and partially furnished
The bench sits alone

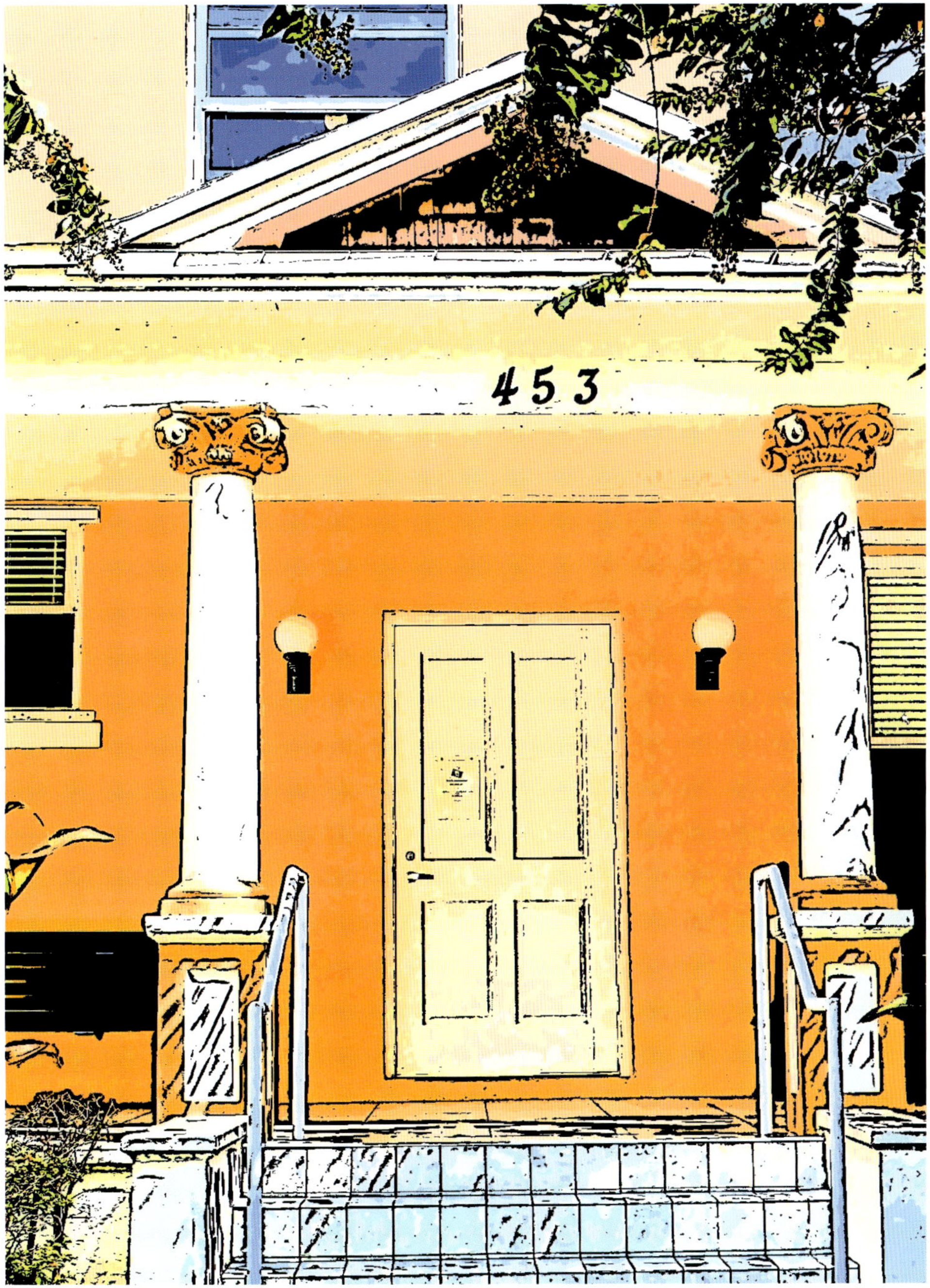

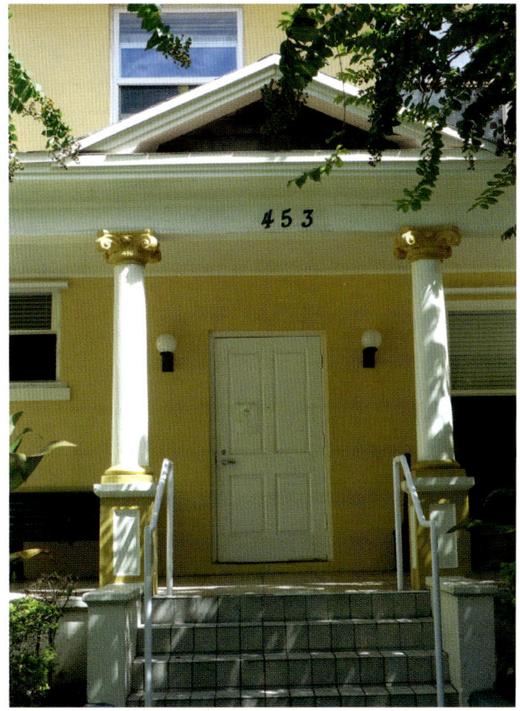

AT HOME

An inviting house
Goes from classic and soft-spoken
To articulated
Like an old storybook drawing

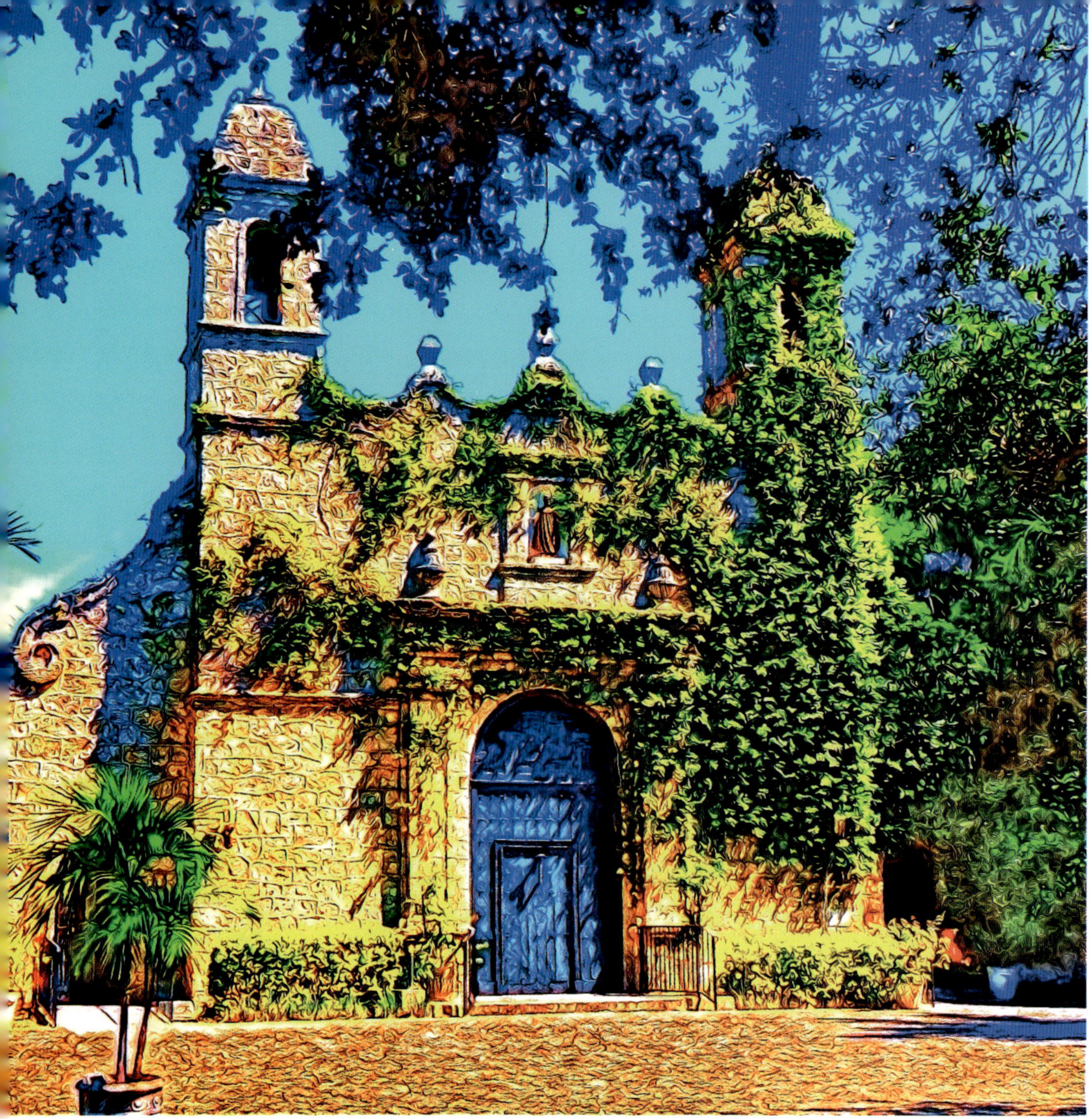

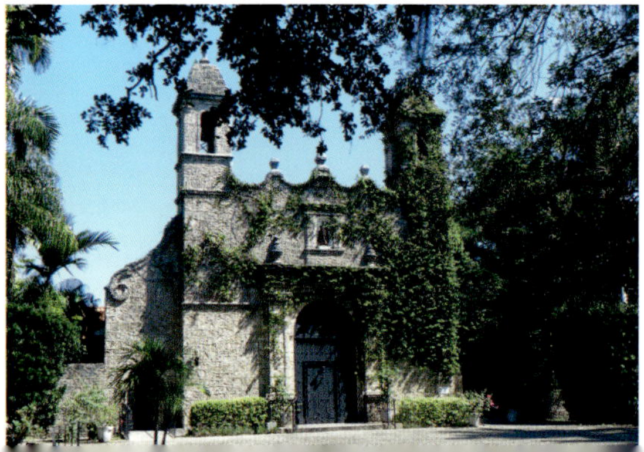

PLYMOUTH CHURCH I

A charming congregational church

Constructed in 1917

Built by Felix Rebom with basic tools

Foliage adds character

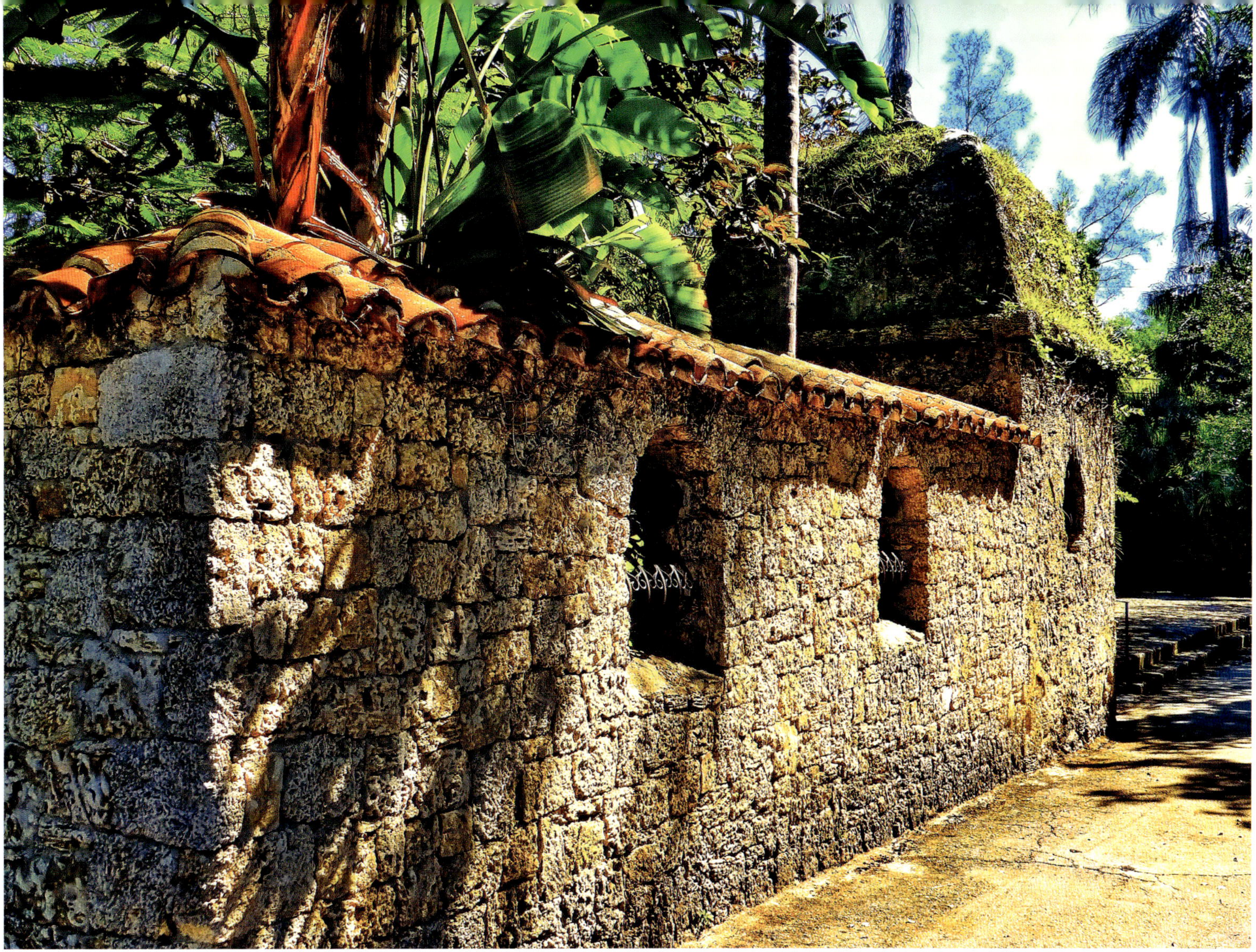

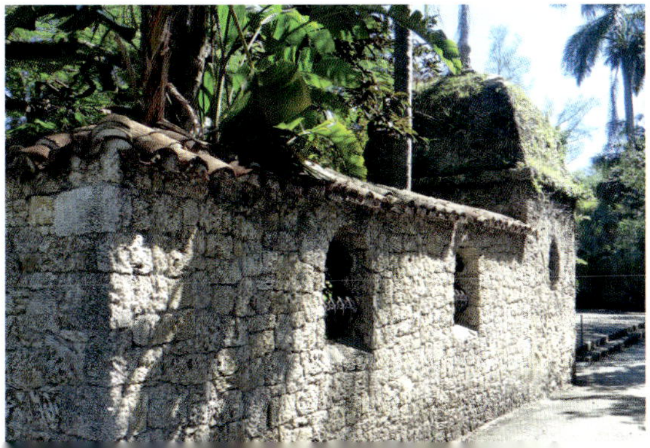

PLYMOUTH CHURCH II

BILTMORE HOTEL

Built in 1926

The tallest building in Miami at the time

Viewed from the golf course

Radiant colors

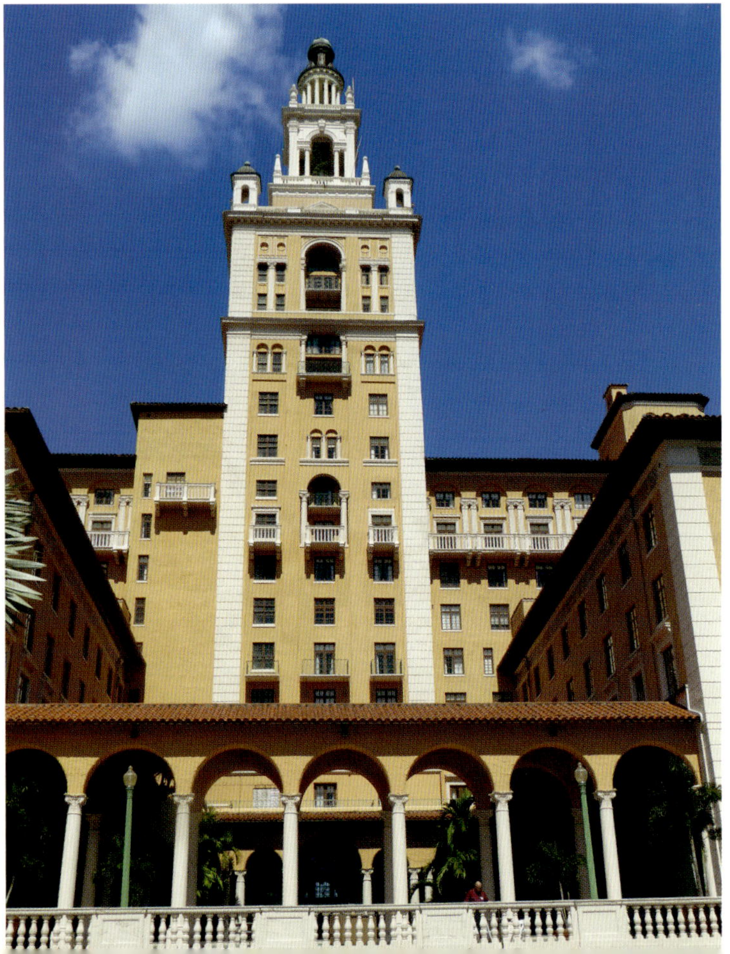

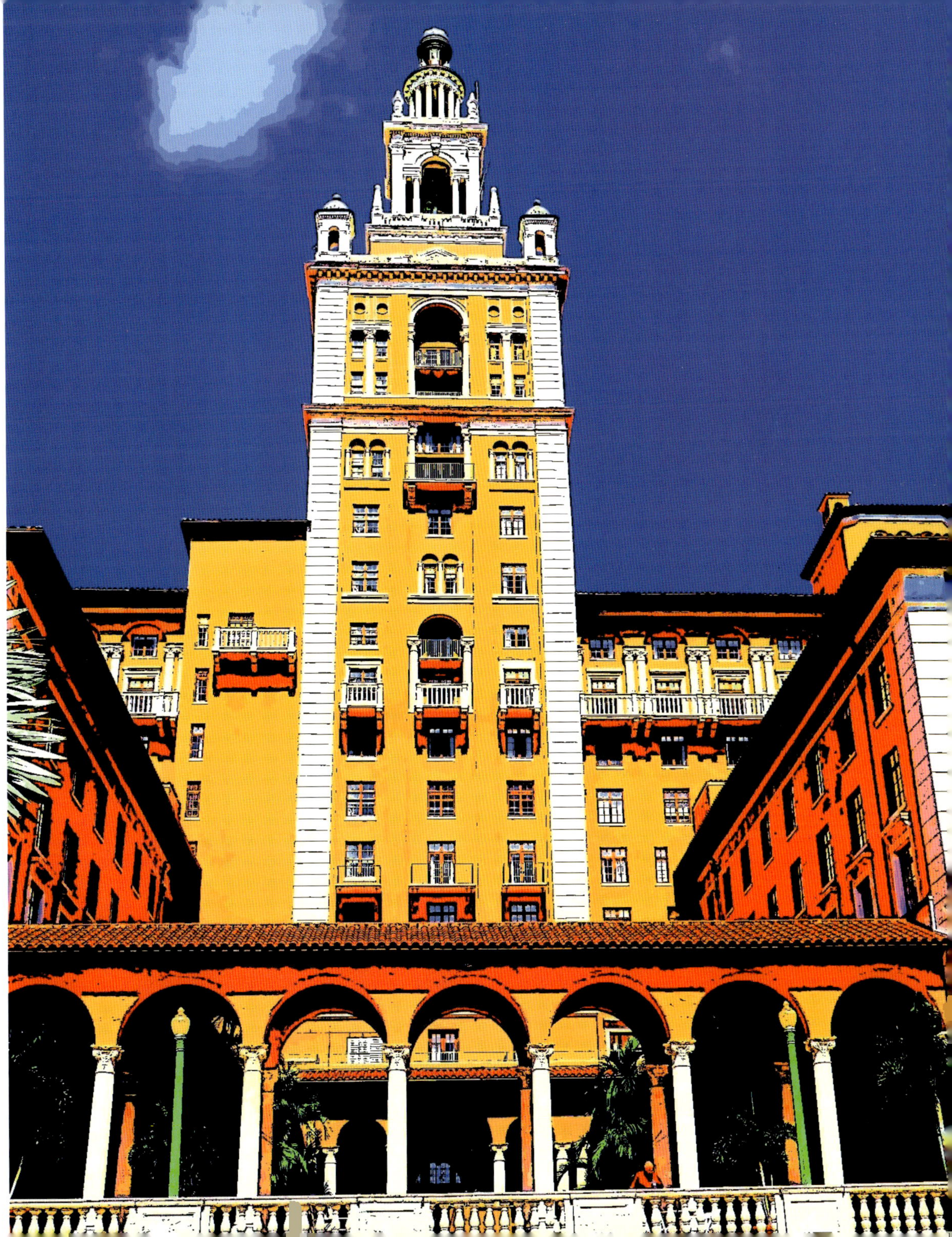

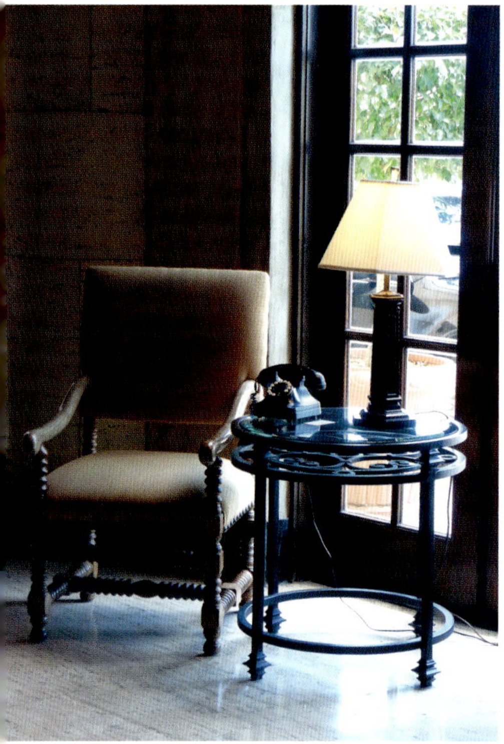

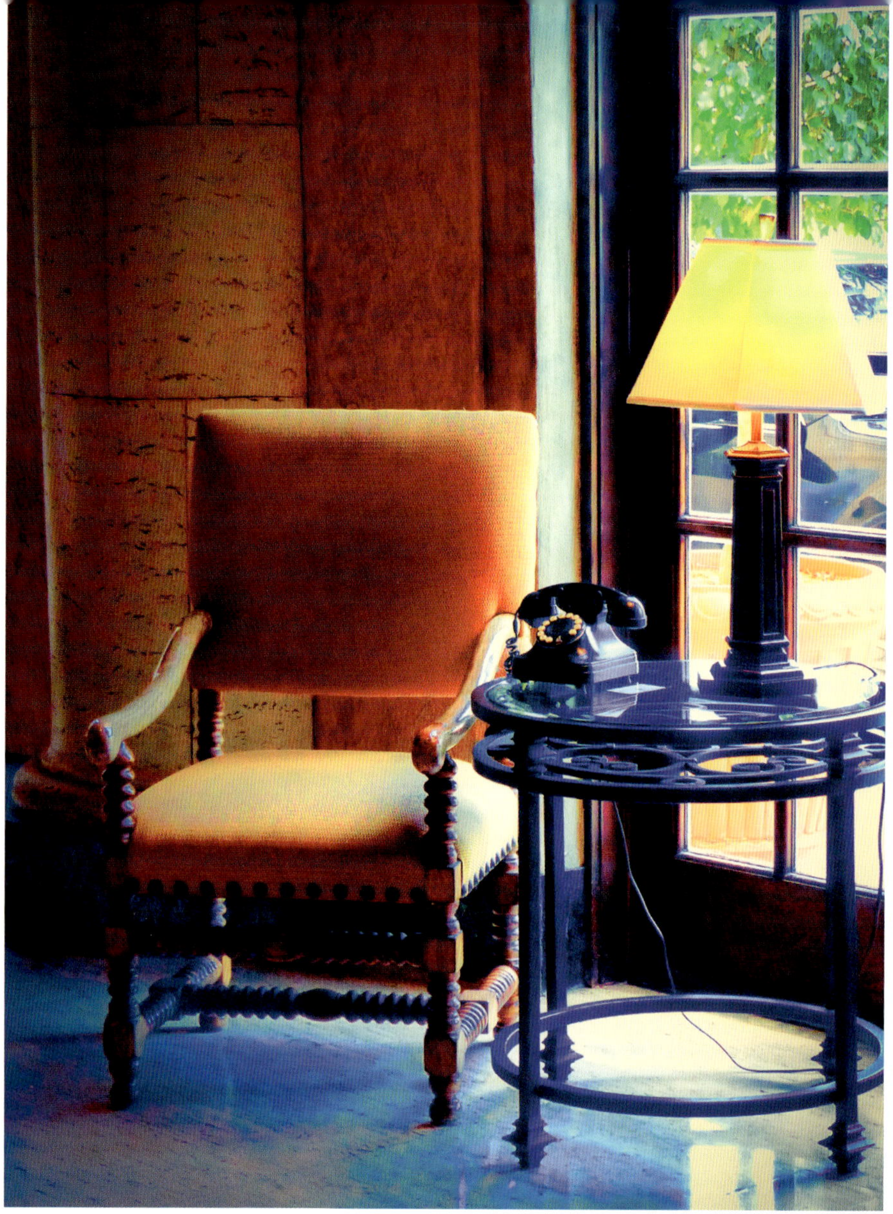

LOBBY I

Classic scene from the Biltmore Hotel lobby

A chair telephone and lamp

Convey history

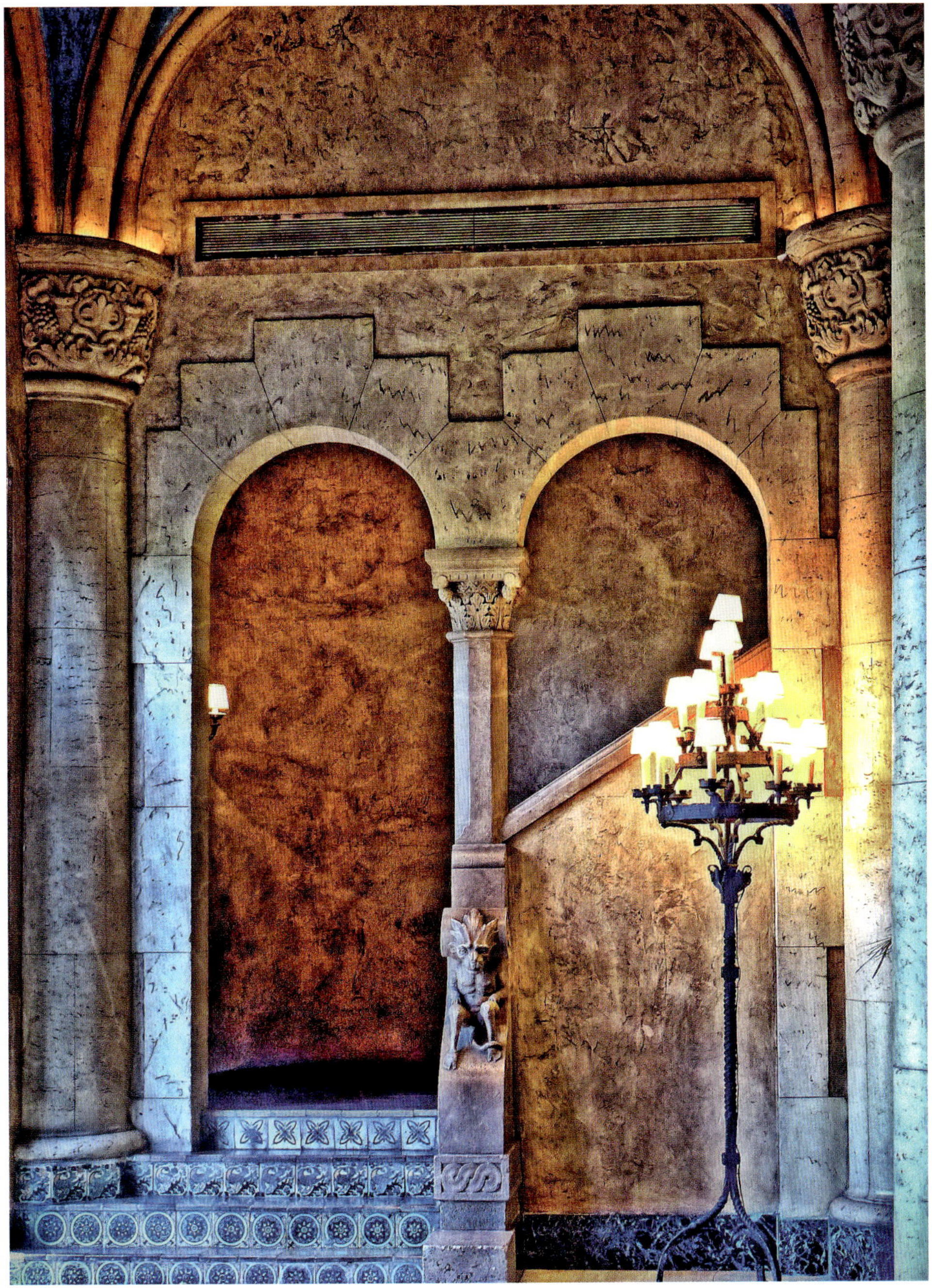

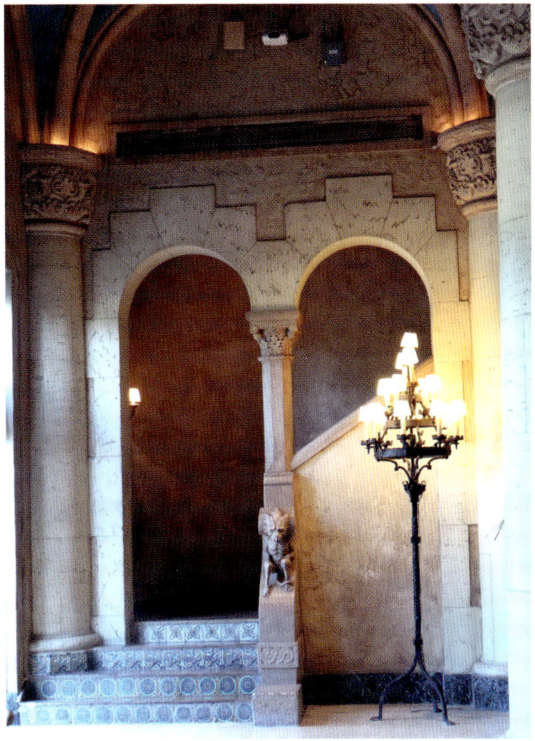

LOBBY II

Stairs to nowhere
Beckon
A gargoyle on guard
Says stay away

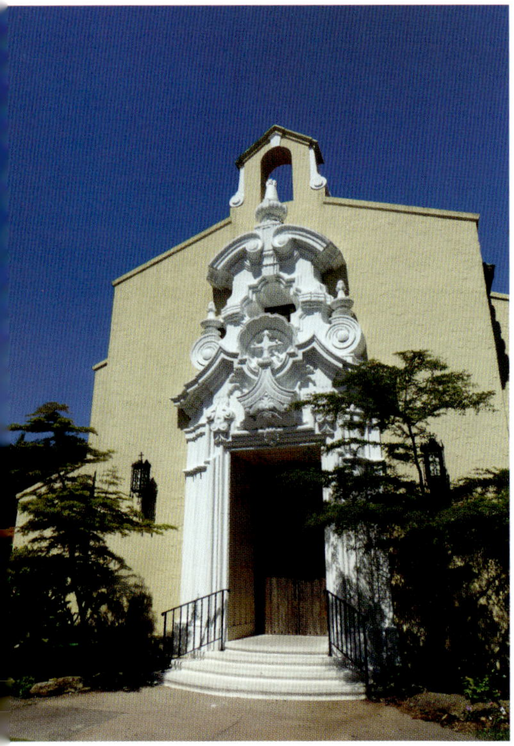

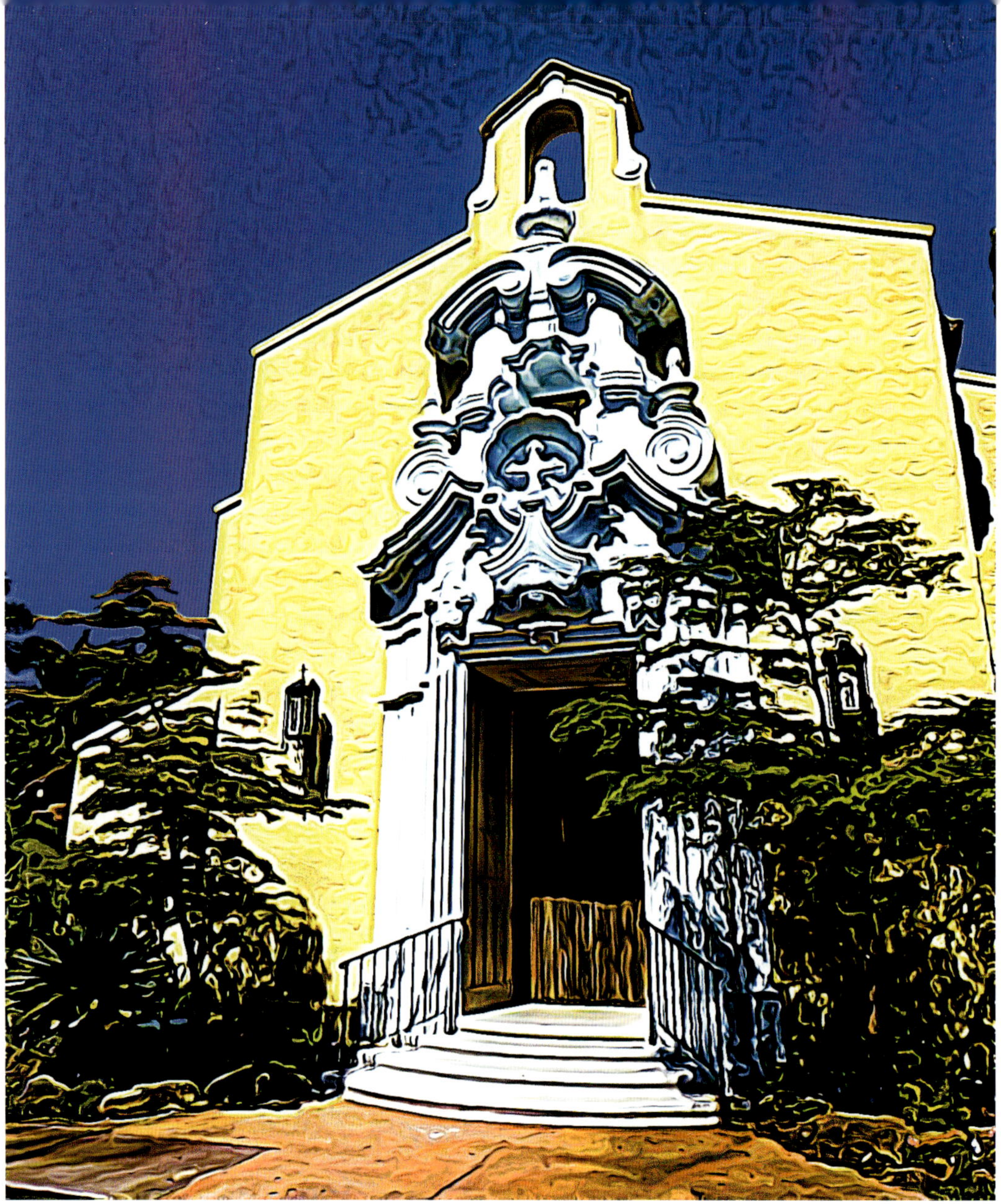

BANYAN CONGREGATIONAL CHURCH I

Historic church constructed in 1924

Contrasting colors pop

Against a cobalt sky

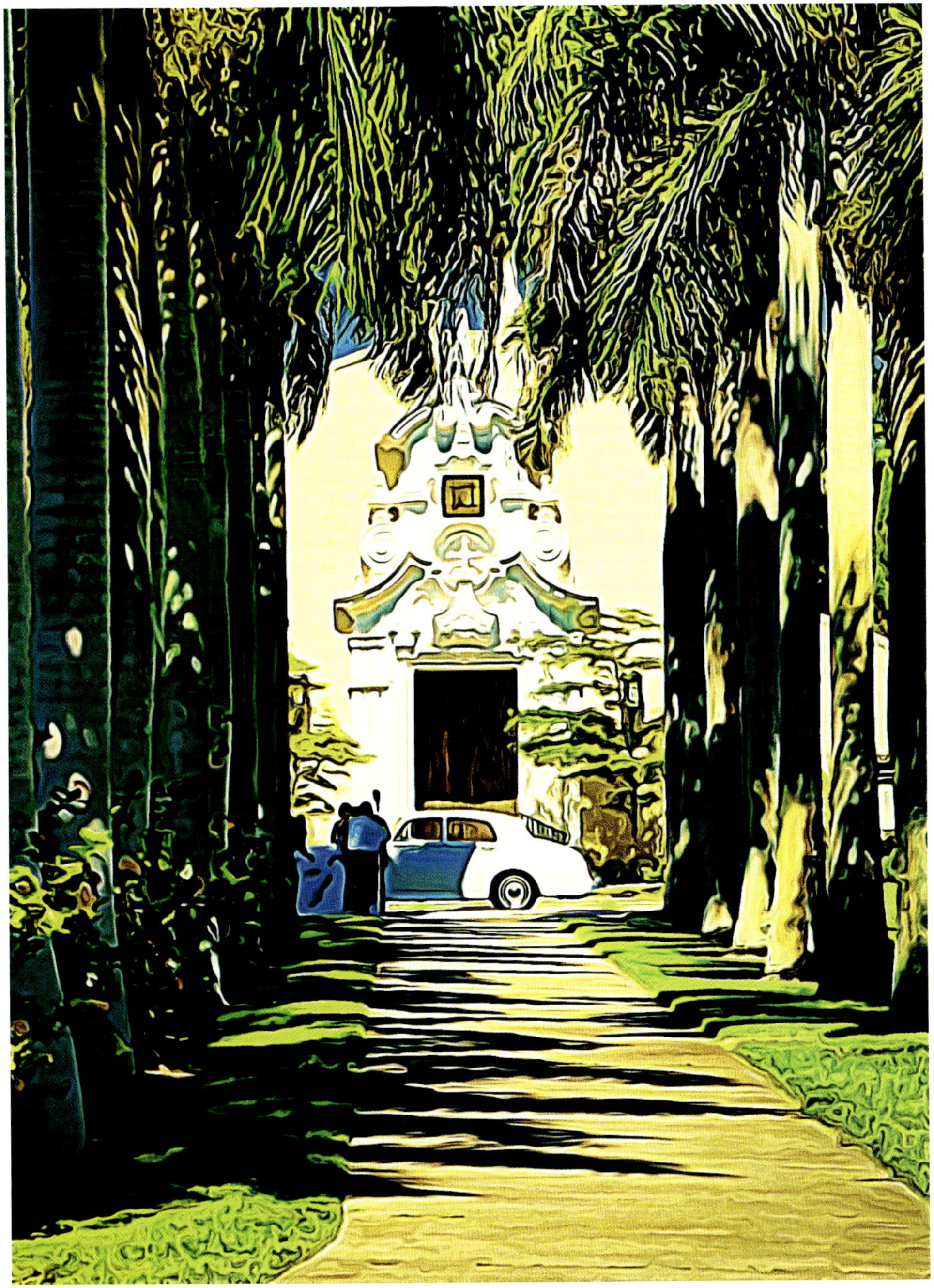

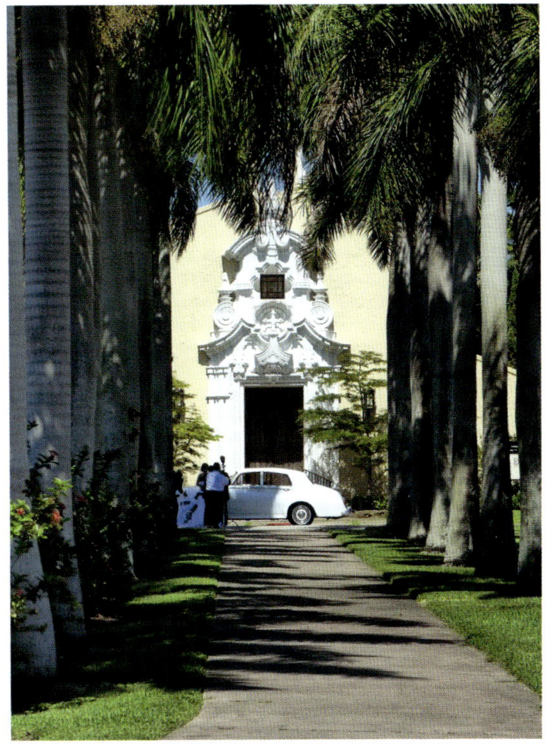

BANYAN CONGREGATIONAL CHURCH II

Royal palms

Frame a wedding party

Nature lends a supportive presence

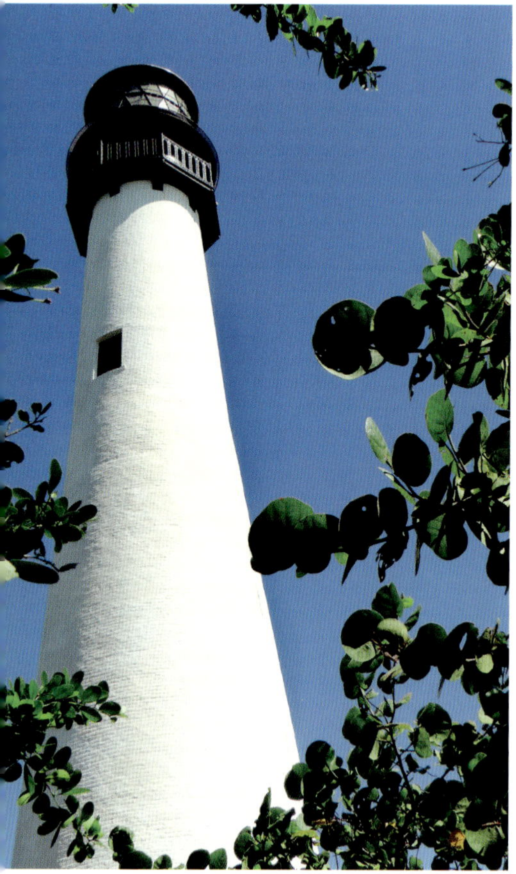

HISTORIC LIGHTHOUSE

Built in the early nineteenth century
On the site of a bloody battle
With the Seminole Indians
Remembrance and wonder

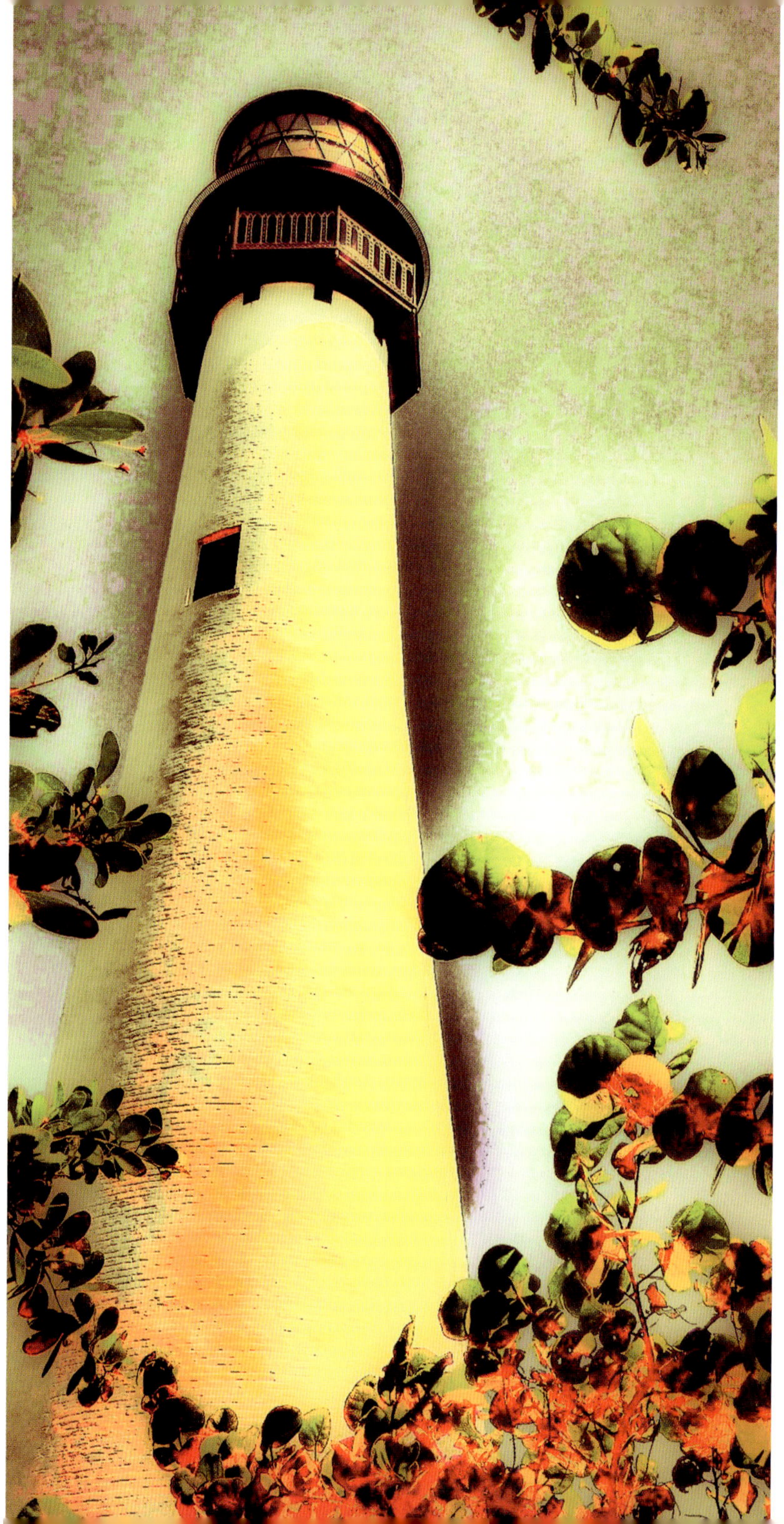

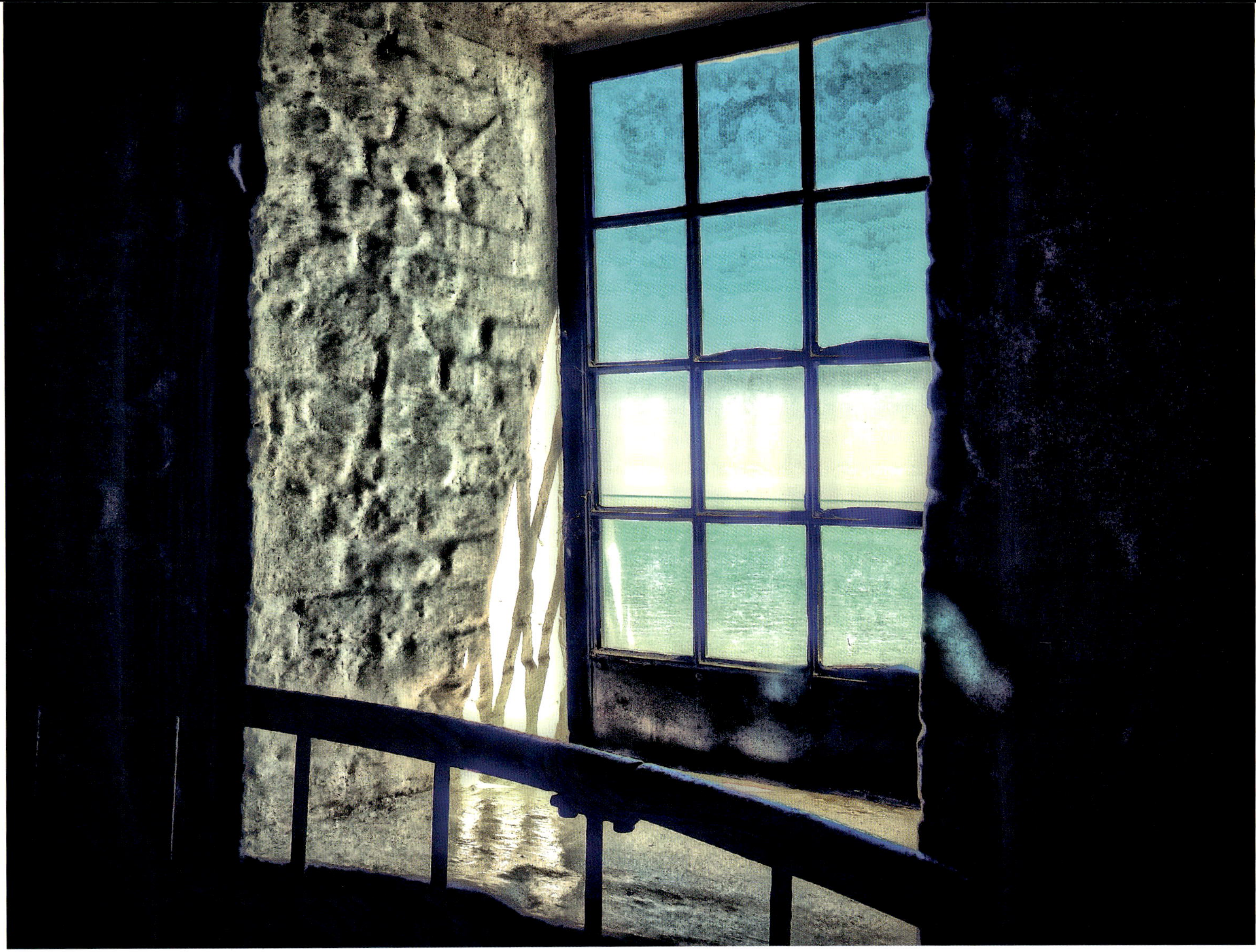

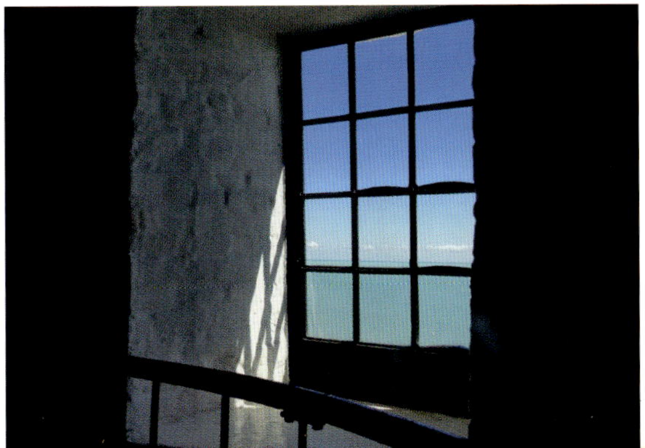

LIGHTHOUSE II

CORAL CASTLE I

Finished in the 1930s
It took a Latvian refugee twenty-eight years to build
Single-handedly
Amazing

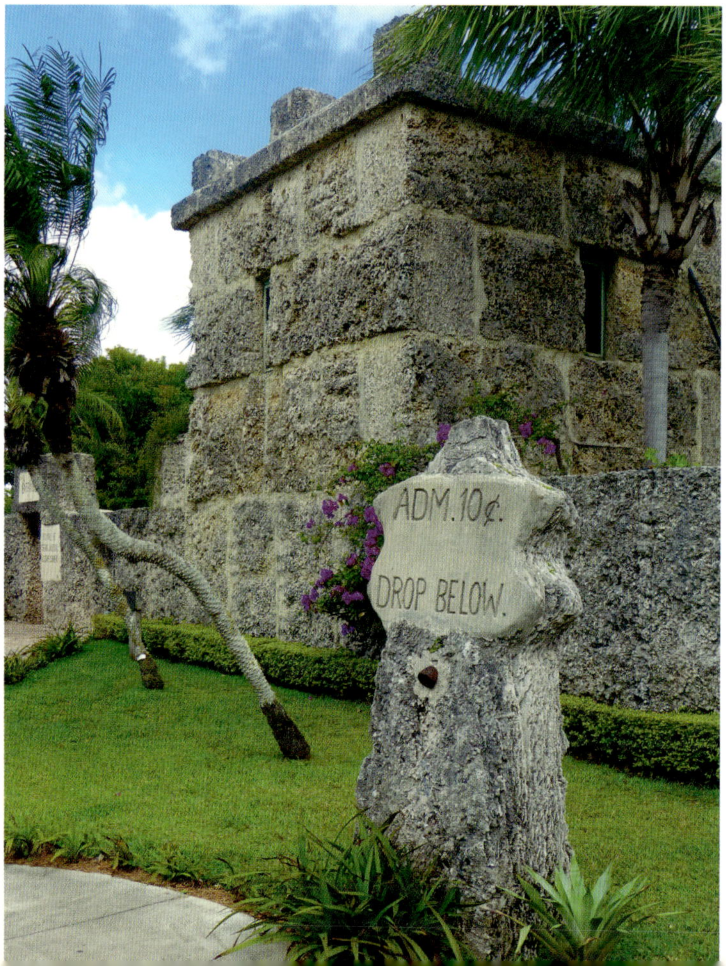

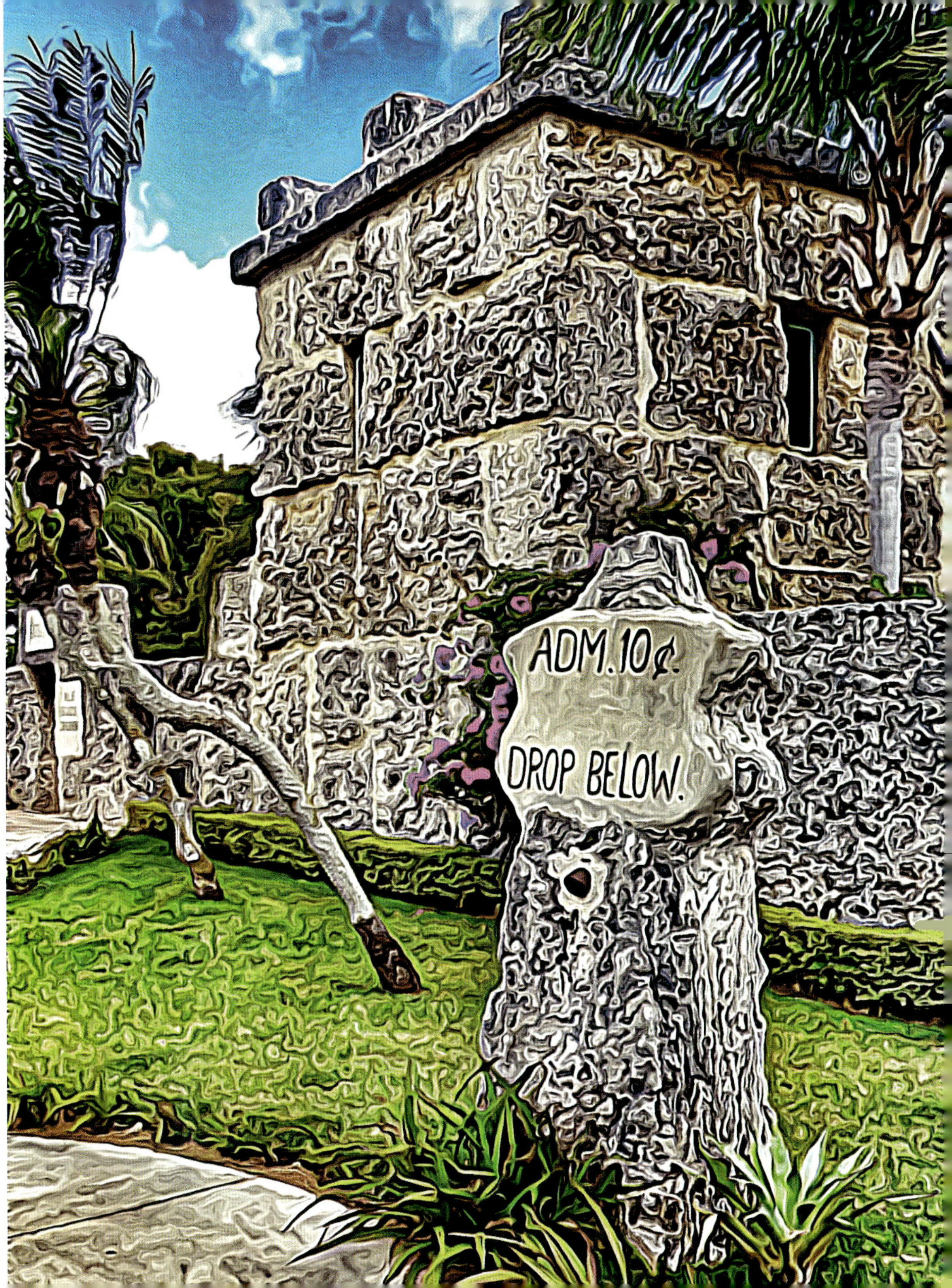
ADM. 10¢.
DROP BELOW.

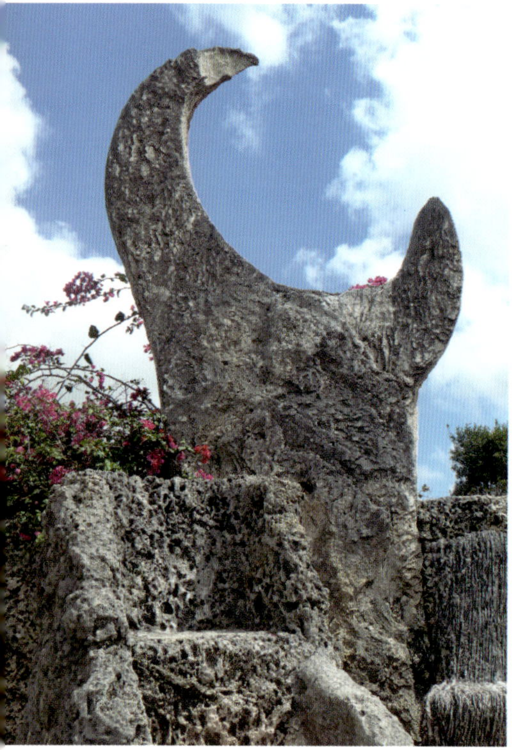

CORAL CASTLE II

Constructed and carved by a man
Jilted by a young woman
He was unhappy and worked alone
Sad

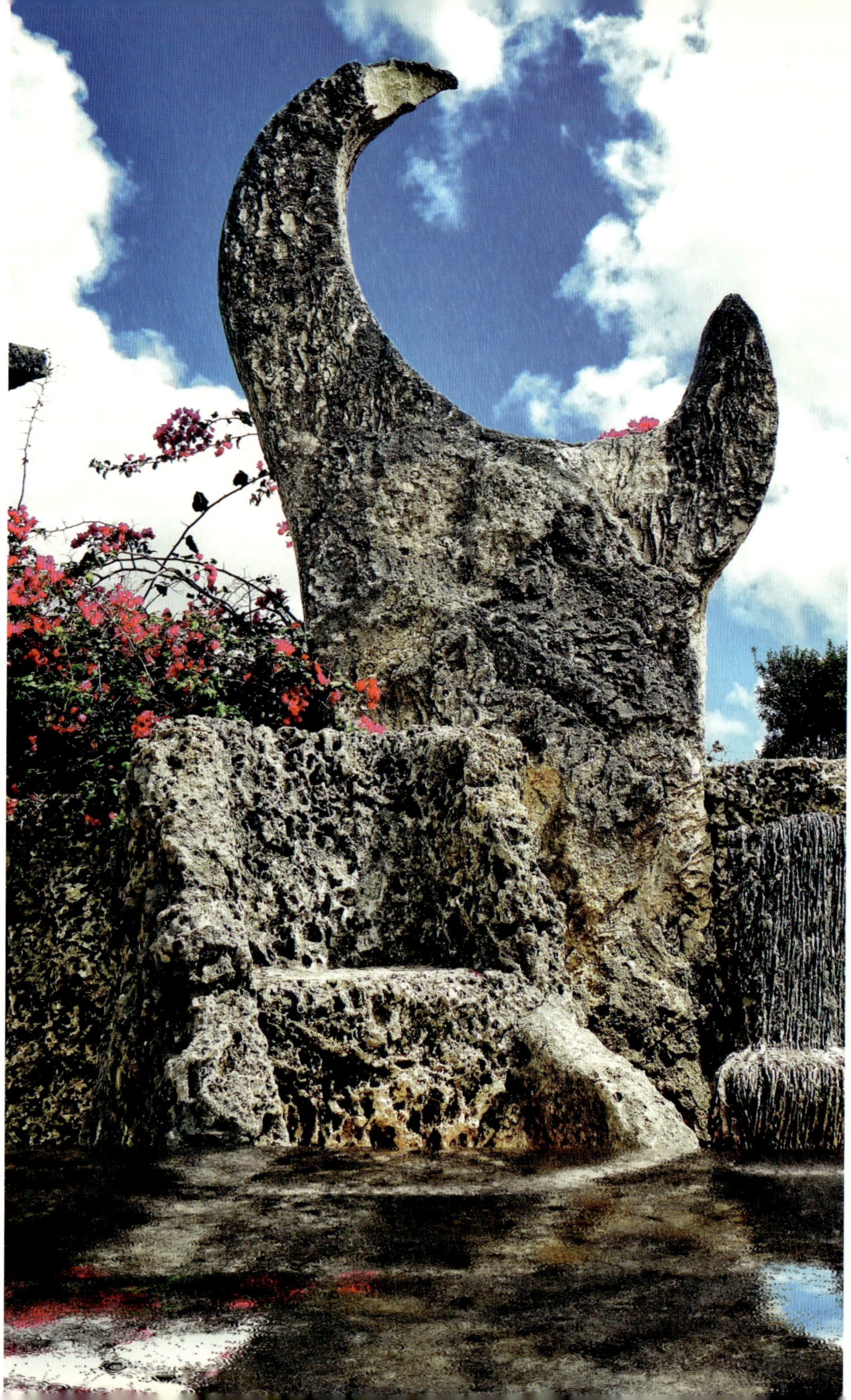

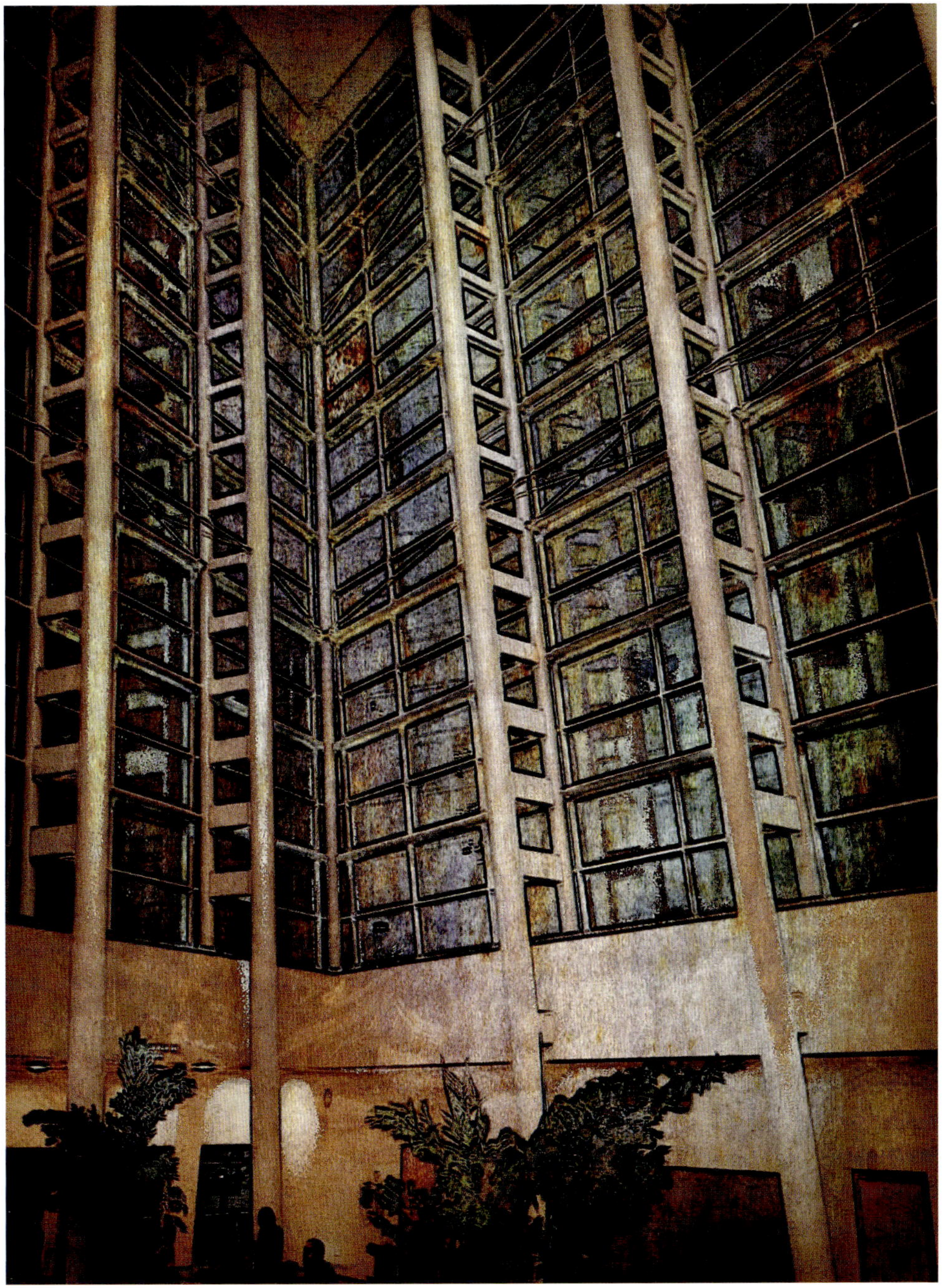

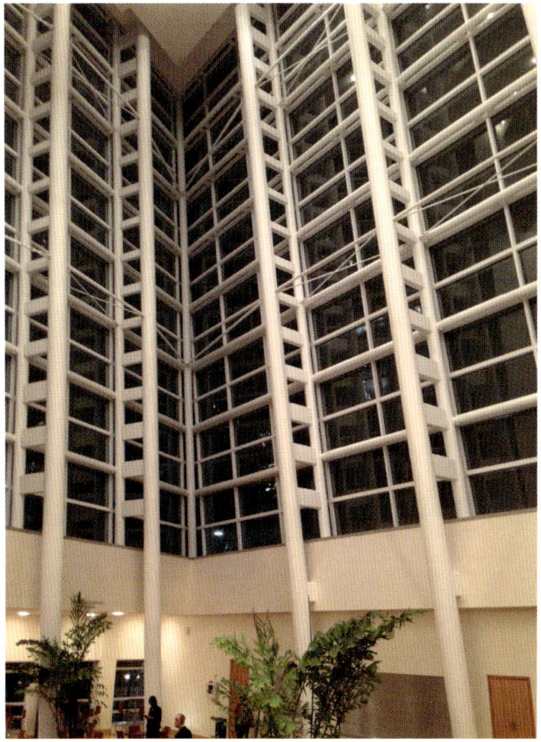

THE KNIGHT HALL

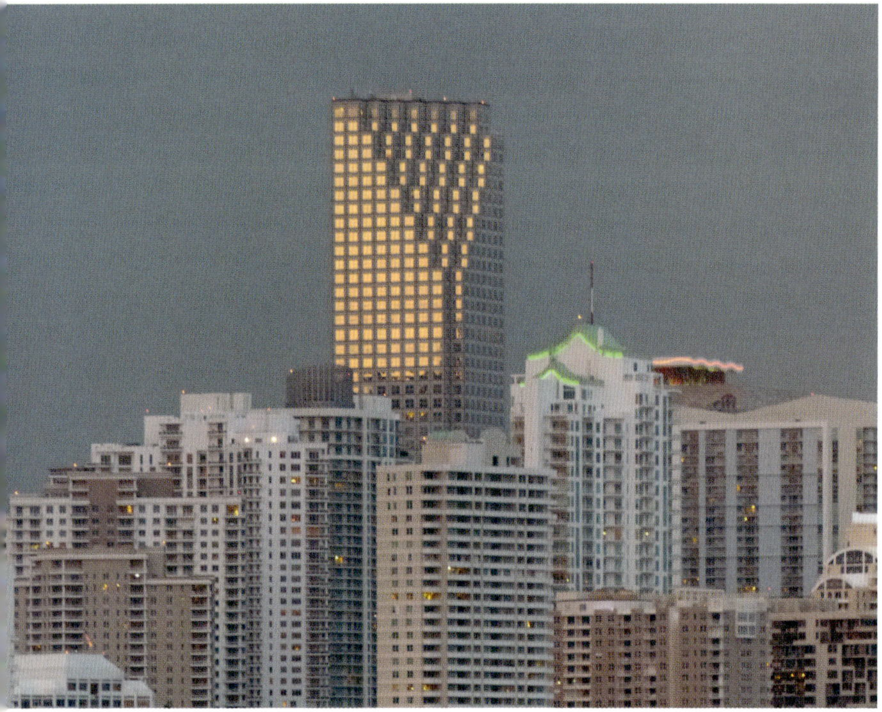

DOWNTOWN

Congested buildings
Fight to reach the sky
One rises above the others
One million square feet
Tall

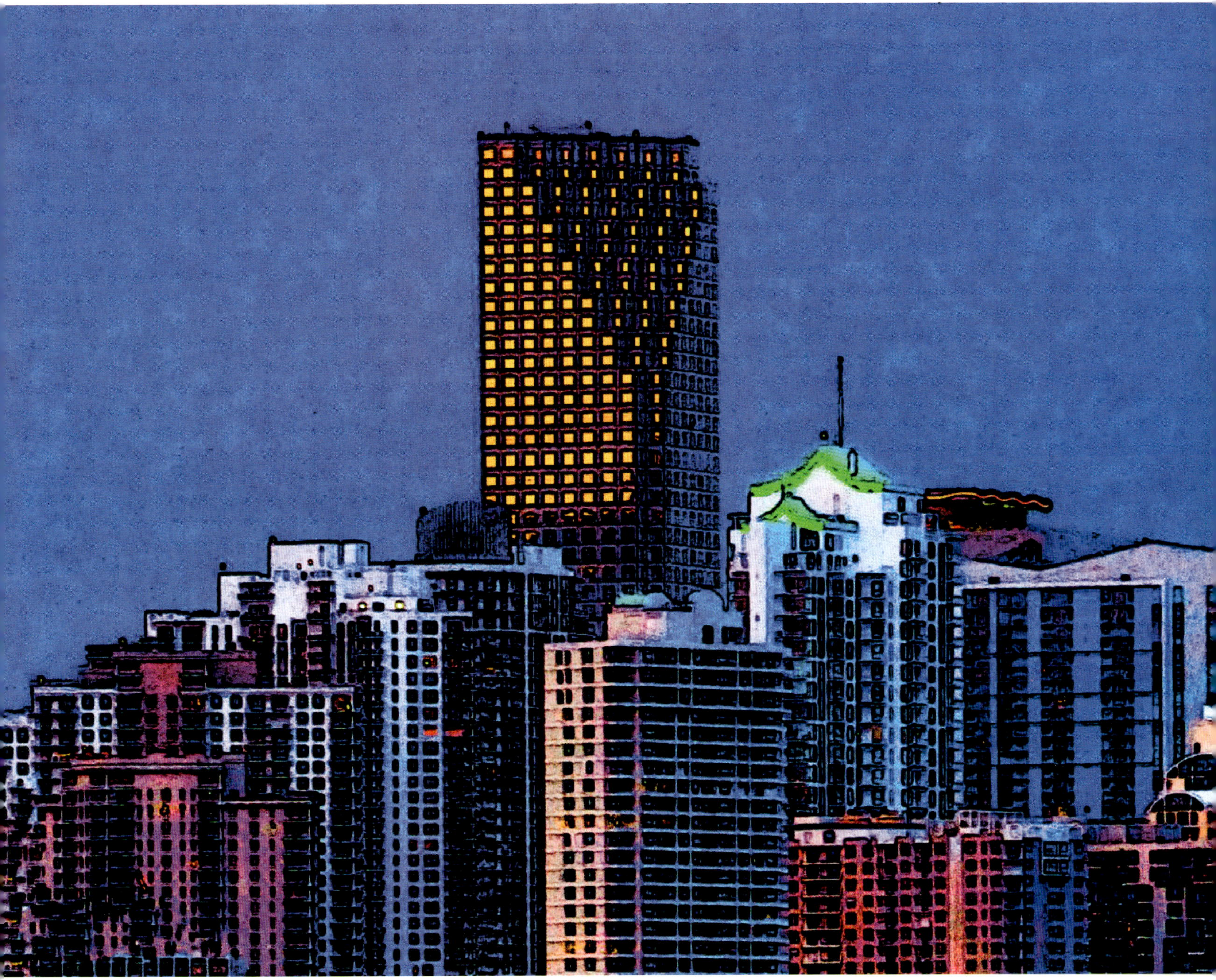

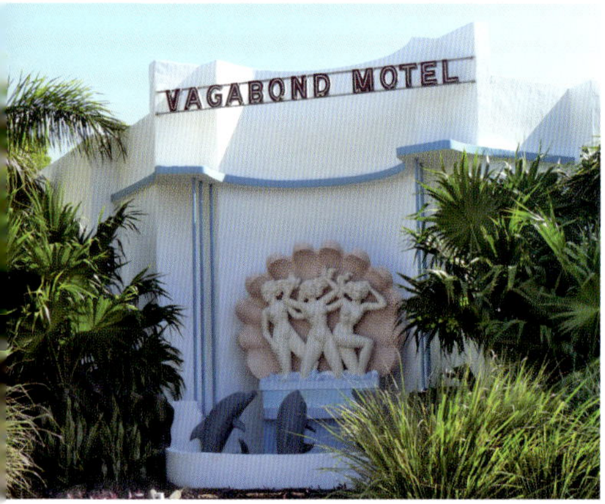

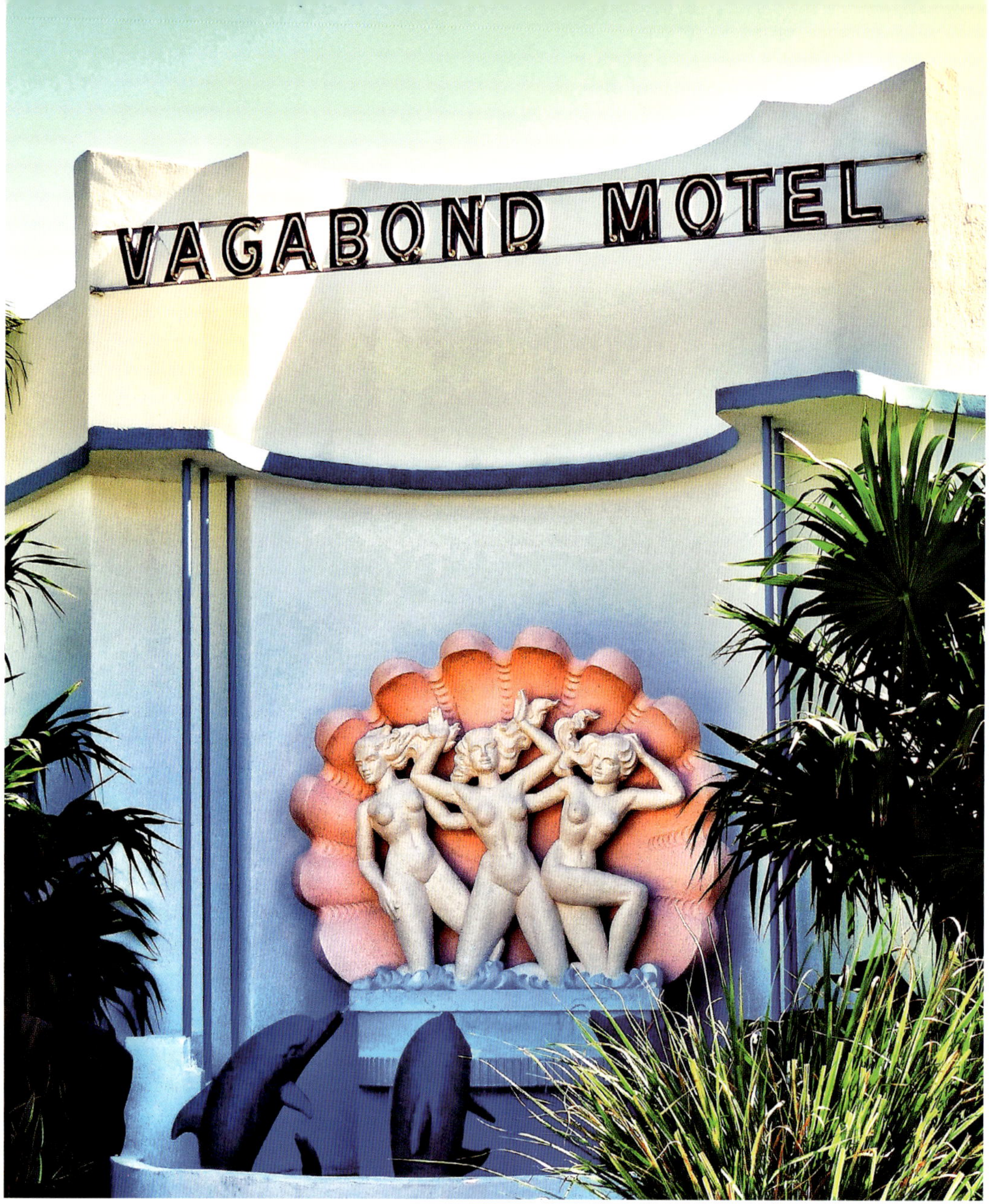

VAGABOND MOTEL

An old motel on Biscayne Boulevard
New restaurant, rooms, and pool
Not just for vagabonds anymore

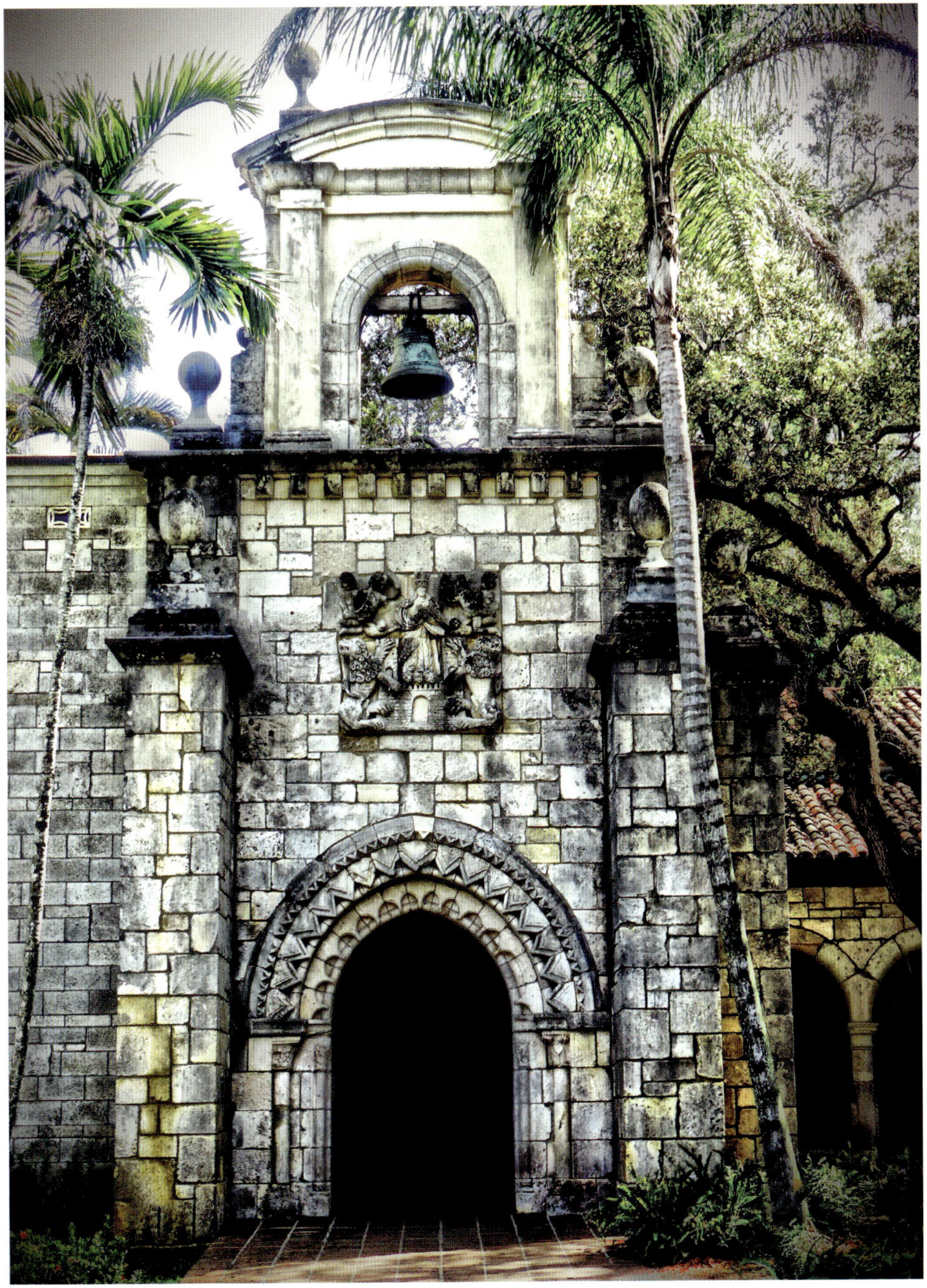

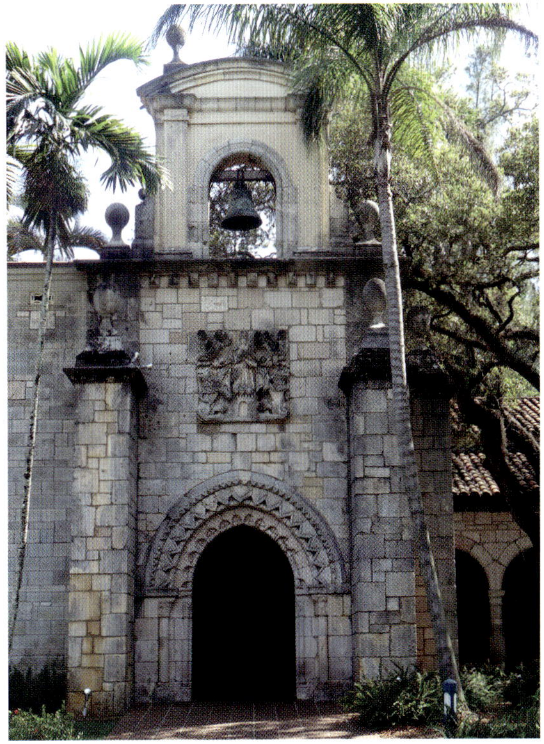

SPANISH MONASTERY I

Built by Spain in the twelfth century
Bought by William Randolph Hearst in 1931
Sold in 1952
Reconstructed in 1964
What a history

SPANISH MONASTERY II

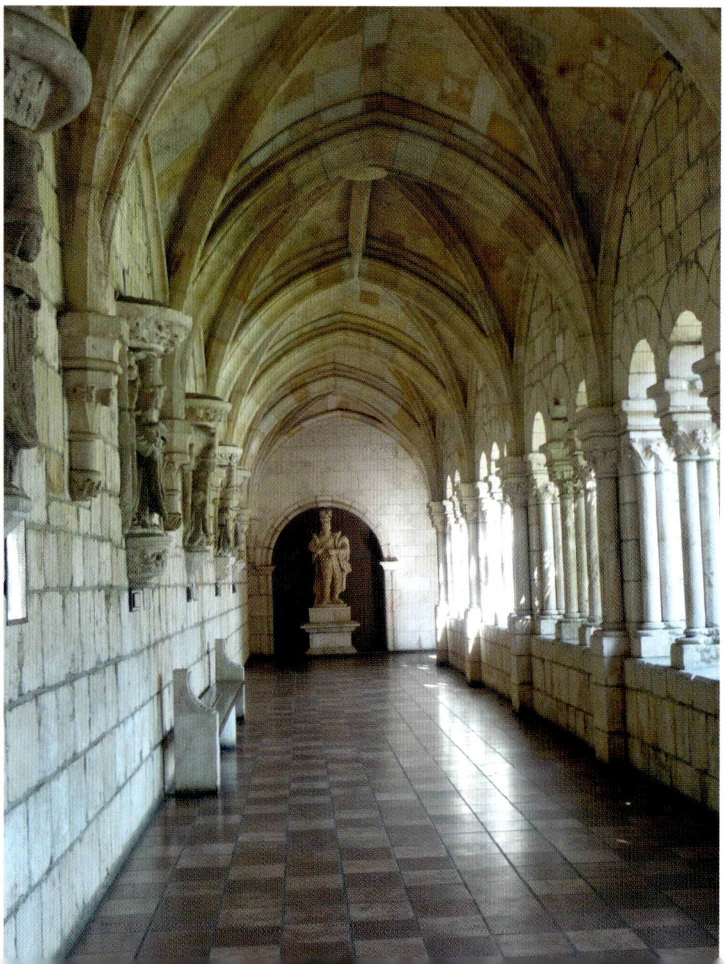

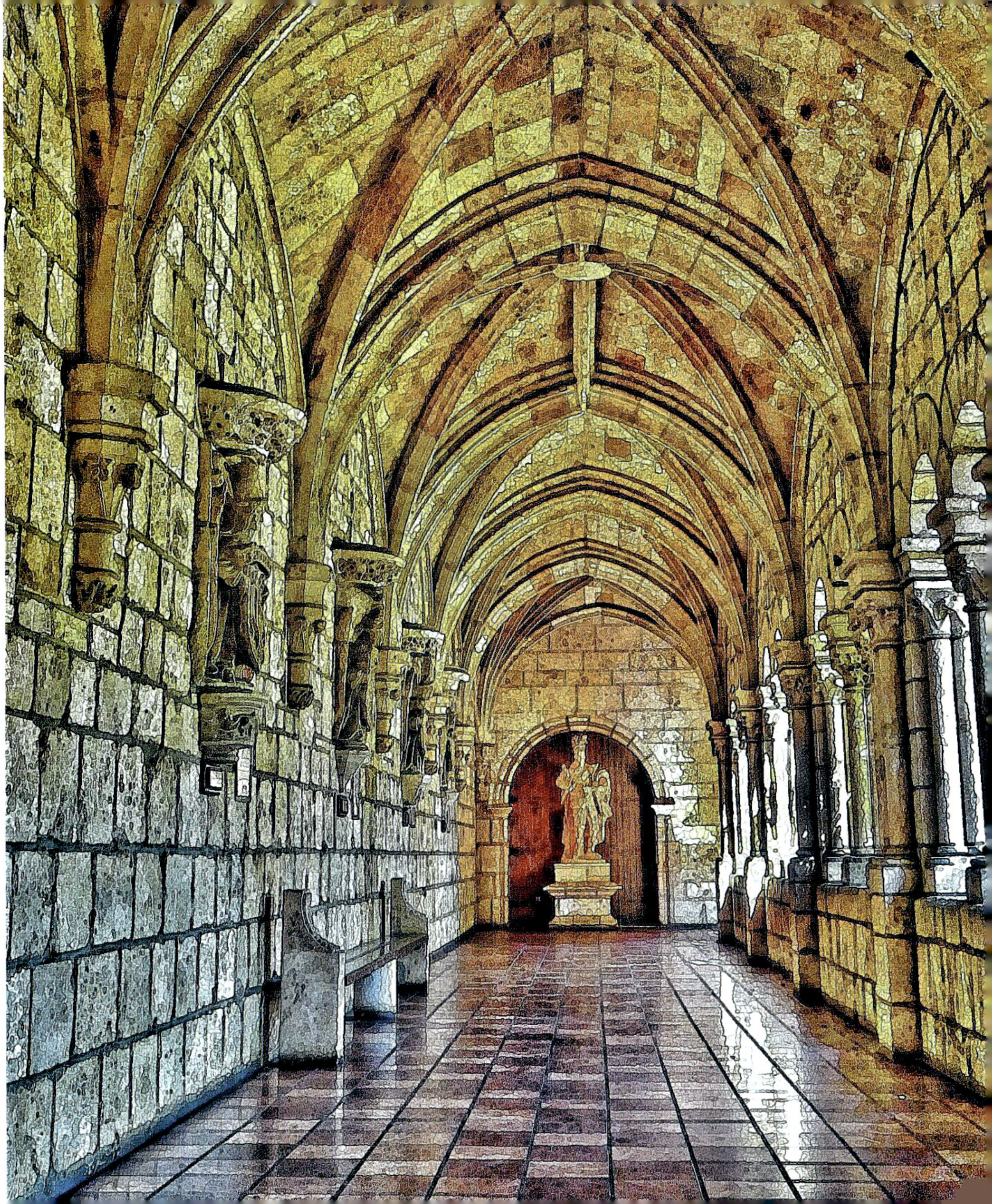

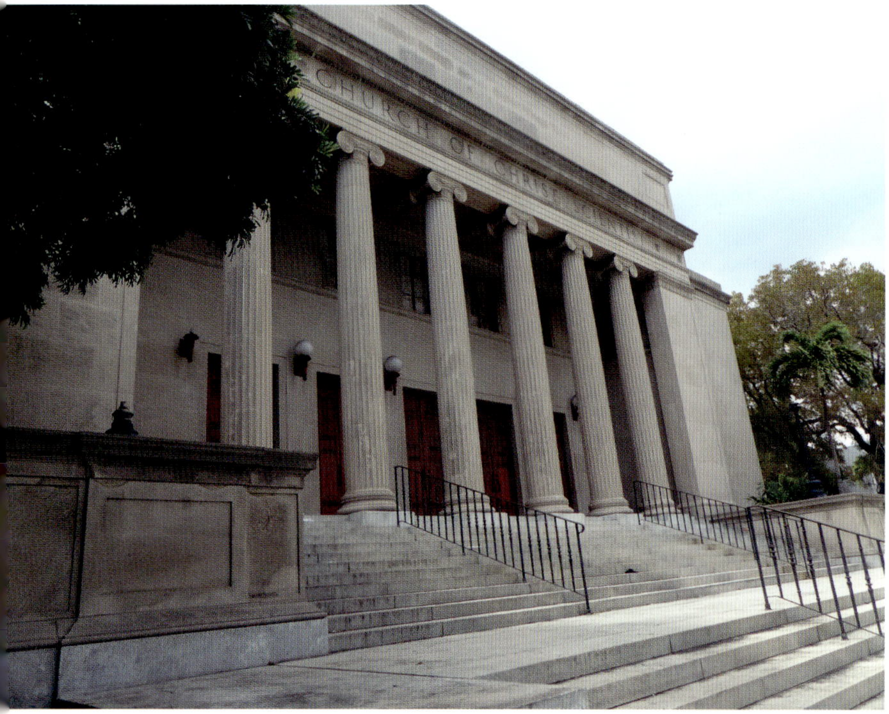

FIRST CHURCH OF CHRIST SCIENTIST

Abandoned church on Biscayne Boulevard

It will live as a part of a new development

Majestic

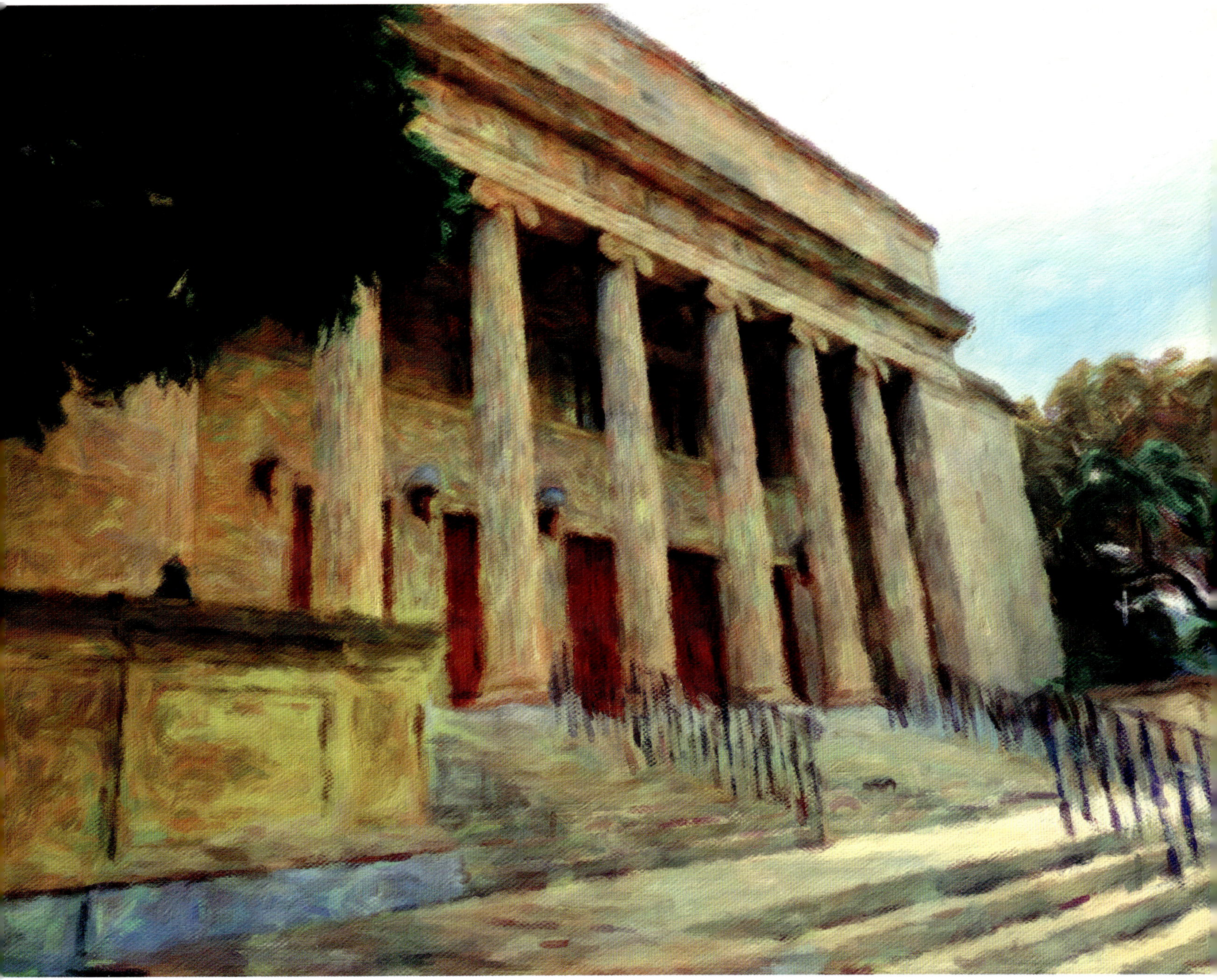

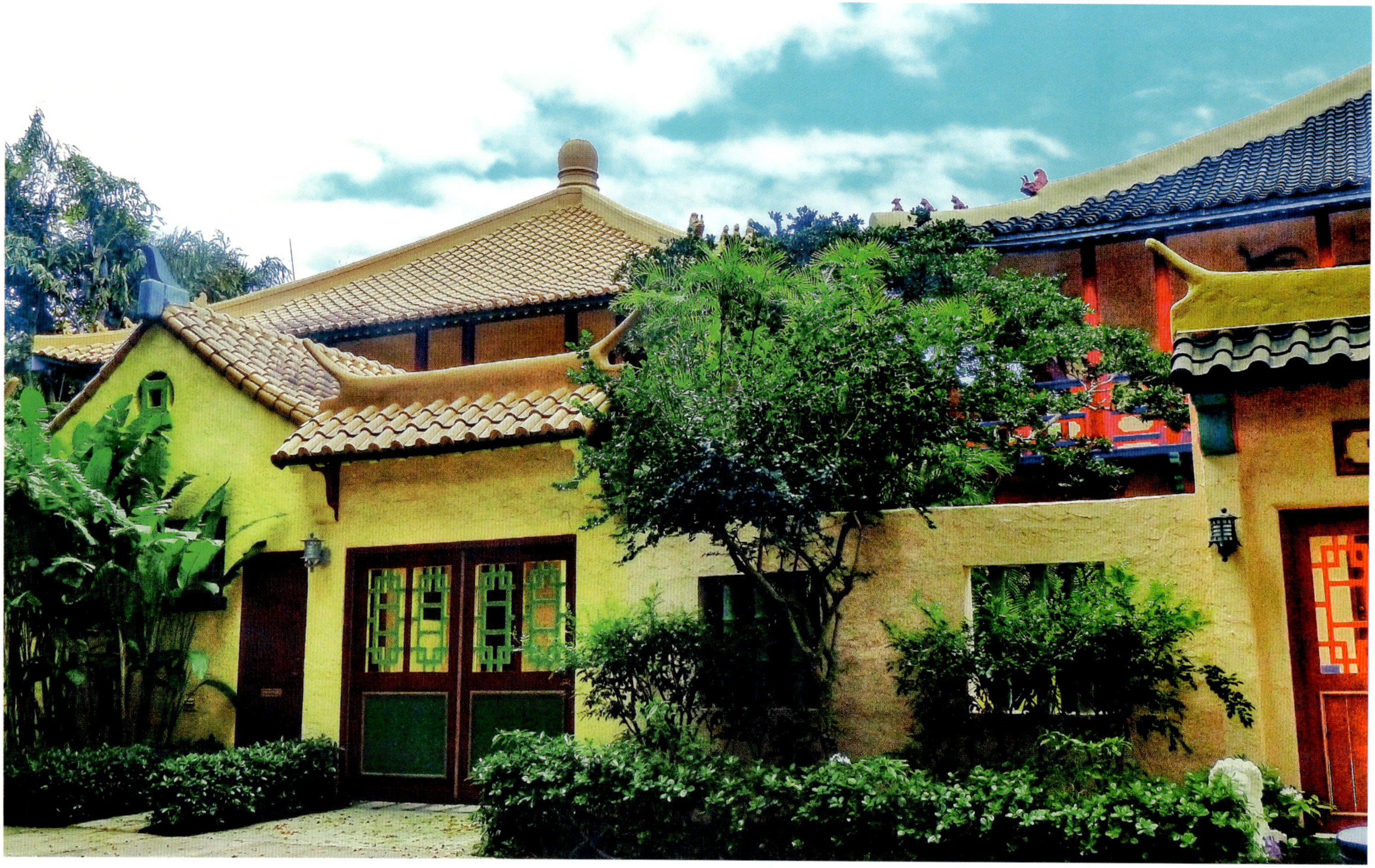

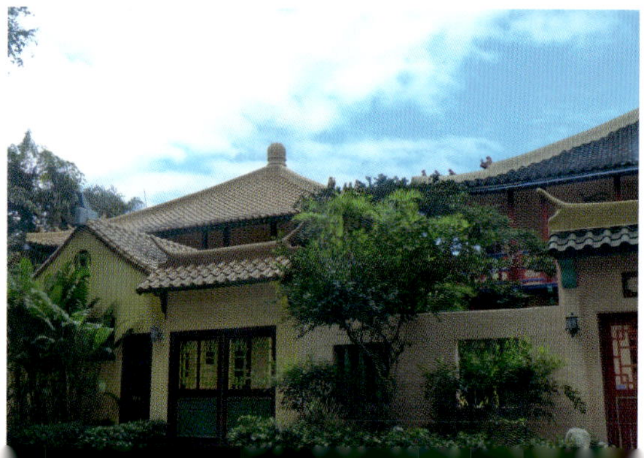

CHINESE VILLAGE

One of the thematic villages in Coral Gables
Built in 1925 by George Merrick
Diversity in a Mediterranean-style neighborhood
Friendly

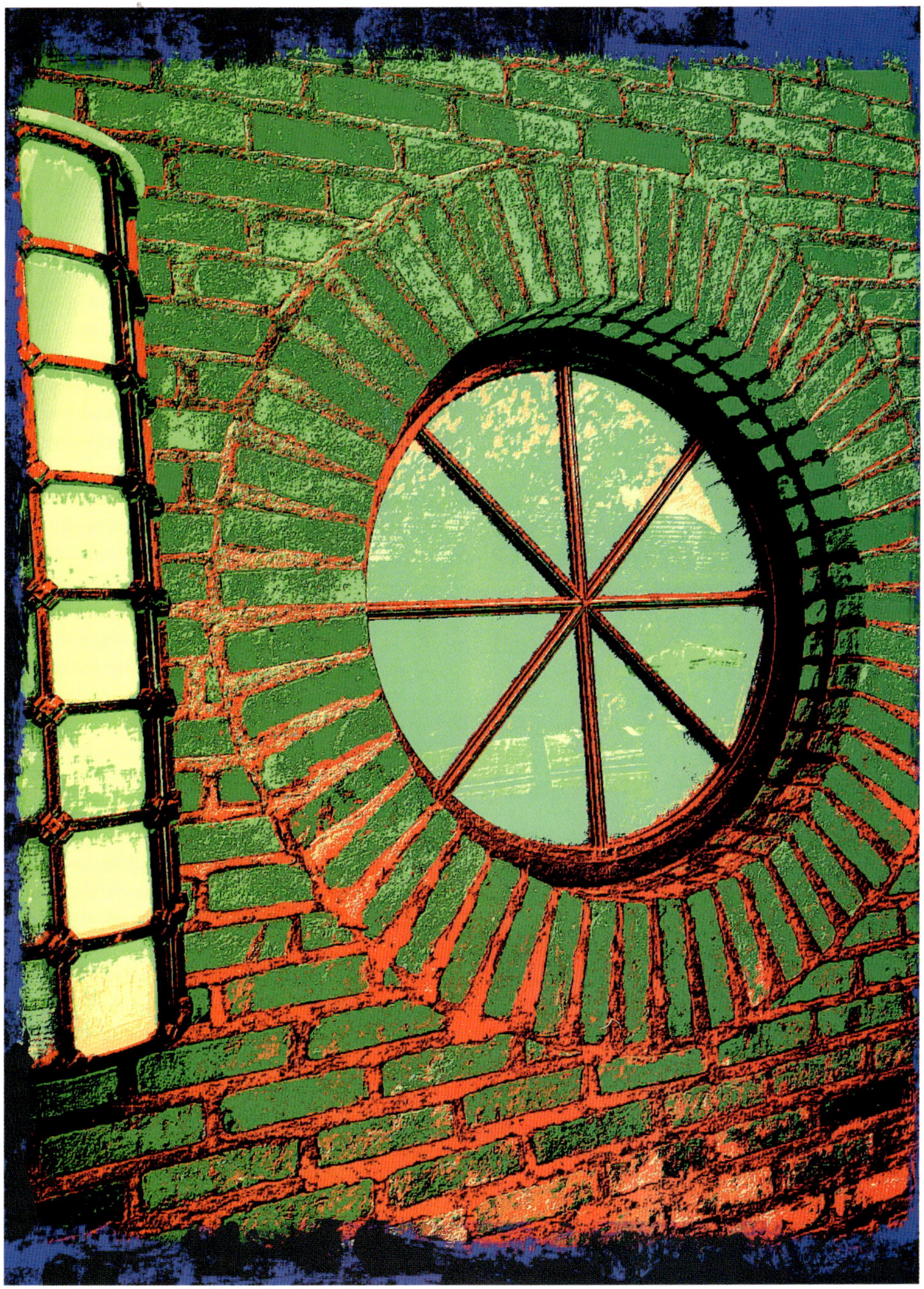

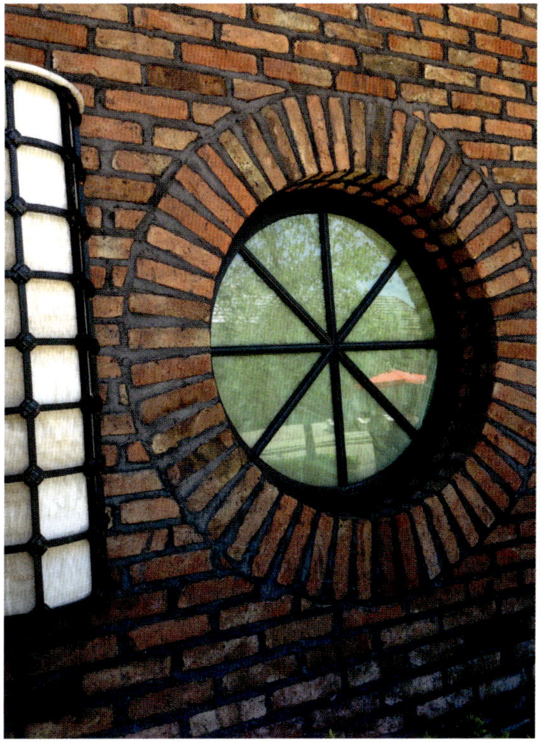

ROUND WINDOW

Brick surrounding a restaurant window
Goes green with red grout
And from ordinary to ooh-la-la

BACARDI BUILDING

International-style architecture

Built in the 1960s

A statement of Miami's tropical modernism

Rum

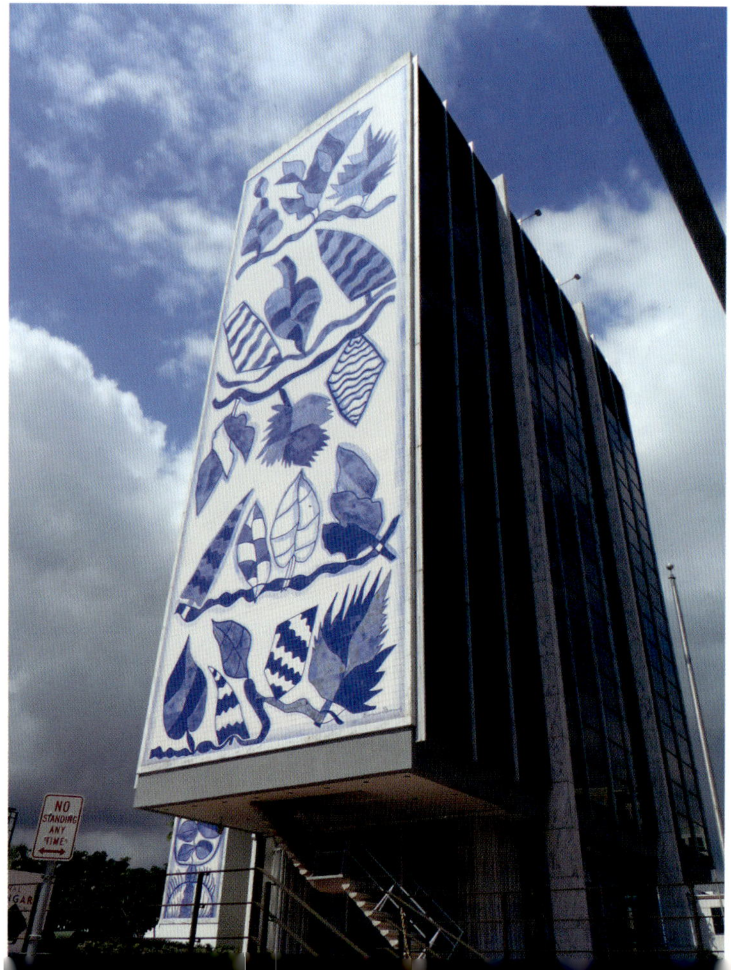

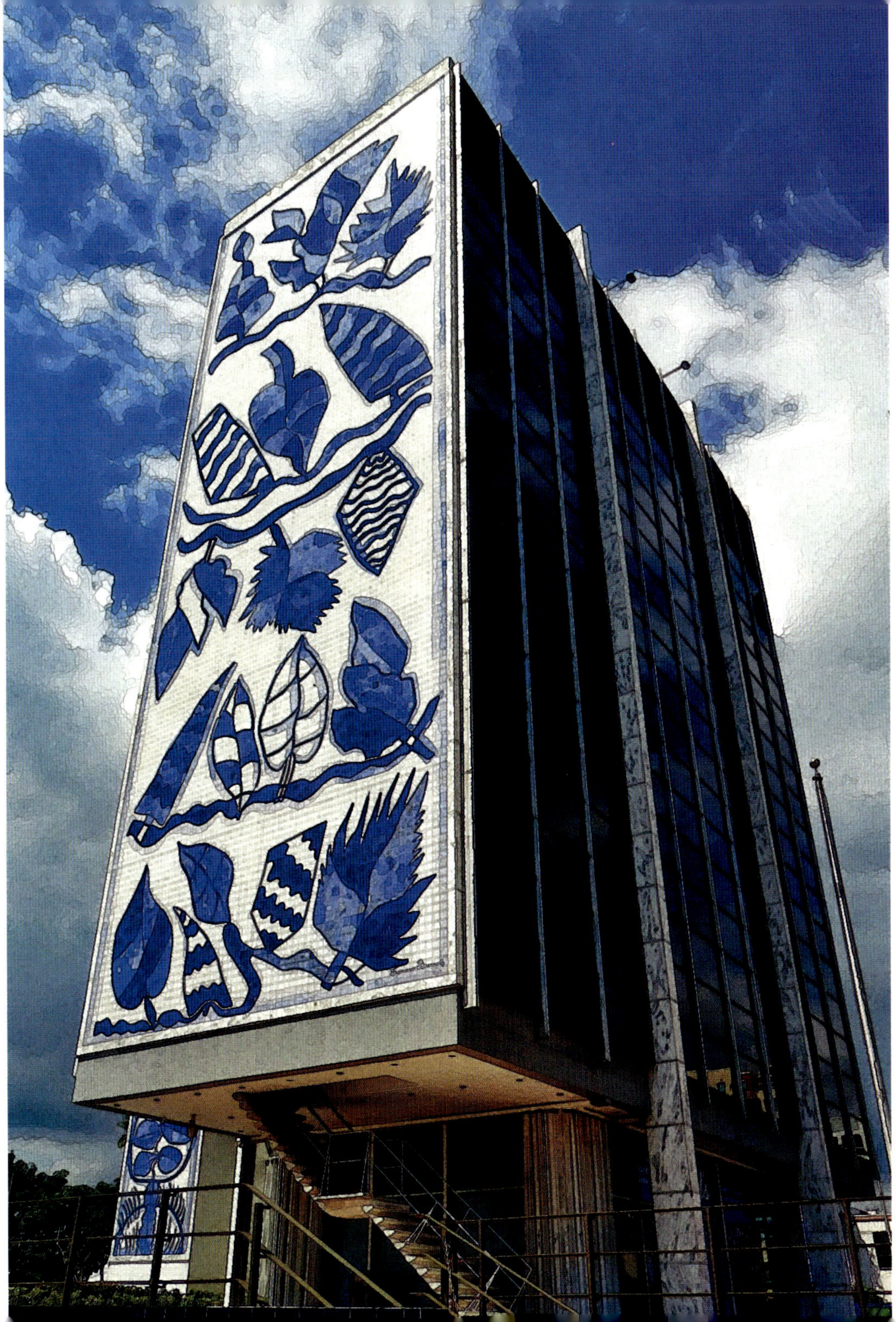

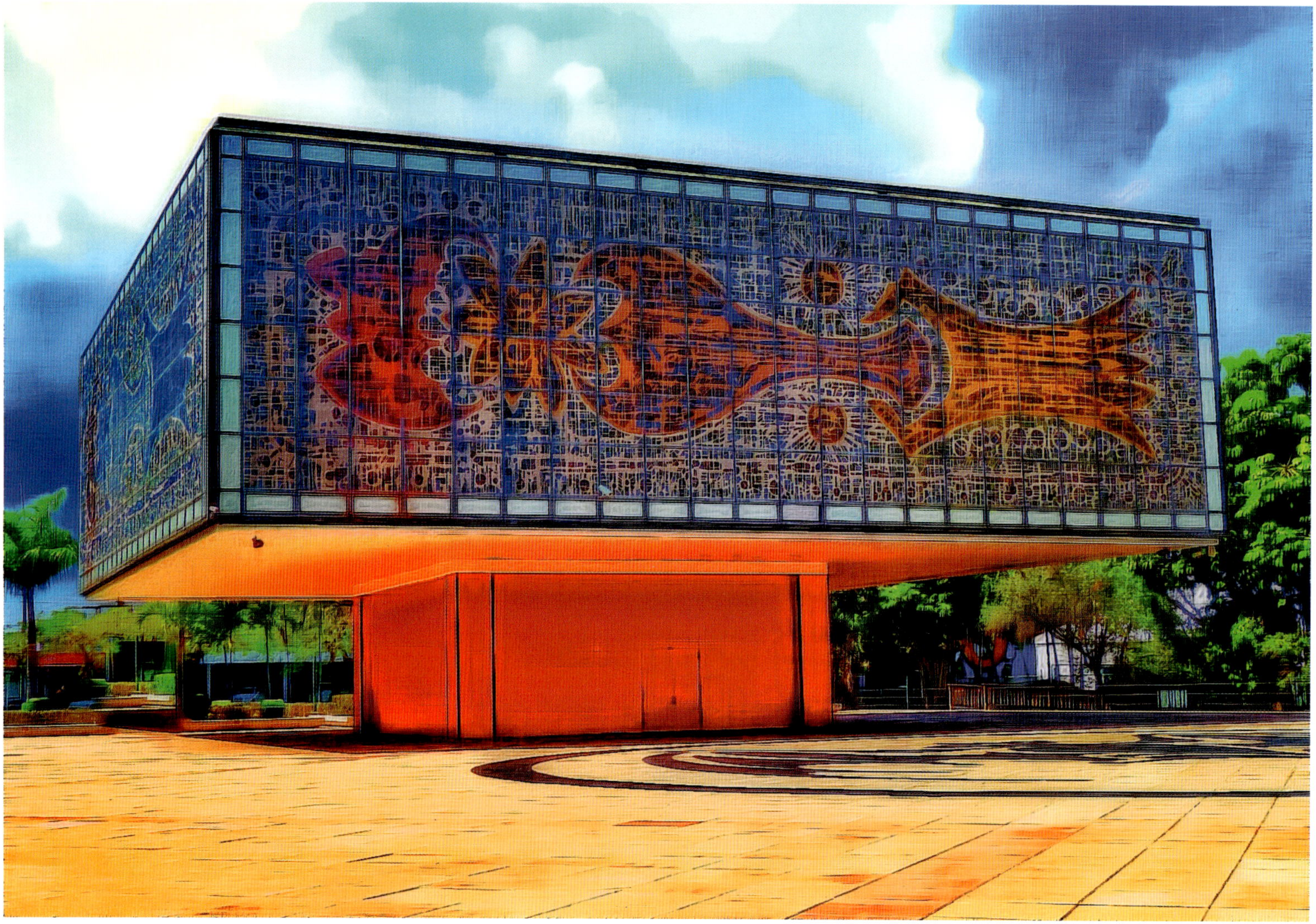

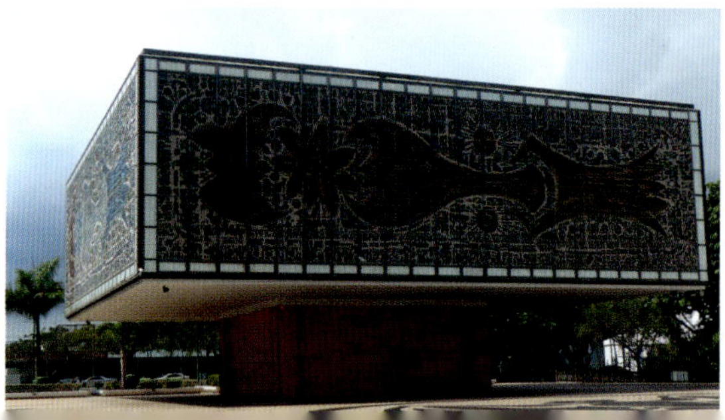

BACARDI II

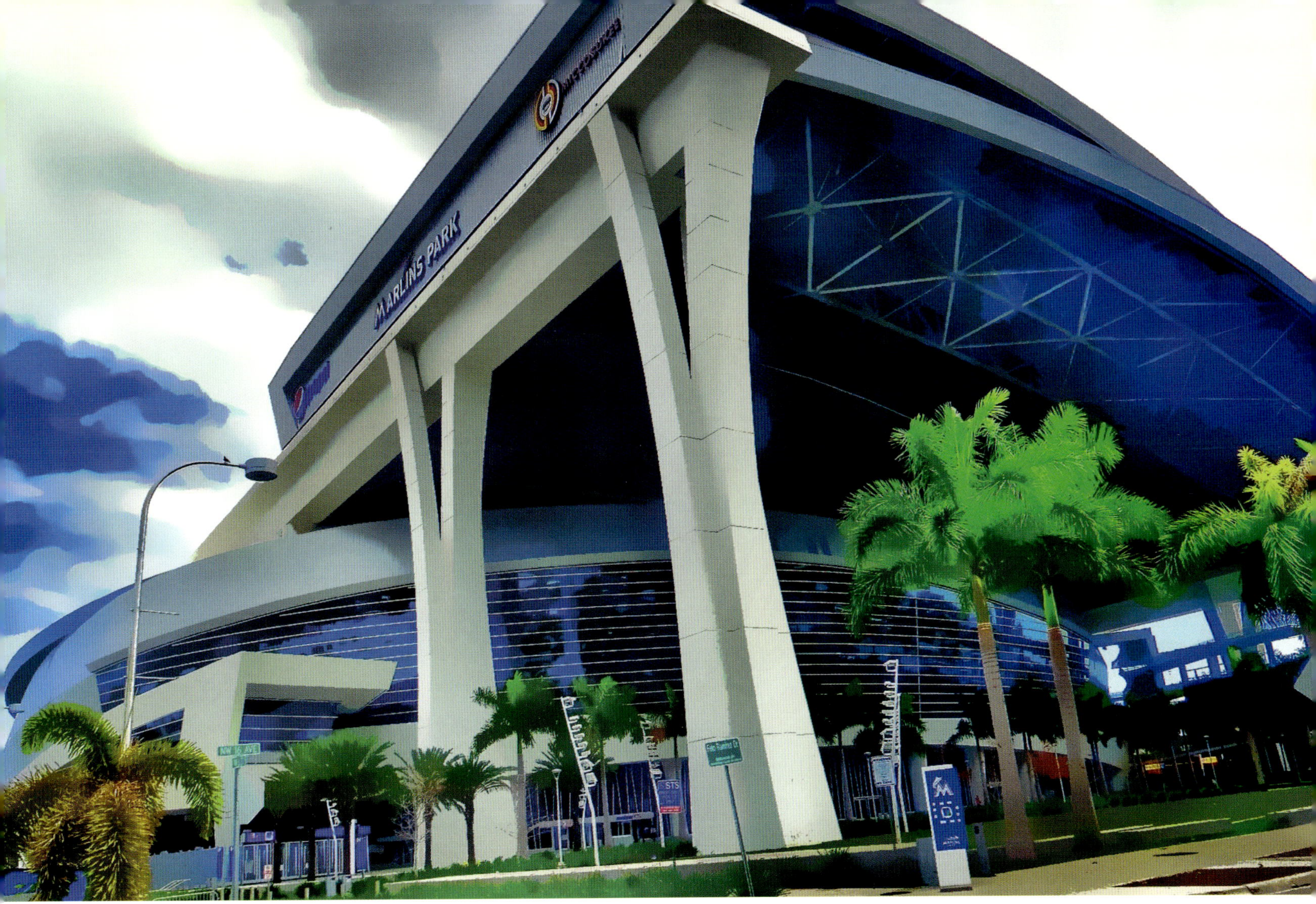

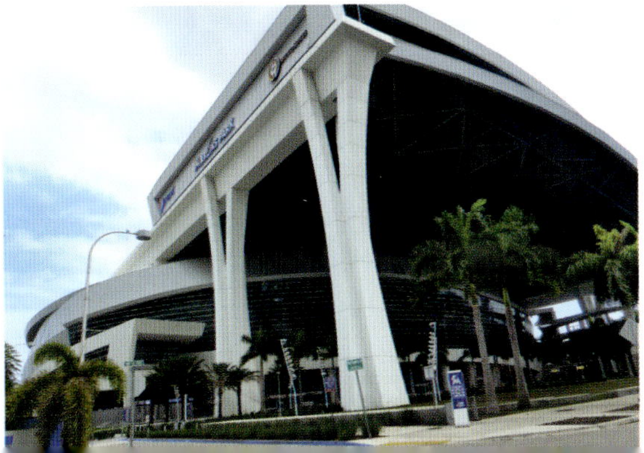

MIAMI MARLINS PARK I

Miami Marlins baseball stadium built in 2012

Originally the Orange Bowl football stadium

A real home run

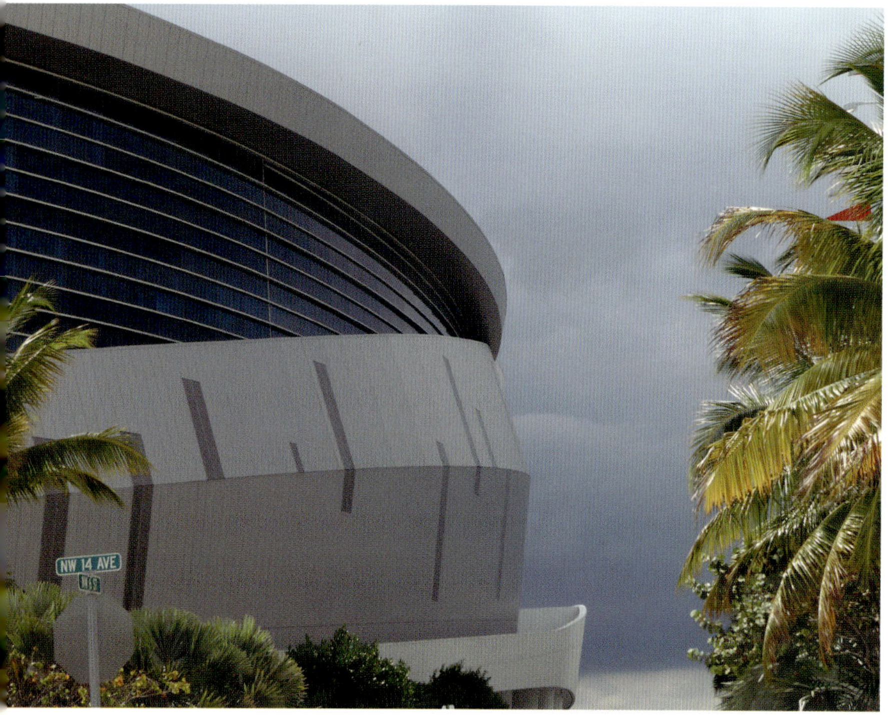

MIAMI MARLINS PARK II

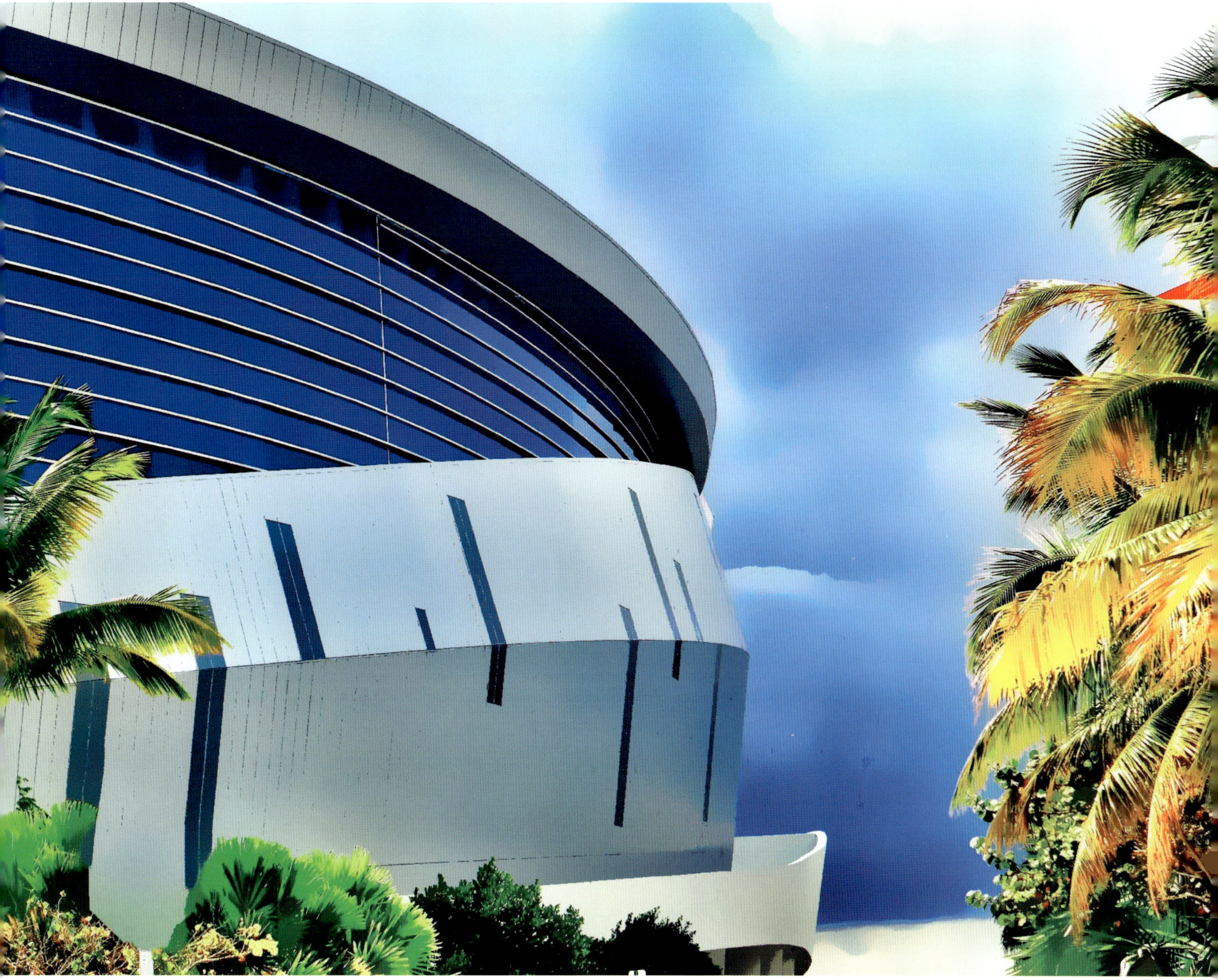

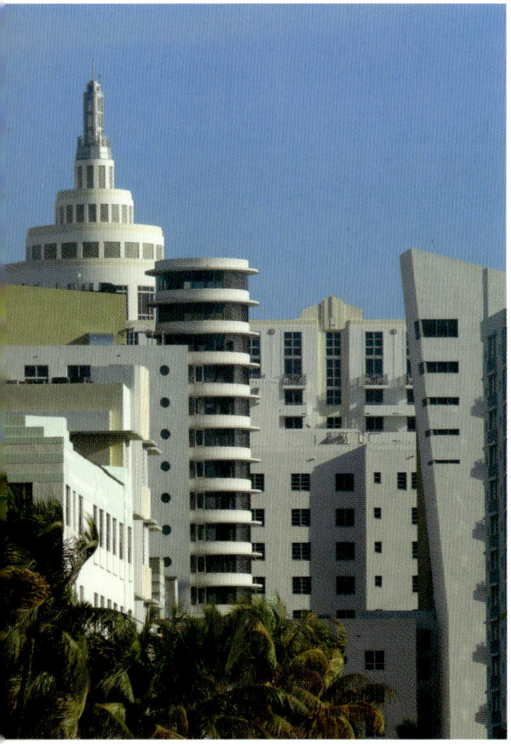

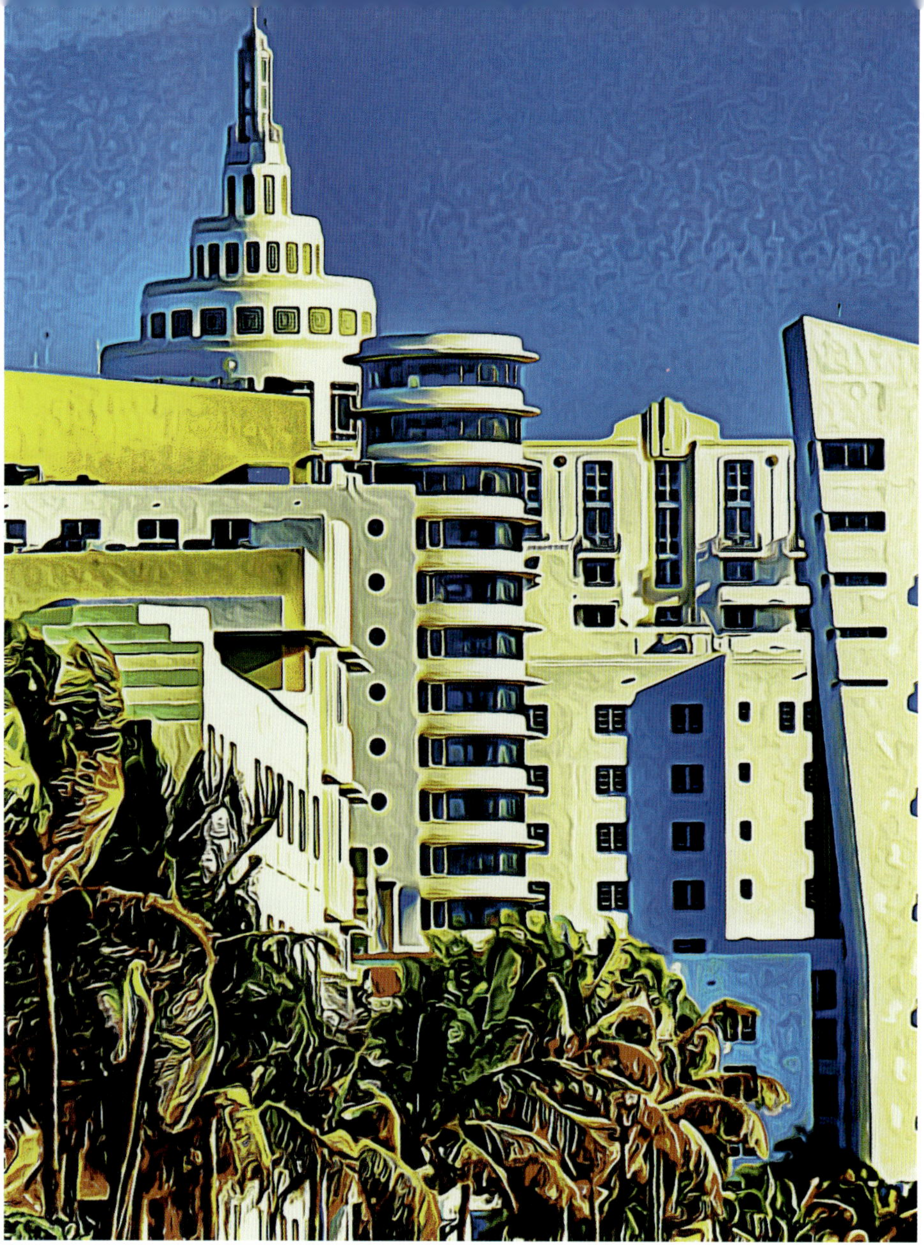

DECO BUILDINGS

A collection of buildings from the 1930s
Set off by palm trees and a blue sky
Composed

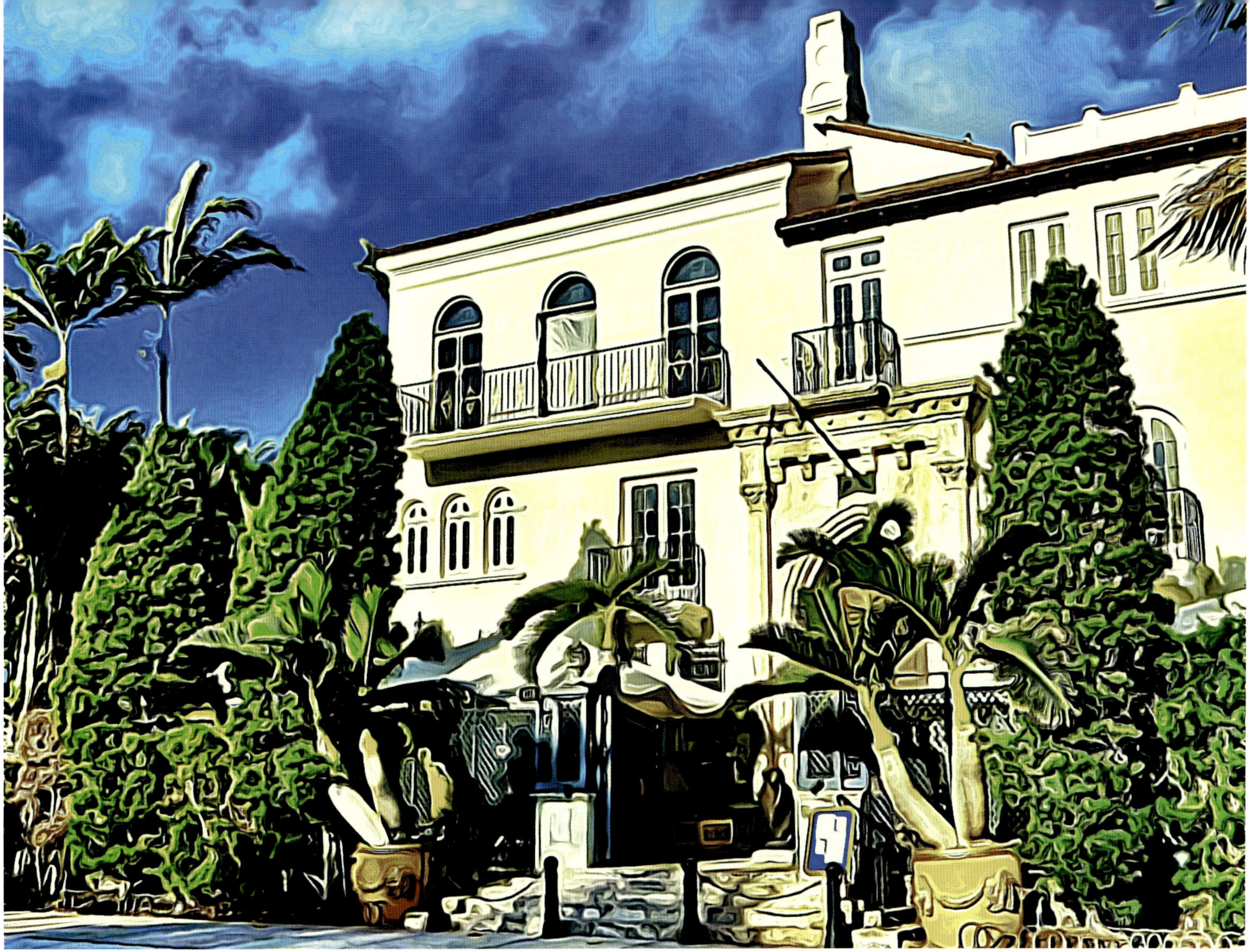

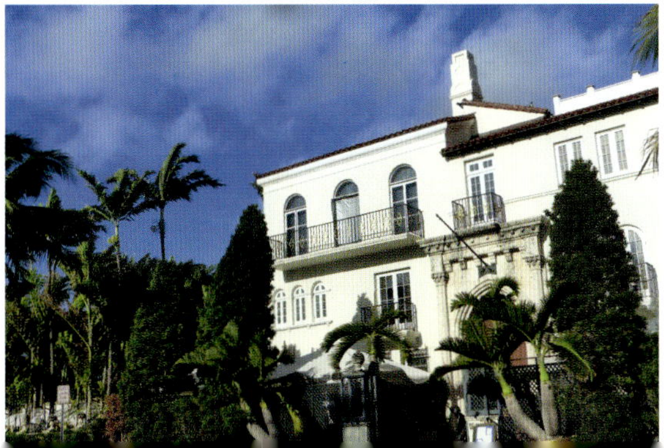

VERSACE MANSION

Beautiful hotel

Home of Gianni Versace

He was murdered at the mansion

Tragic

BREAKWATER HOTEL

South Beach art deco icon

Breezy palm trees

Blue sky

Old sign

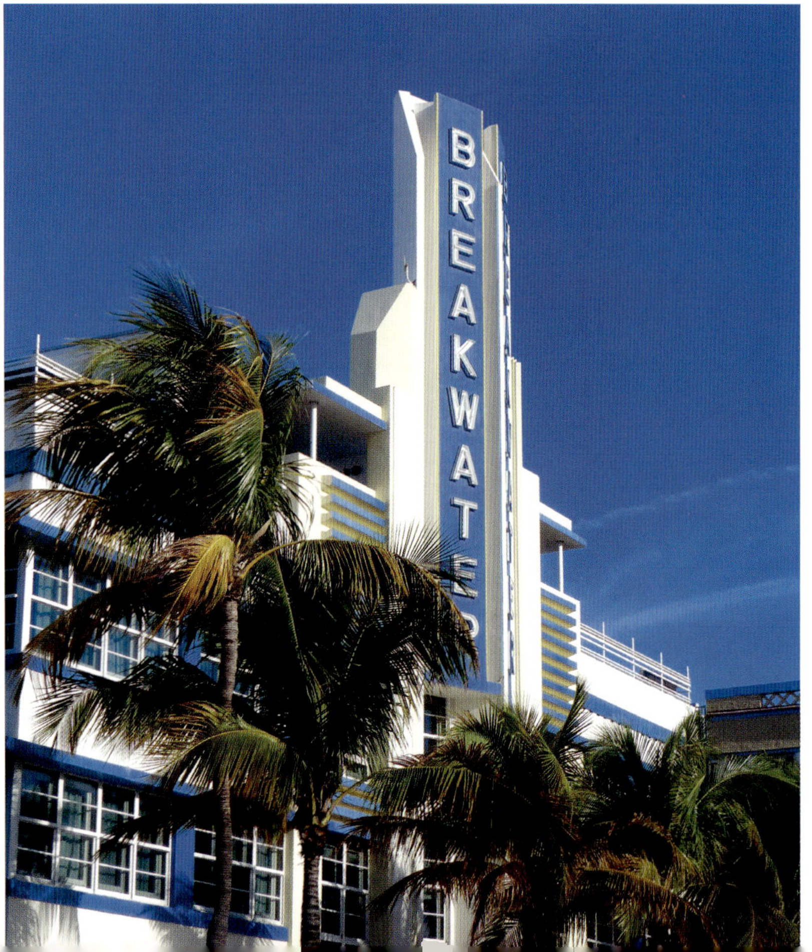

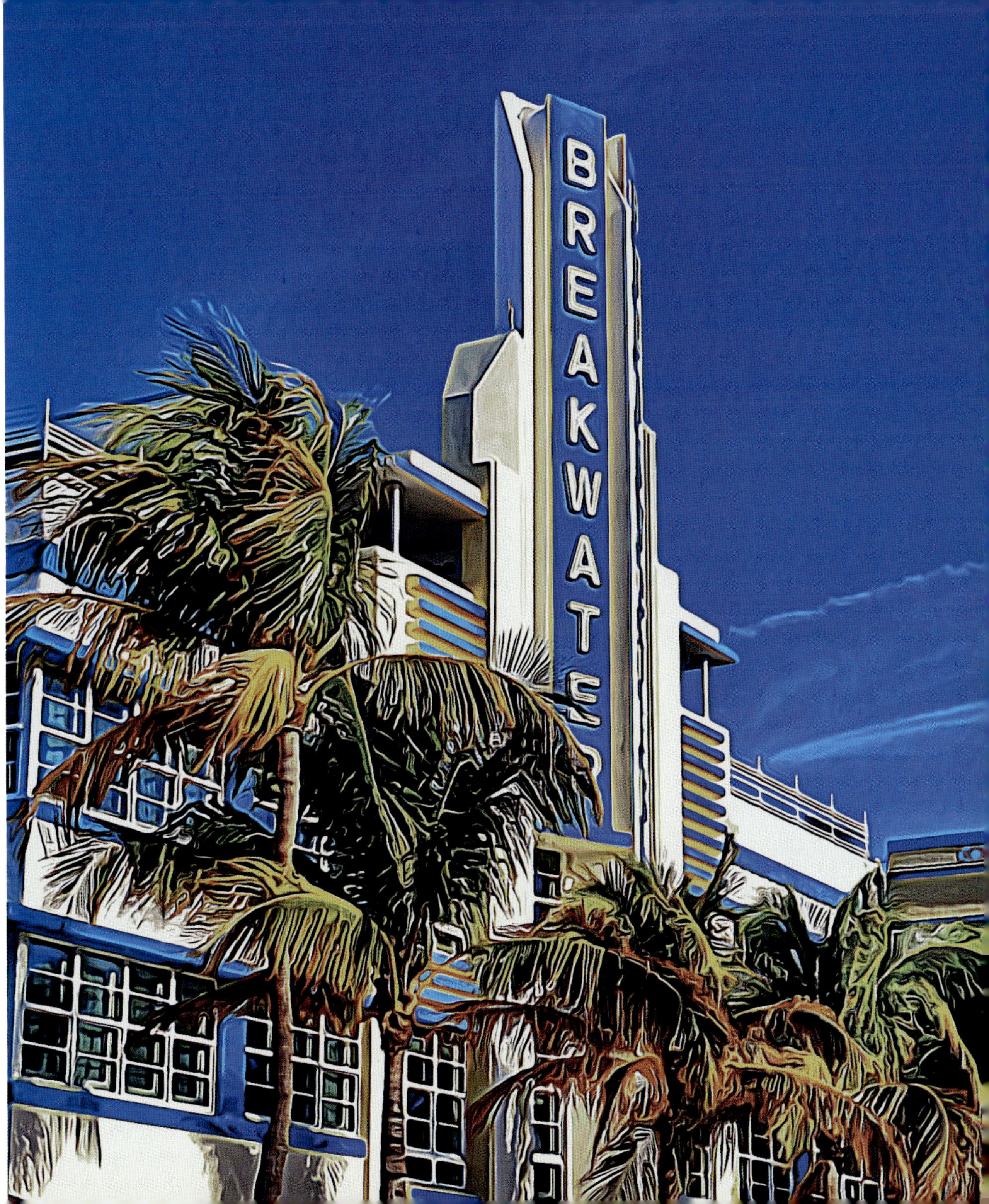
BREAKWATE

OCEAN DRIVE

Park Central Hotel on Ocean Drive

Strong breezes, blues

Painterly

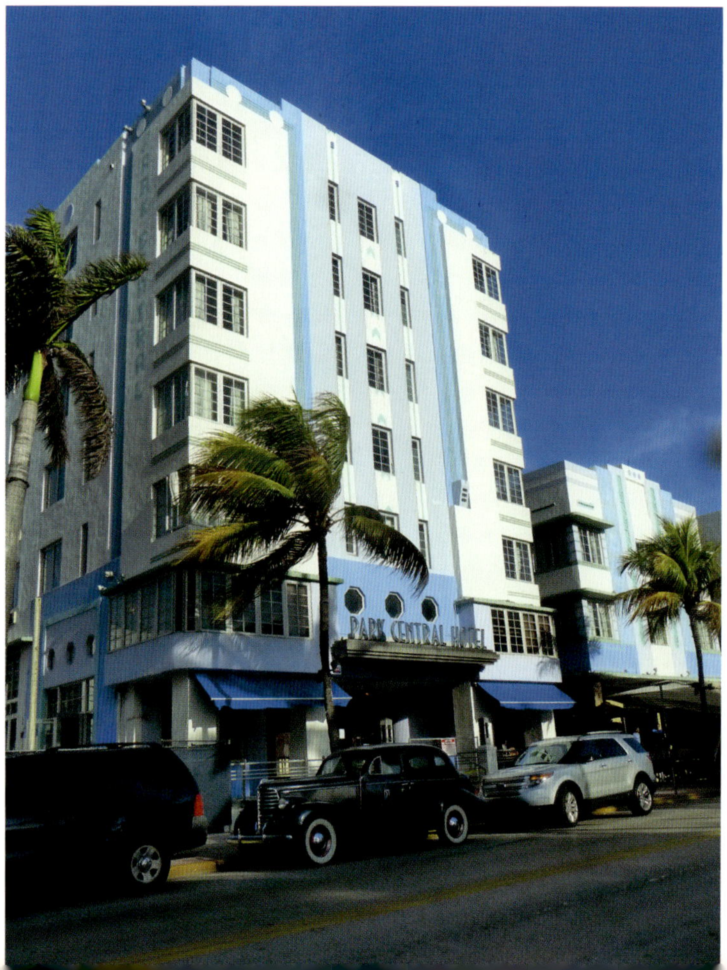

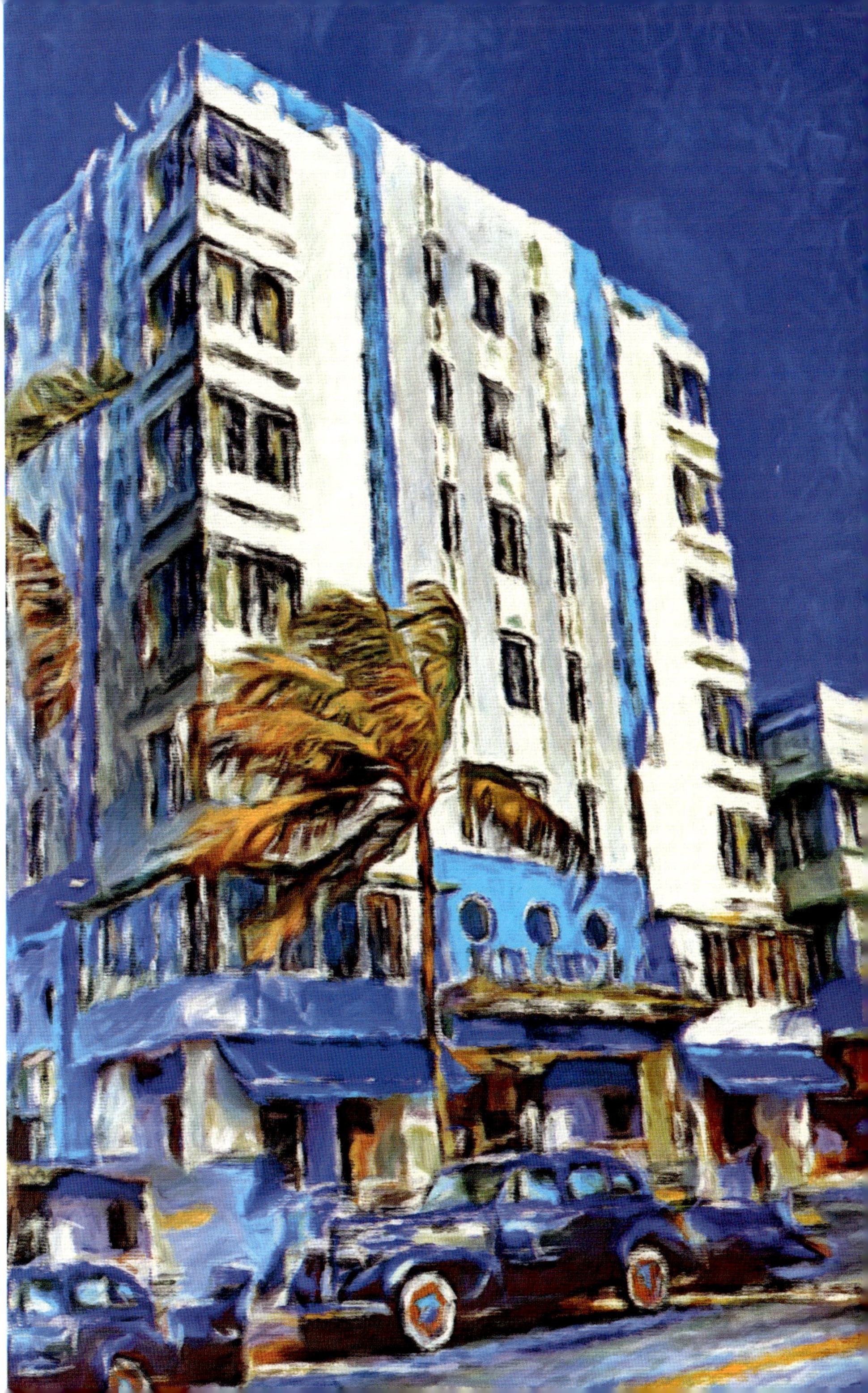

COLONY HOTEL

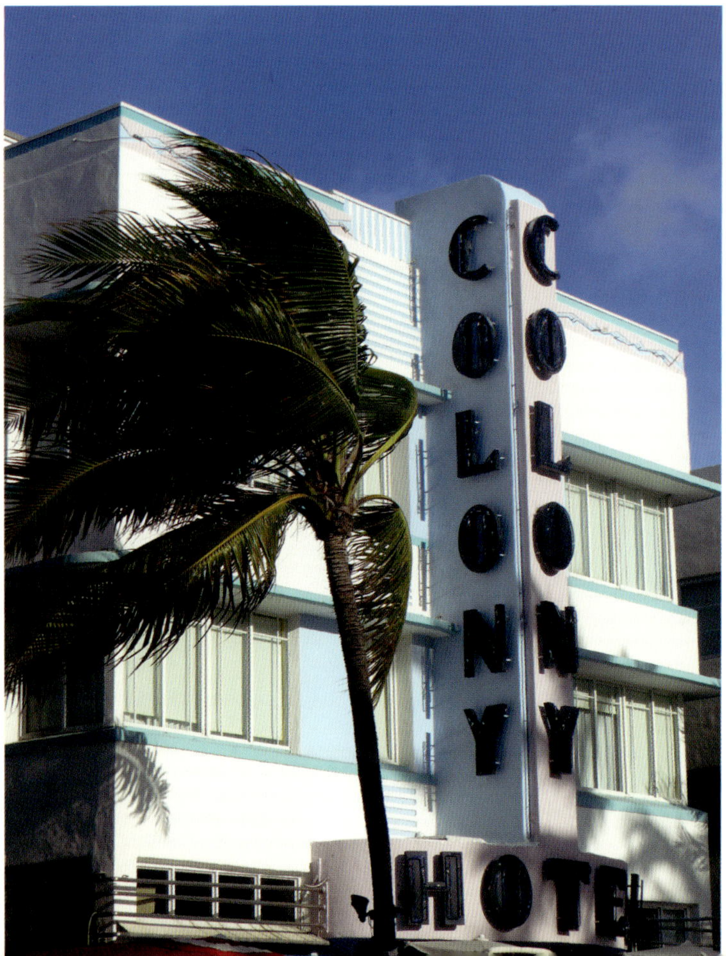

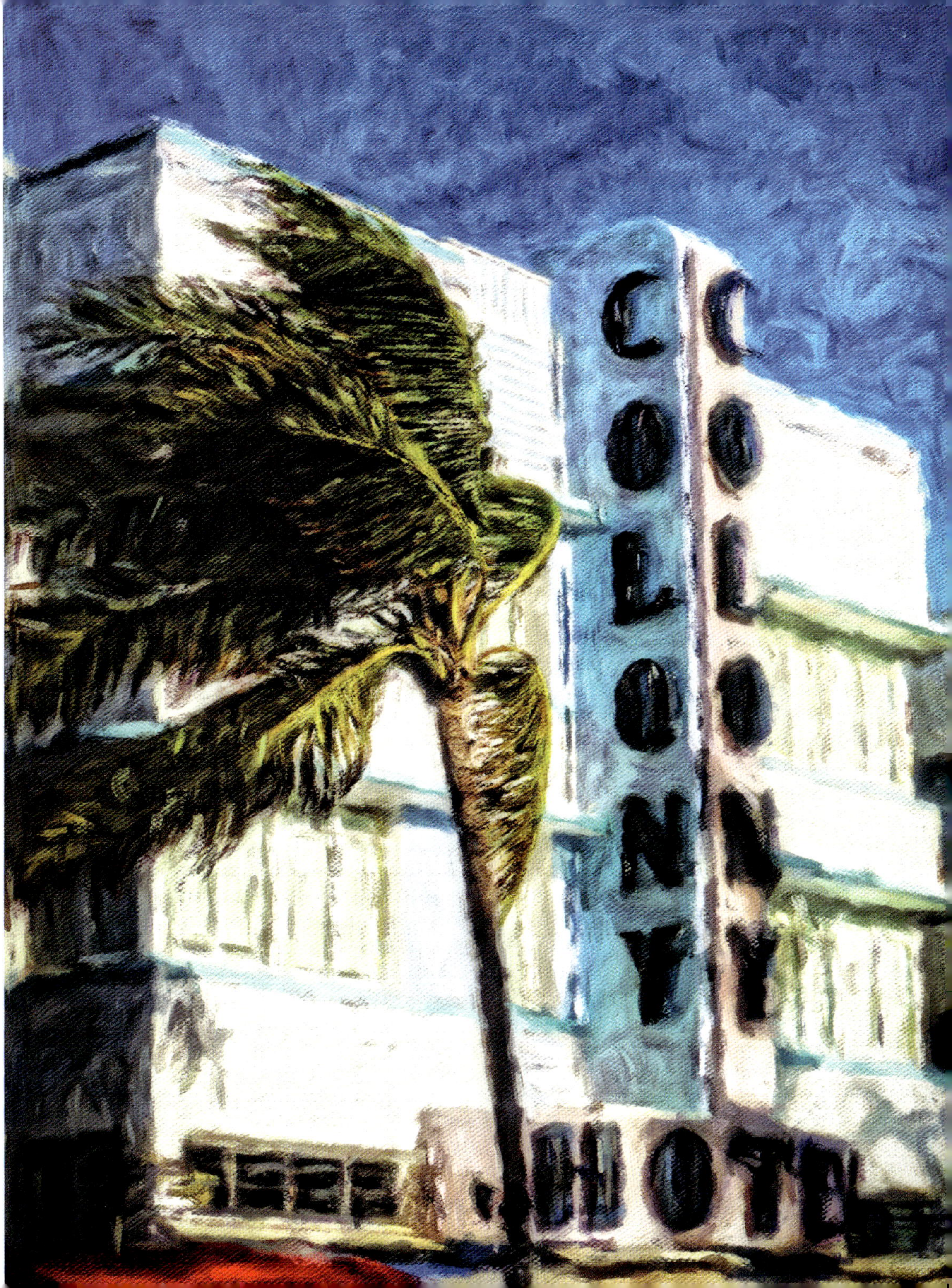
COLONY
COLONY

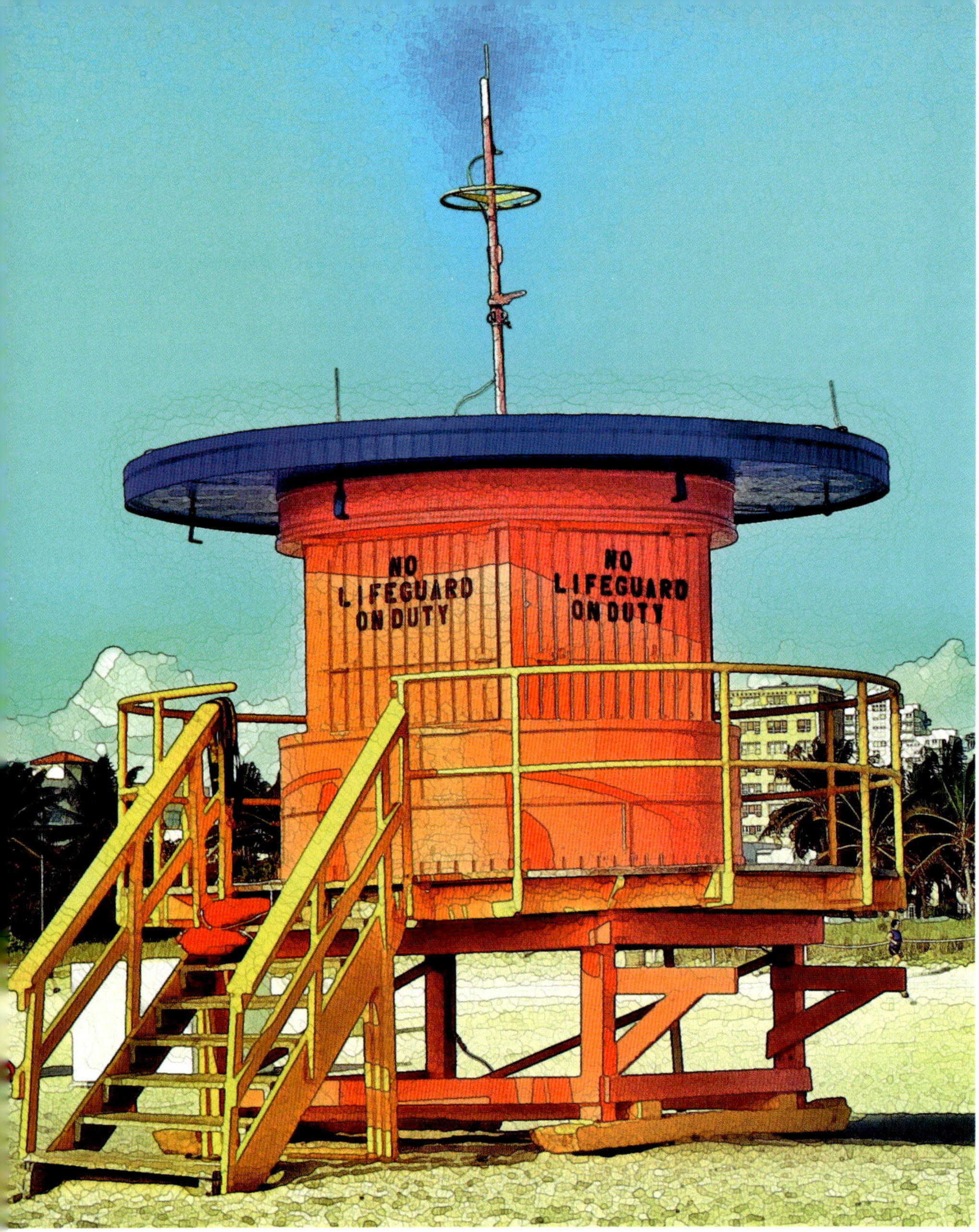

LIFEGUARD STATION

Across from the hotels on Ocean Drive
Lifeguard stations are ready
No lifeguards yet
No drowning

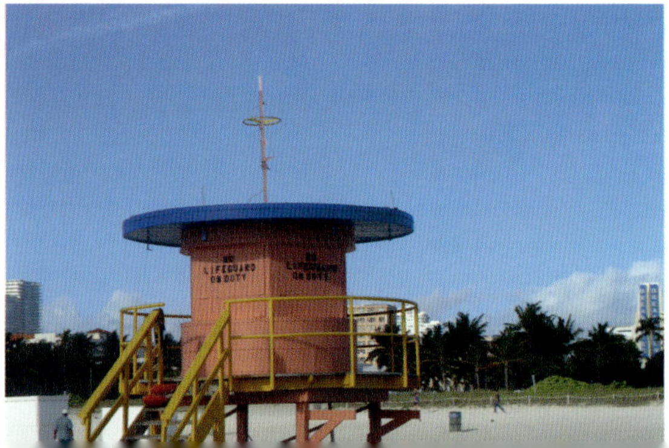

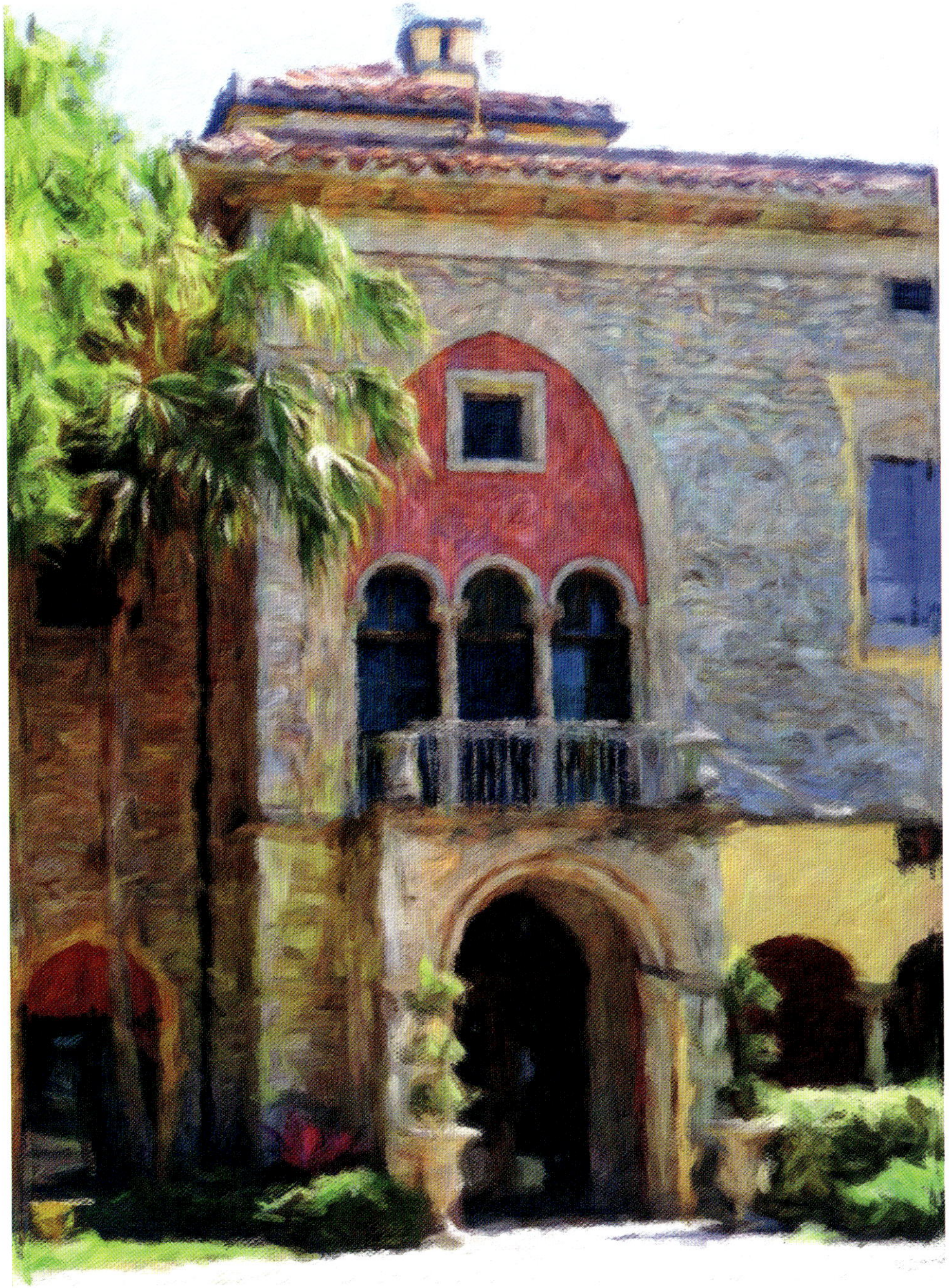

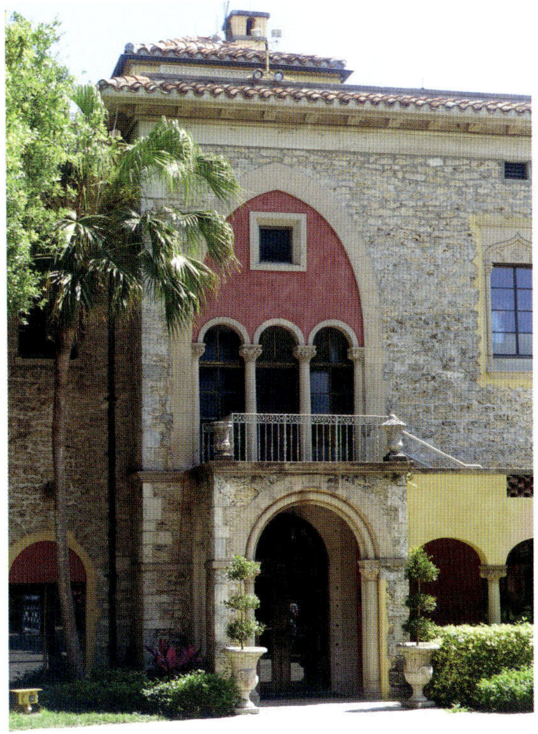

CHARLES DEERING ESTATE

Built in 1927

Destroyed by Hurricane Andrew in 1992

After a seven-year restoration

History is back

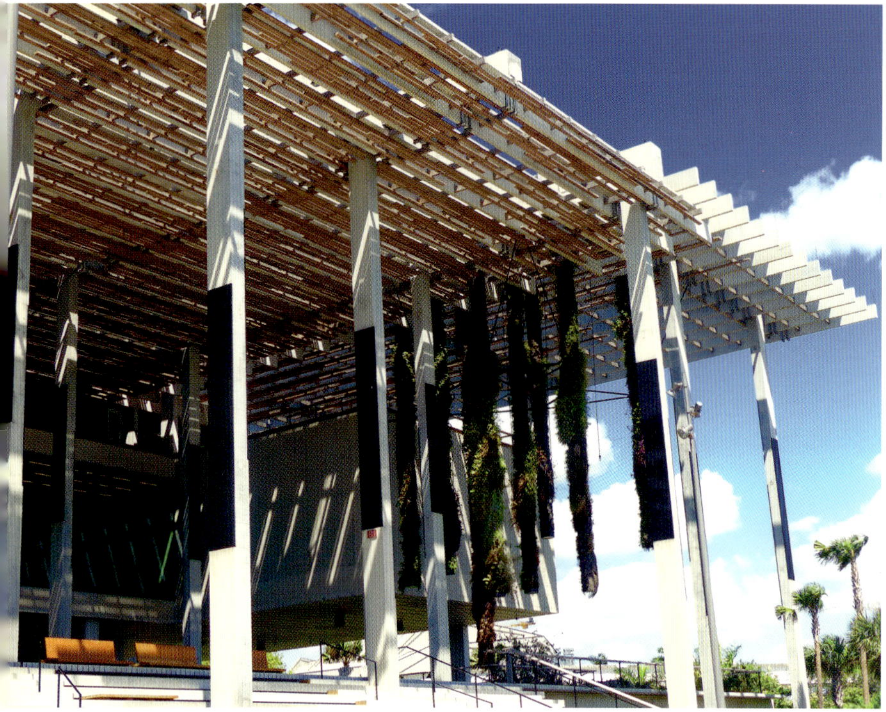

PEREZ ART MUSEUM MIAMI

Future icon

By architects Herzog & de Meuron

View art and hang out

Welcoming

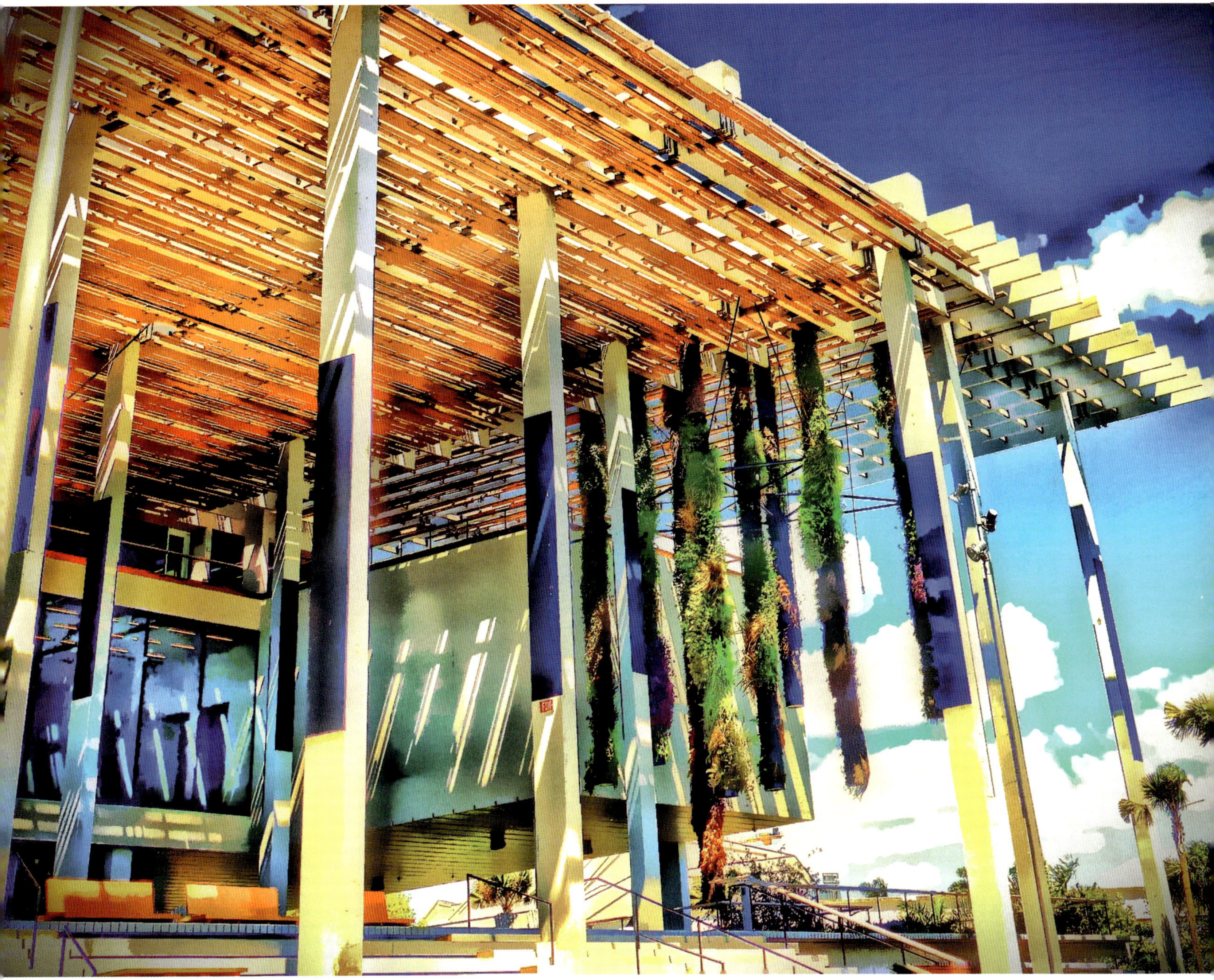

Chapter Two
ANIMALS

The animals featured in this chapter are a mixture of those indigenous to South Florida and "newcomers" who have made this tropical state their home. Some, like the alligators, white and blue herons, and an anhinga, live in the Everglades, Florida's river of grass, while others, like the lion, tiger, and donkey, call the Miami Zoo their home. The beautiful butterfly—the smallest member of this animal kingdom collection—joins us from Fairchild Tropical Gardens Wings of the Tropics exhibit. It may appear as though these animals posed for the photos, as they sit with grace, dignity, strength, and even humor.

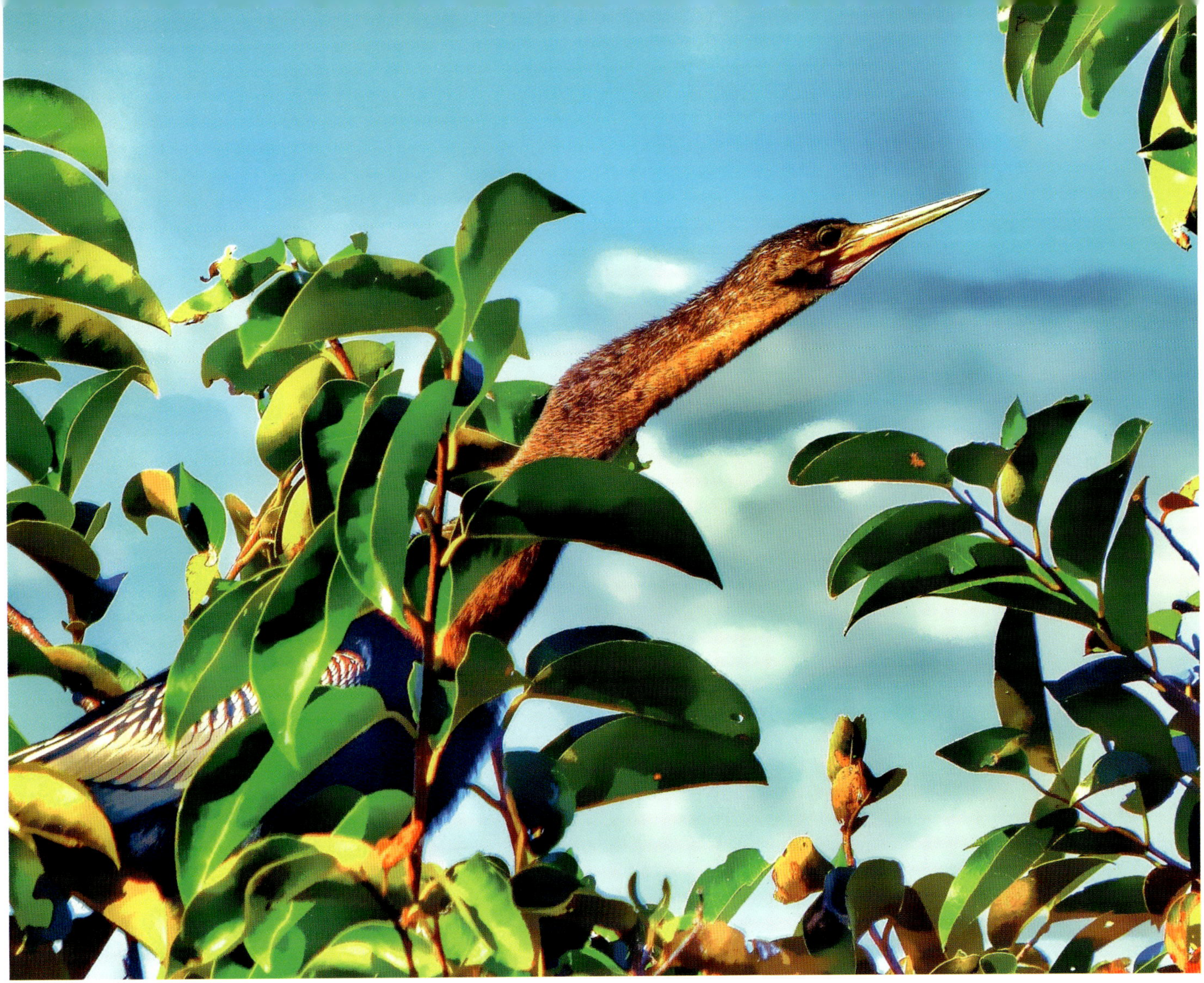

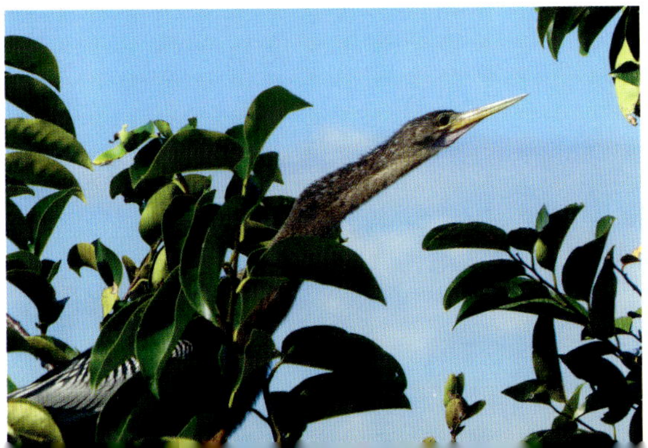

ANHINGA

This is a snakebird
He loves the Everglades
Stretches his neck
Looking for a snack

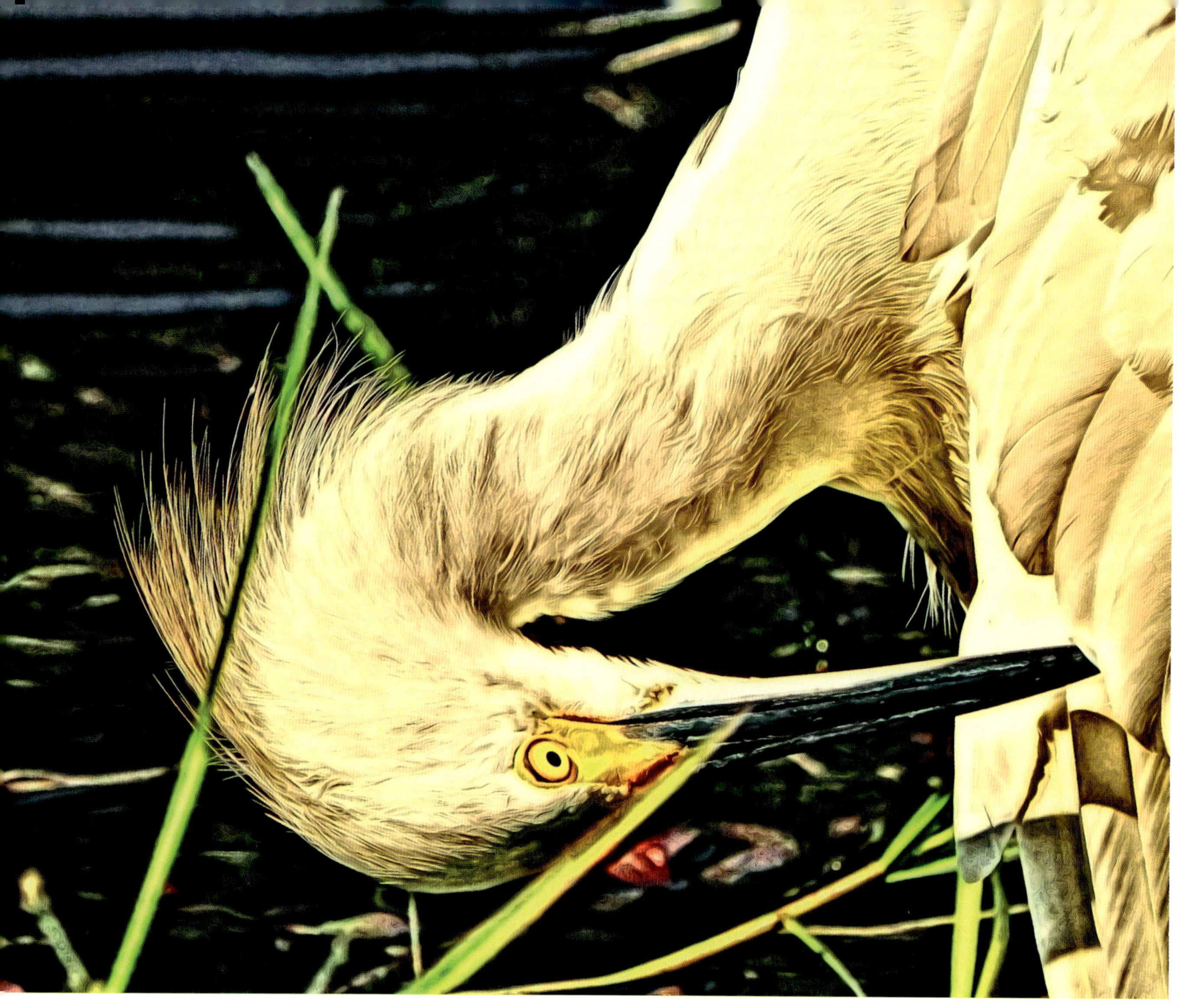

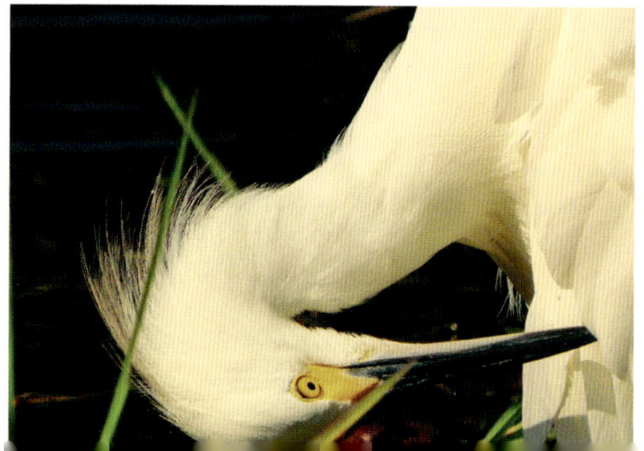

EVERGLADES WHITE HERON

An Everglades white heron
Searching for a bug on his chest
A mini meal

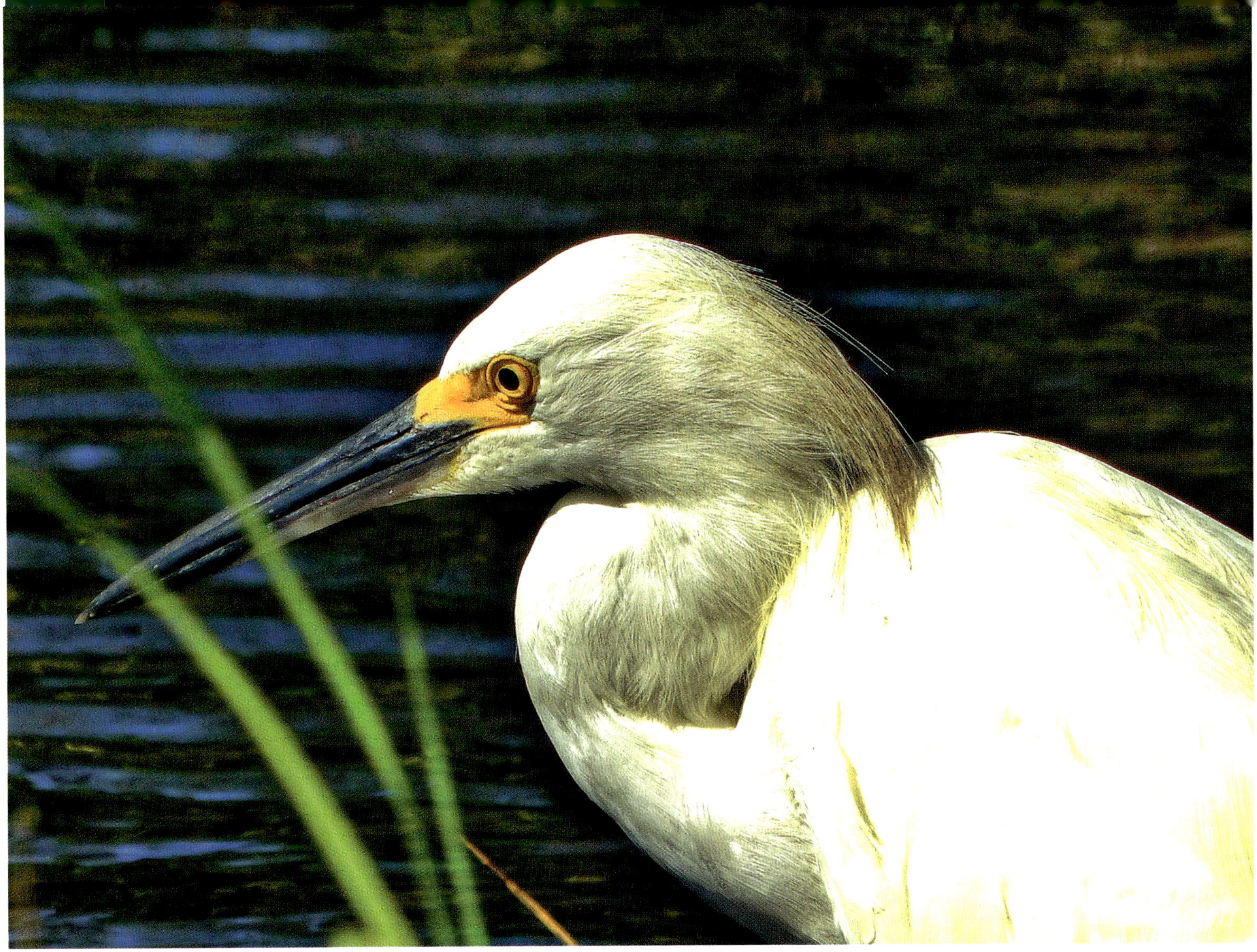

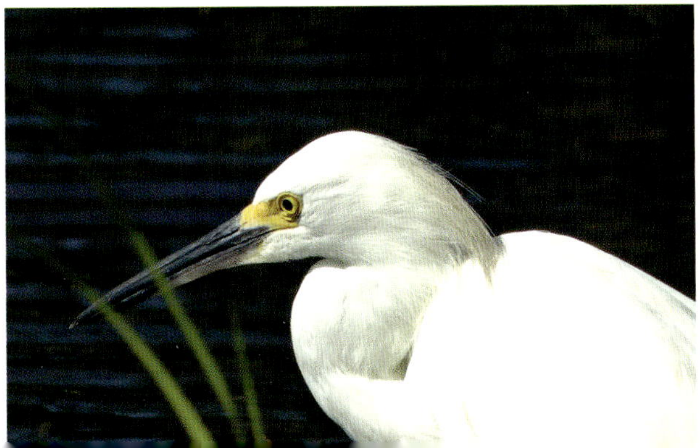

EVERGLADES WHITE HERON II

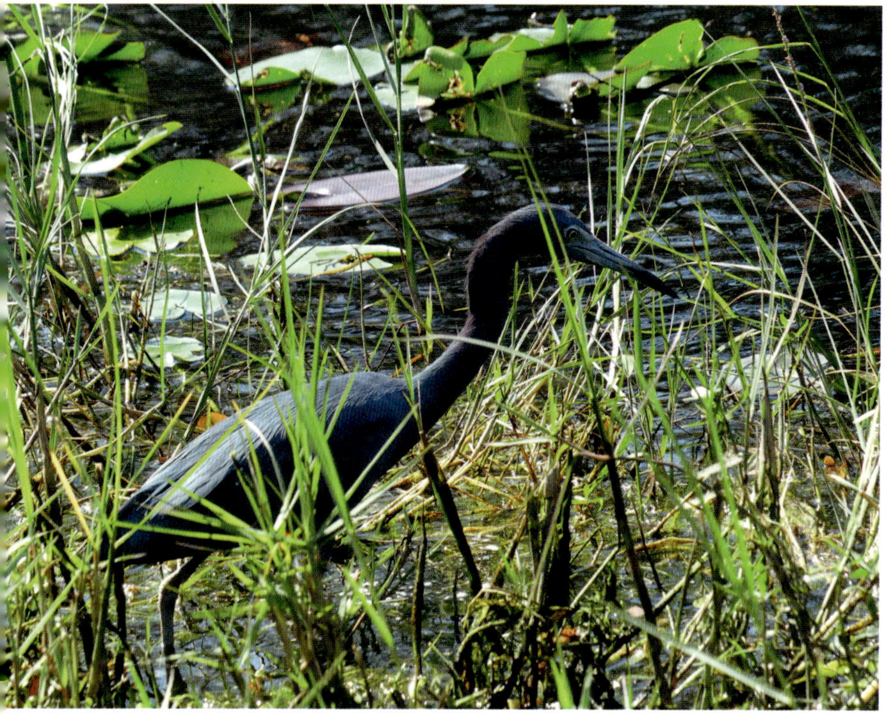

GREAT BLUE HERON

Everglades wading bird

Looking for food

Cousin of the great white heron

Breathtaking in blue

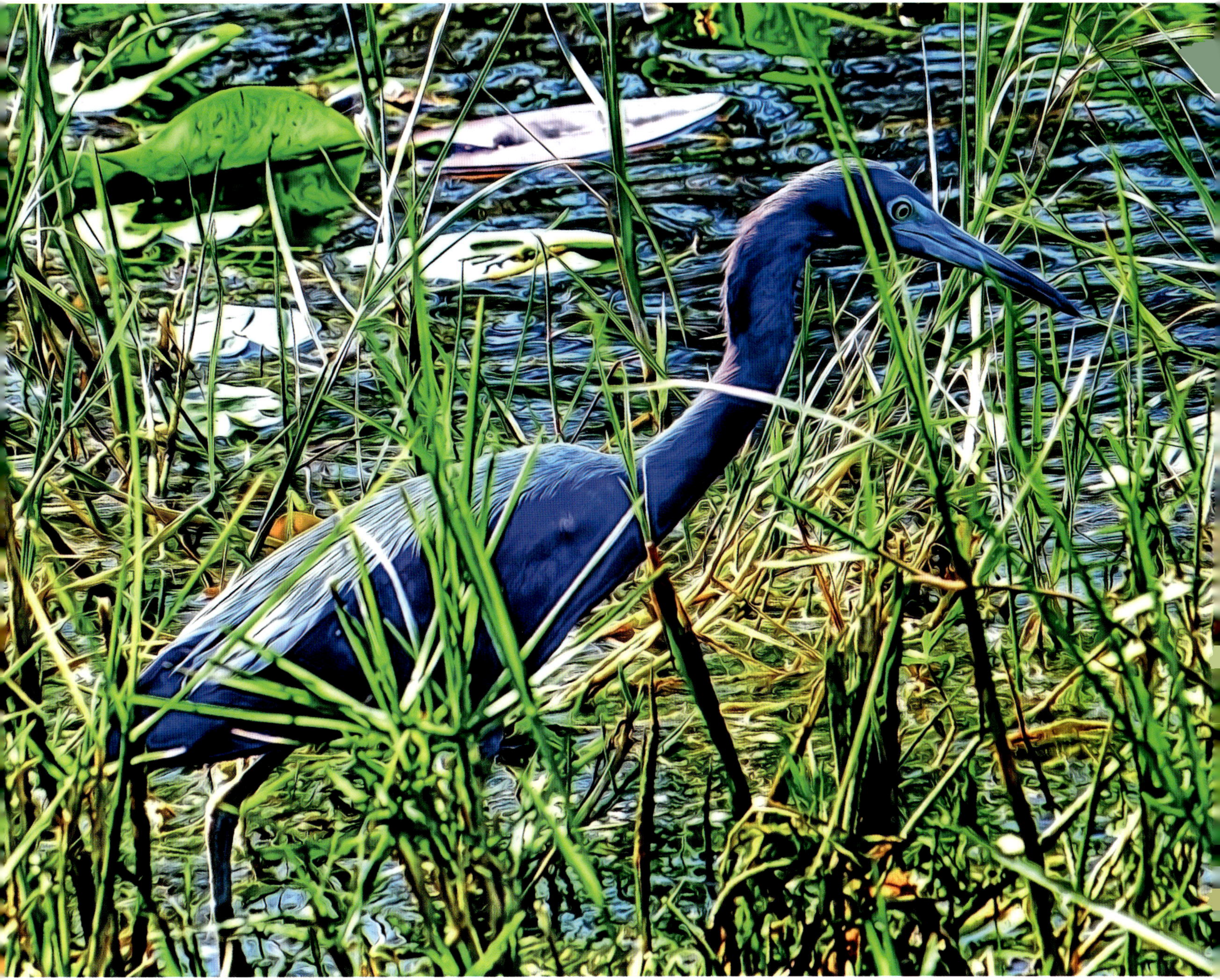

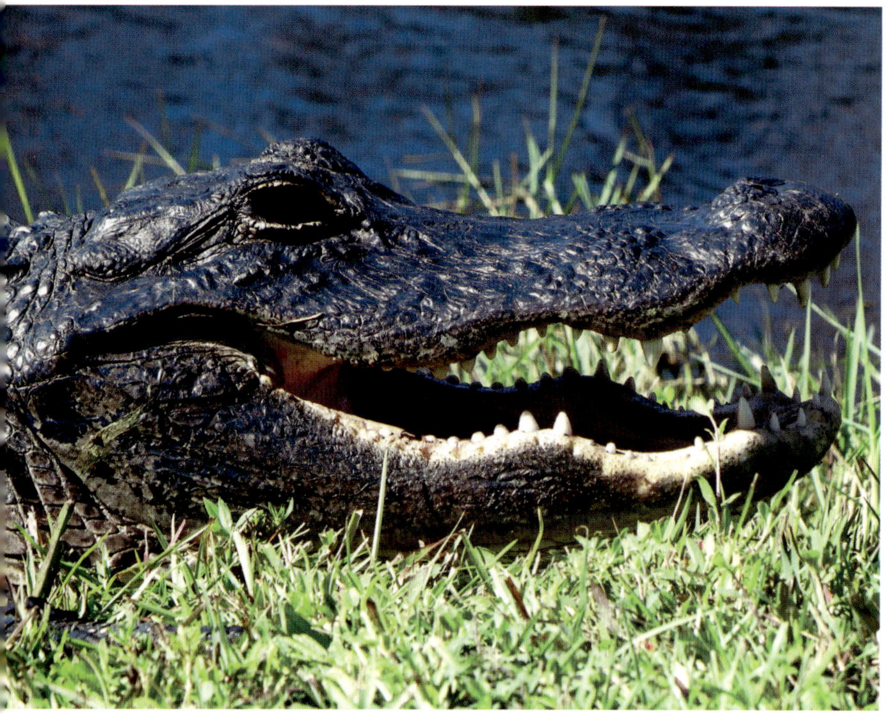

ALLIGATOR I

An alligator is smiling
Trying to make friends
No thanks
Too close for comfort

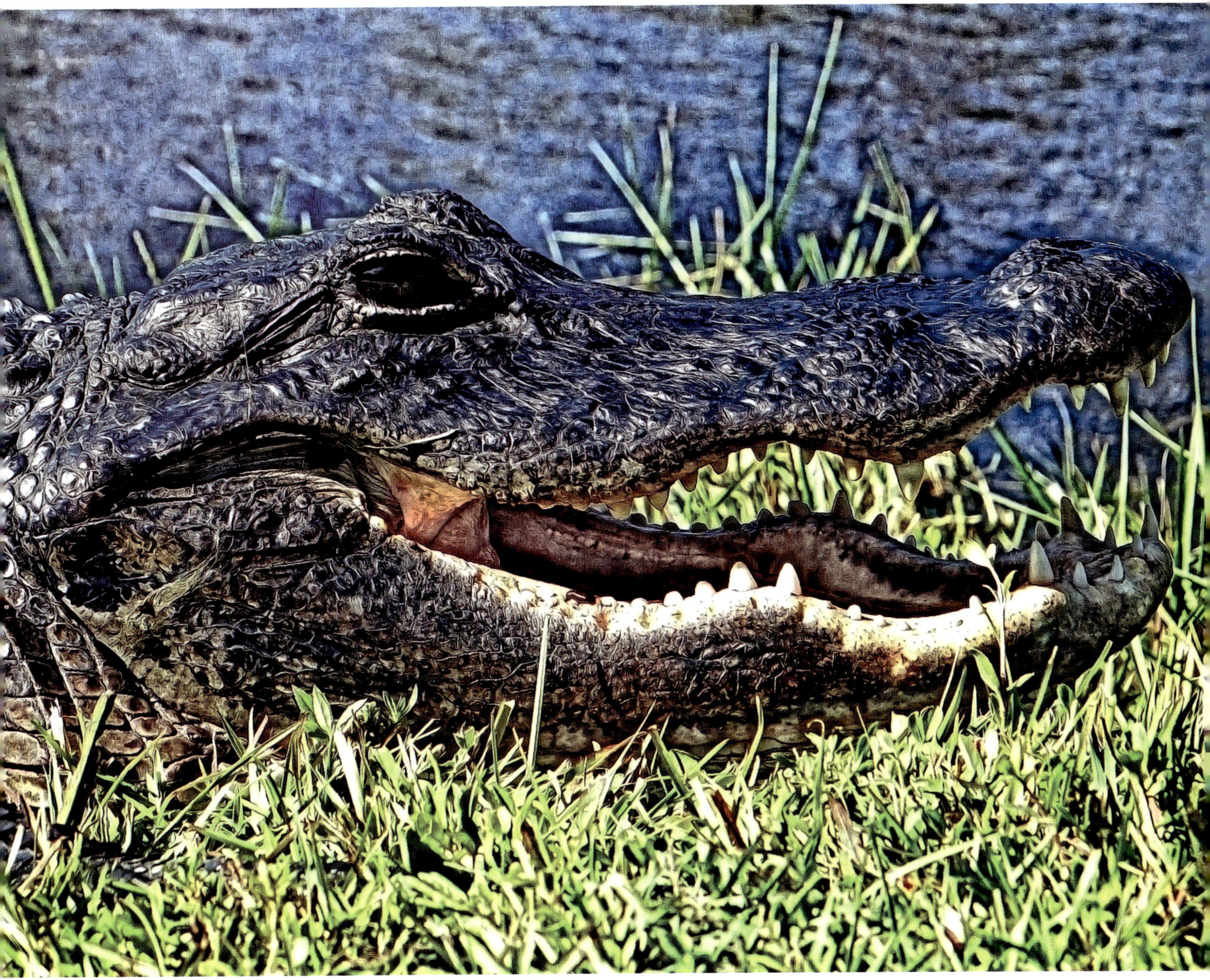

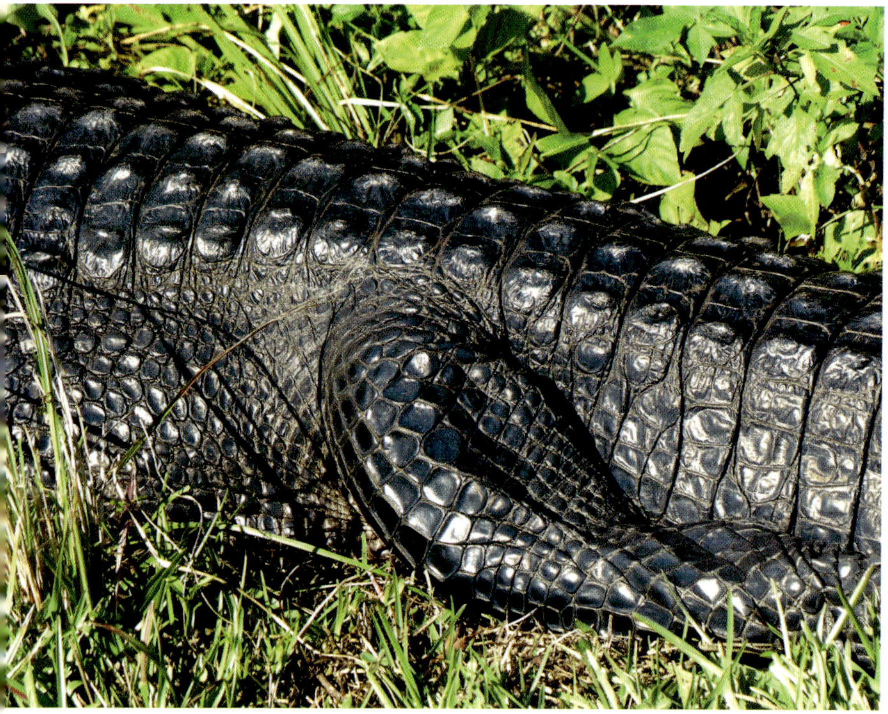

ALLIGATOR II

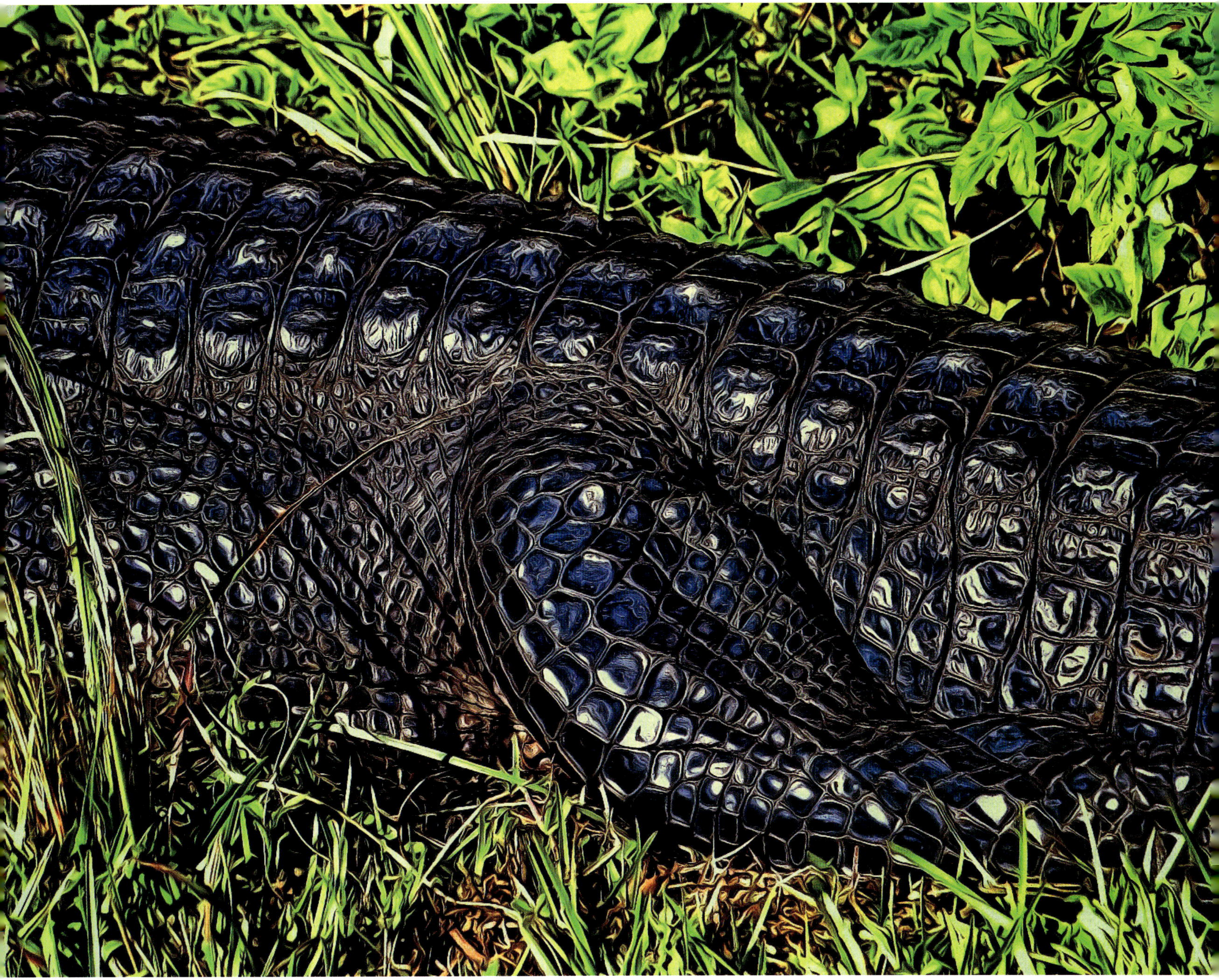

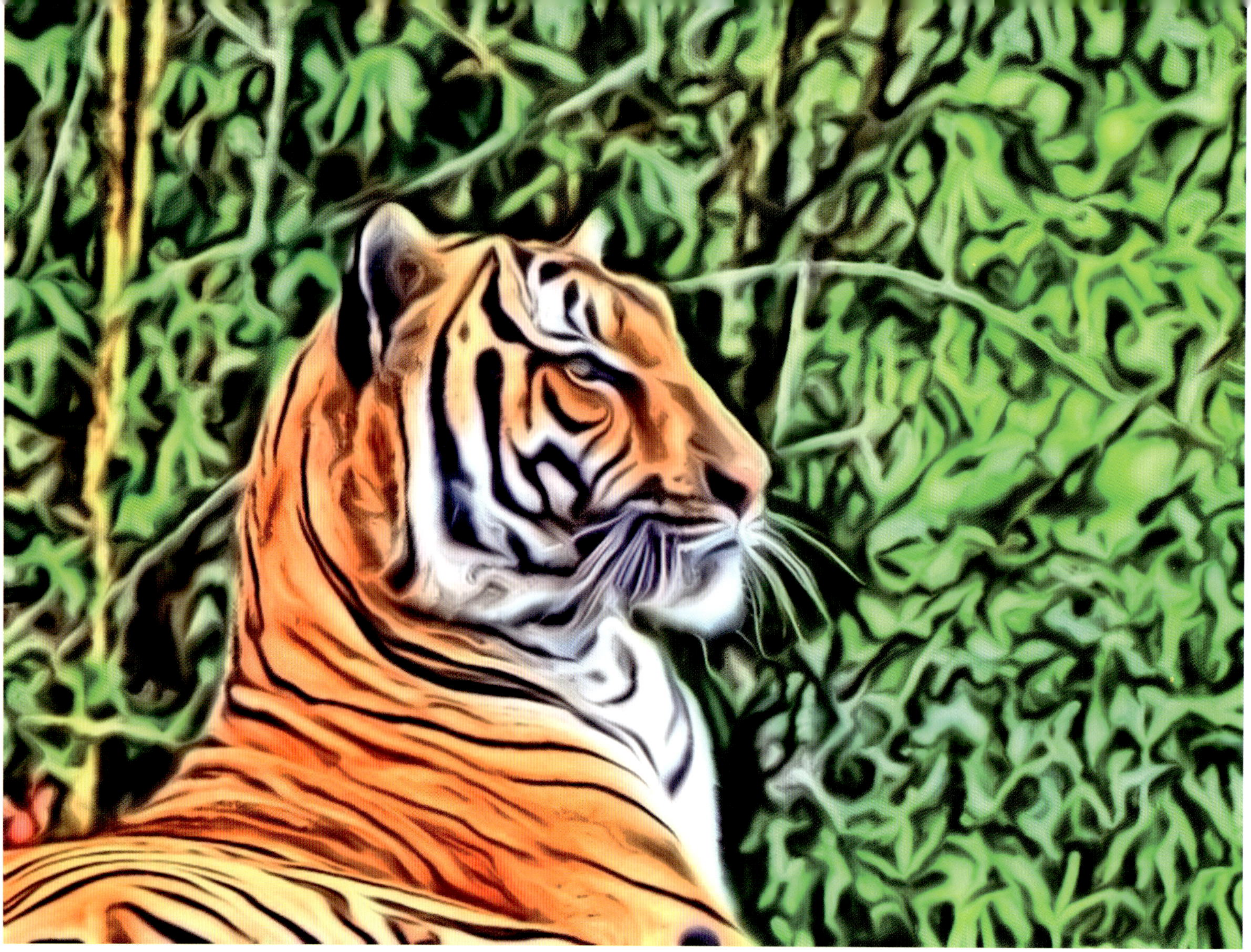

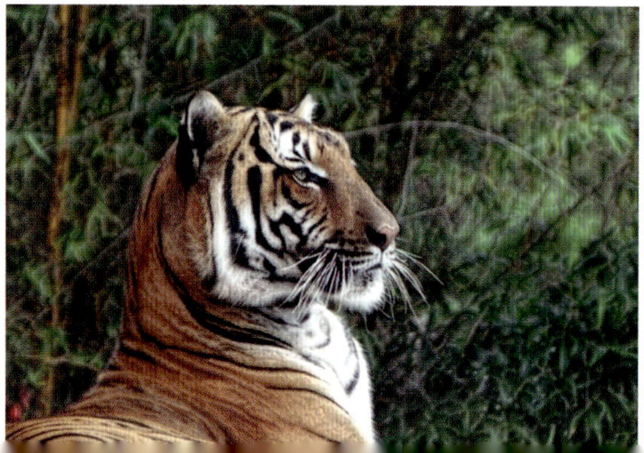

BENGAL TIGER

Stately pose
On alert for his next meal
Powerful and intense

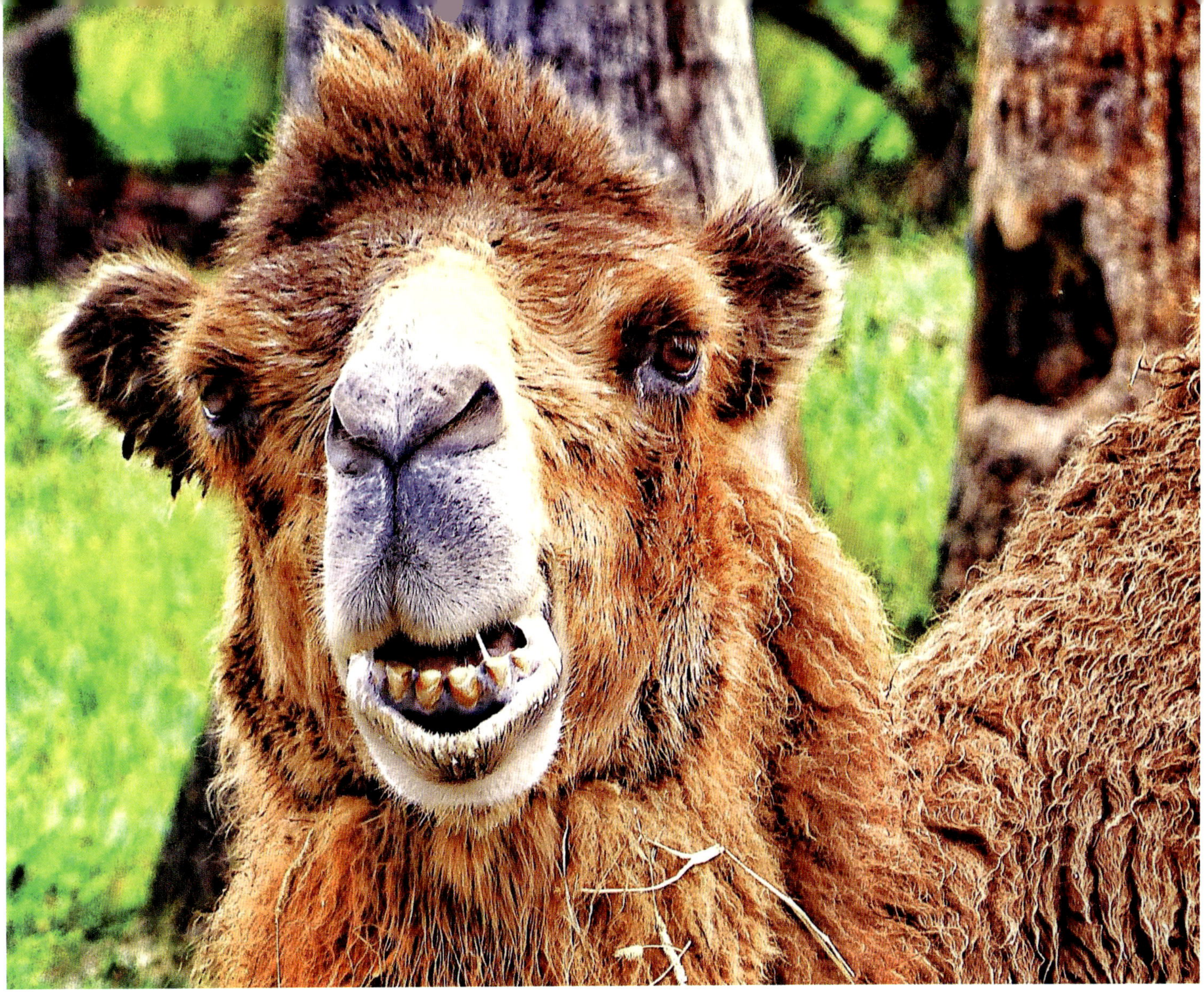

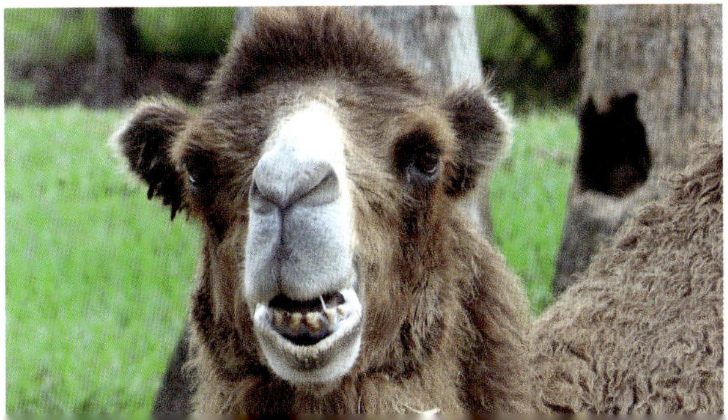

CAMEL

Checking out a human intruder

Not happy

He's going to spit

Watch out!

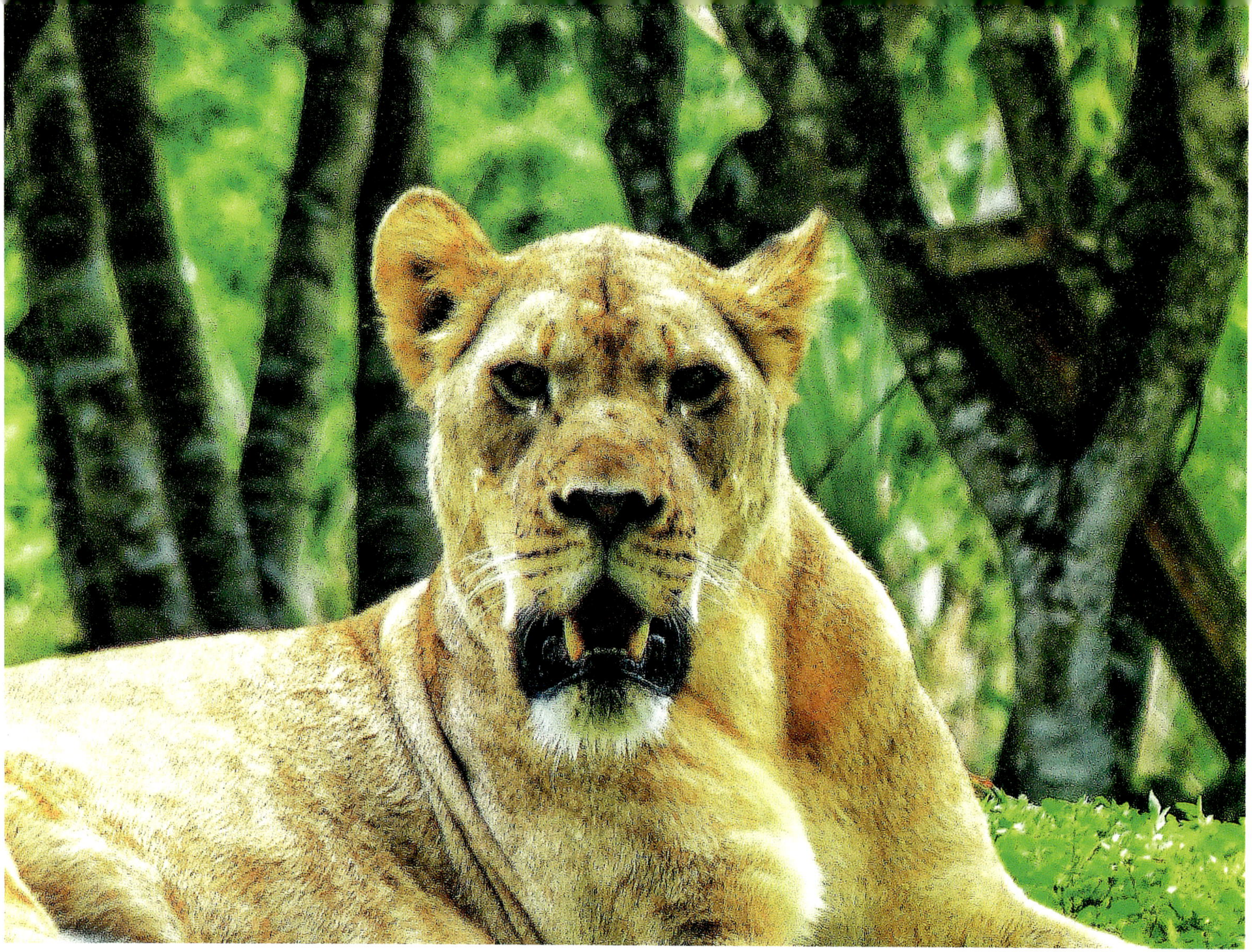

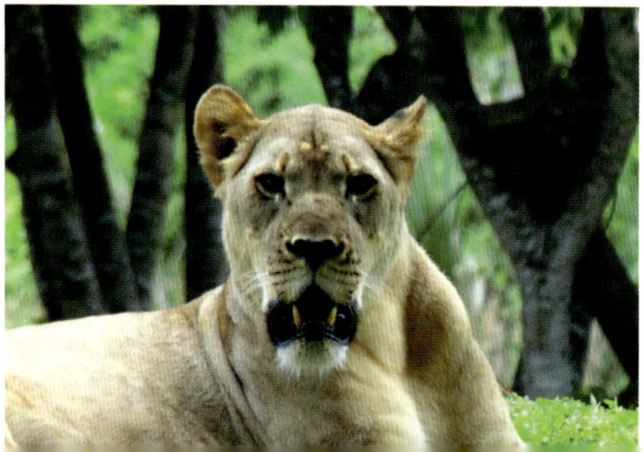

LIONESS

Flashing two front teeth
Looking at someone
Who might become her next appetizer

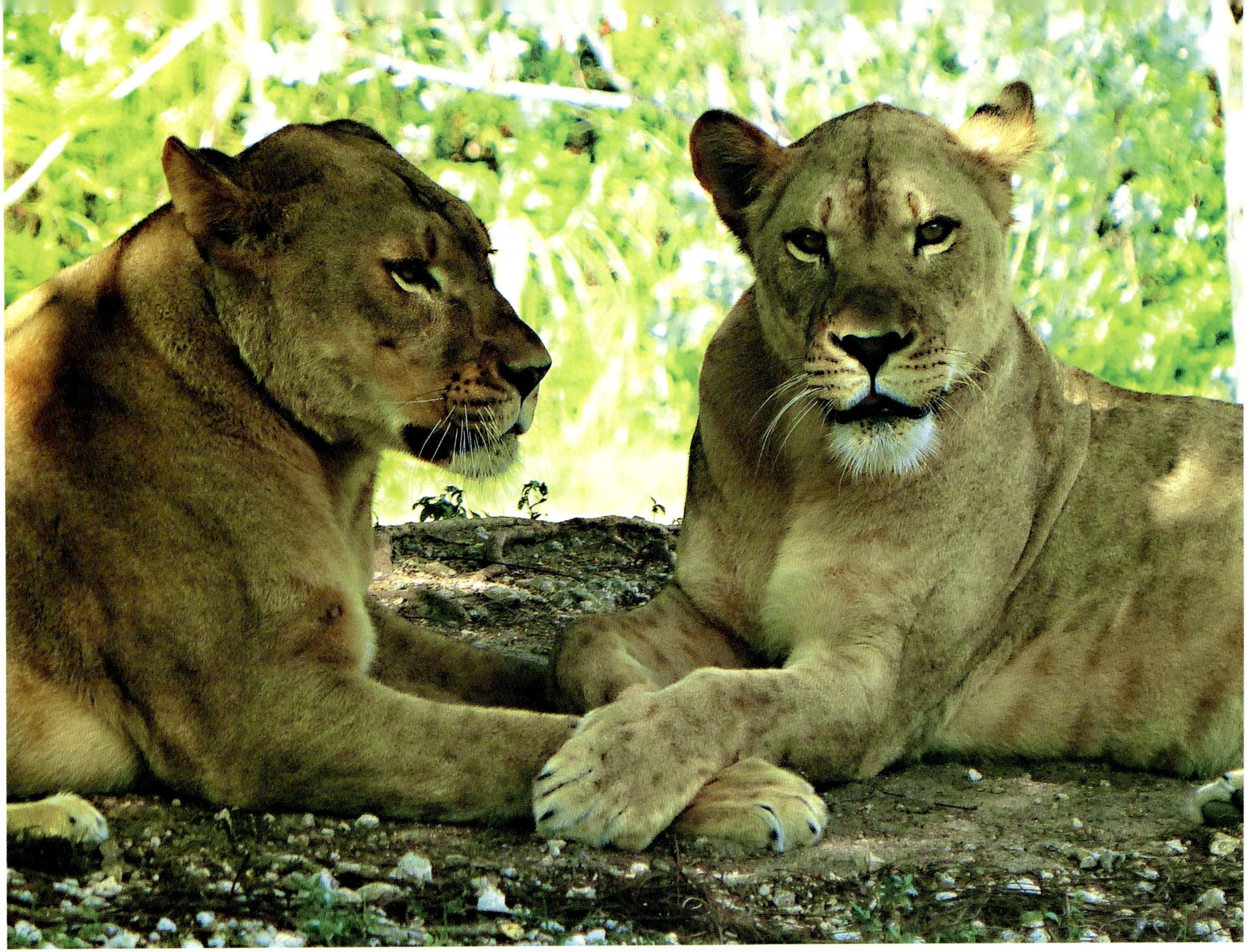

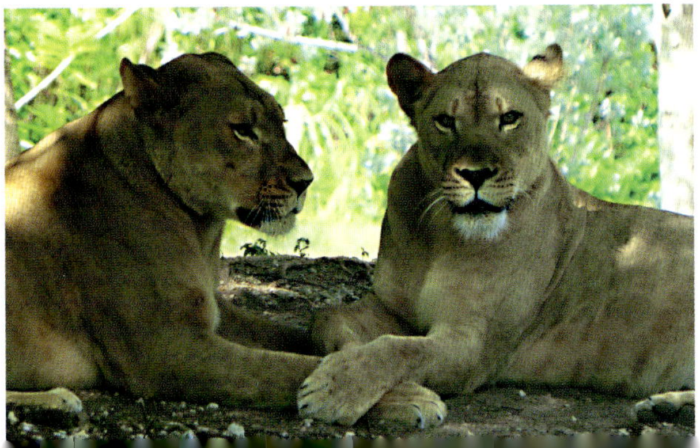

LIONESS COUPLE

Two female lions
Holding hands or paws
Buddies

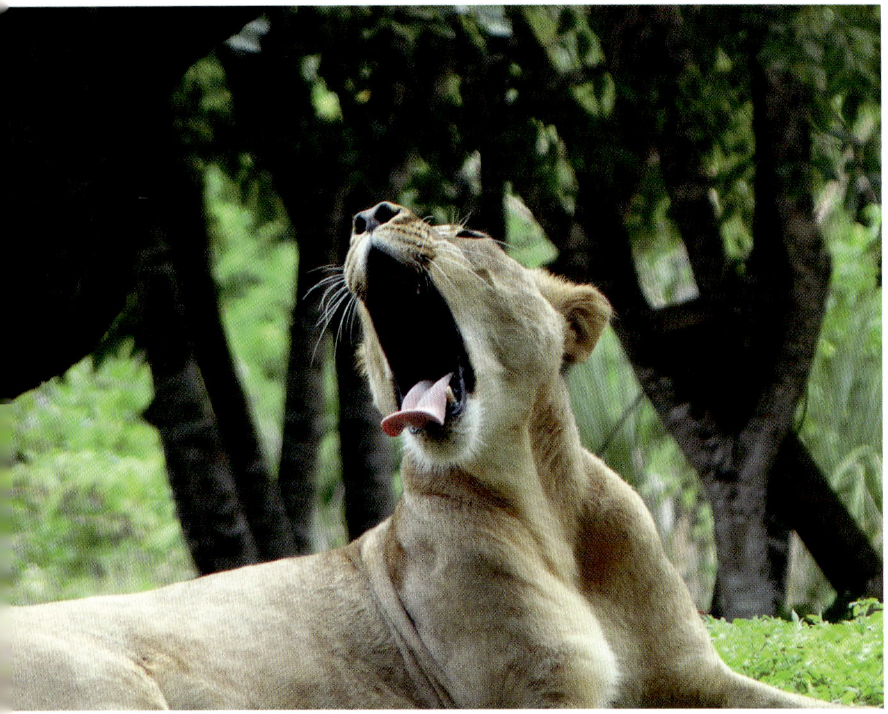

LION YAWNING

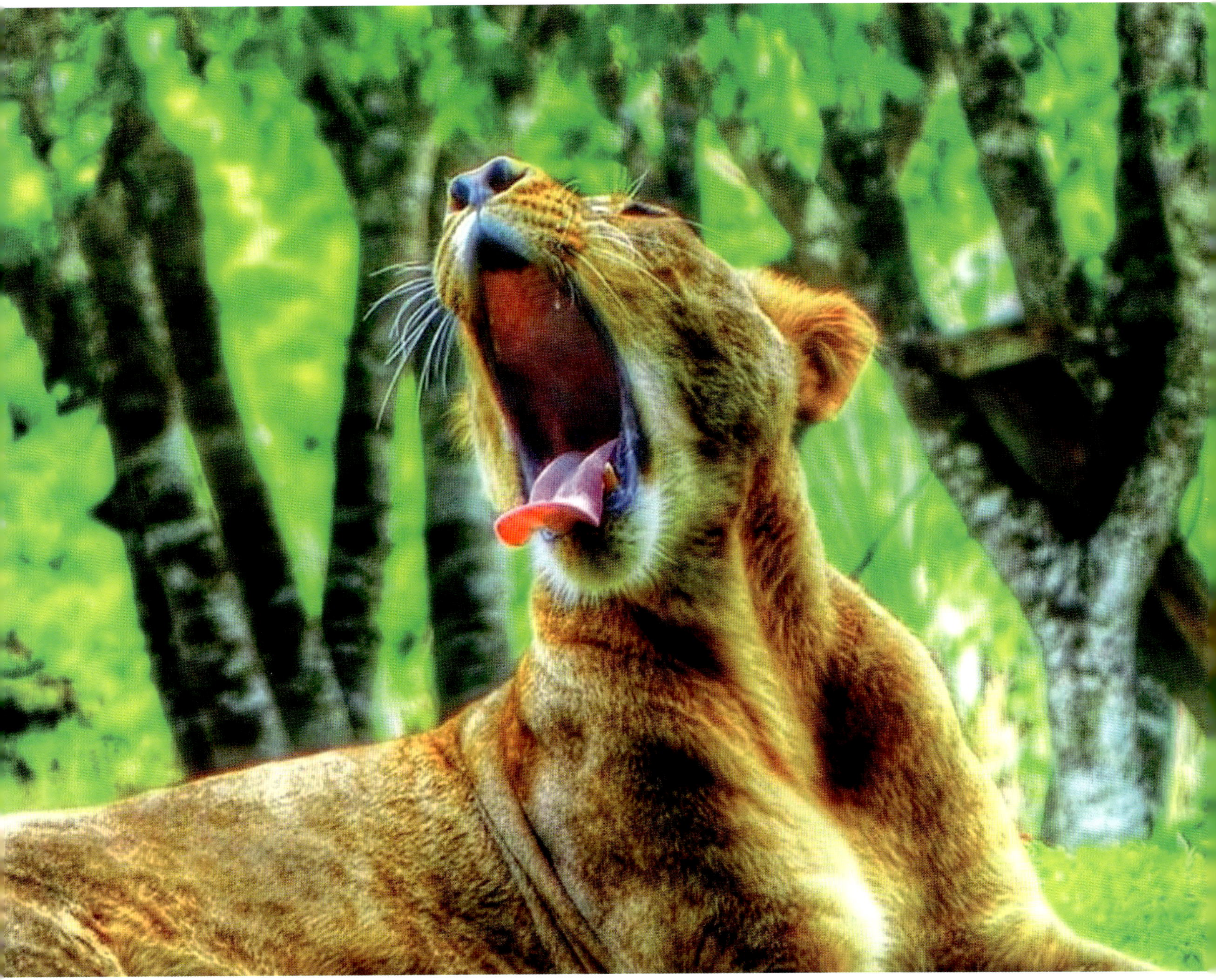

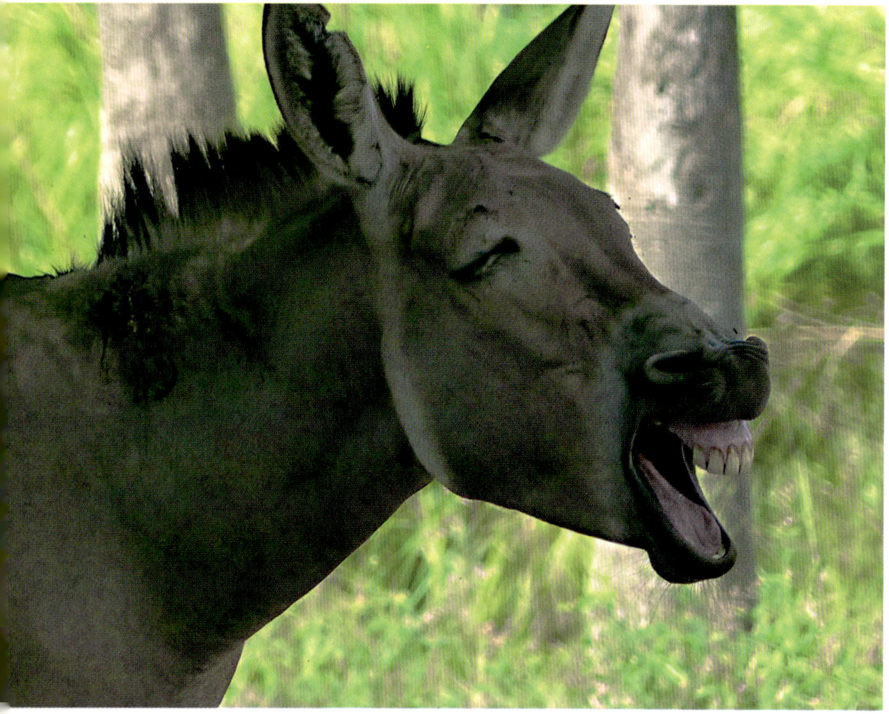

DONKEY

Hee haw
He's laughing at me
Toothy

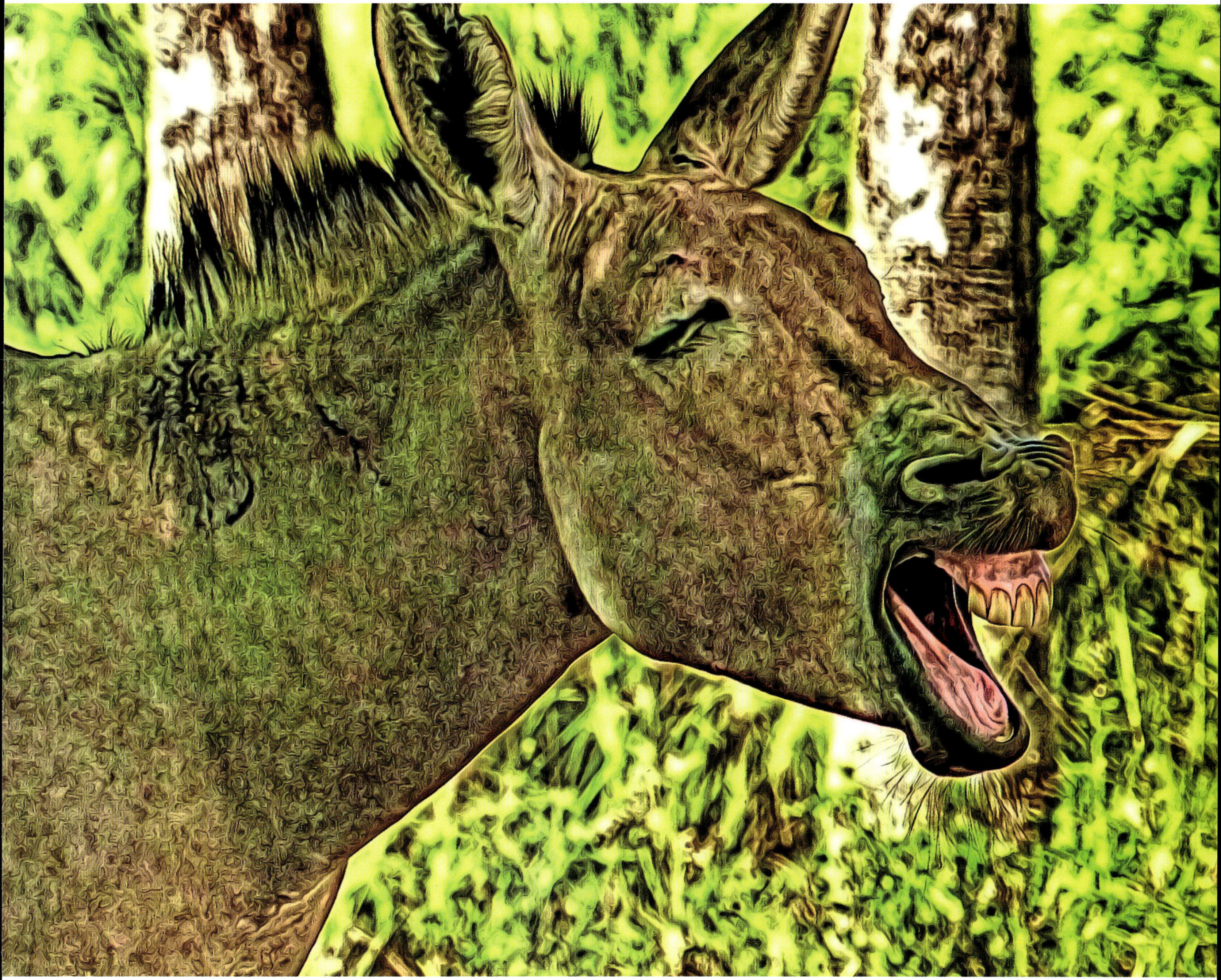

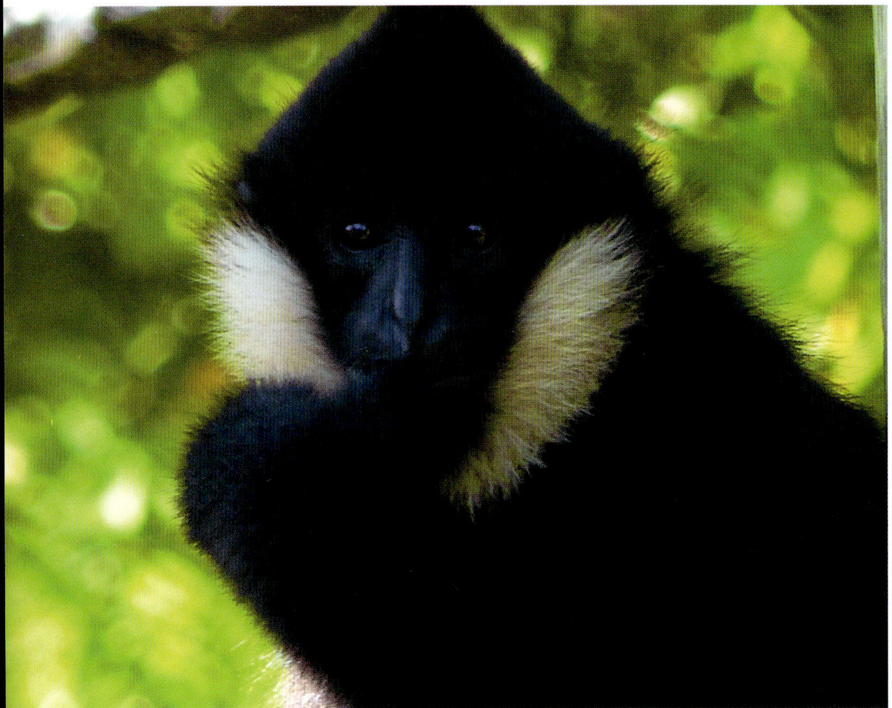

BLUE MONKEY

A monkey staring
Sucking his thumb
Focused

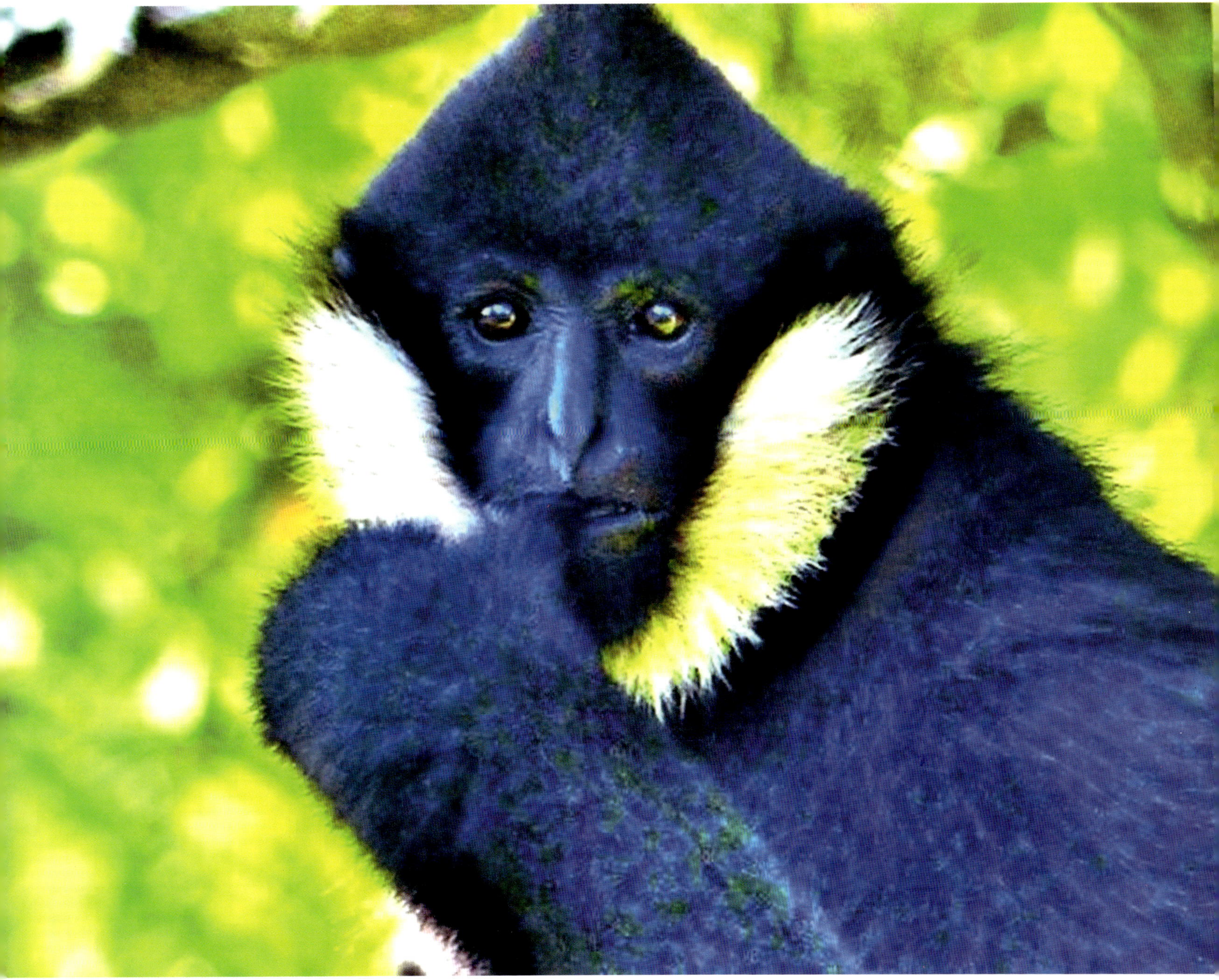

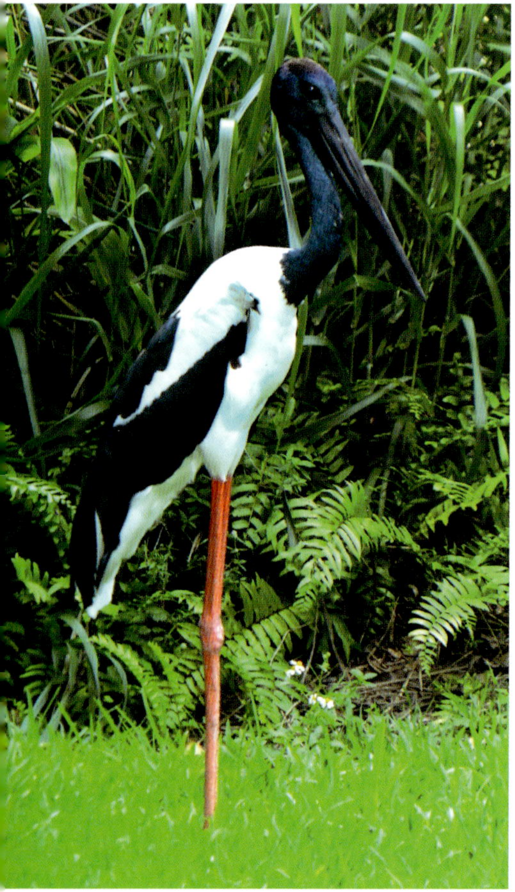

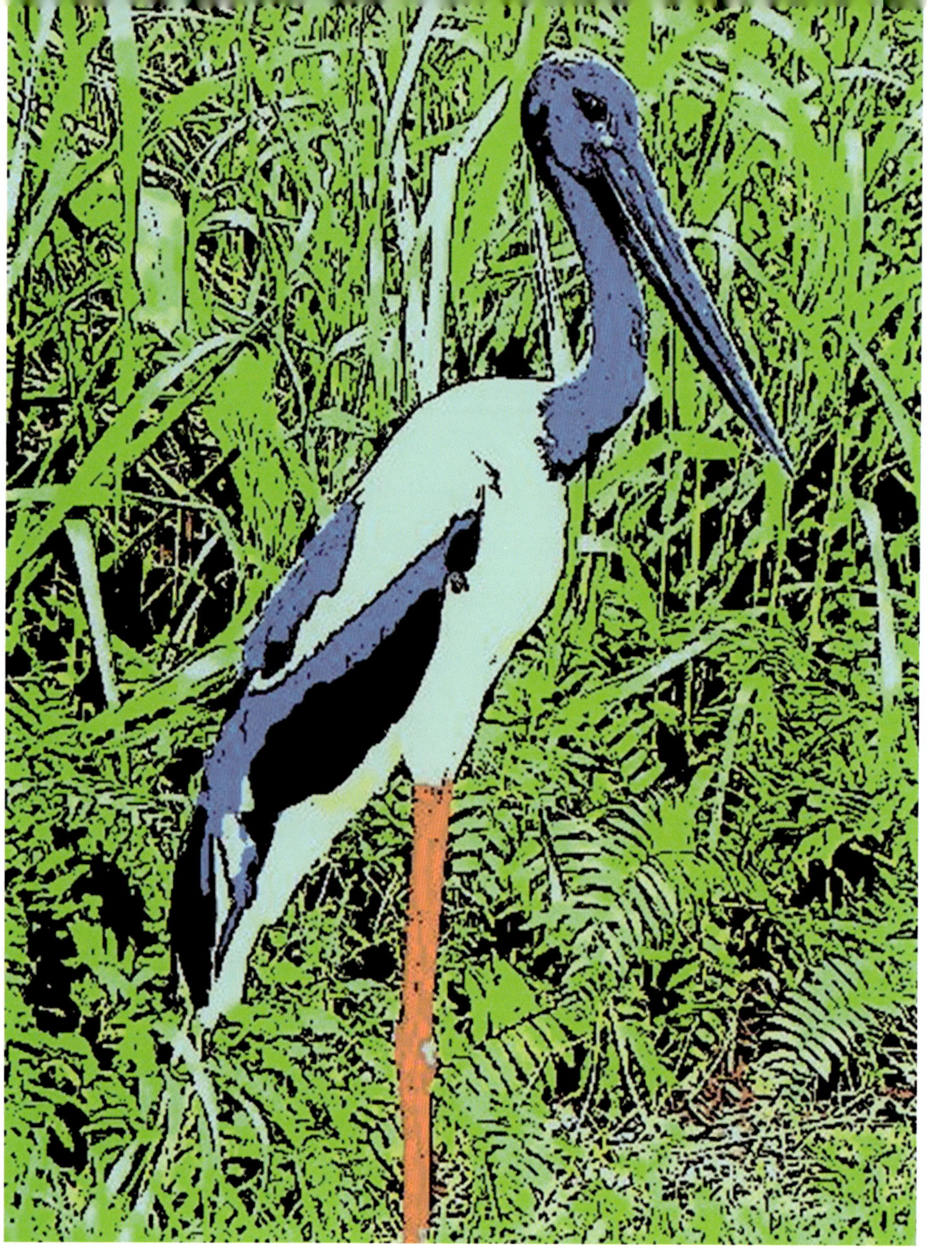

STORK

Where's the other leg?

No one really knows

Amazing

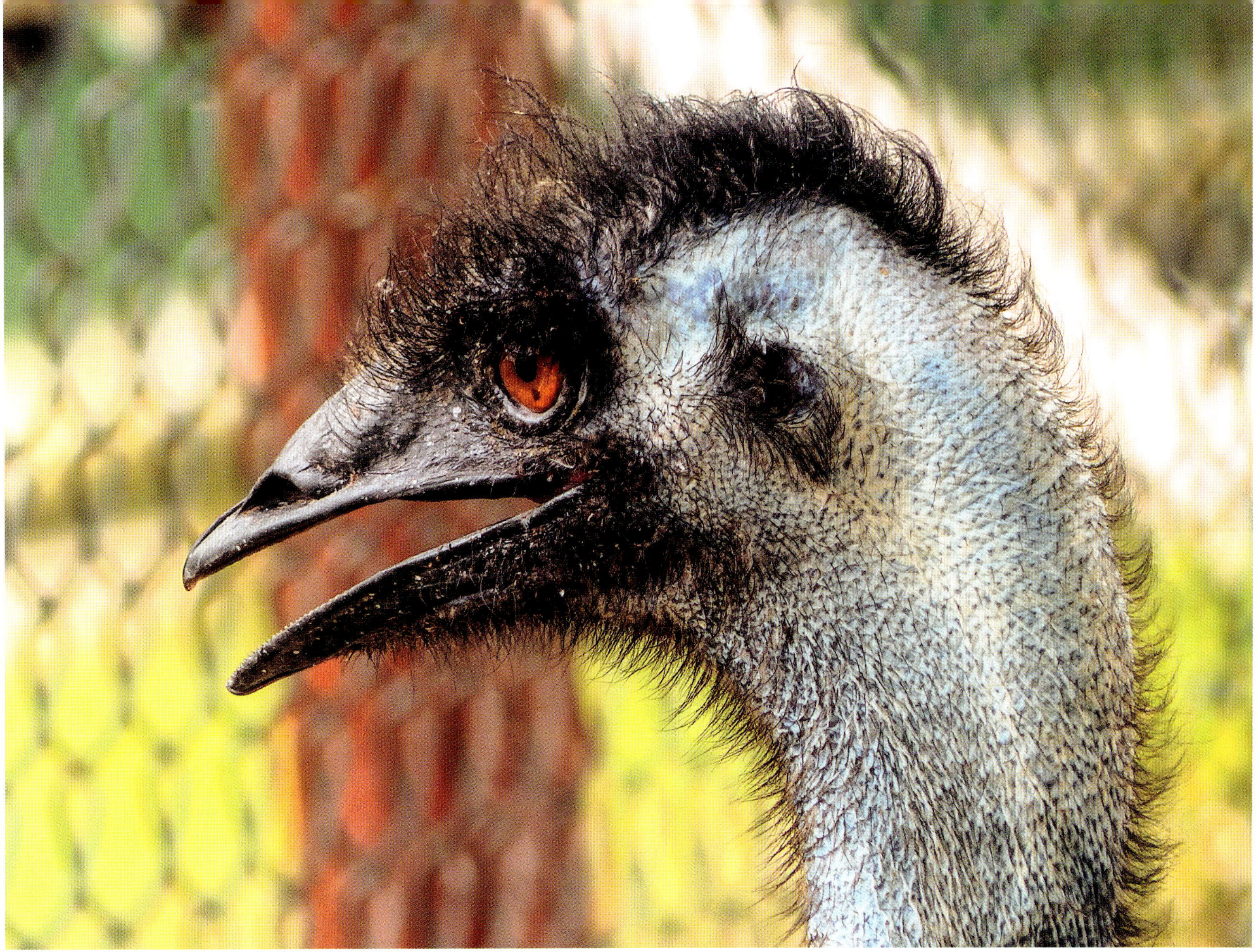

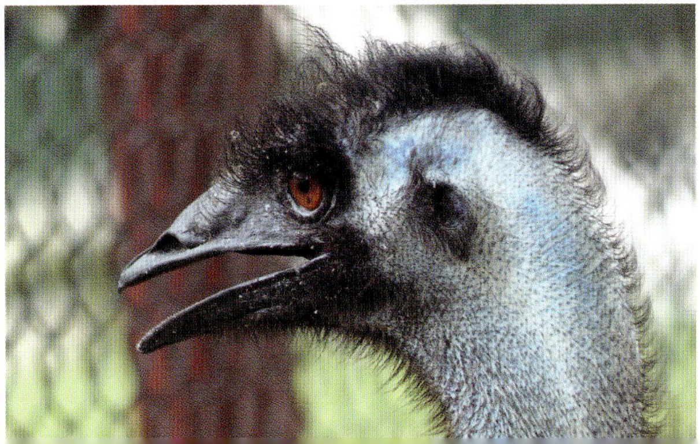

EMU

A cousin to the ostrich
At the fruit stand Robert Is Here
Australian native
Not very pretty, but pretty cool

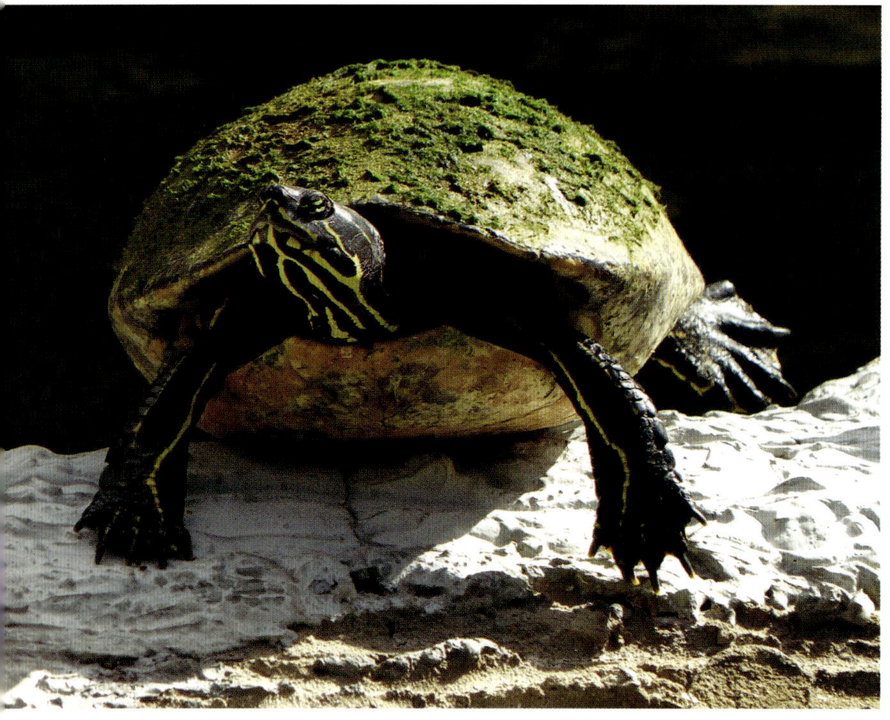

TURTLE

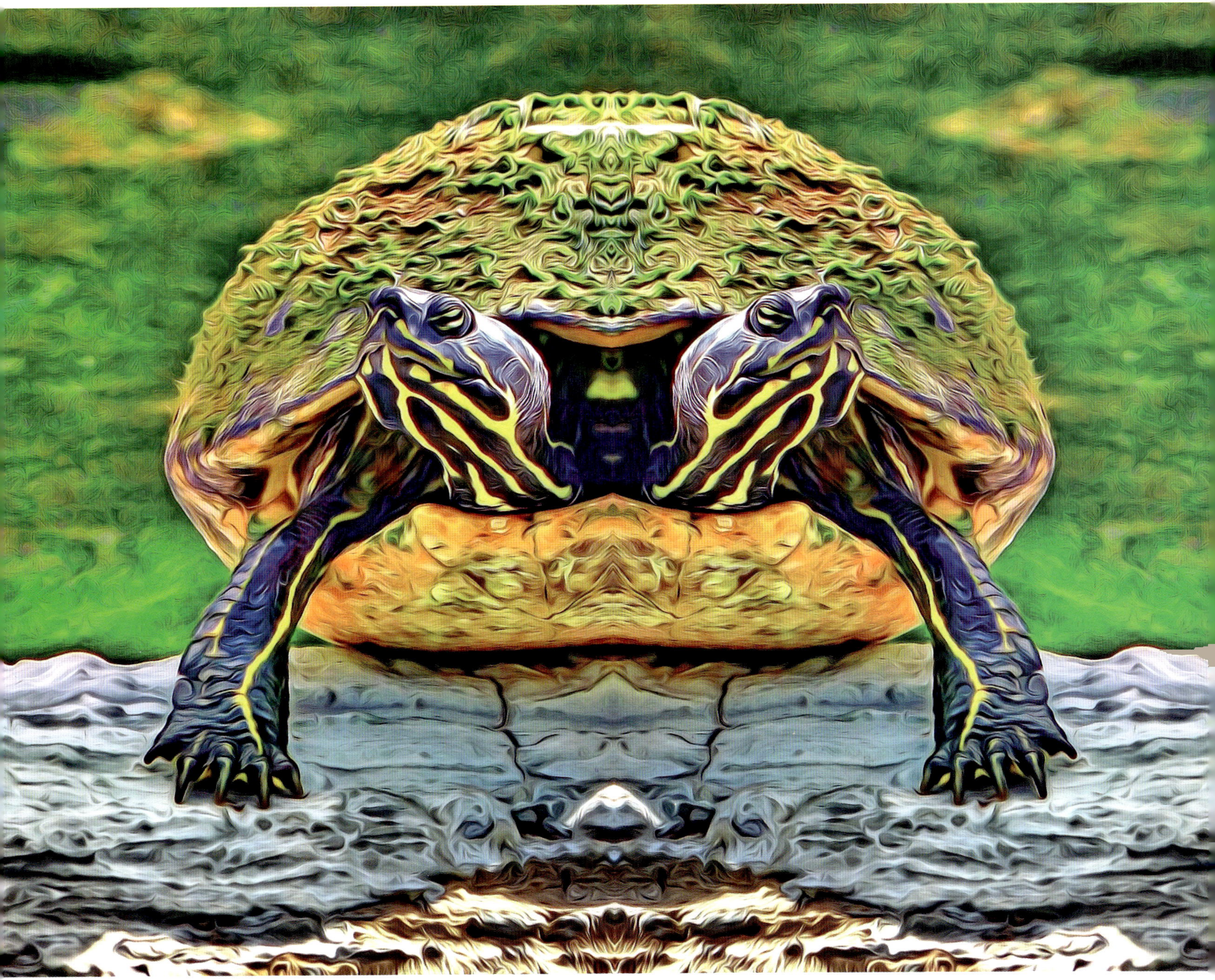

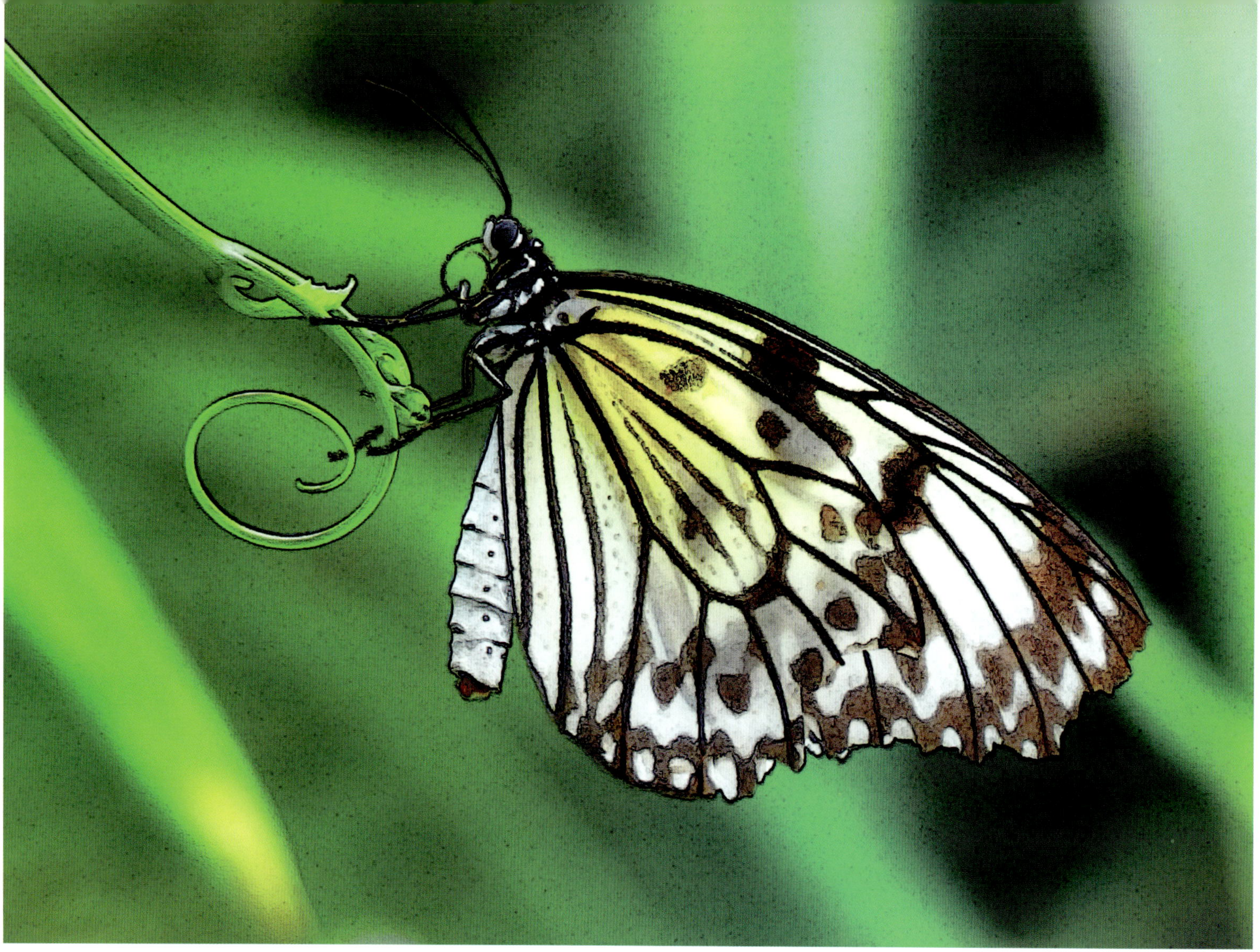

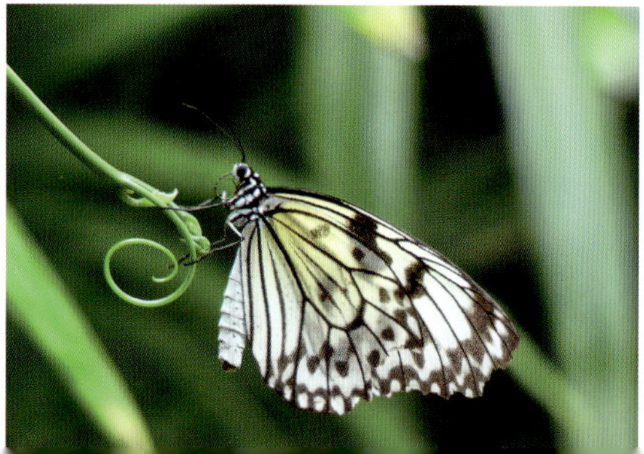

BUTTERFLY

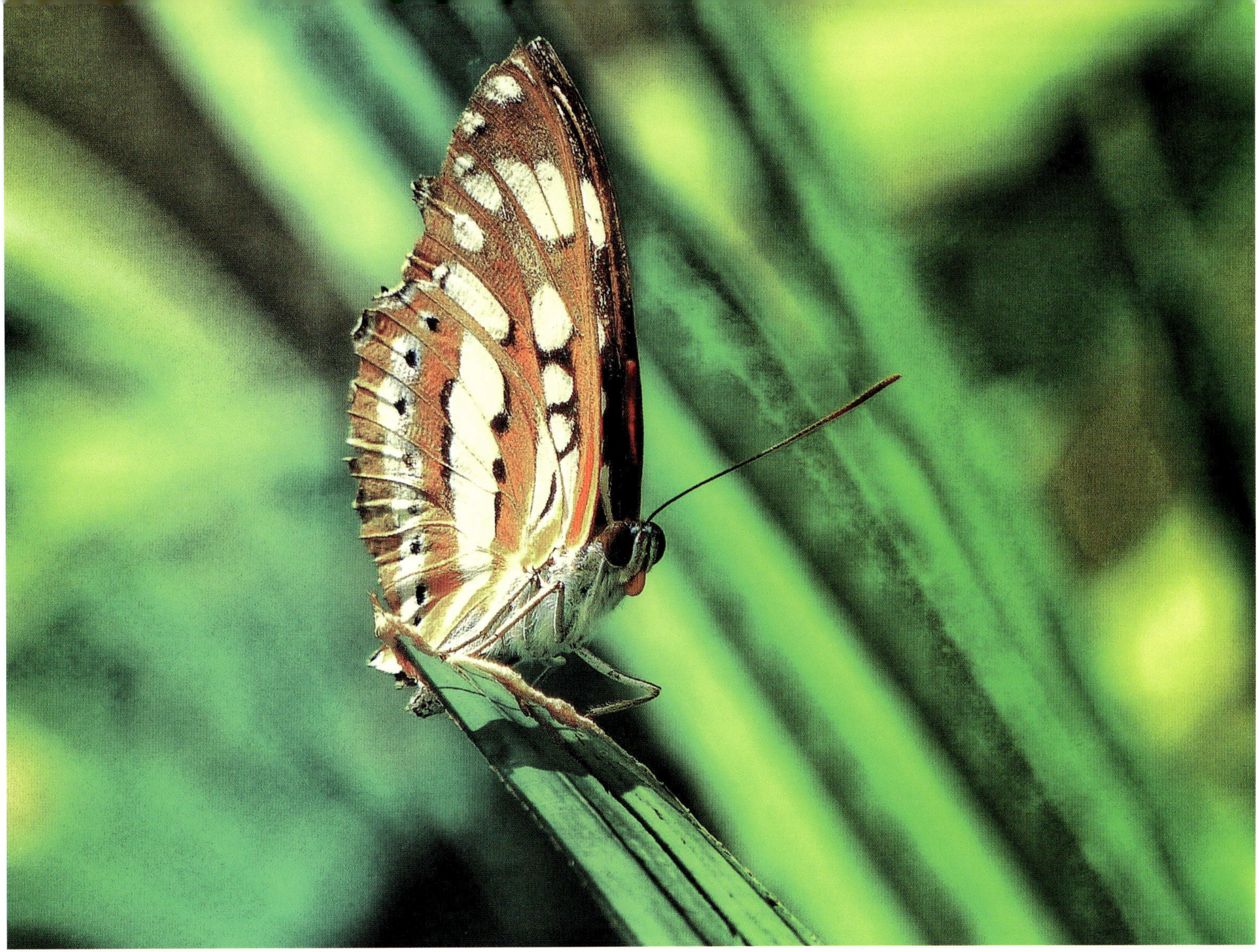

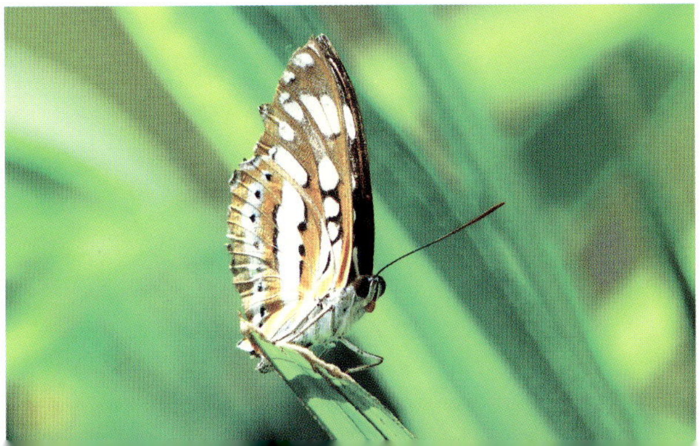

BUTTERFLY
ON A LEAF

Chapter Three

PEOPLE & CULTURE

What shapes a city's culture? In Miami, it is unmistakably the year-round sunny, warm weather and the vibrancy of our multicultural population—from the locals whose families have called Miami home for generations, to the Cubans who came to our shores seeking freedom, to the Haitians in search of economic opportunities, to the South Americans, snowbirds, Russians, French Canadians, and those from countries all over the globe. We see the impact of both climate and multiculturalism in our fashion and food, the enjoyment of the great outdoors, and the intellectual pursuits of art lovers and book lovers. Miamians live life to the fullest—sailing on the beautiful waters of the bay, playing a friendly game of Dominos, hanging out at their favorite outdoor cafe, or relaxing on the beach.

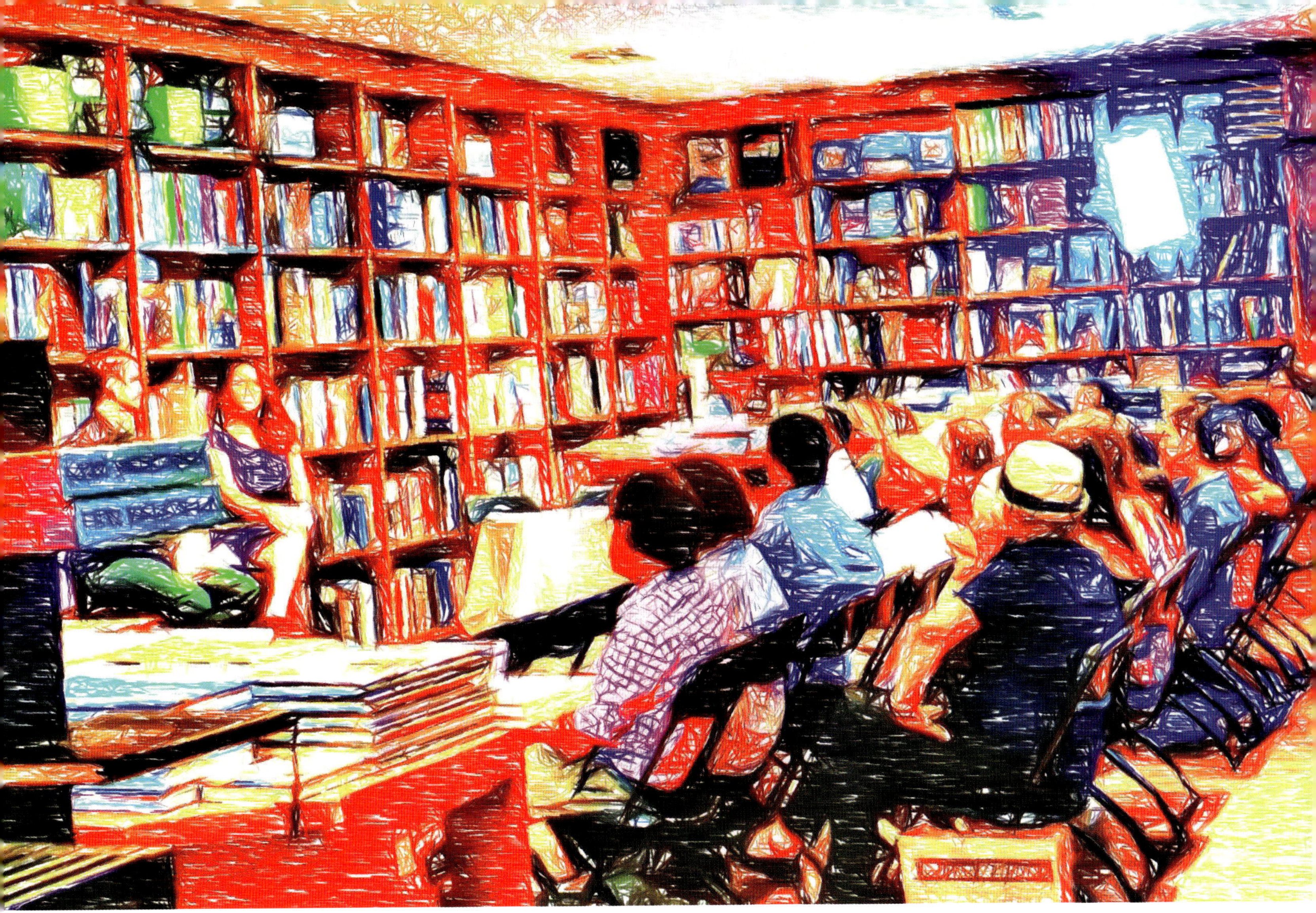

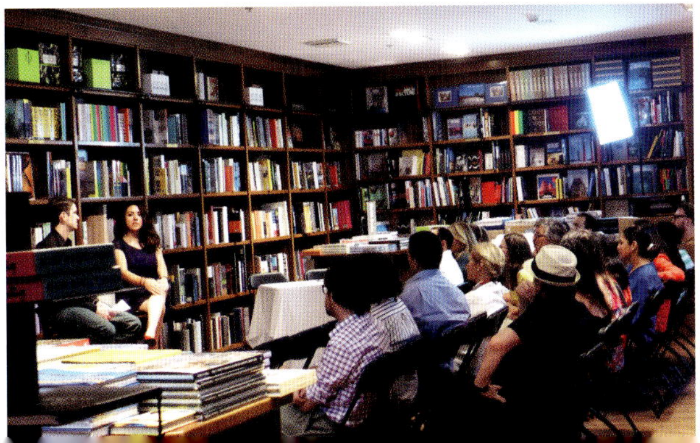

BOOKS & BOOKS

Independent bookstore

Bringing together authors and readers

Ideas and debate

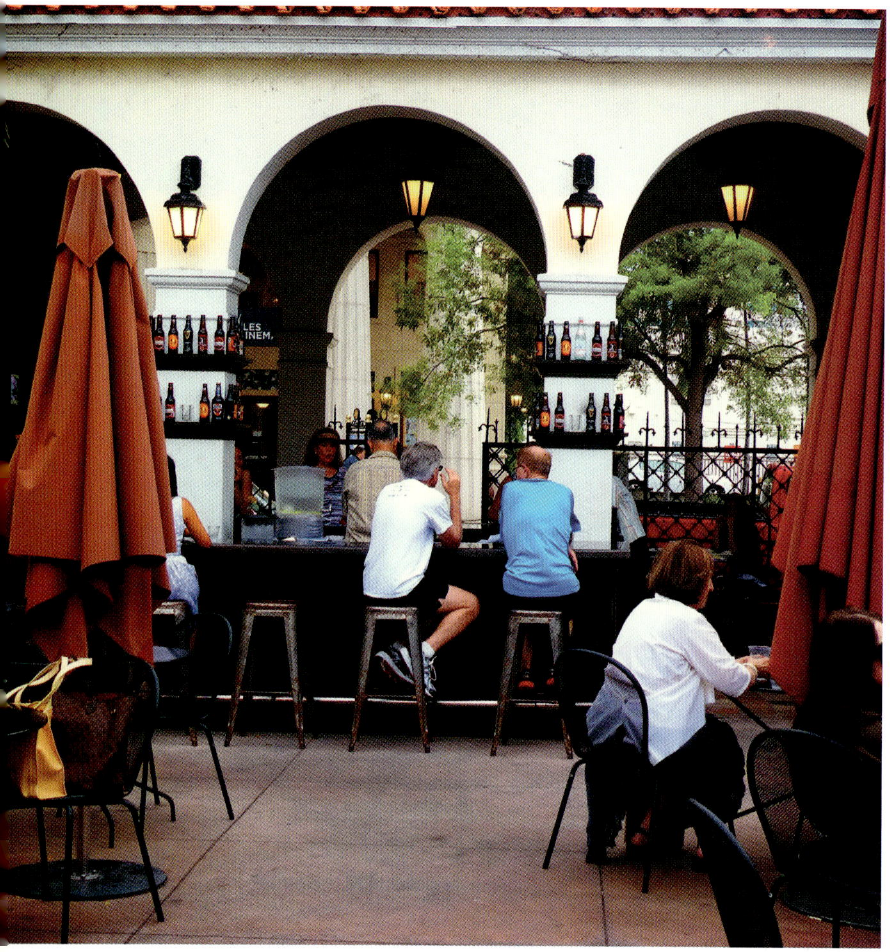

SUNNY AFTERNOON AT BOOKS & BOOKS COURTYARD

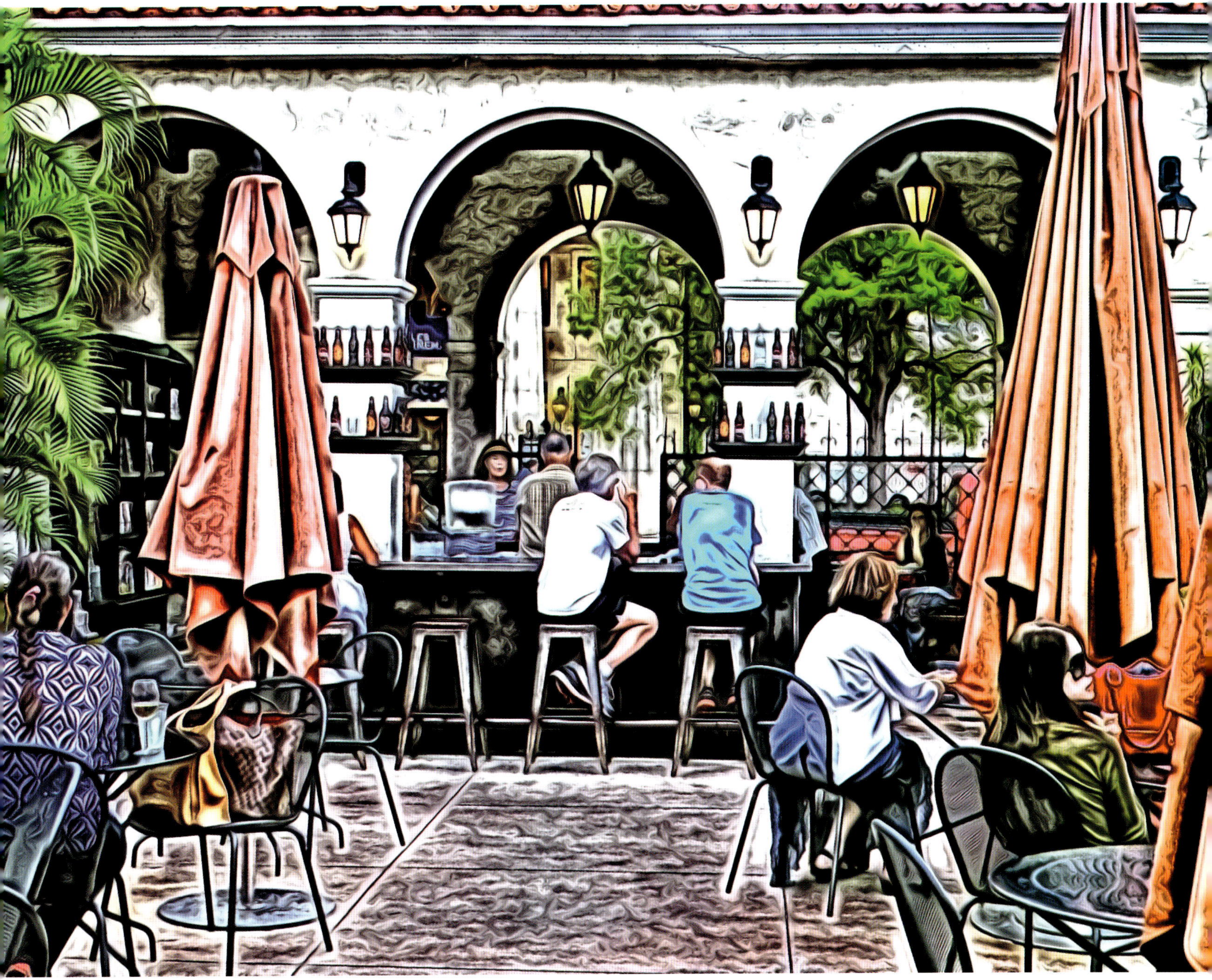

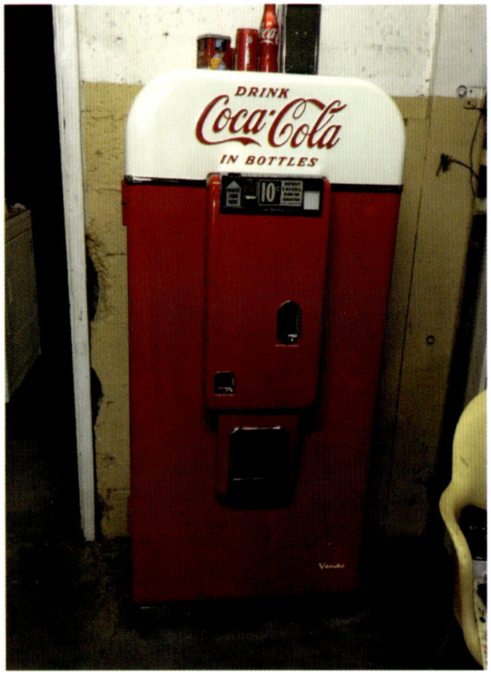

COKE MACHINES

Bud's Paint & Body shop, circa 1937
Formerly industrial section of Coral Gables
Now a hip neighborhood
A dime for a Coke
What a bargain

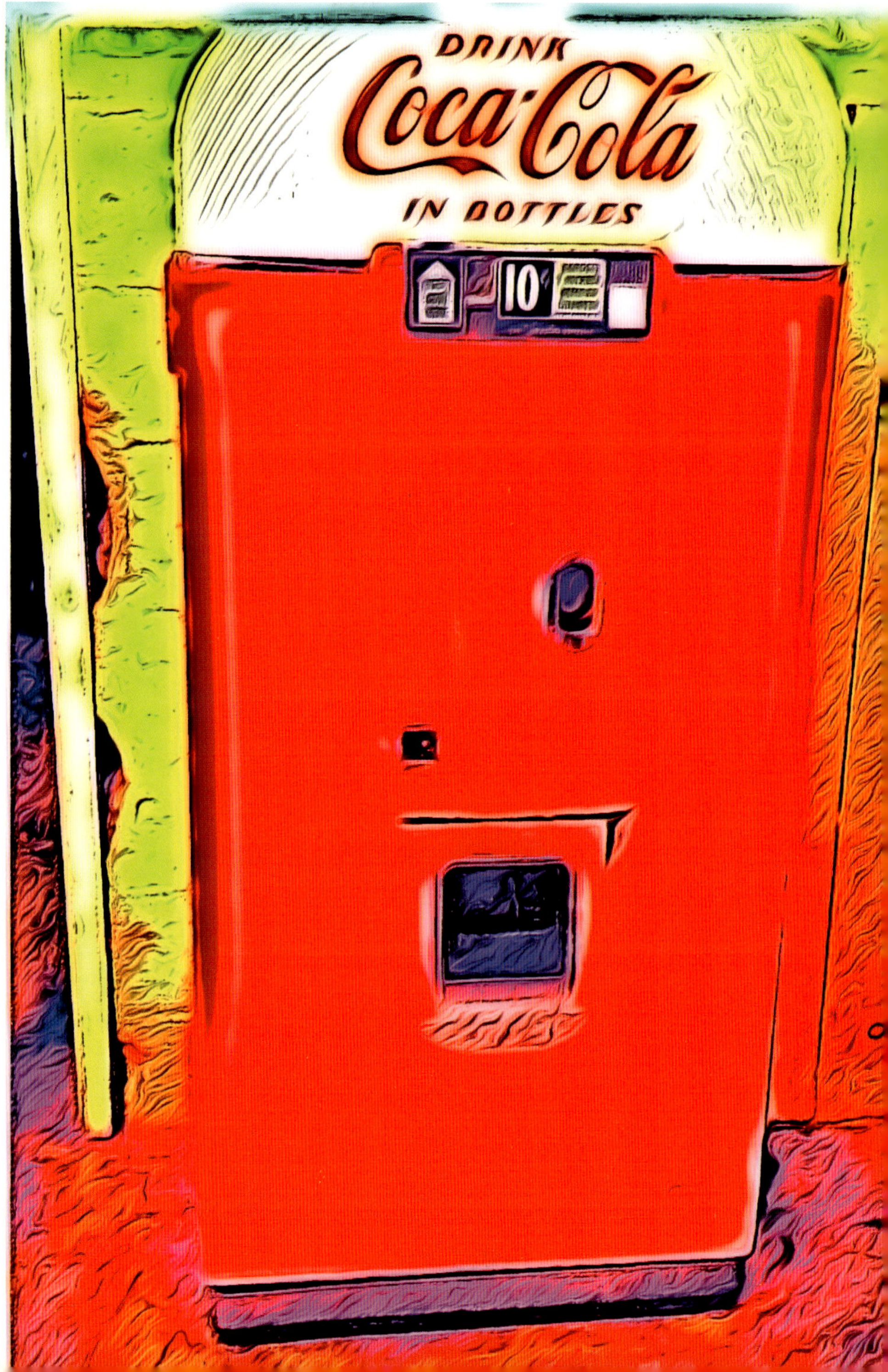

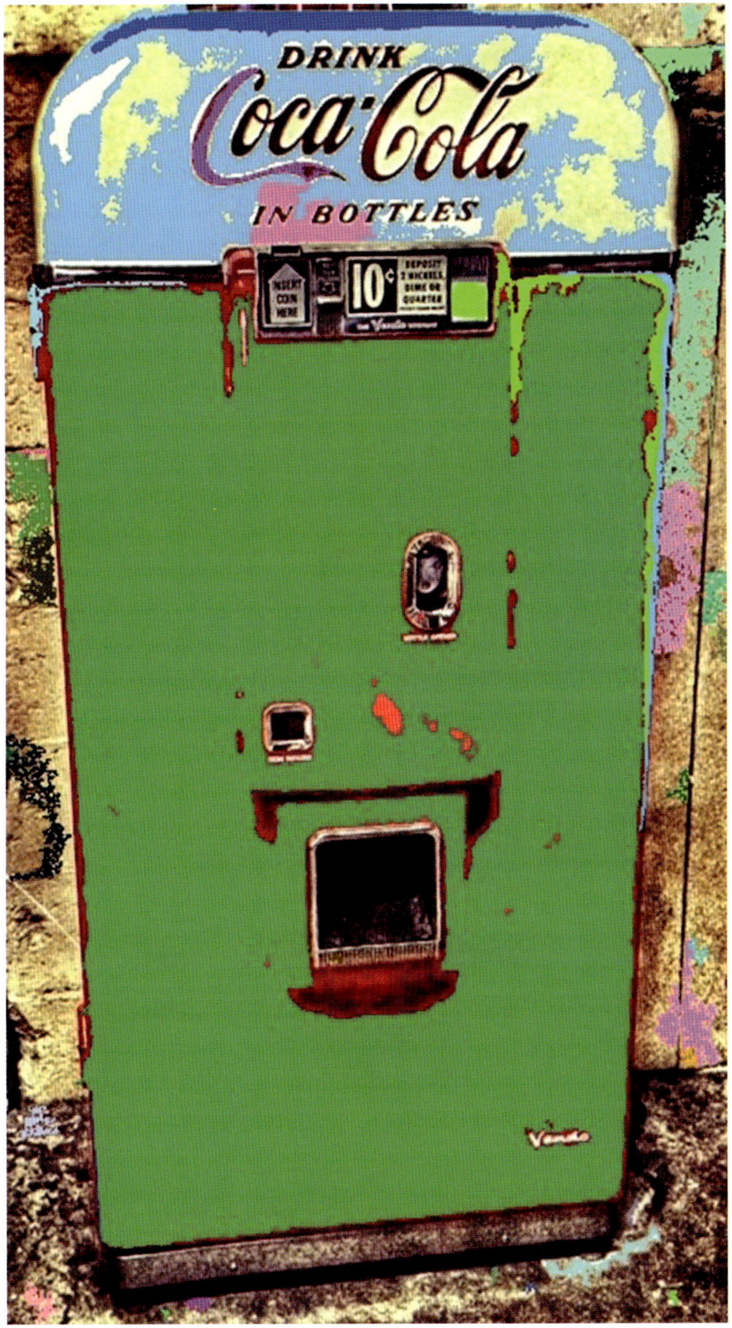
DRINK
Coca-Cola
IN BOTTLES
10¢

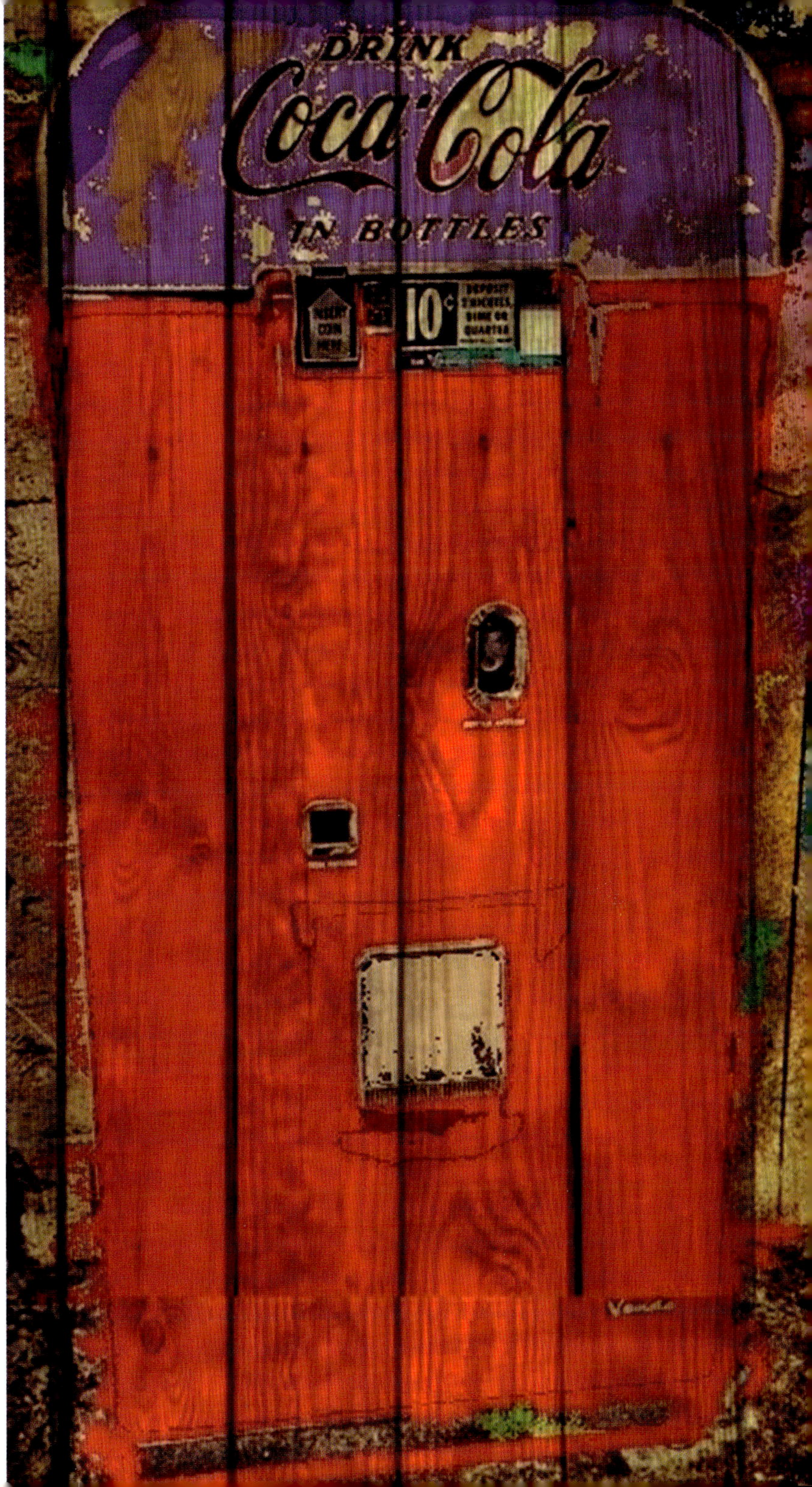
DRINK
Coca-Cola
IN BOTTLES
10¢

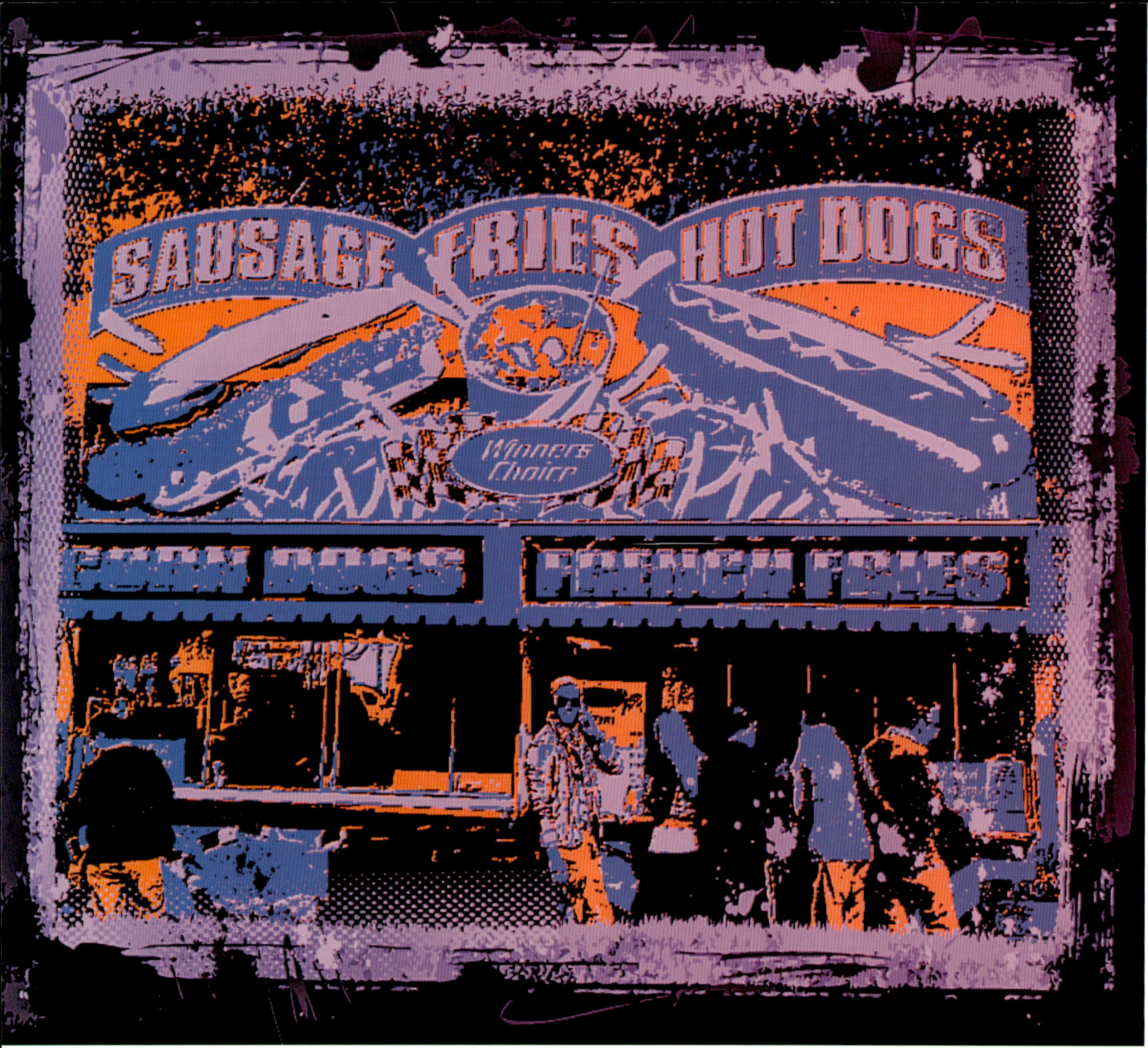

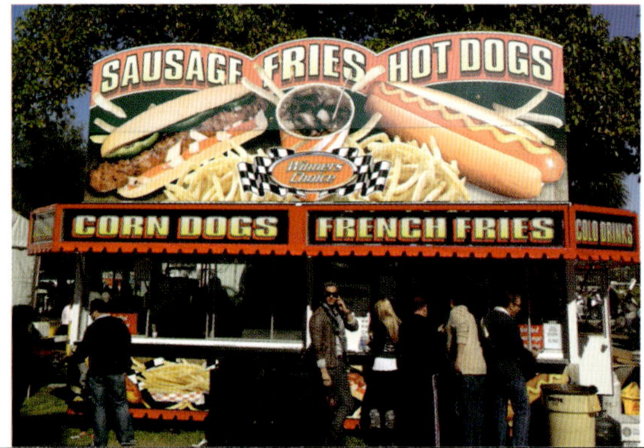

COCONUT GROVE ARTS FESTIVAL

Over 100,000 people visit the festival
To see the work of more than 300 artists
Then there's the food
Sausage, hot dogs, and fries
Fine dining

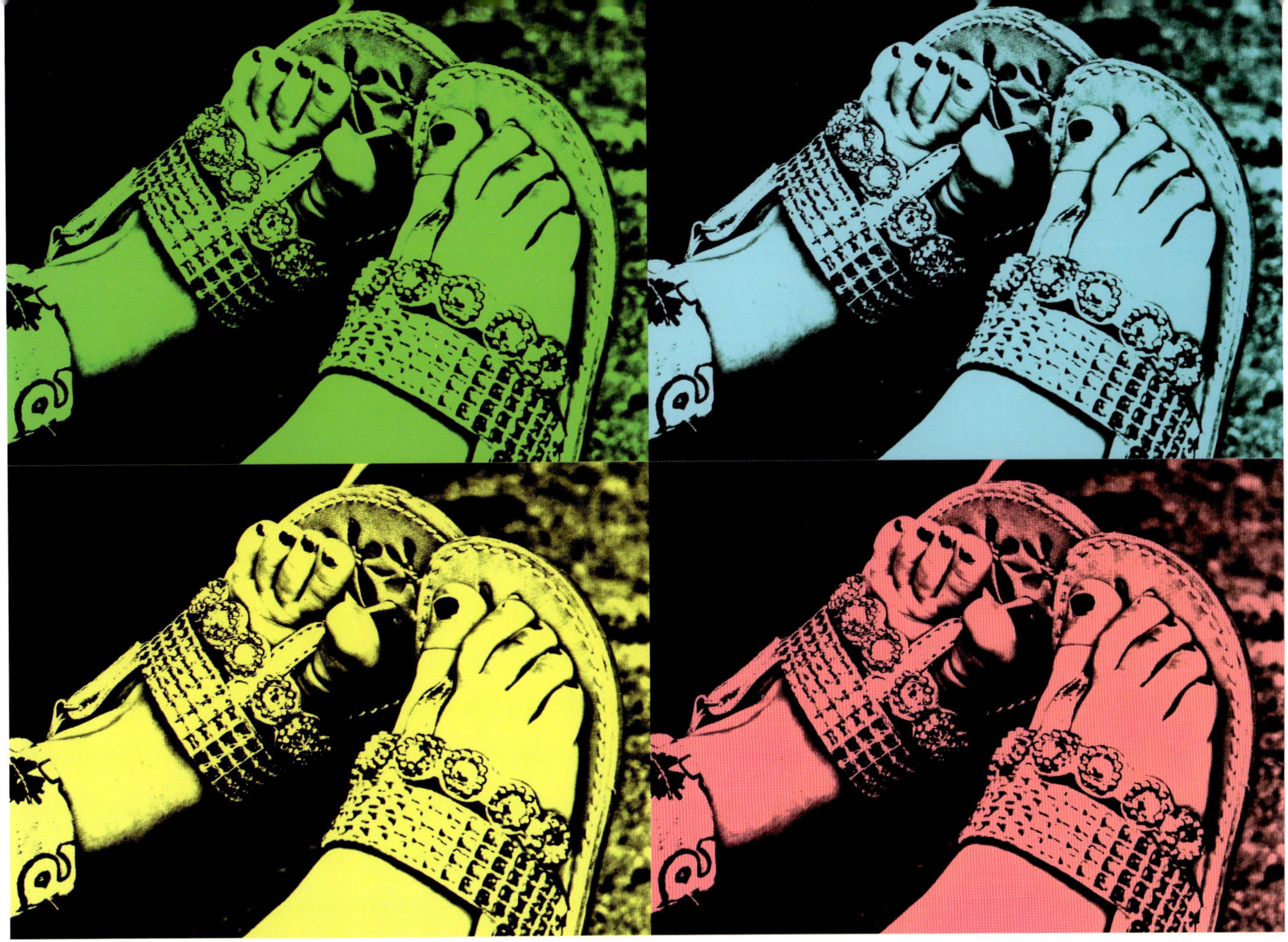

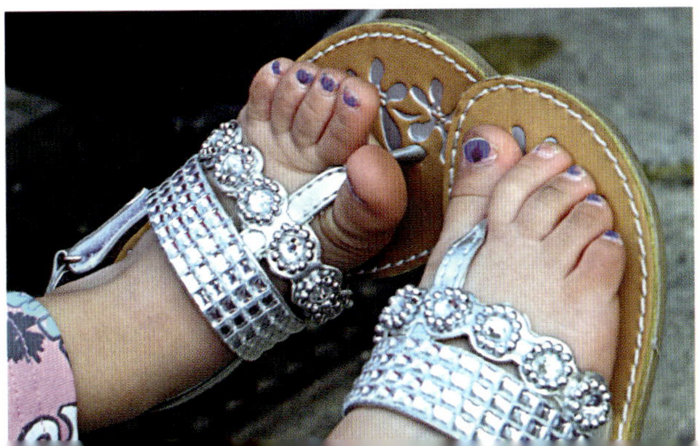

A CHILD'S TOES

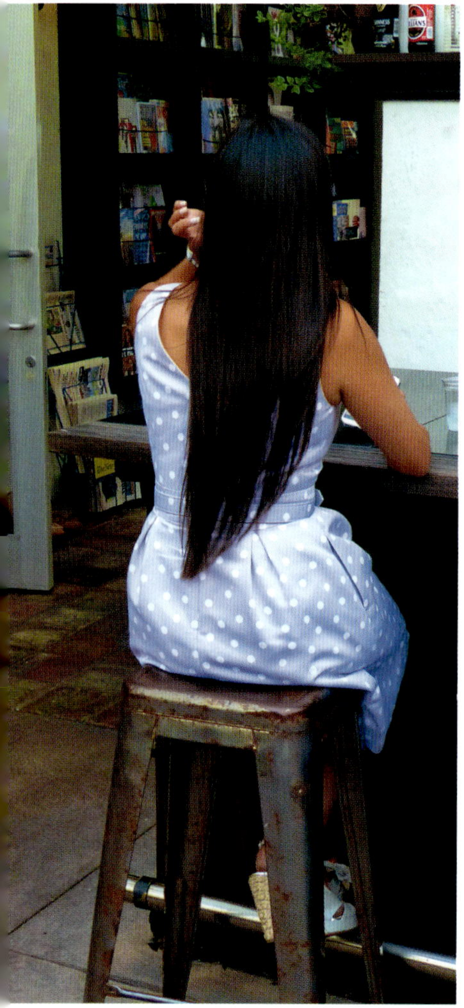

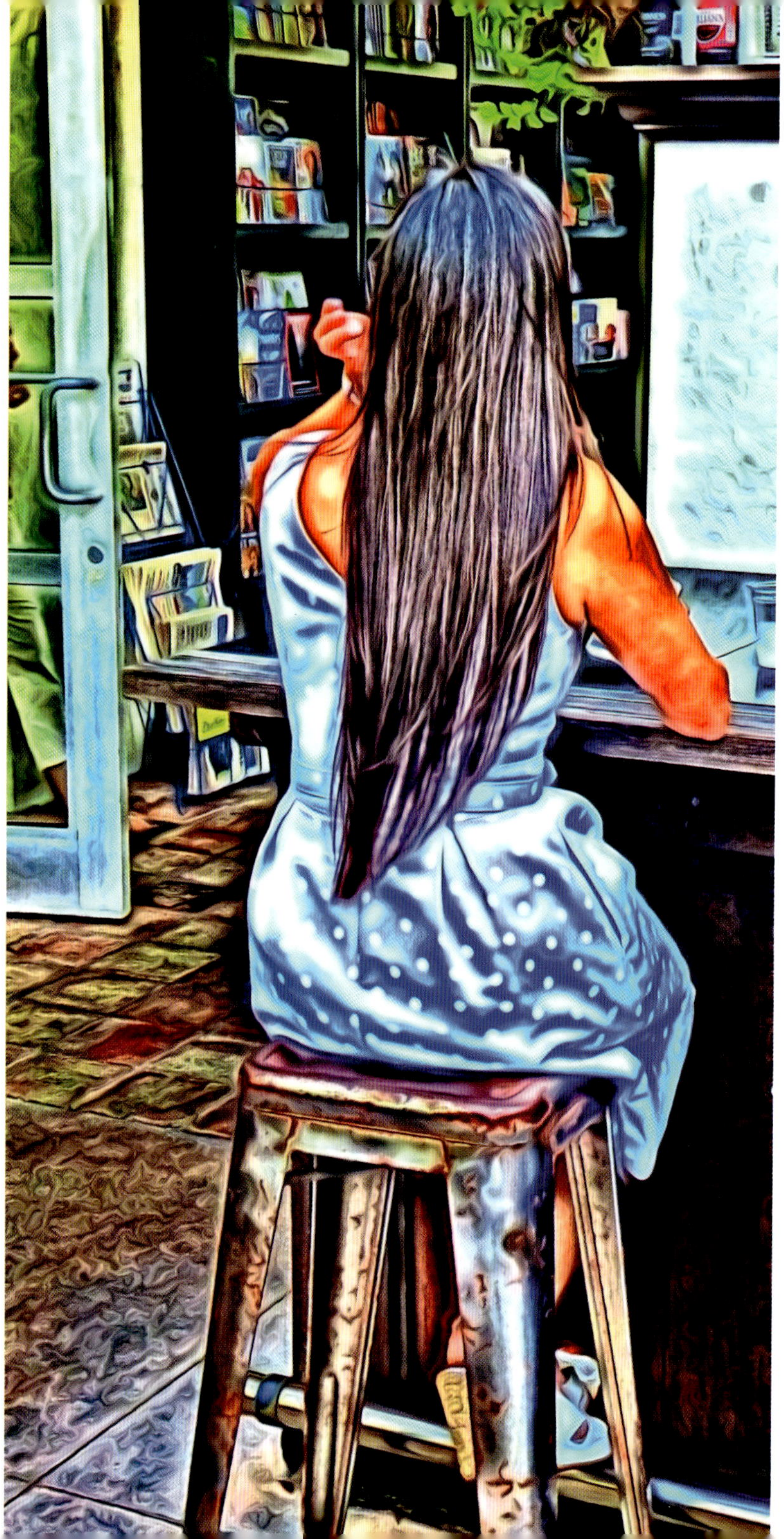

YOUNG WOMAN AT A BOOKSTORE

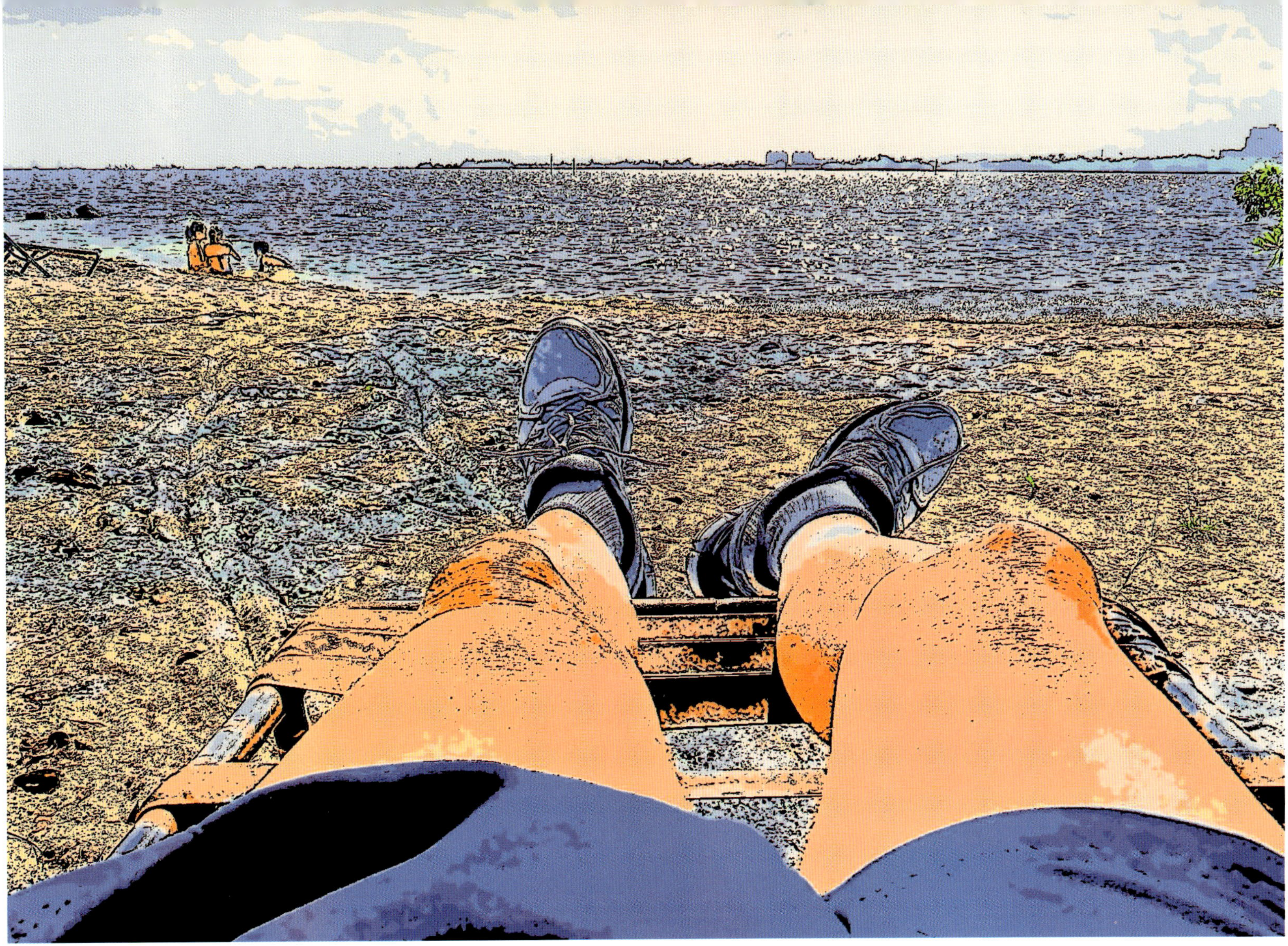

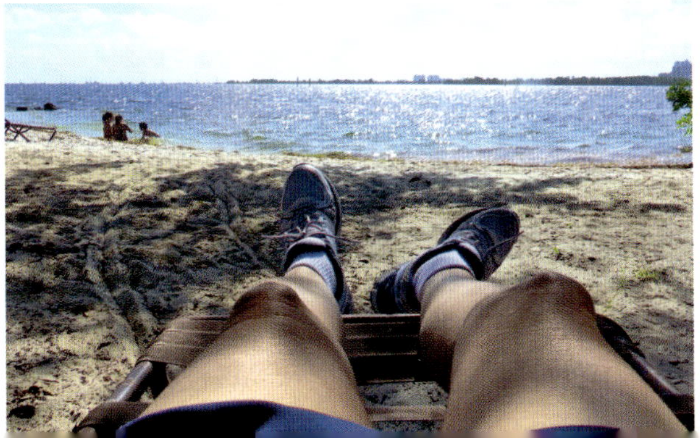

SELF PORTRAIT

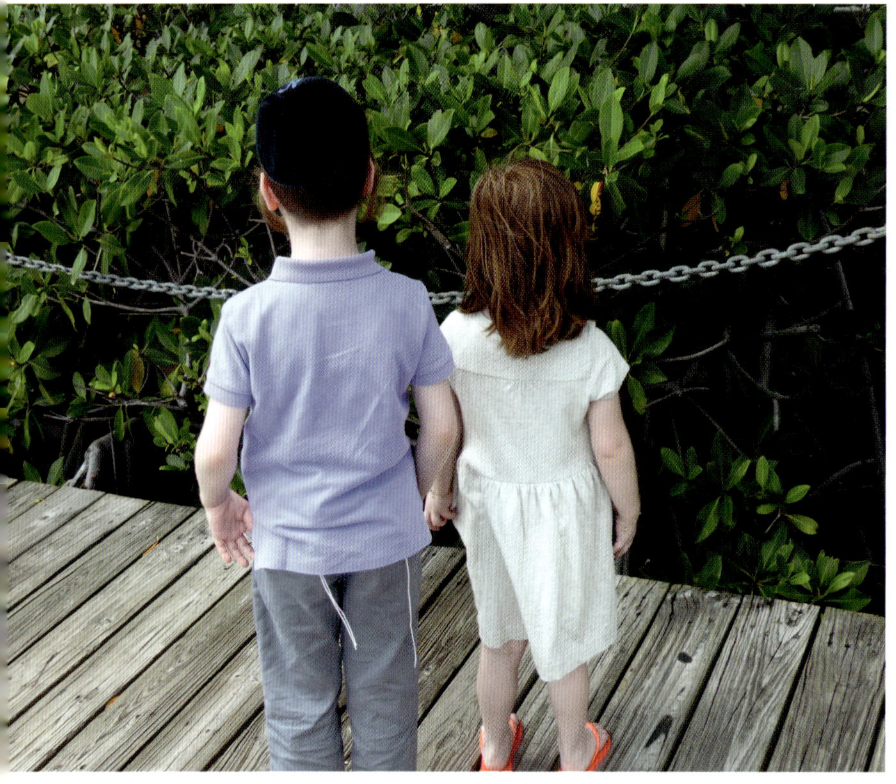

TWO KIDS ADMIRING
THE MANGROVES

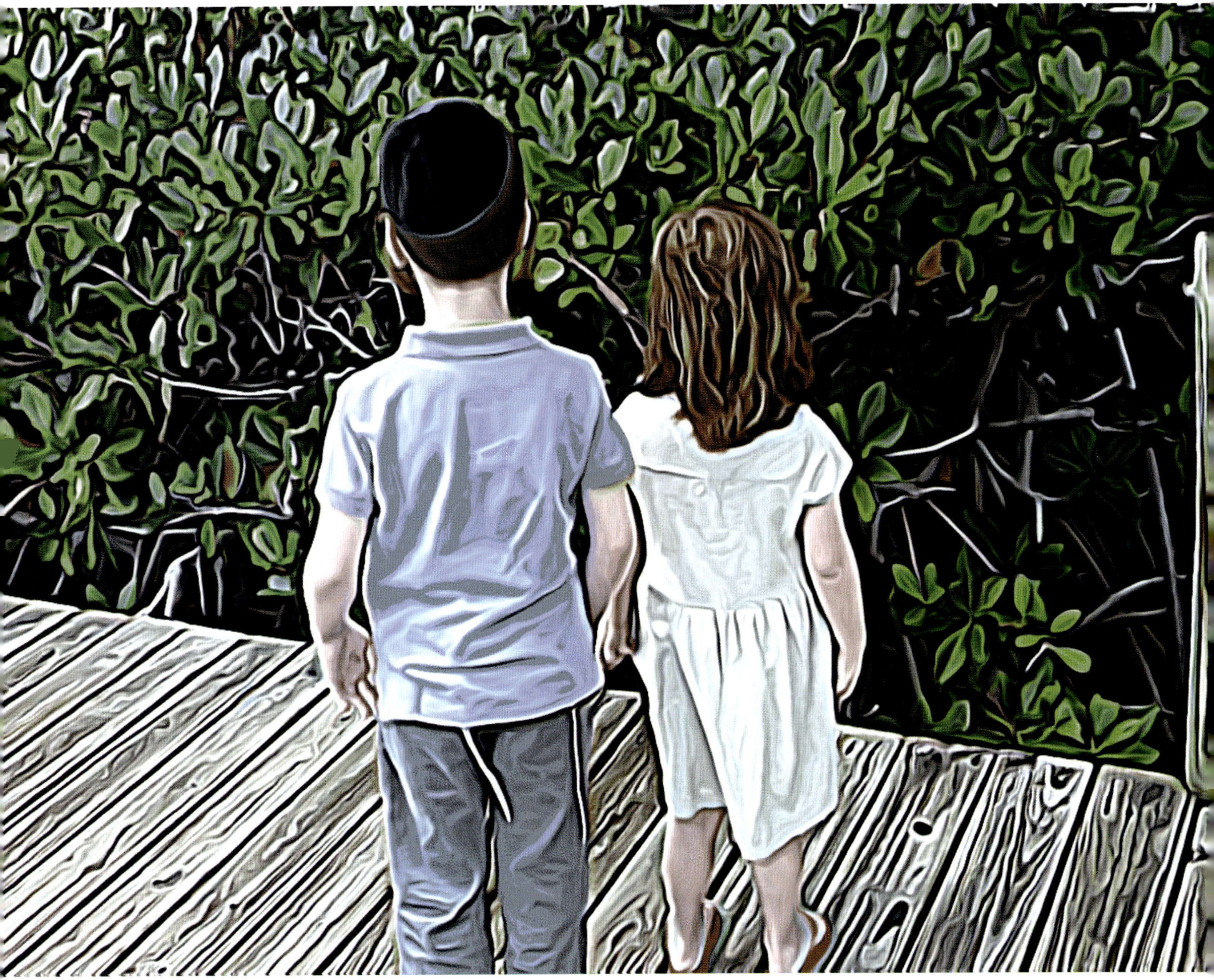

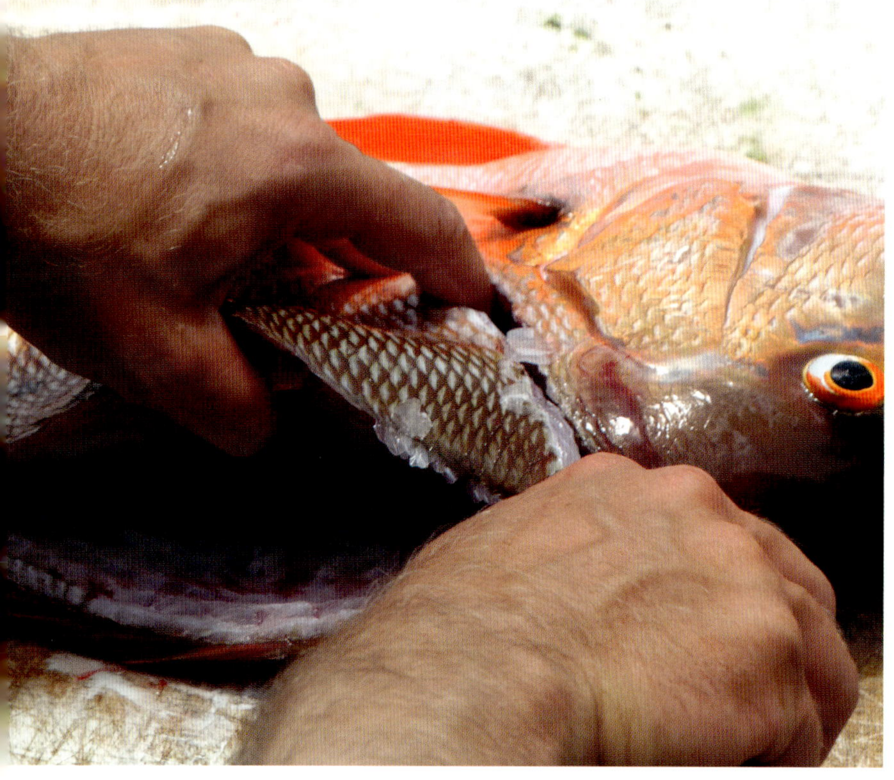

FABULOUS FILET

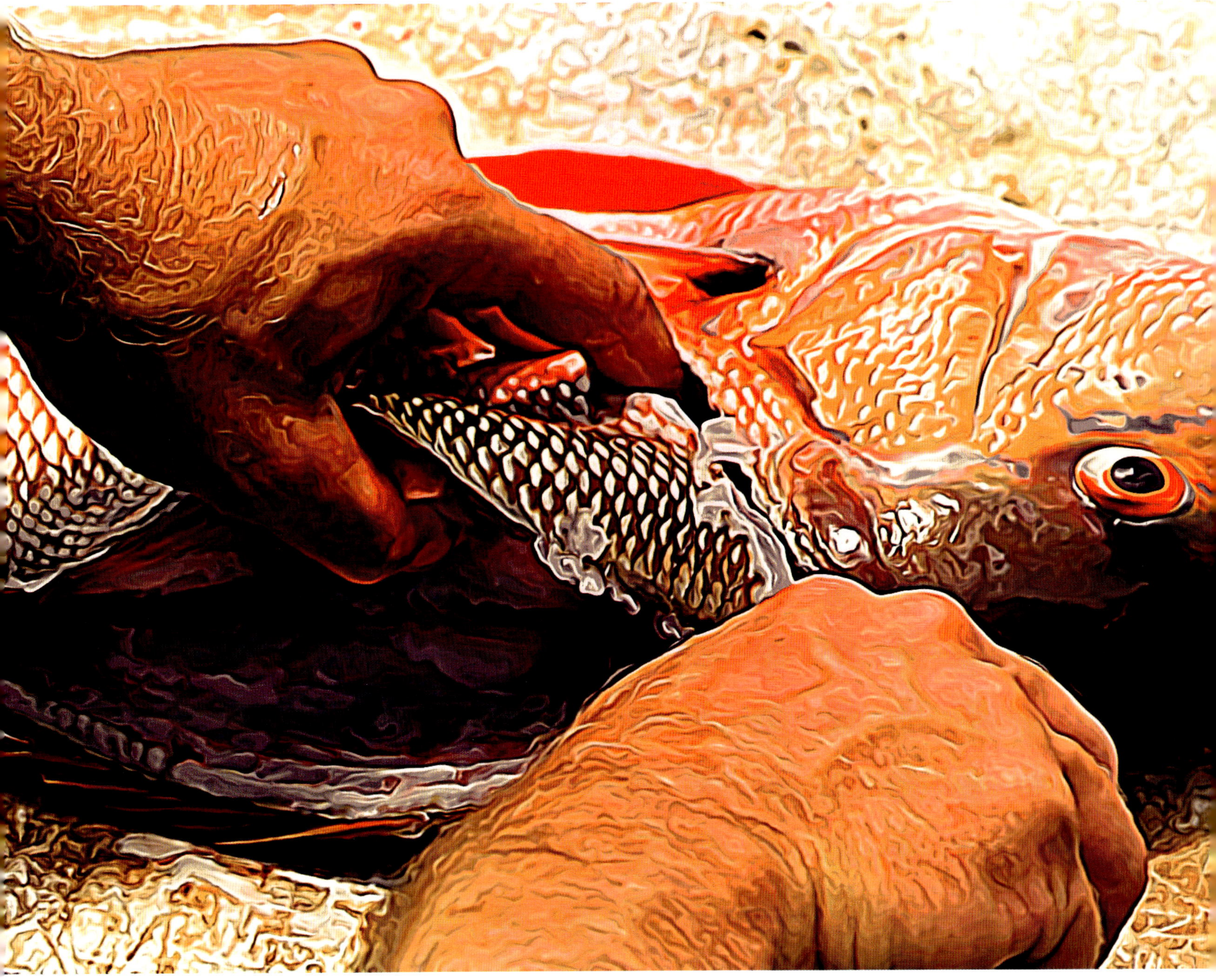

WYNWOOD KITCHEN

Excellent food and good service
A hip place in Wynwood
New neighborhood
It's cool

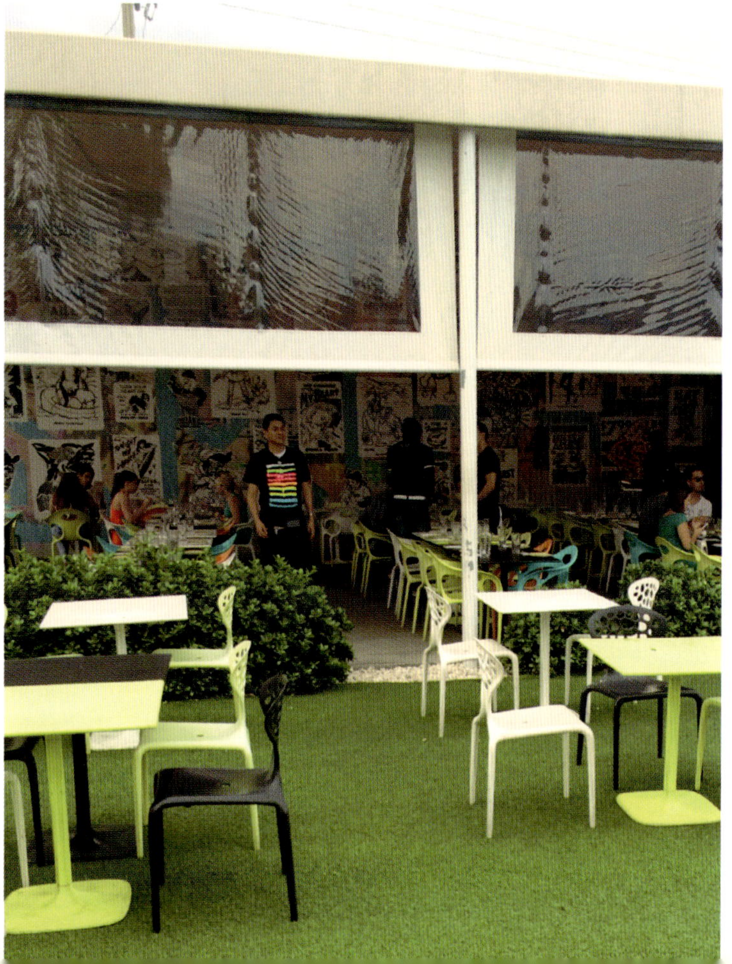

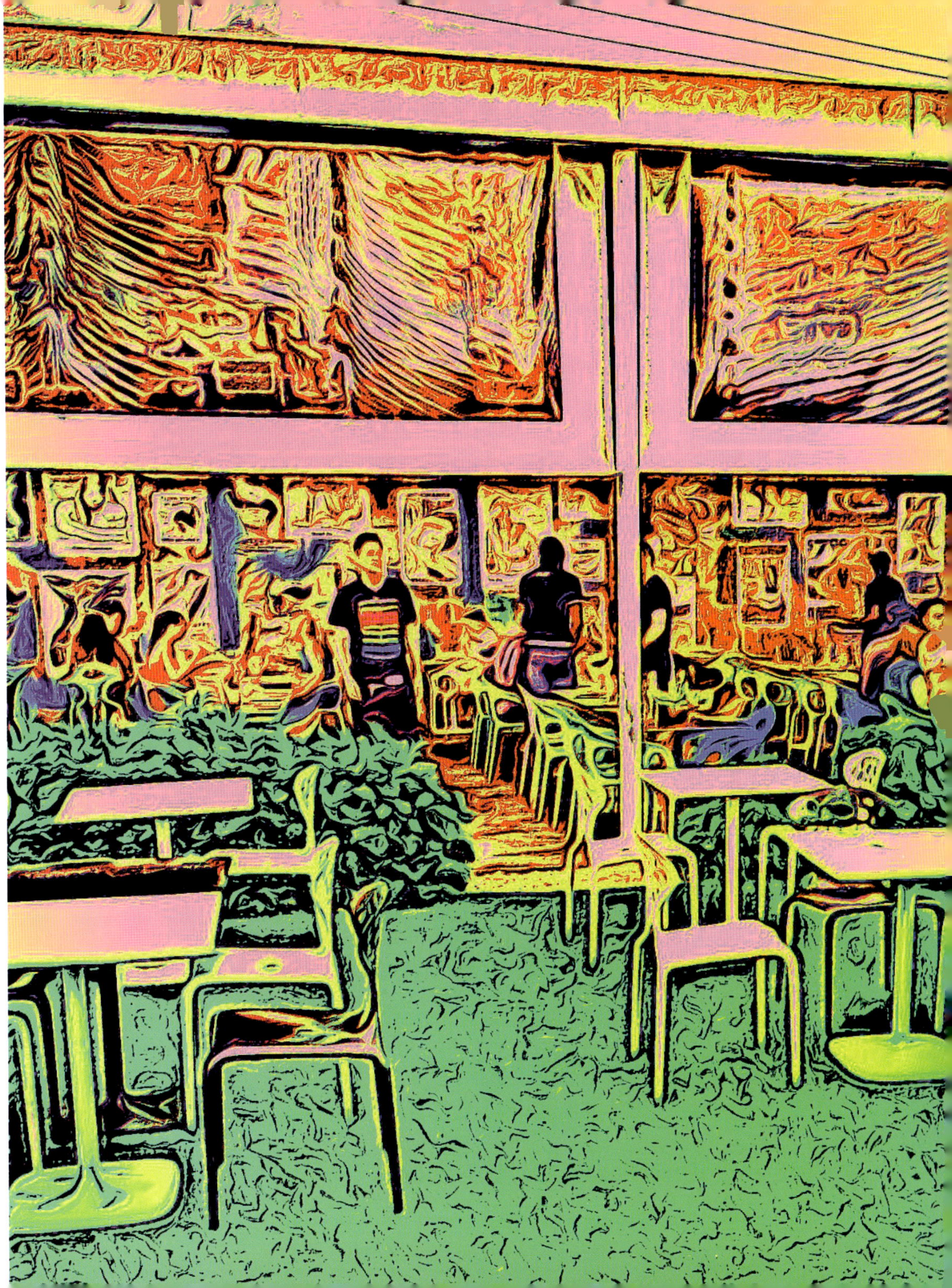

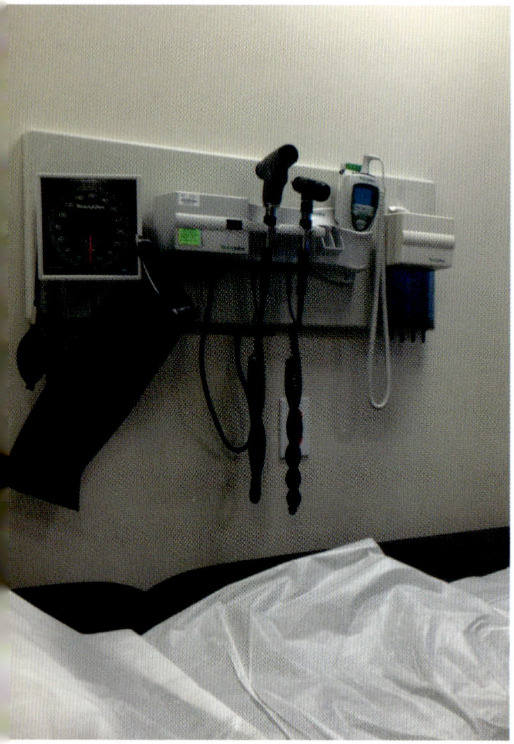

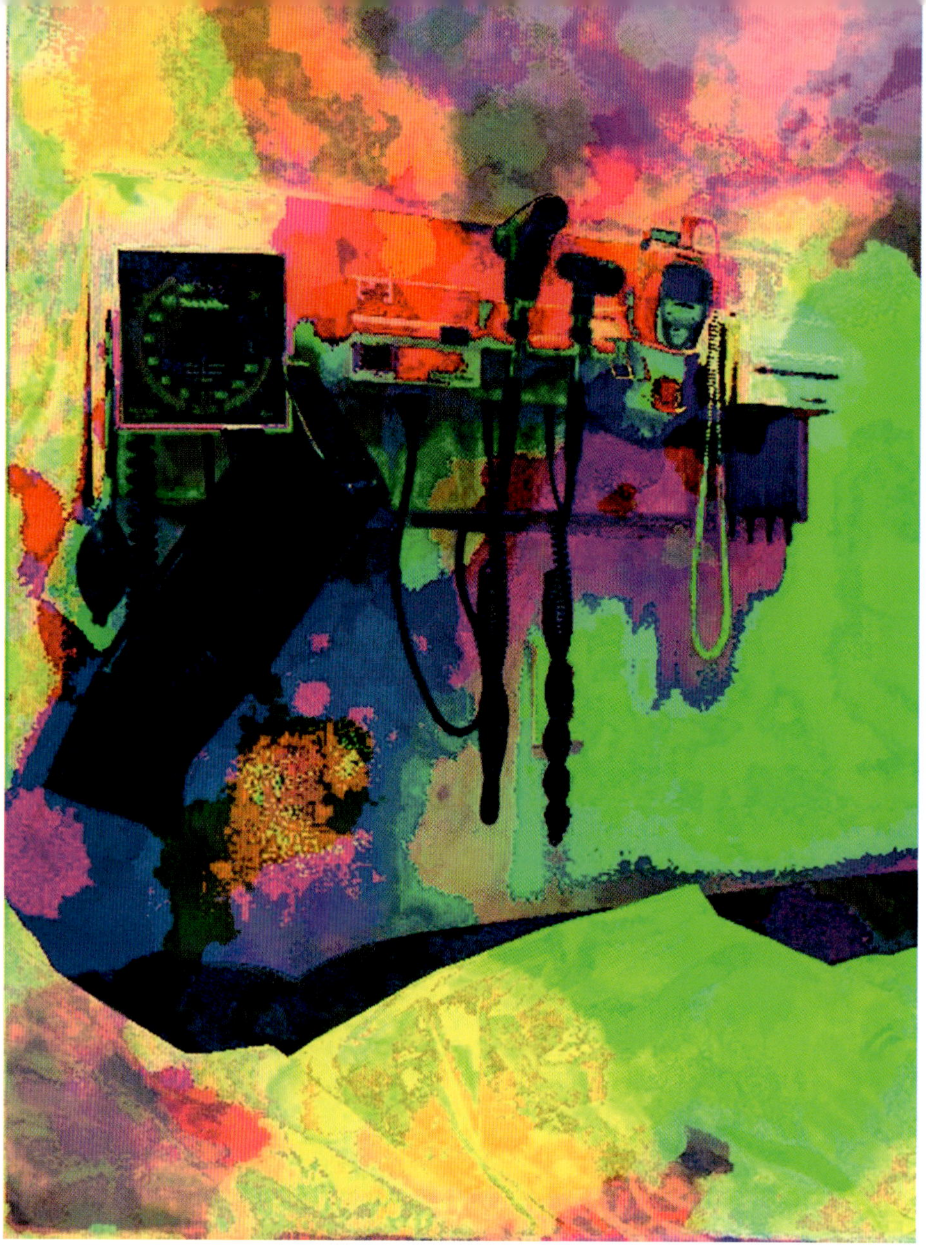

MEDICAL OFFICE

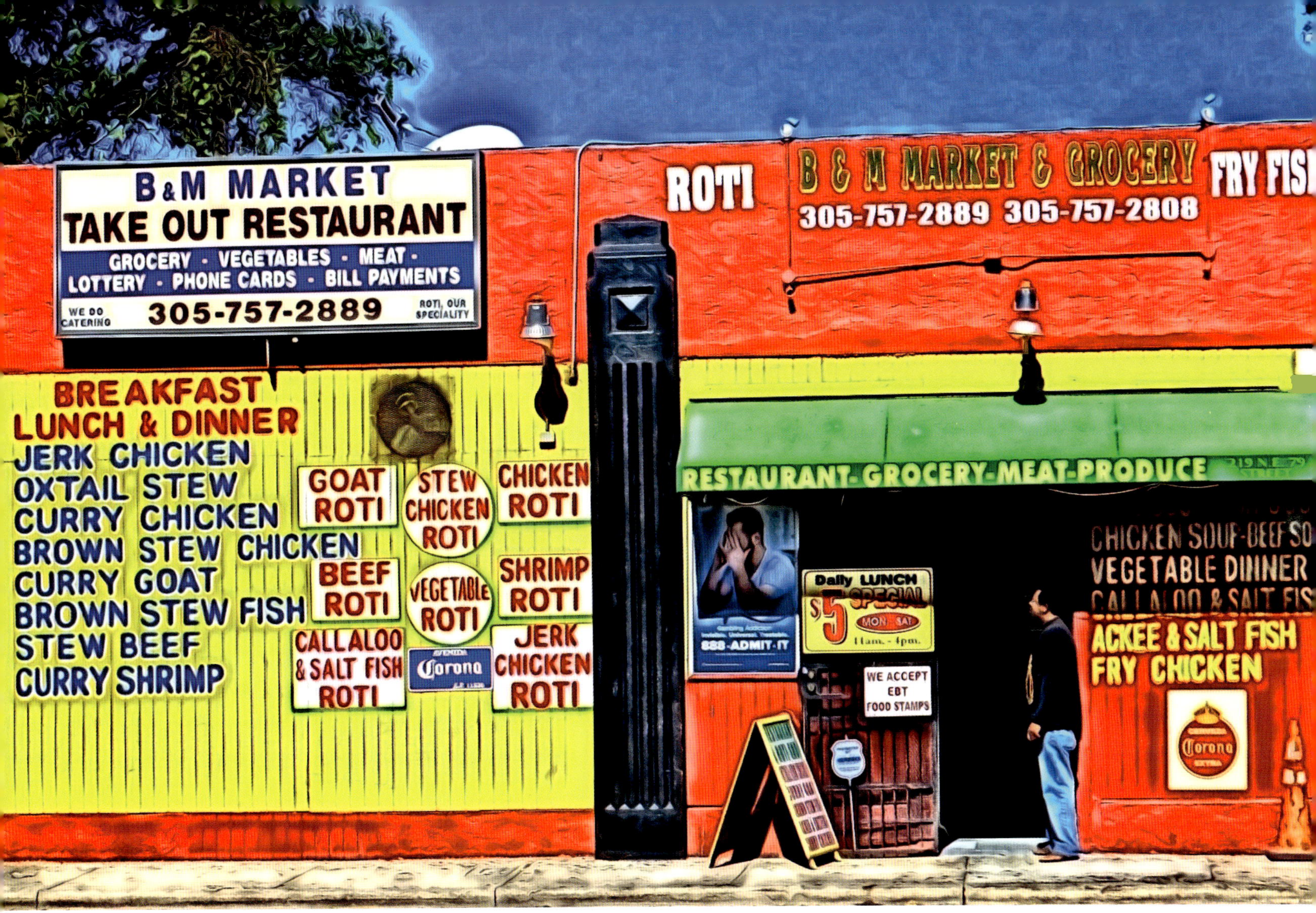

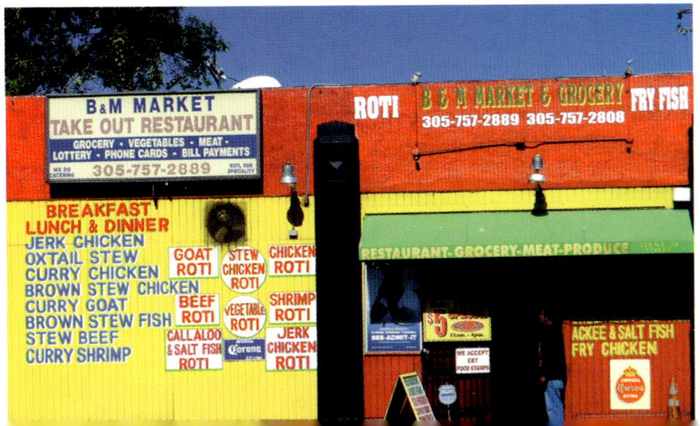

B & M MARKET

Takeout restaurant

Fish, chicken, beef, and goat

Pay bills, too

Full service

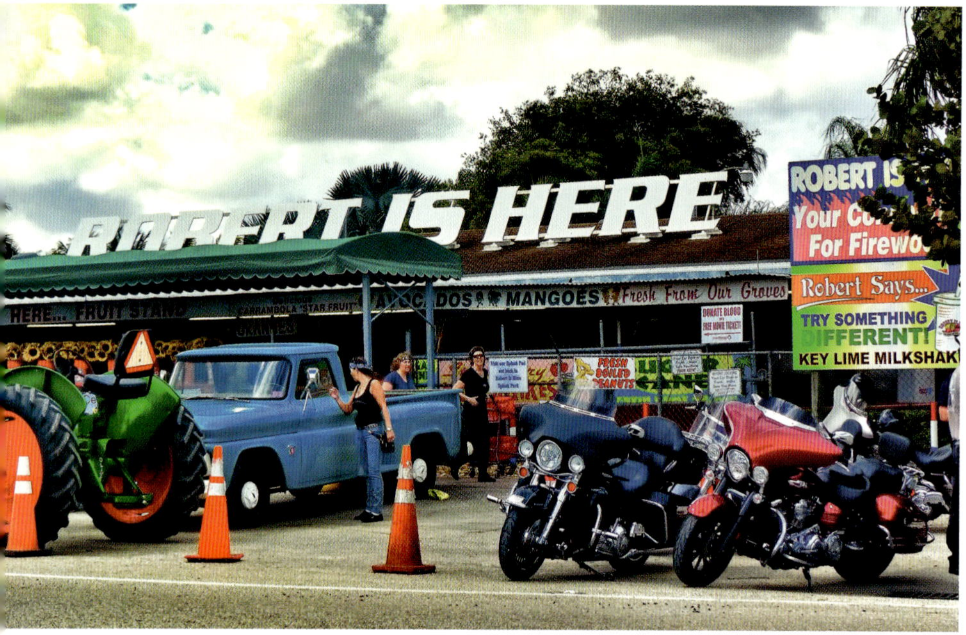

ROBERT IS HERE

Homestead, Florida

Original home of the famous fruit and veggie stand

Where is it?

It's here

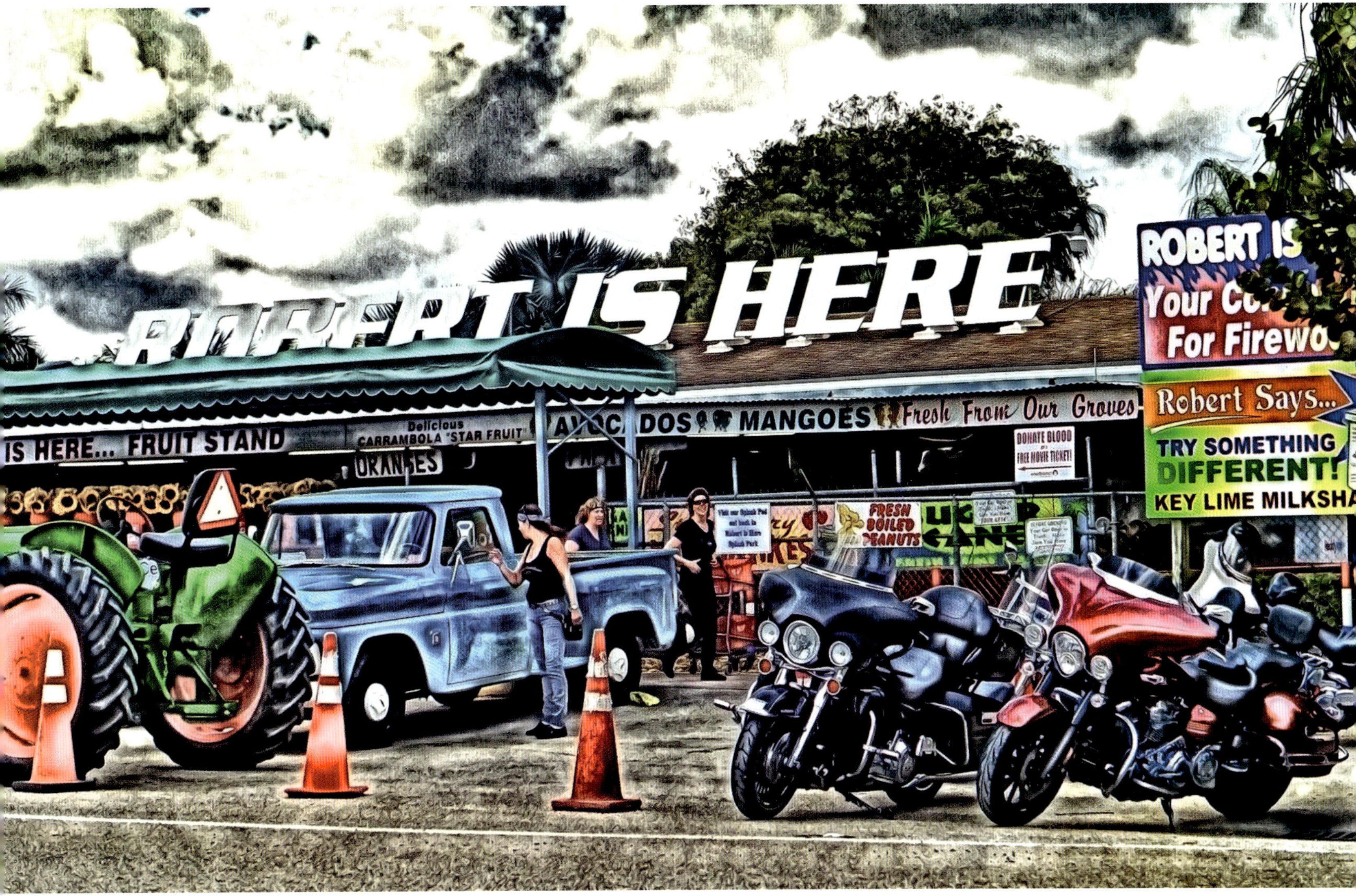
IS HERE
IS HERE... FRUIT STAND
Delicious
CARRAMBOLA "STAR FRUIT"
MANGOES
Fresh From Our Groves
DONATE BLOOD
FREE MOVIE TICKET!
FRESH BOILED PEANUTS
Robert Says...
TRY SOMETHING DIFFERENT!

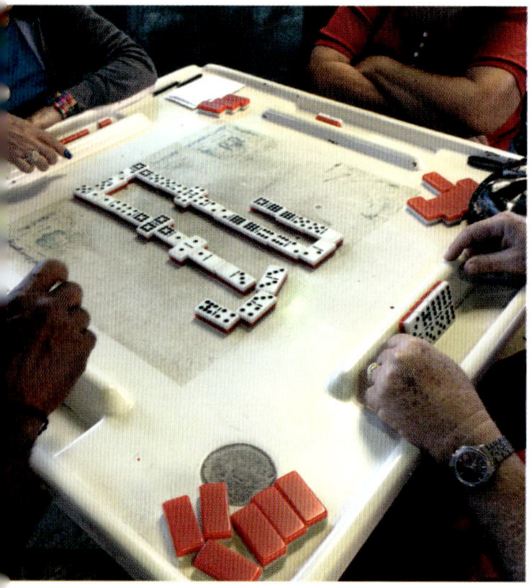

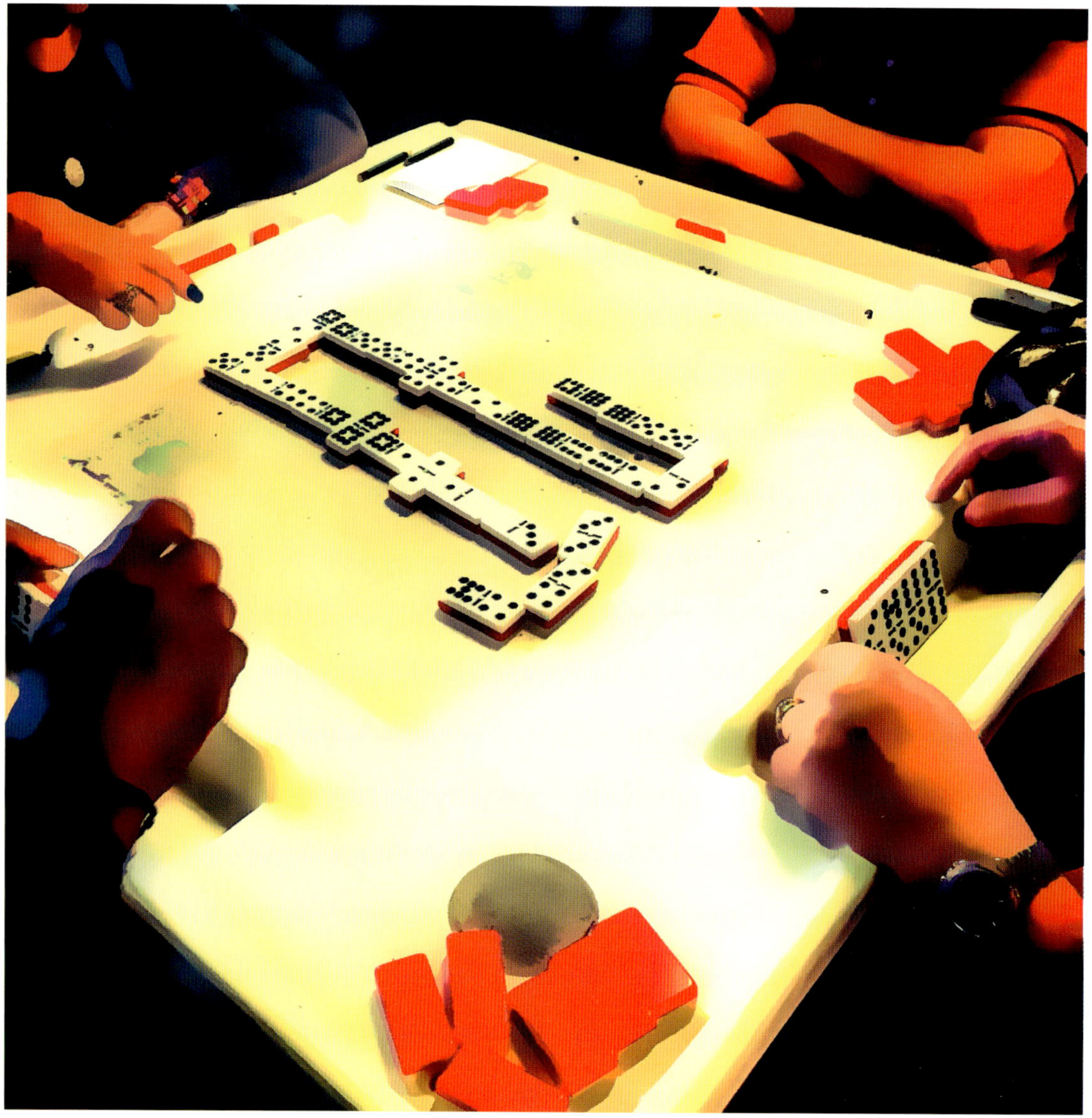

DOMINOES

At Dominoes Park

On Eighth Street, better known as Calle Ocho

A player gestures with a painted nail

Competitive

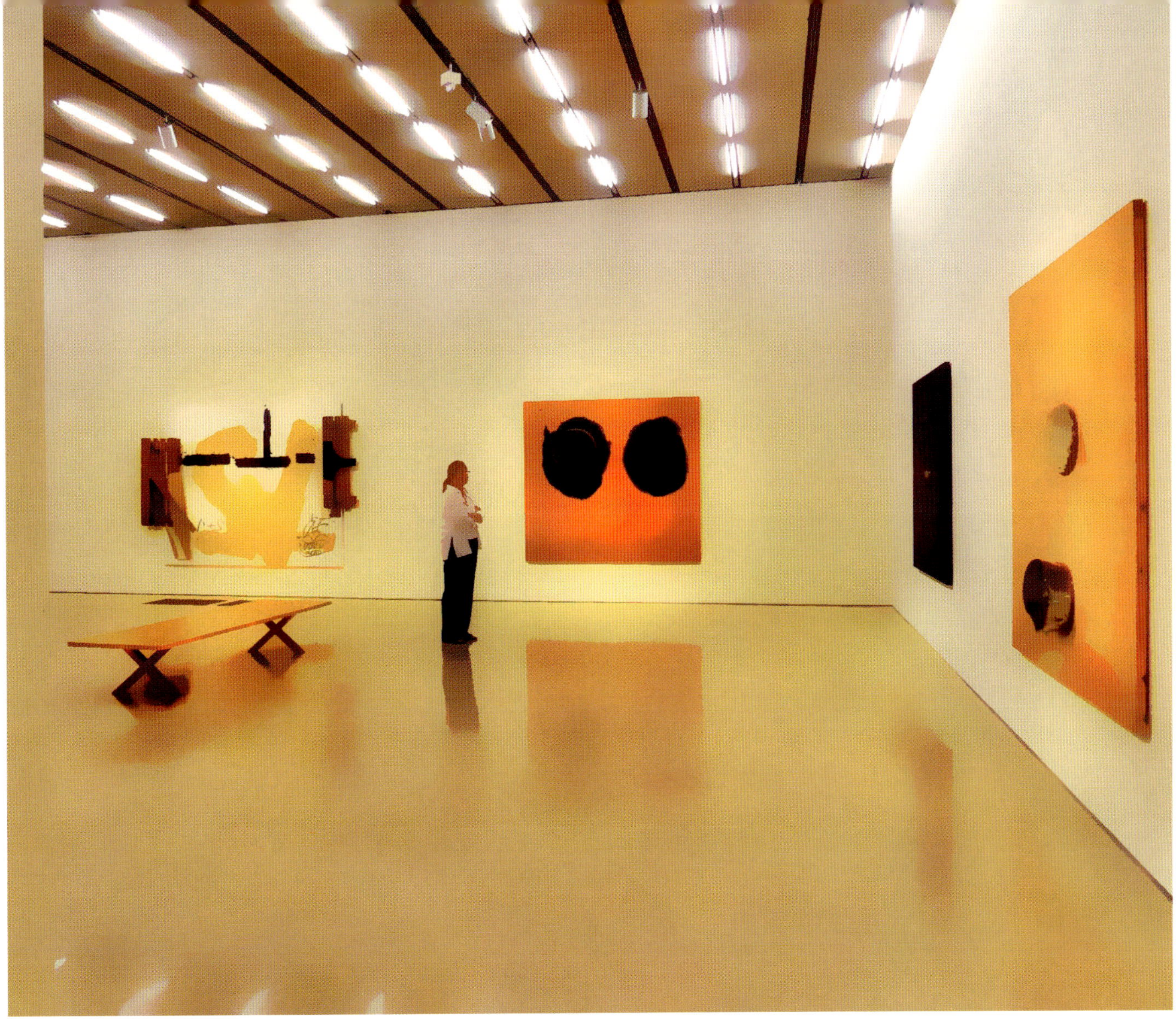

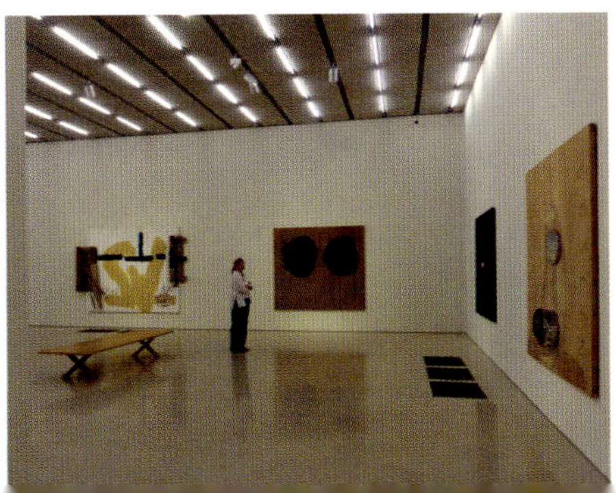

PAMM

ZIFF BALLET HOUSE

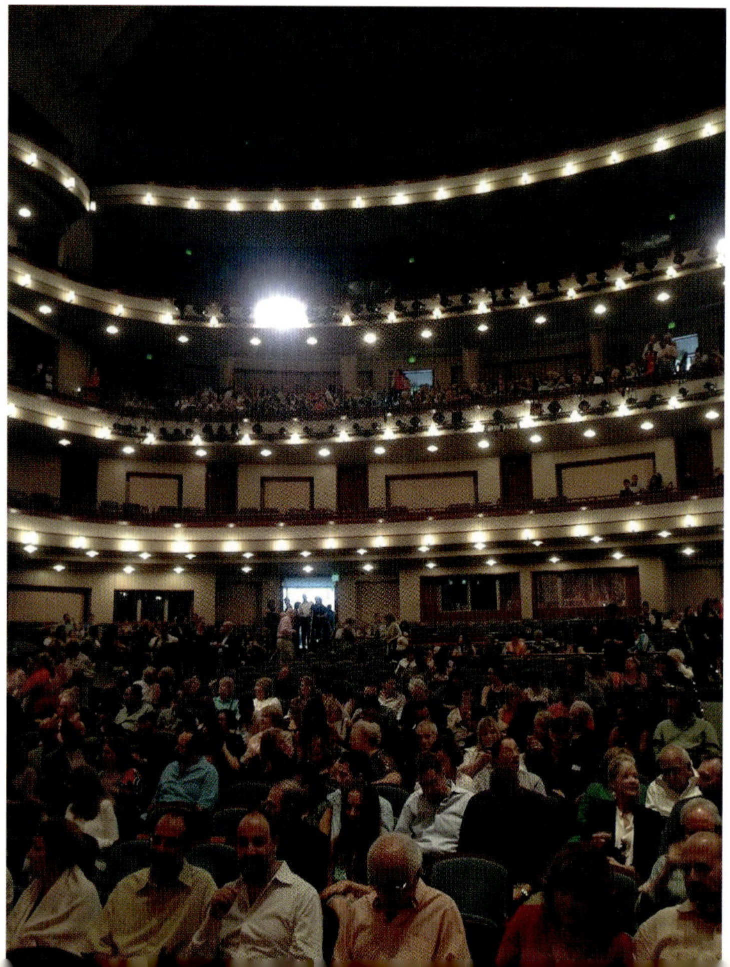

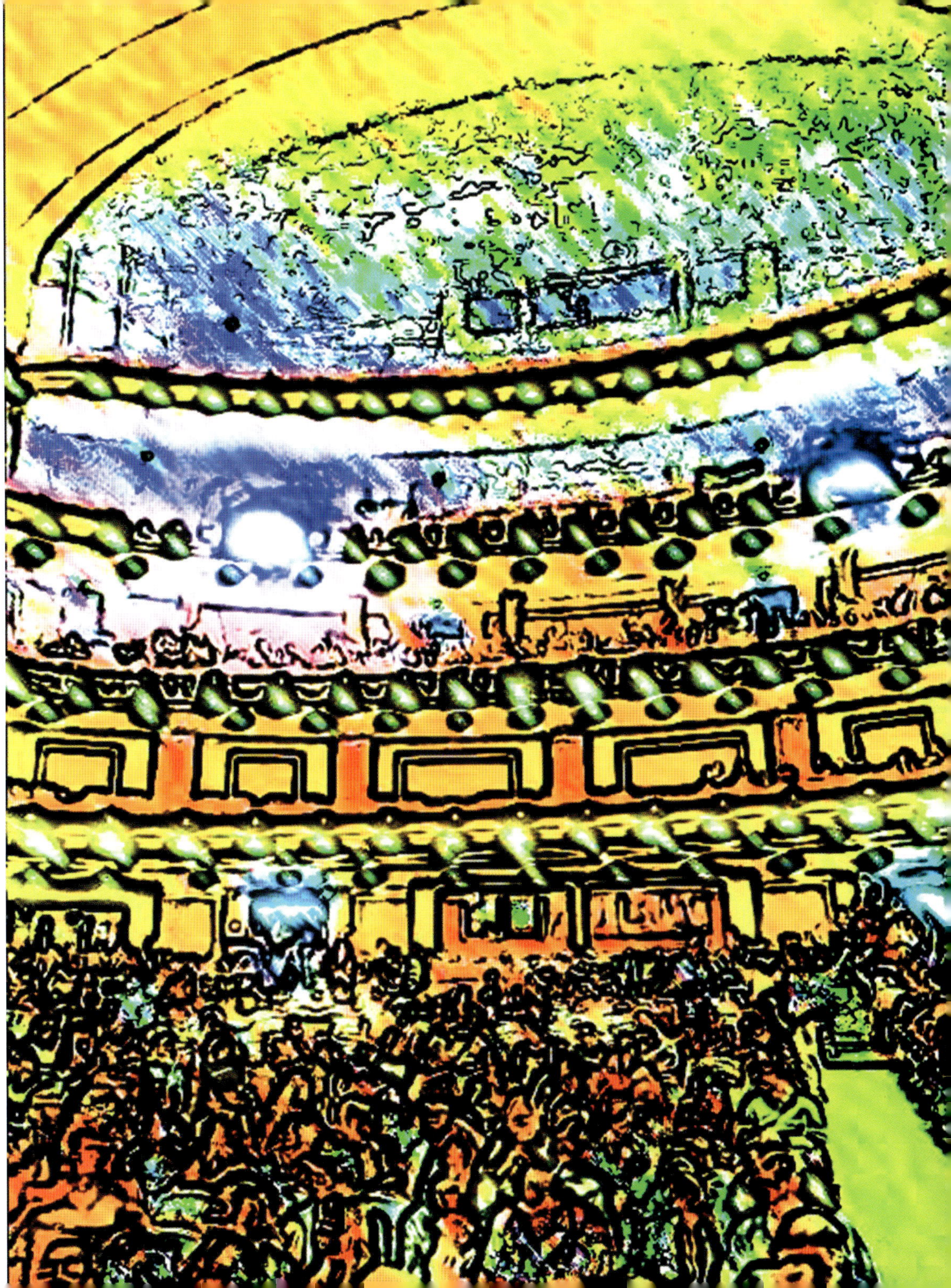

ADRIENNE ARSHT CENTER

Watching a dance performance
From a colorful balcony box
Argentinean dancers

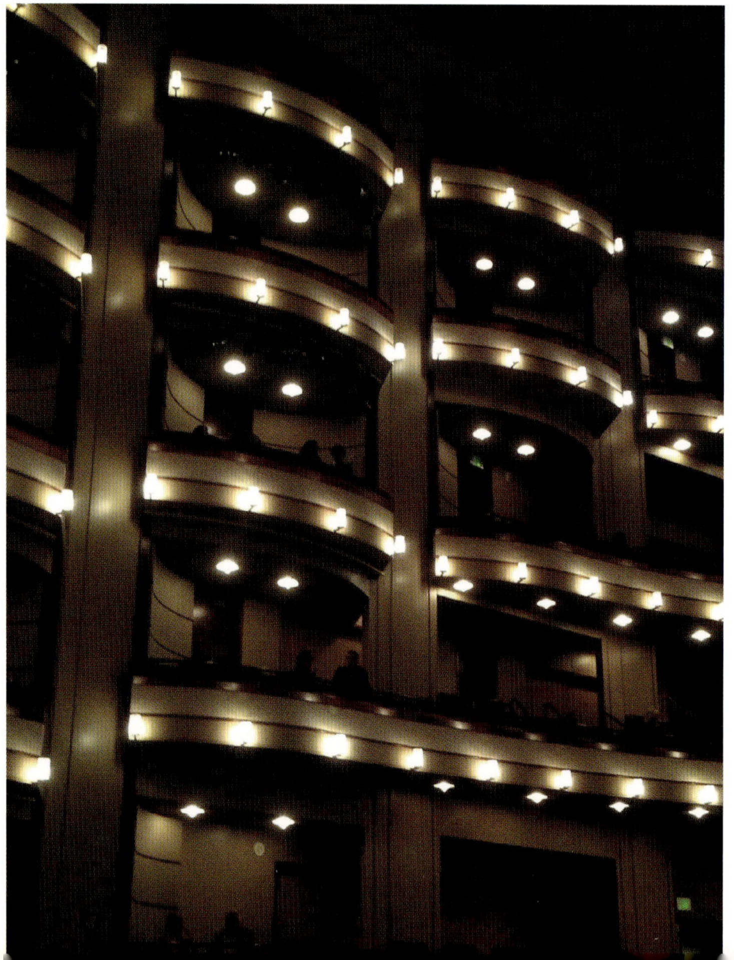

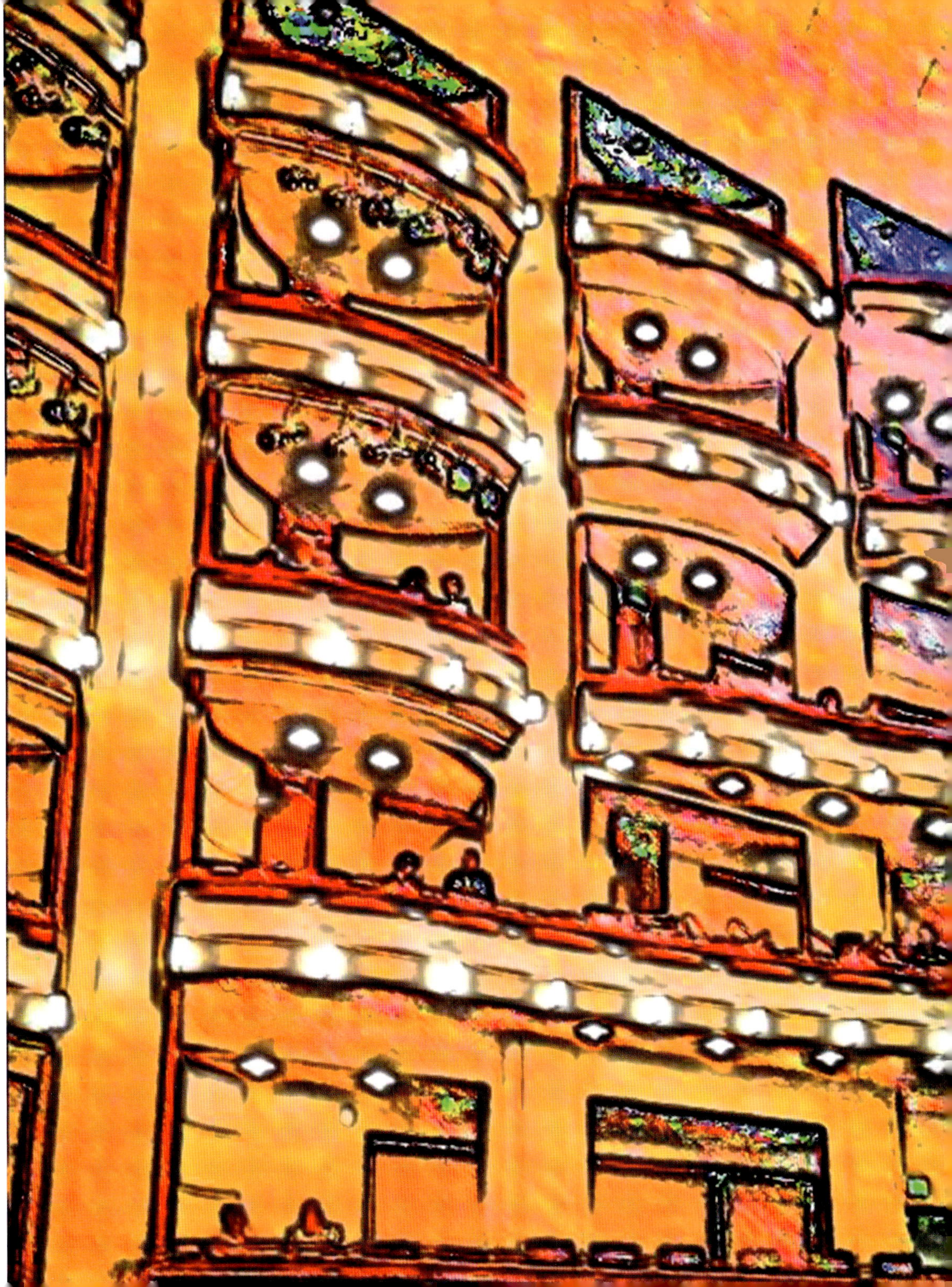

TAILOR

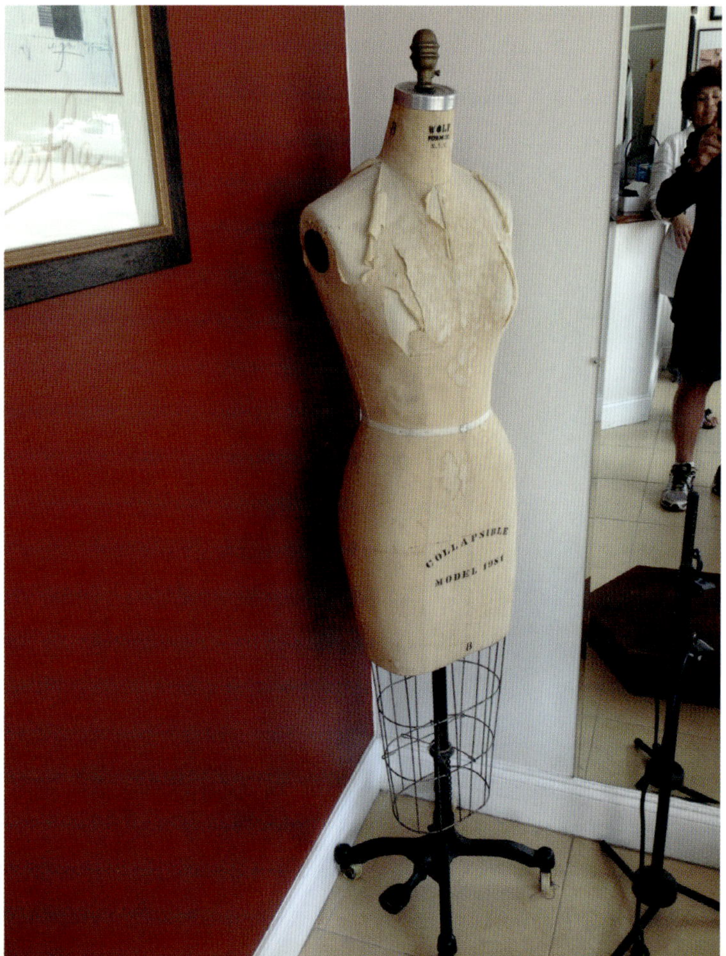

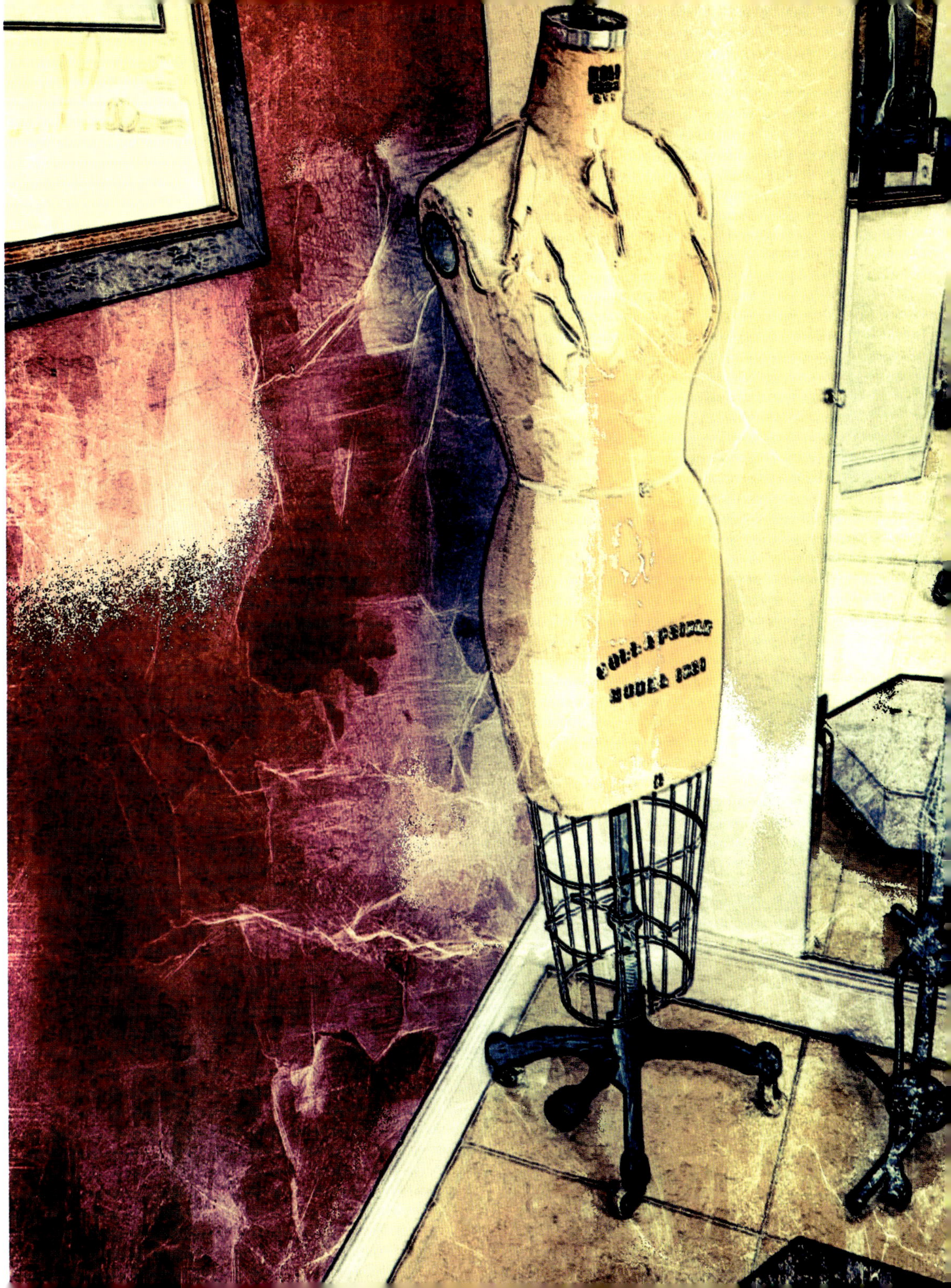

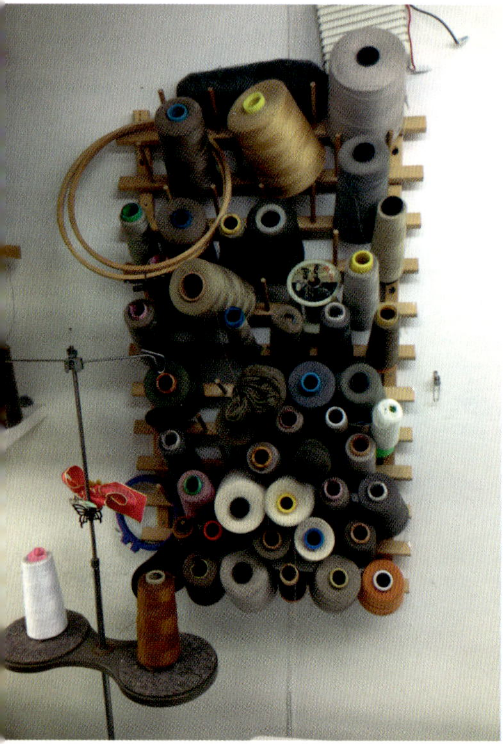

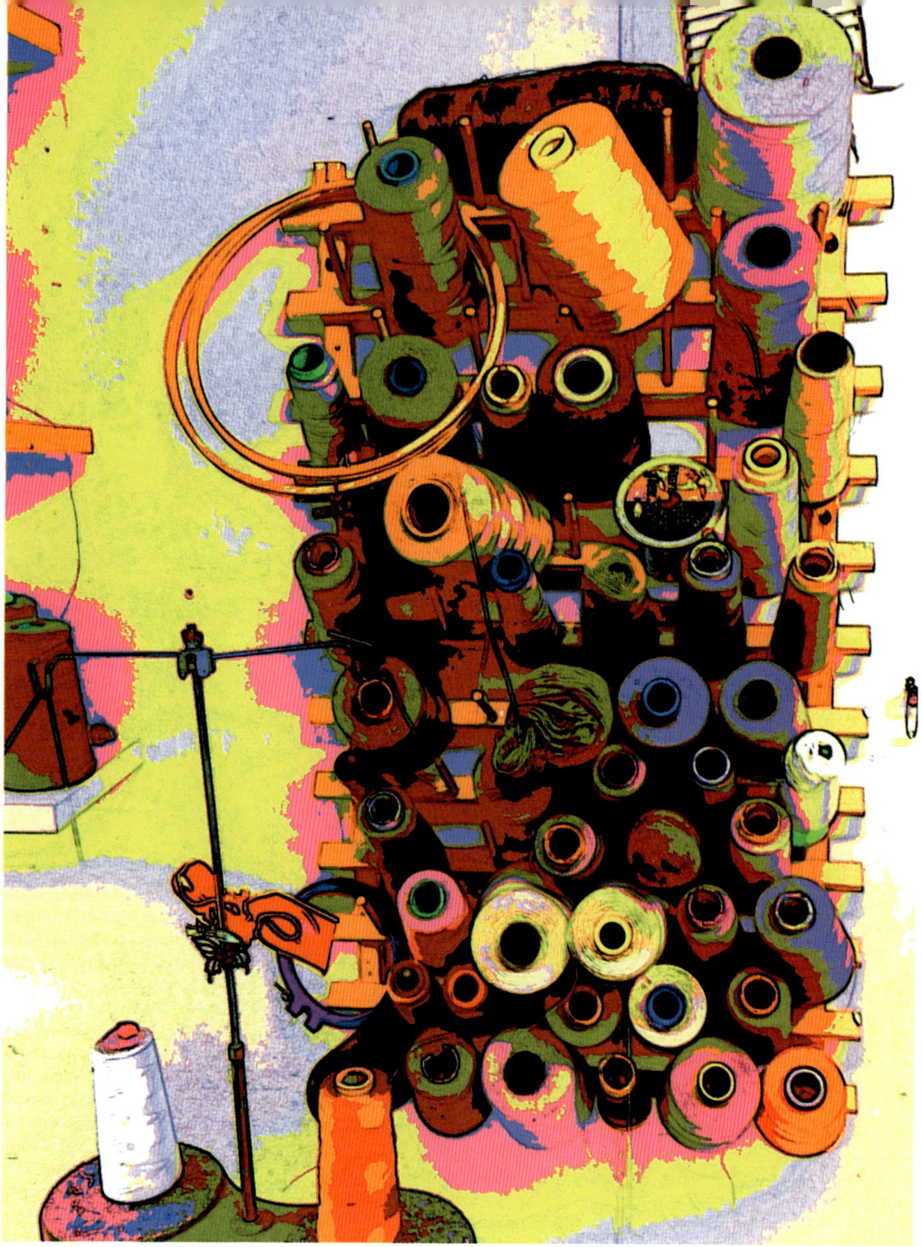

THREAD

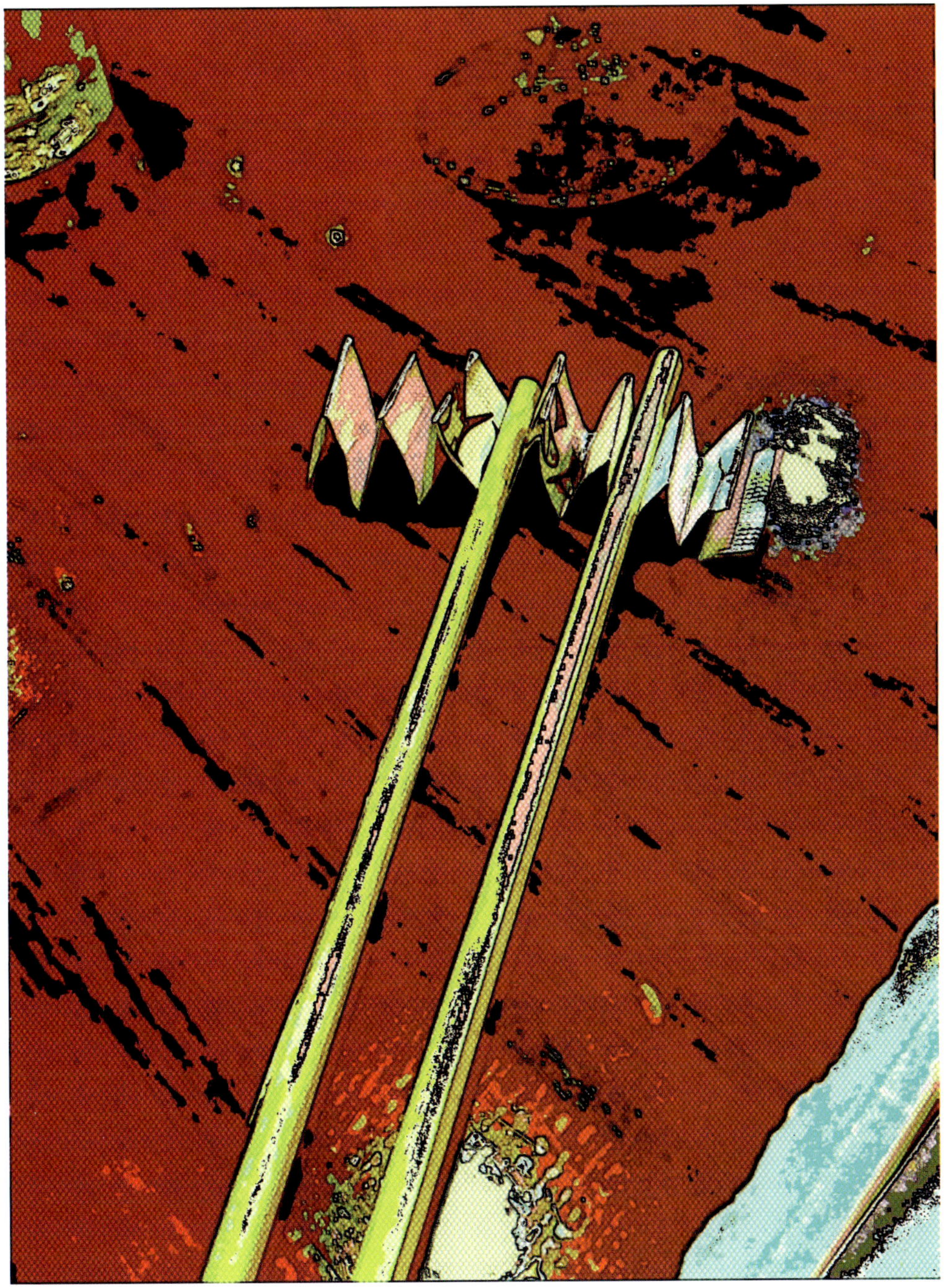

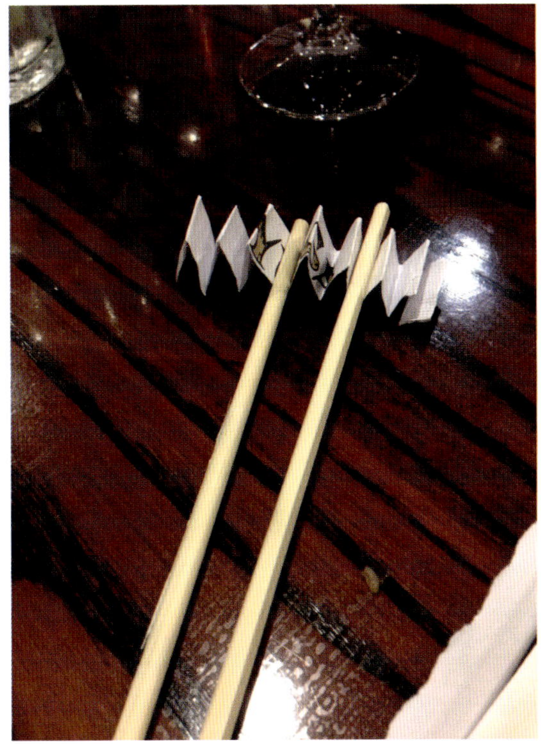

CHOPSTICKS

Eating utensils

They're for sushi

Not soup

PAY PHONE

Don't see them much anymore
Who uses them?
Just for exhibit now

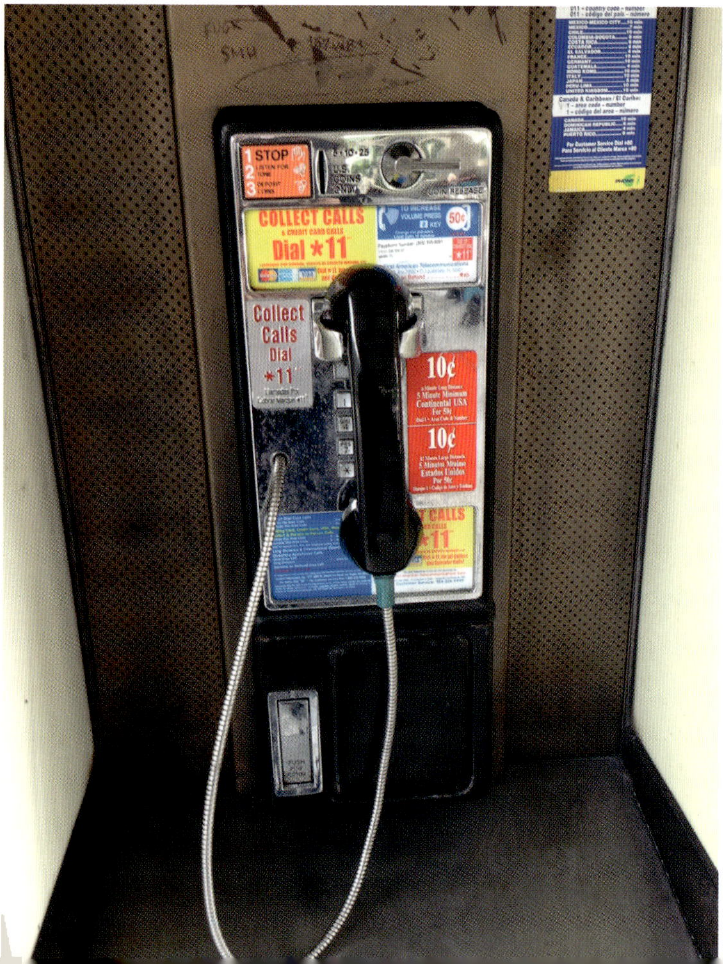

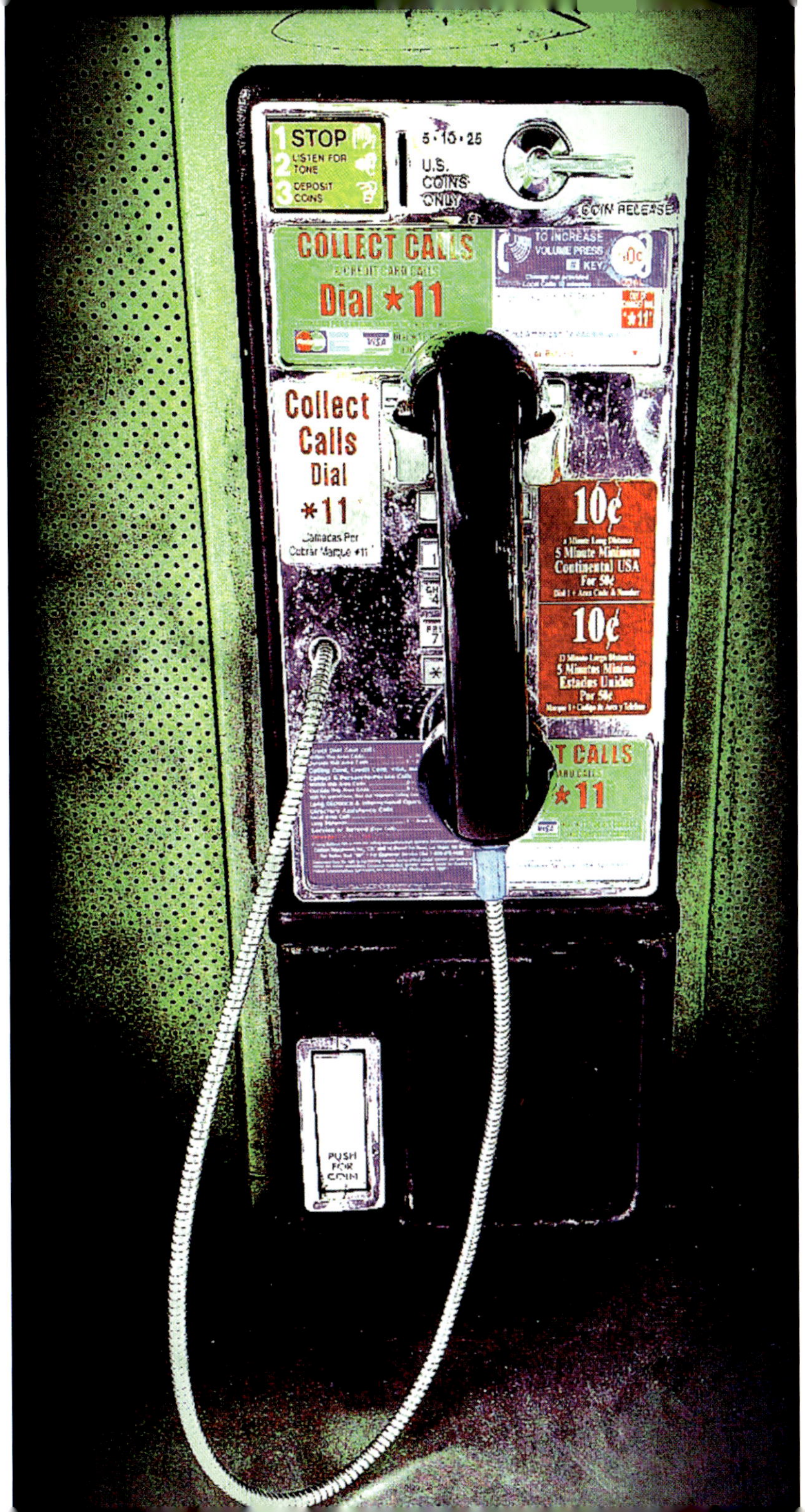
1 STOP
2 LISTEN FOR TONE
3 DEPOSIT COINS
5·10·25
U.S. COINS ONLY
COIN RELEASE
COLLECT CALLS
Dial *11
TO INCREASE VOLUME PRESS KEY
Collect Calls Dial *11
10¢
5 Minute Minimum Continental USA For 50¢
10¢
5 Minutos Minimo Estados Unidos Por 50¢
PUSH FOR COIN

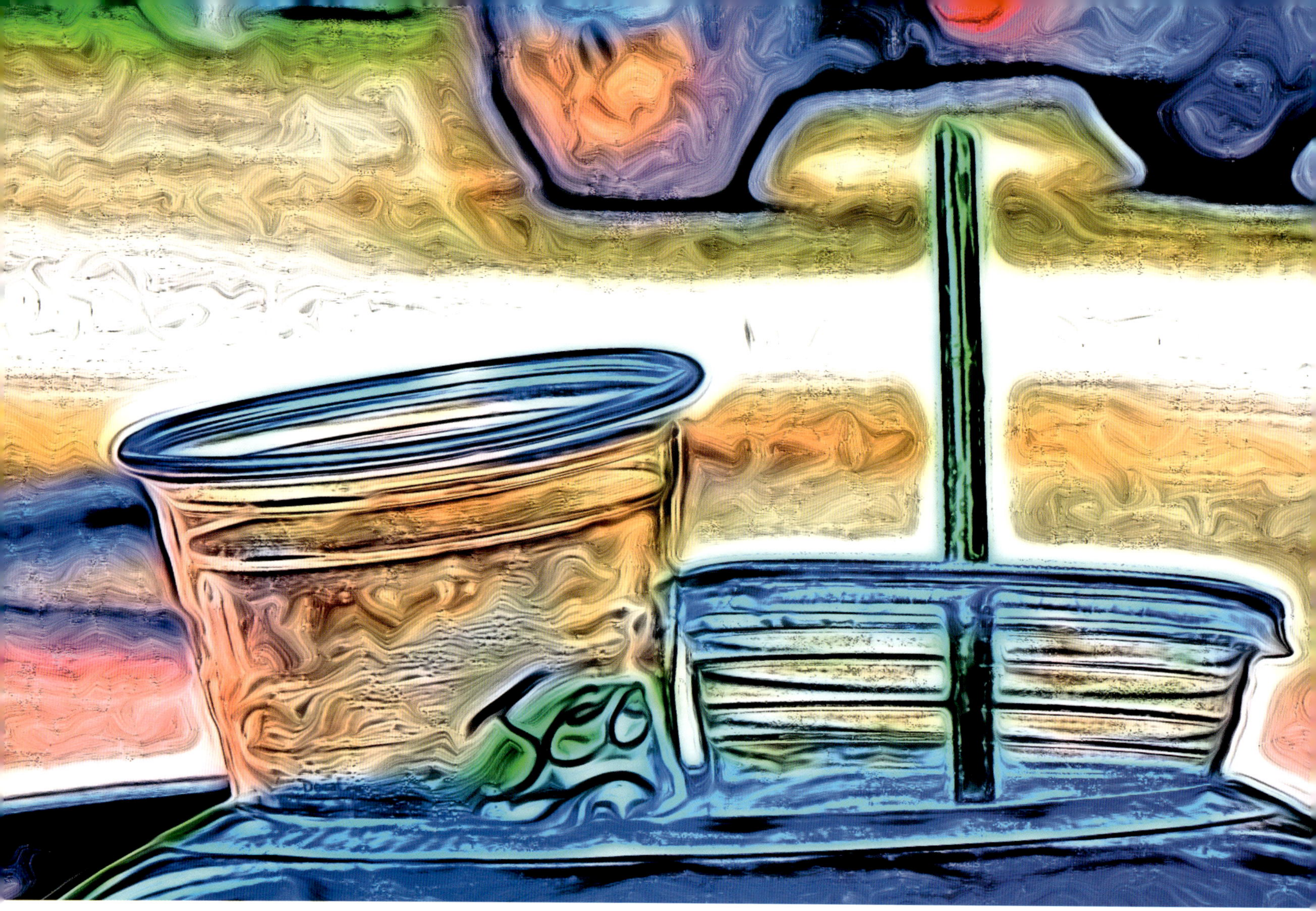

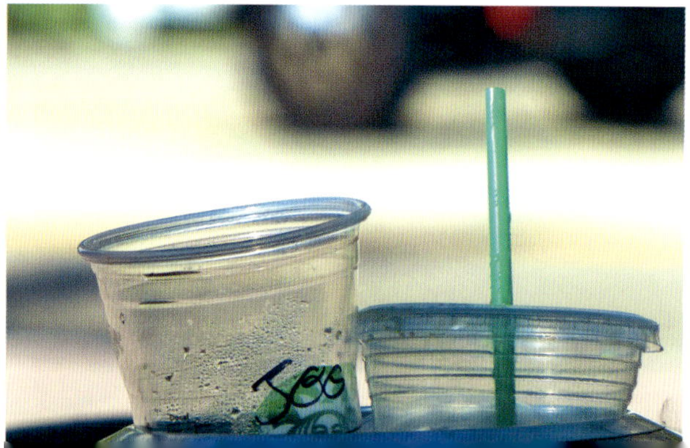

STARBUCKS TRASH

Once a grande mocha iced coffee
Now just a straw drawing attention
Throwaway stuff

Chapter Four

TRANSPORTATION

Miami is a busy city. Whether on the water, on the ground, or in the air, transportation is an essential part of the daily life and history of this fair city. The following photos represent the wide variety of transportation modes that have helped this community grow and thrive. Workaday transportation includes tugboats moving the ships on the Miami River, Air Force F-16s refueling over Homestead Air Force base, police boats protecting our shipping lanes and Biscayne Bay, and trains that move goods from the port throughout the country. Leisure activities revolve around sailboats on Biscayne Bay and bicycles in the streets. Old train cars from the Gold Coast Railroad Museum create a sense of nostalgia and remind us of the debt we owe to Julia Tuttle for convincing Henry Flagler to expand the railroad to Miami in 1896. To some, transportation seems dull and downright boring . . . but if you look closely, you'll see that there is beauty in its form and function.

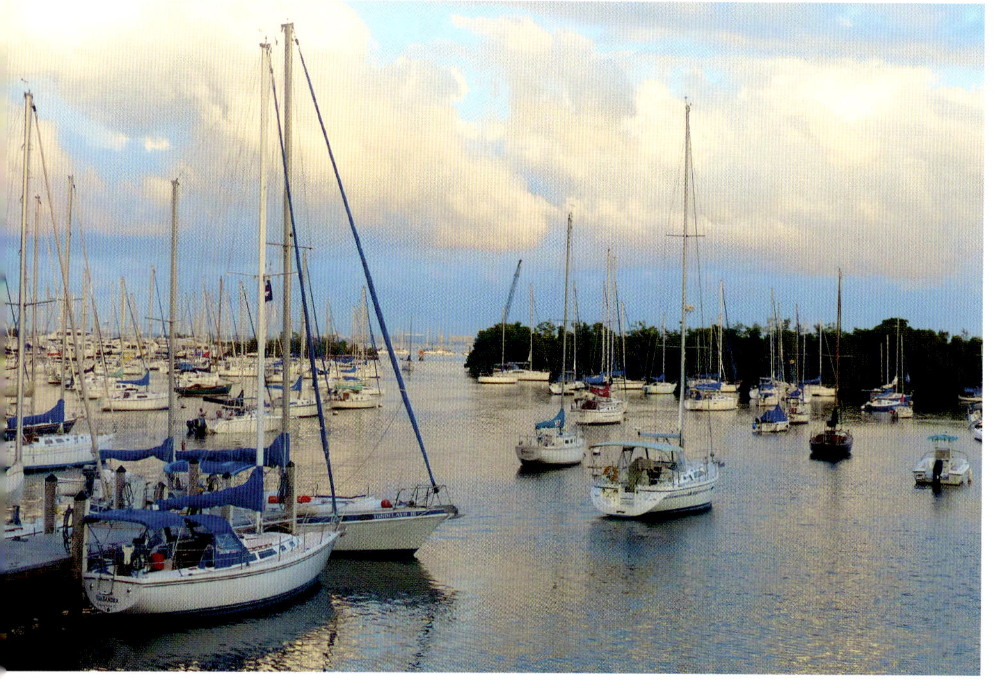

SAILBOATS AT DINNER KEY

Boats at Coconut Grove Sailing Club
Tied up at the dock under peaceful clouds
Awaiting the sailors

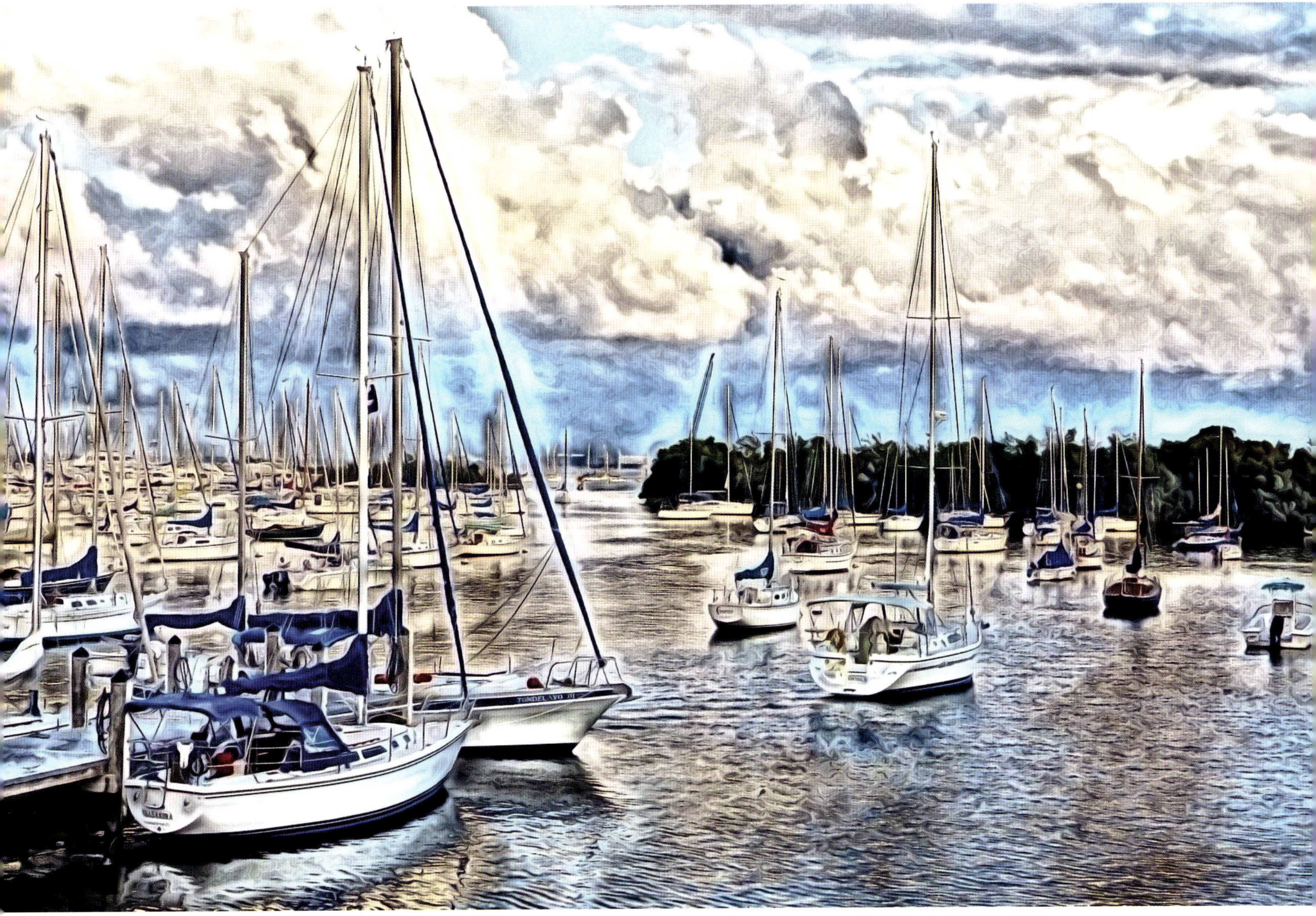

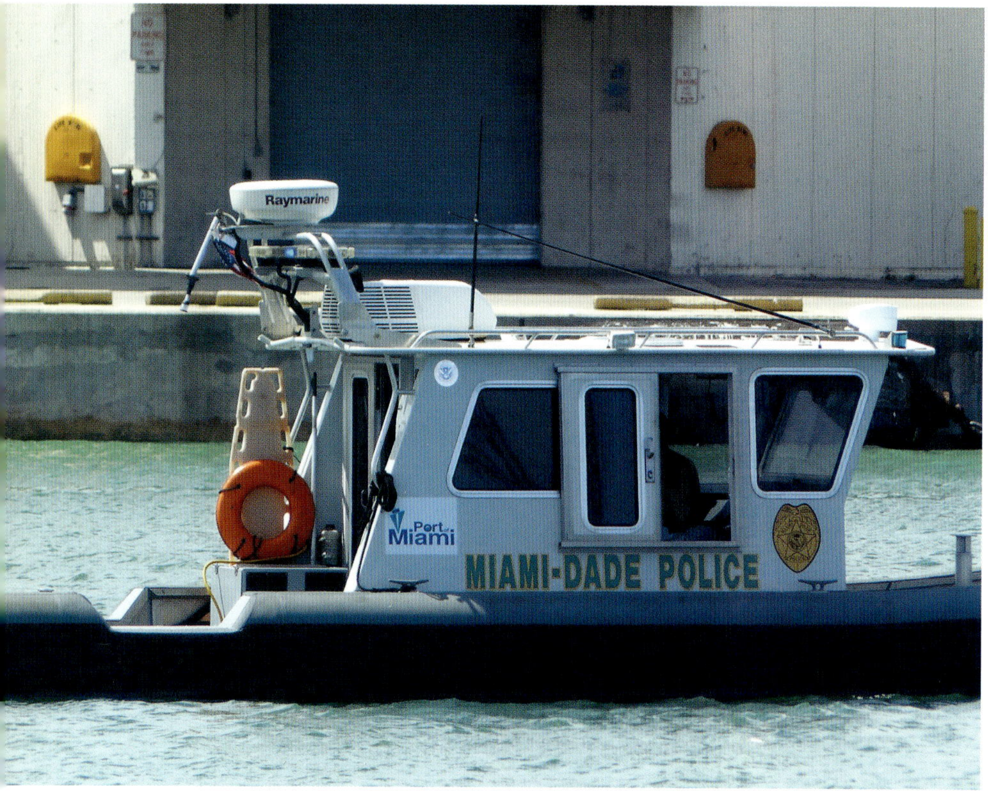

MIAMI DADE POLICE BOAT

Wavy vessel
Colorful cops
Seasick

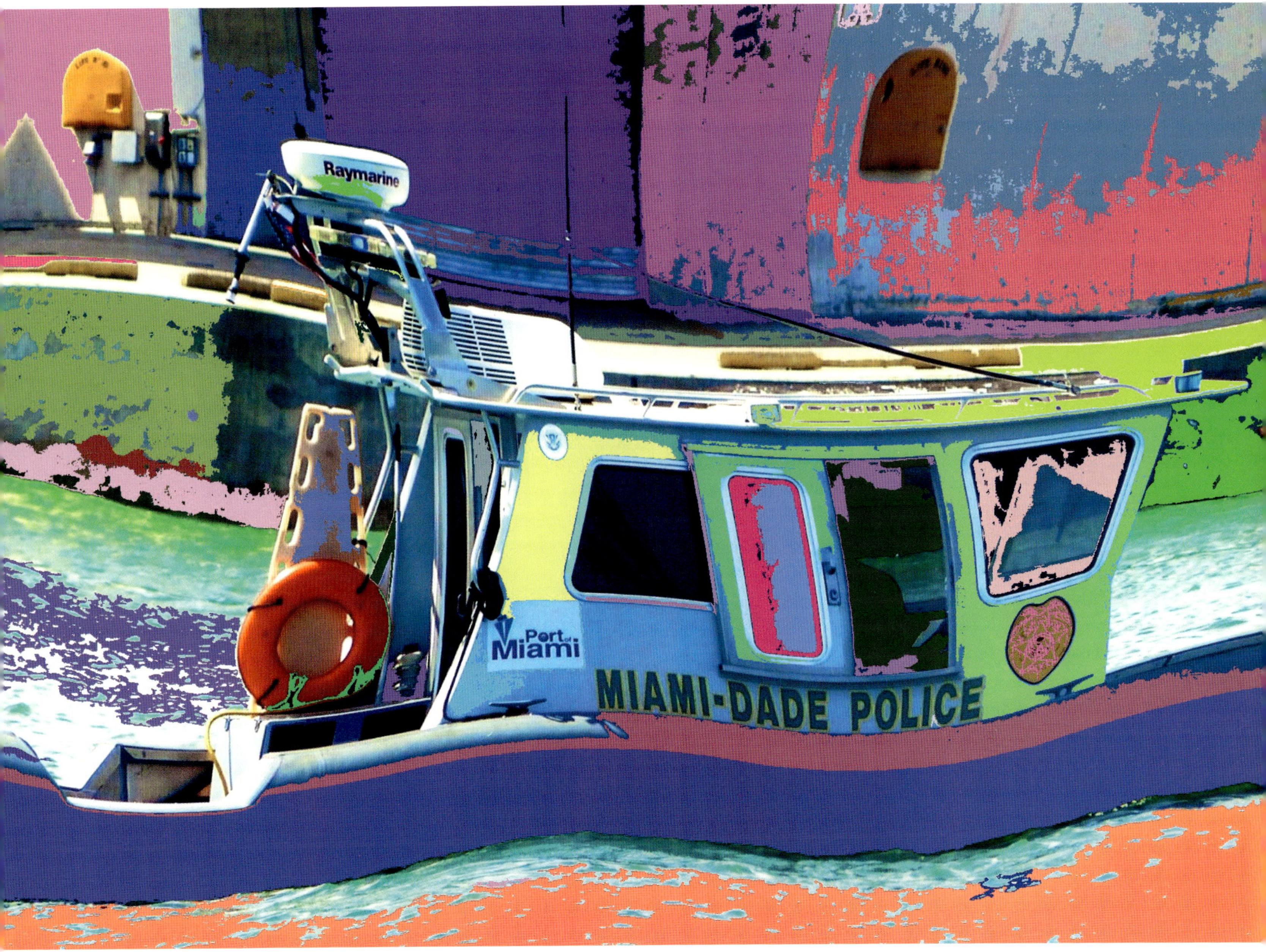
Raymarine
Port of Miami
MIAMI-DADE POLICE

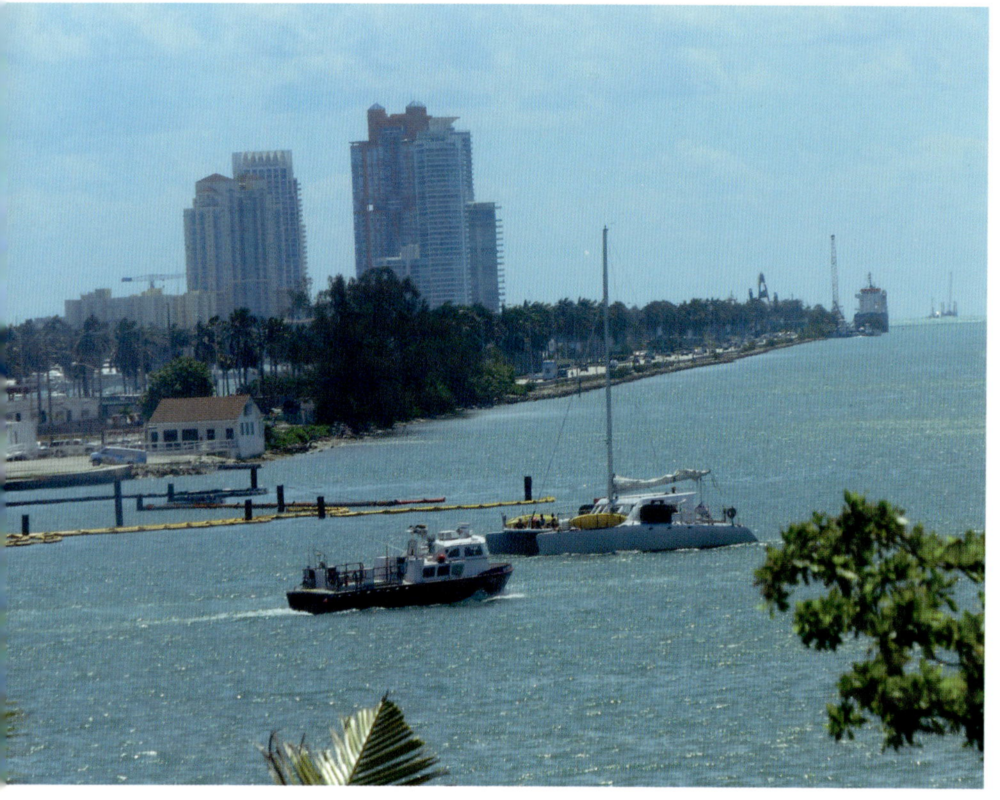

MIAMI PORT

An important economic engine
Raw materials and finished goods
Coming and going
Work becomes art

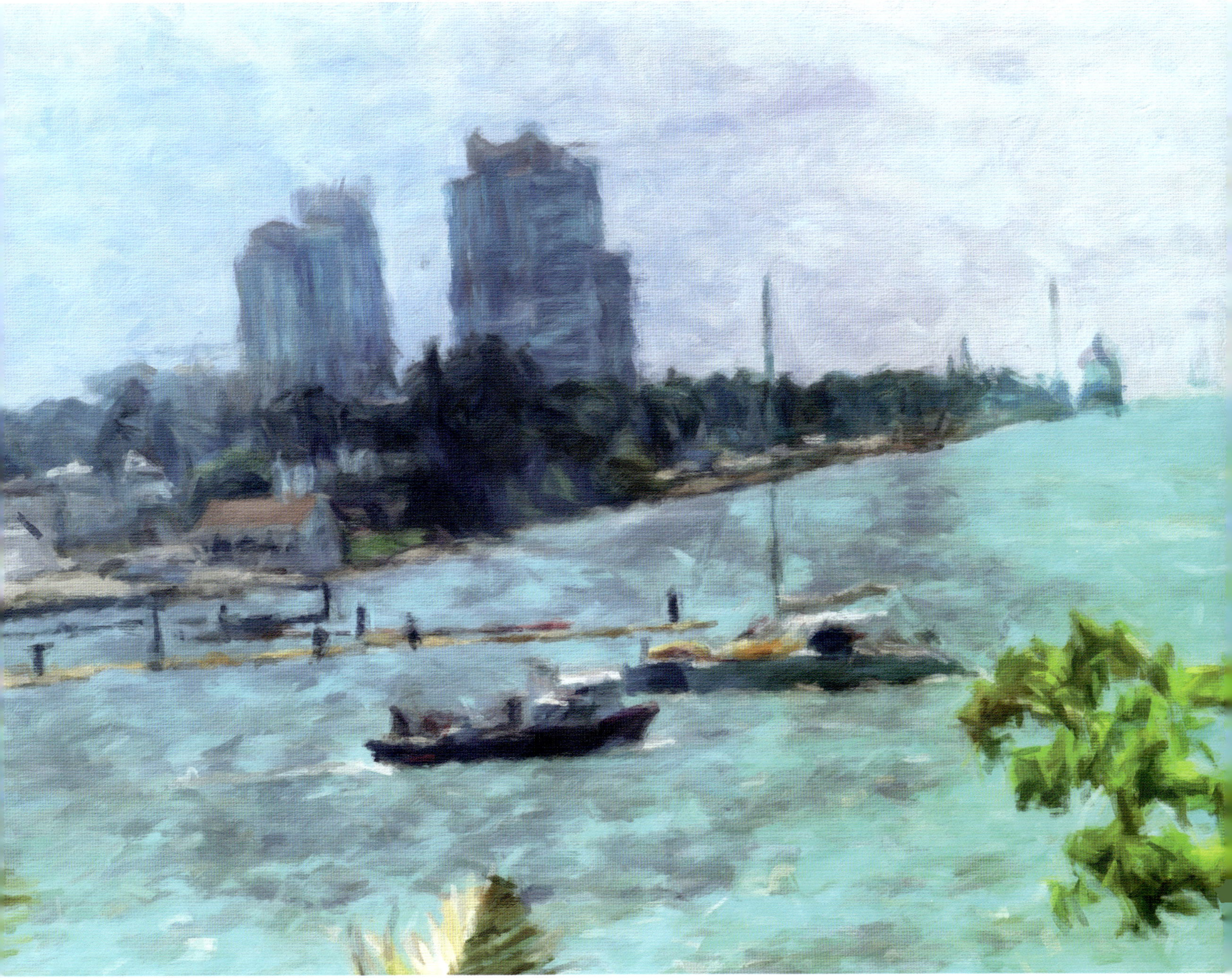

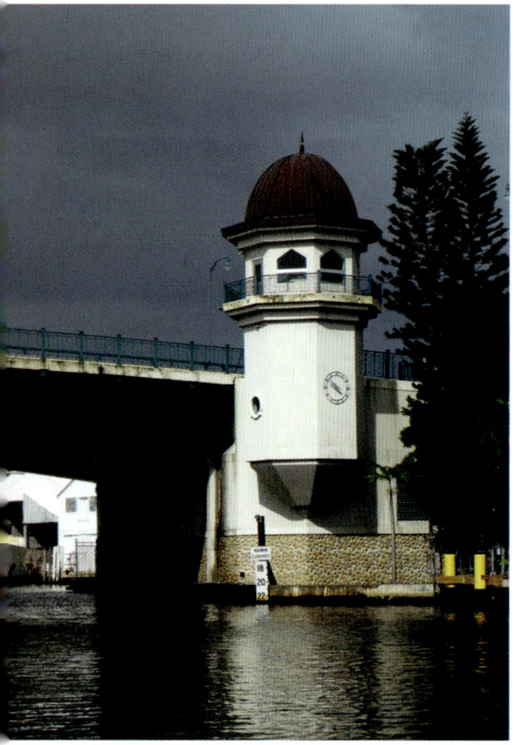

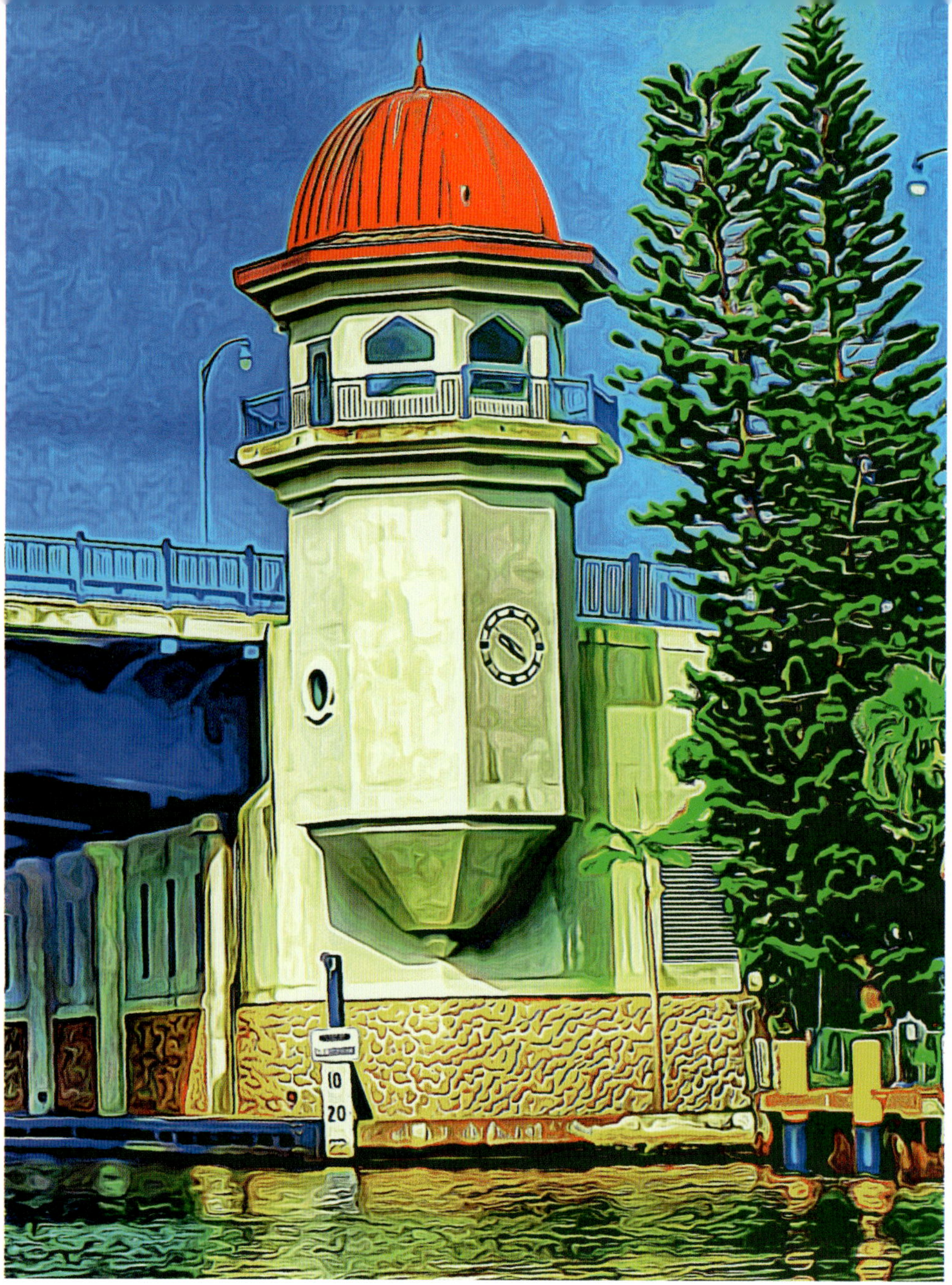

12TH AVENUE BRIDGE

A drawbridge over the Miami River
The operator sits in a small booth
Open and close

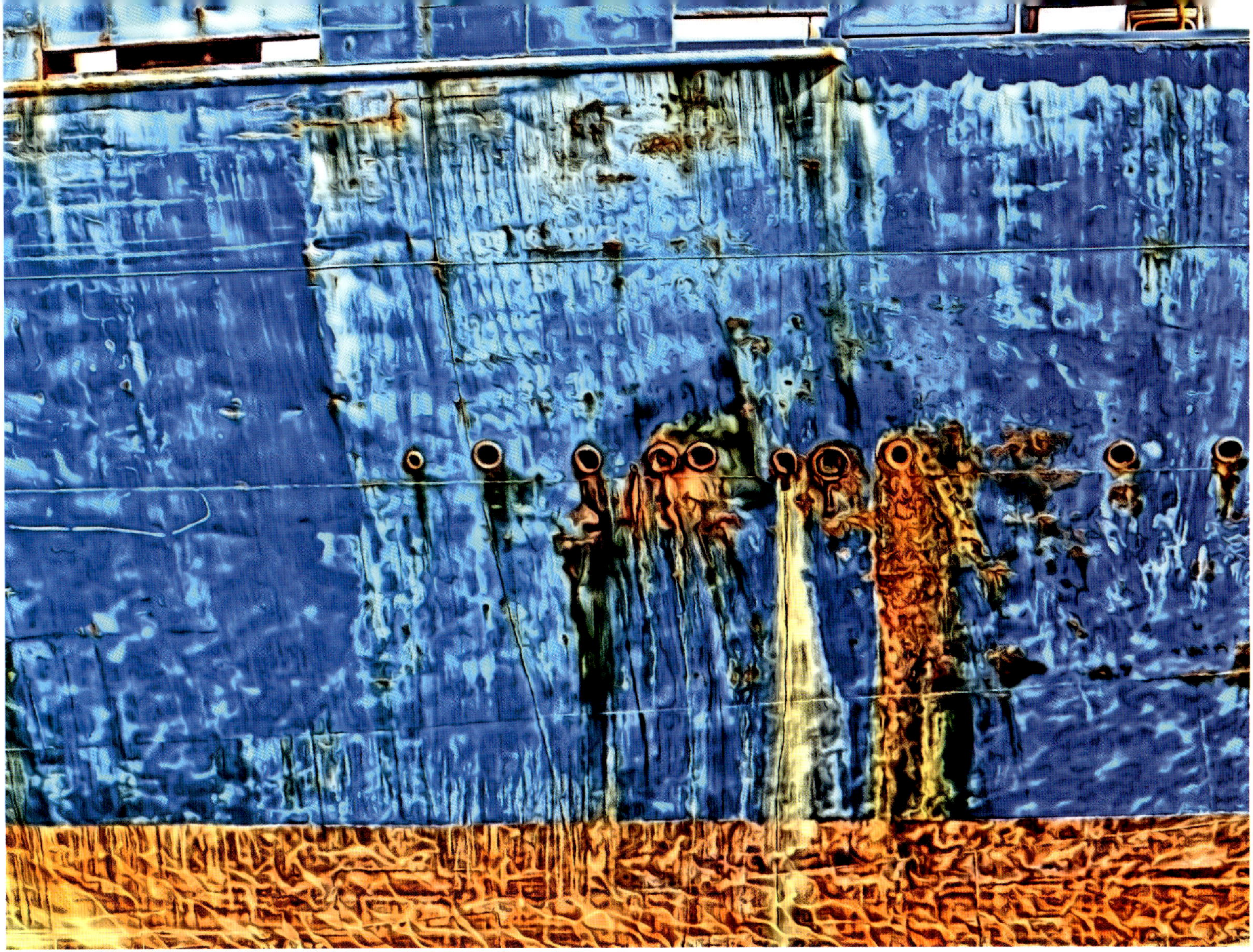

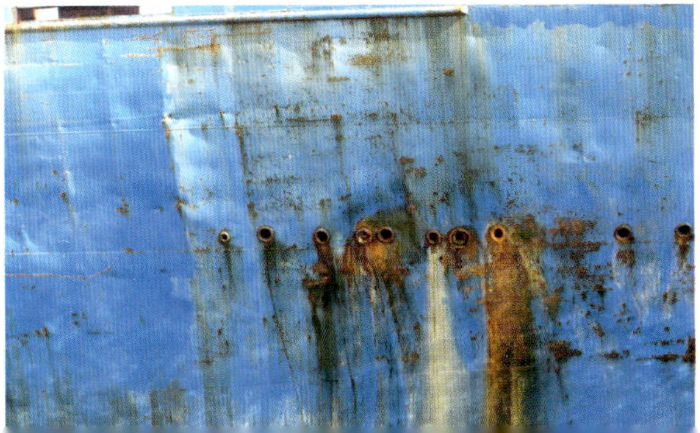

RIVER ART

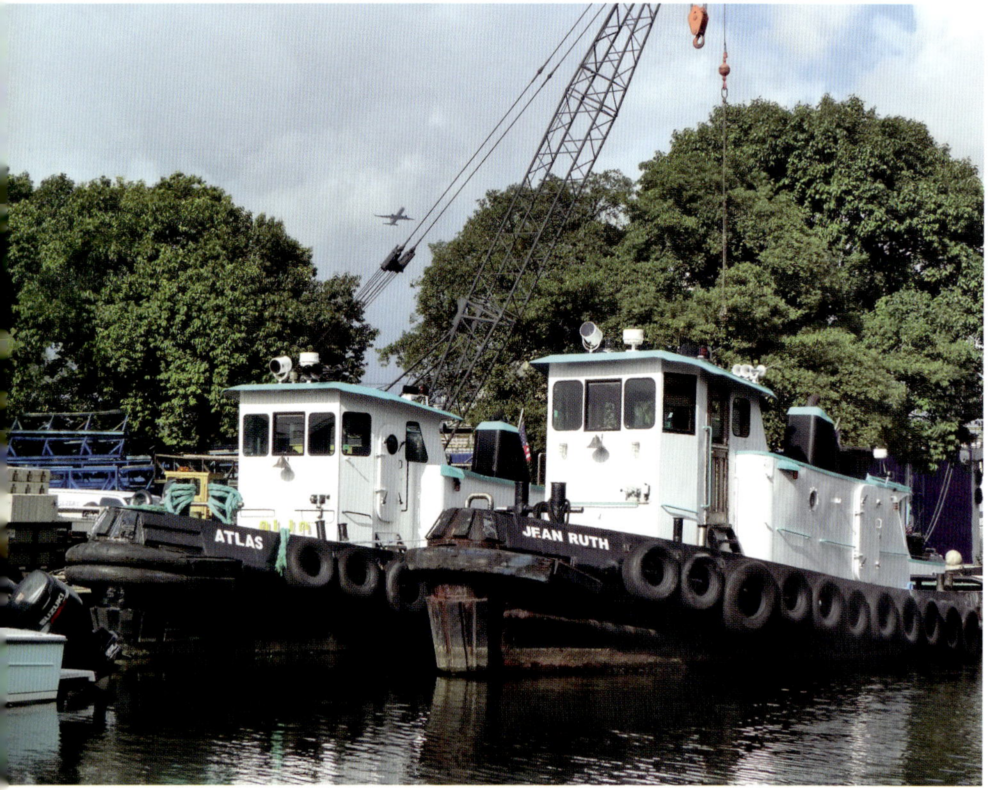

TUGBOATS

Hard-working tugboats
Atlas and *Jean Ruth*
Move large ships
And carry skillful captains

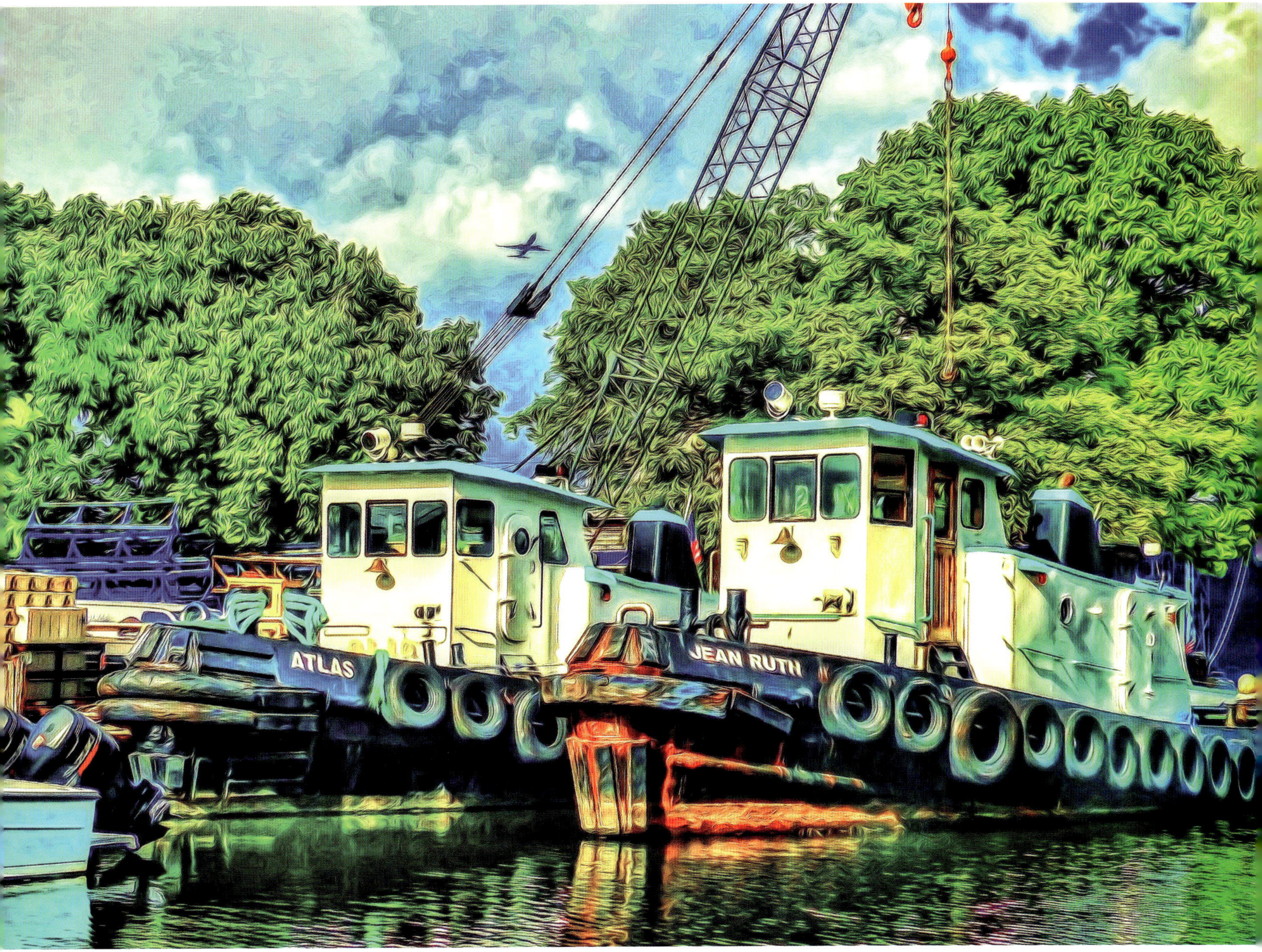
ATLAS
JEAN RUTH

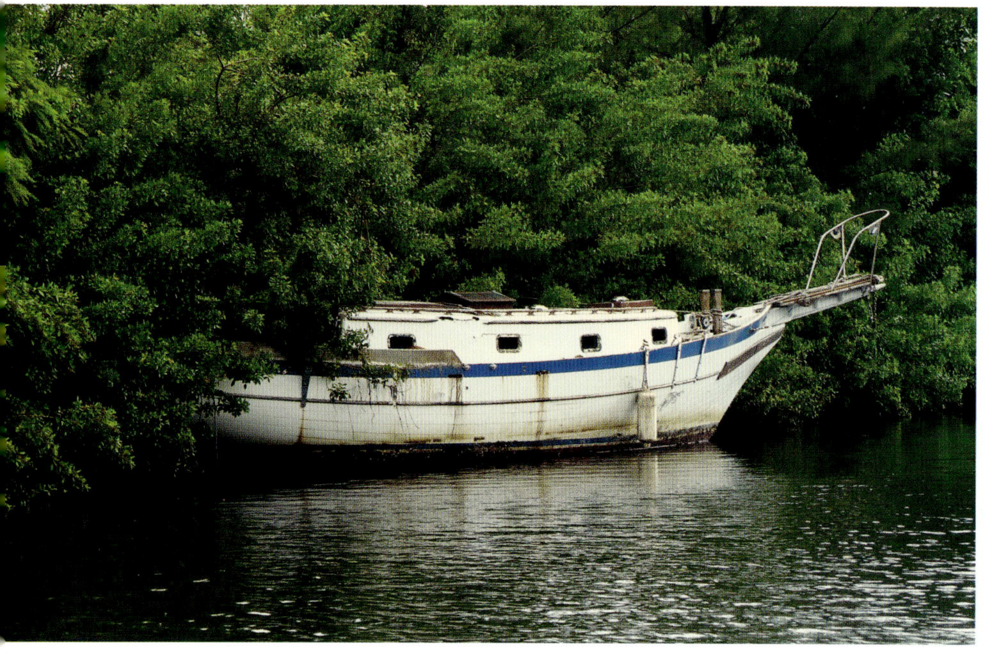

ABANDONED SAILBOAT

Missing its mast
Forgotten in the foliage
Useless

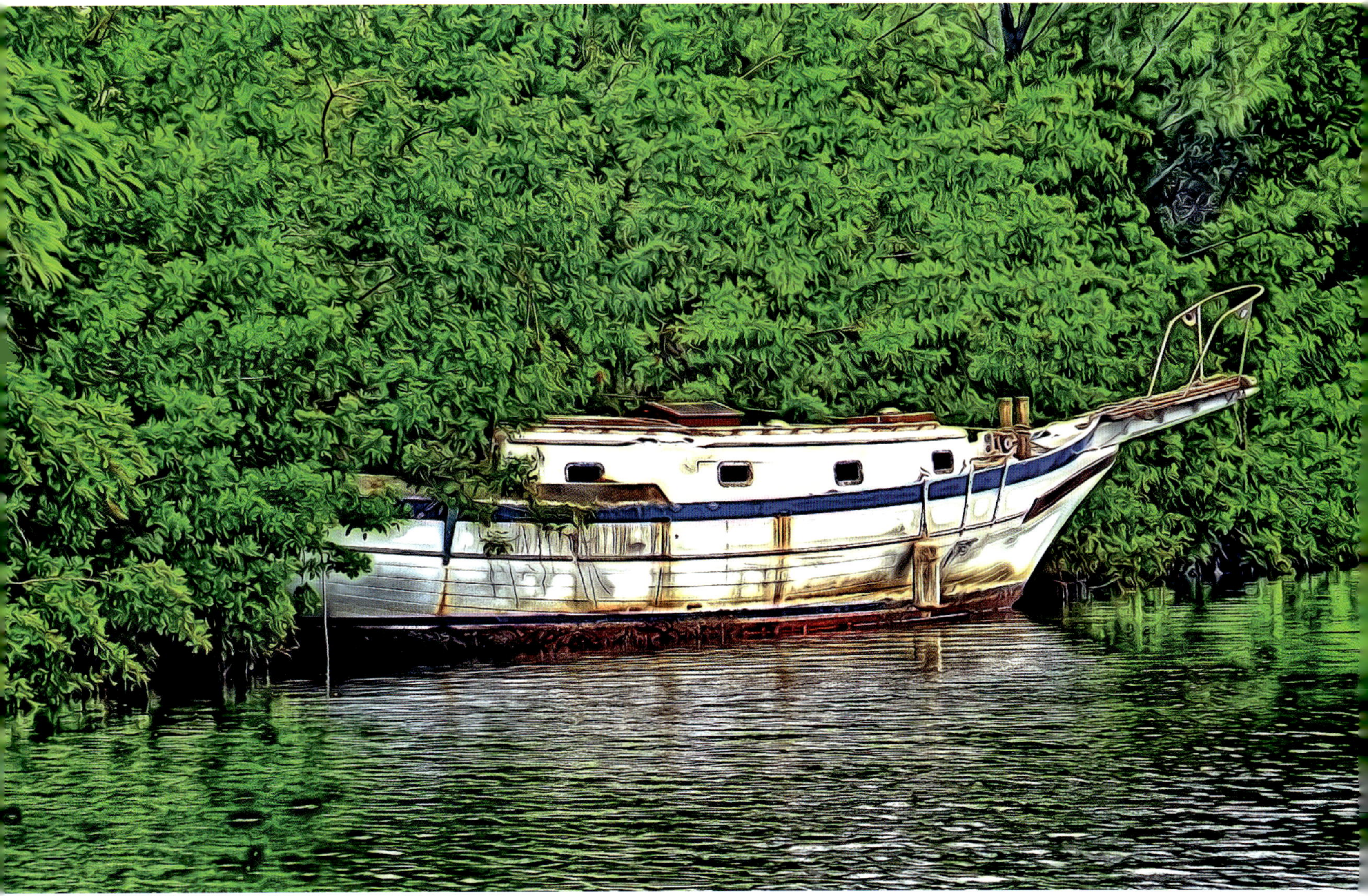

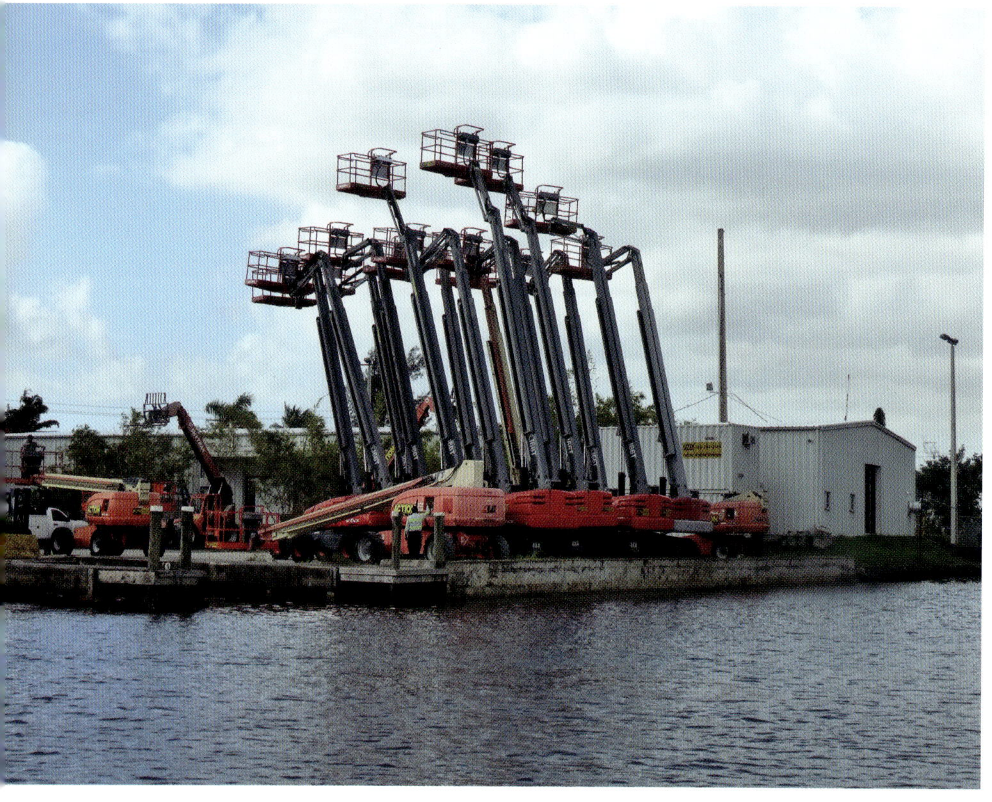

LIFTS FOR RENT

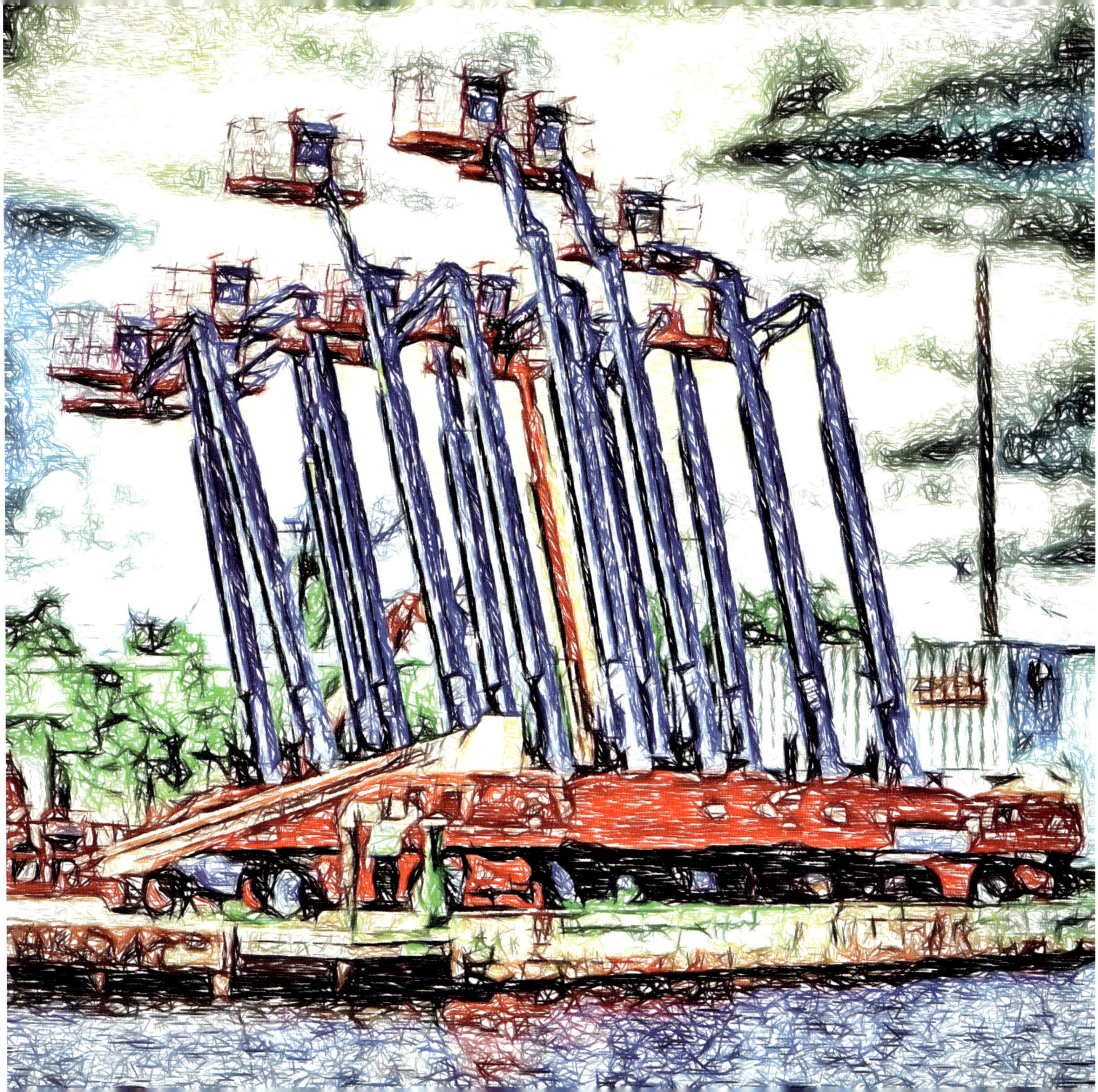

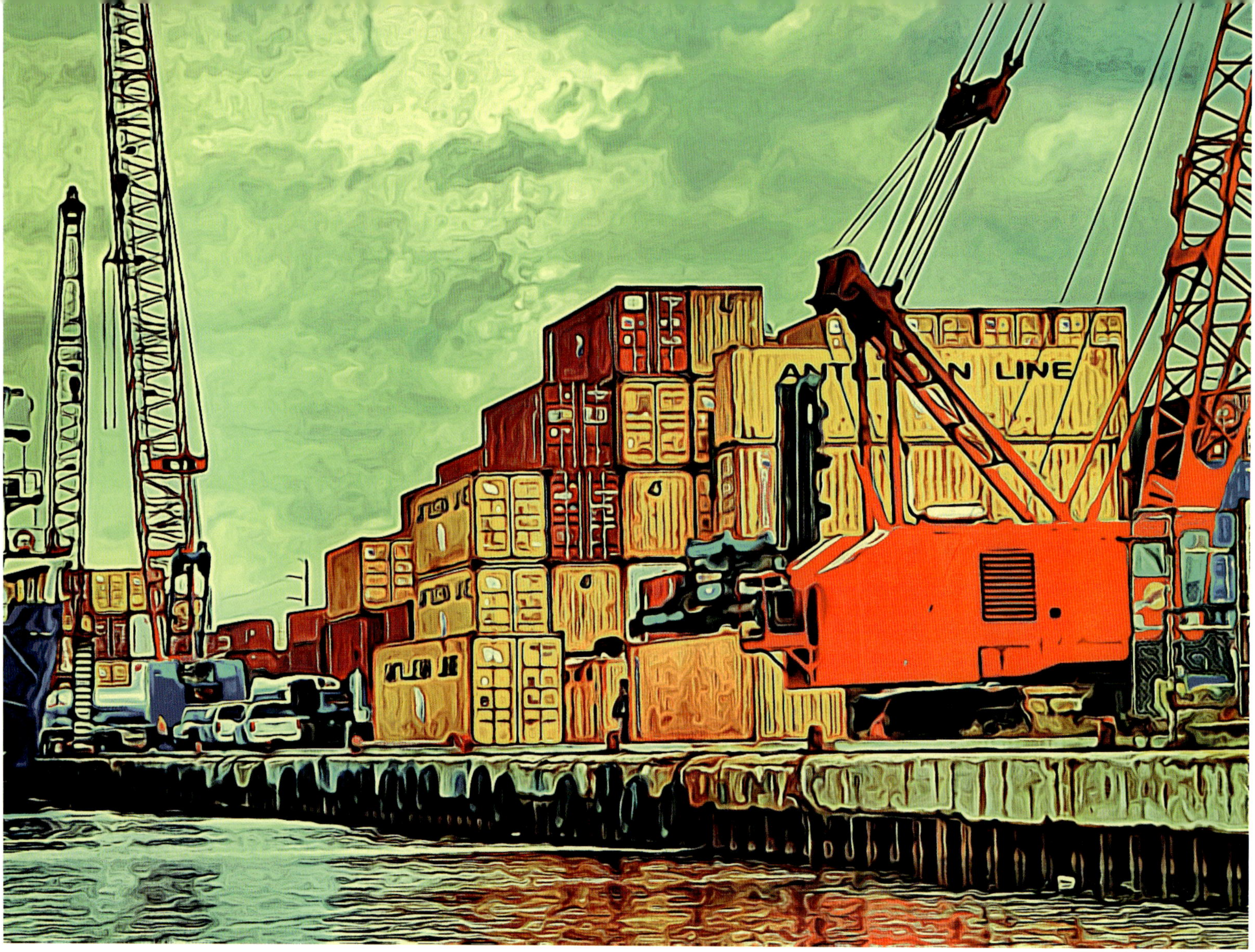

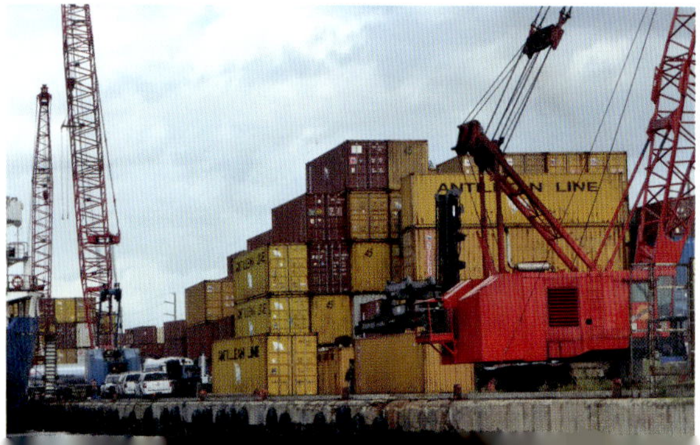

CONTAINERS

Containers are stacked up
Ready for a seagoing vessel
Material goods on the move

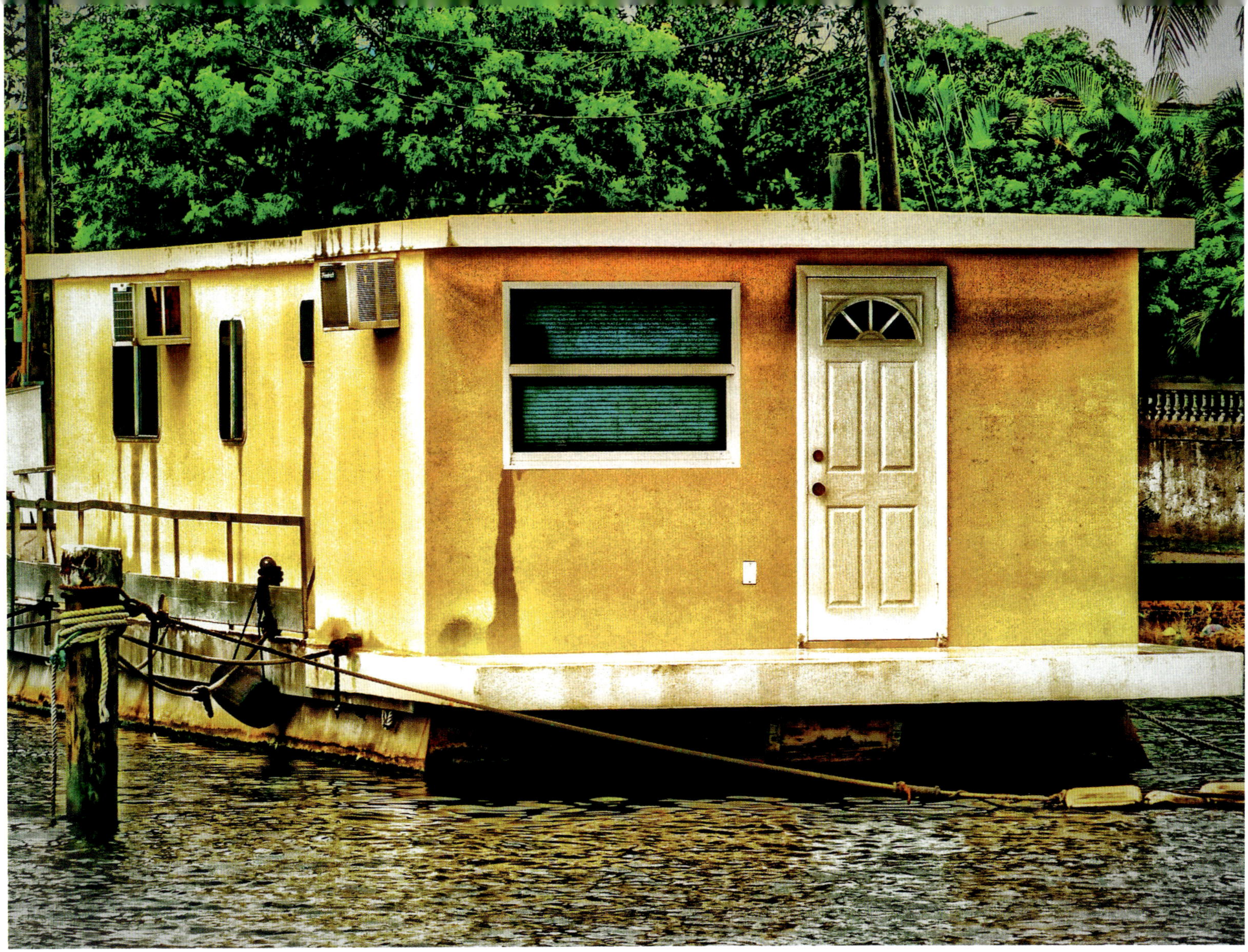

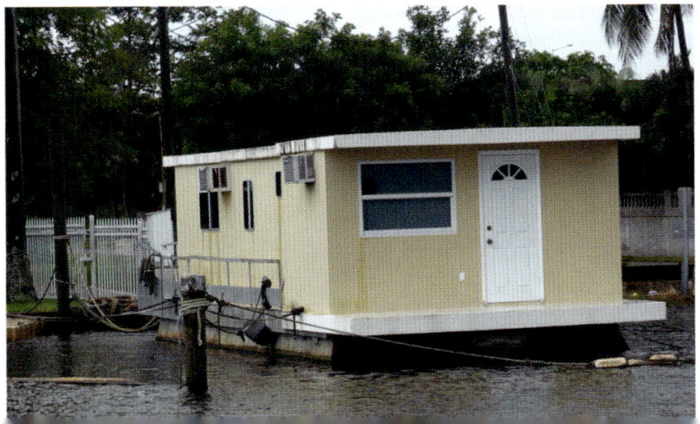

HOUSE BOAT

A lovely home on the water
No front lawn, no backyard
Watch your step

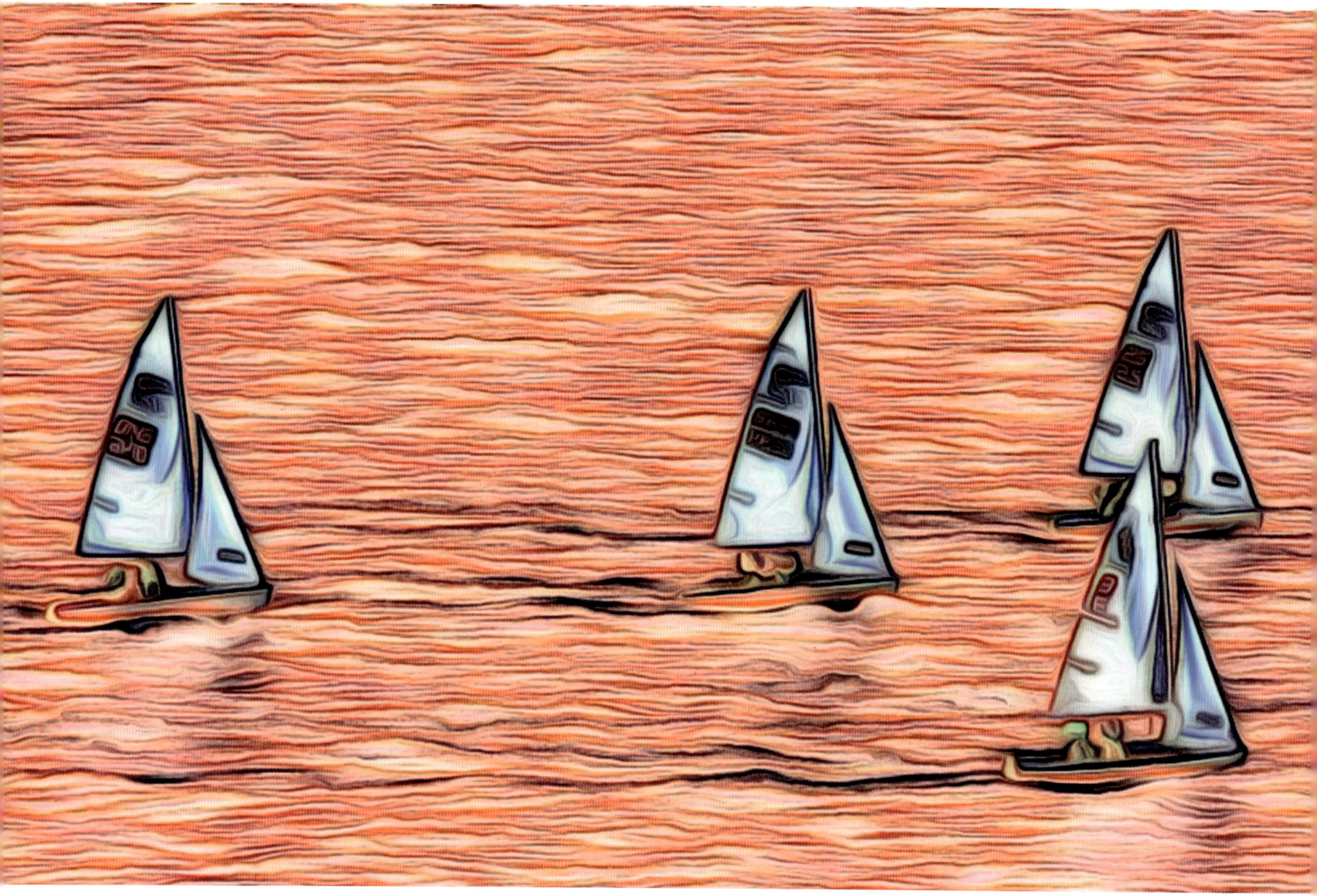

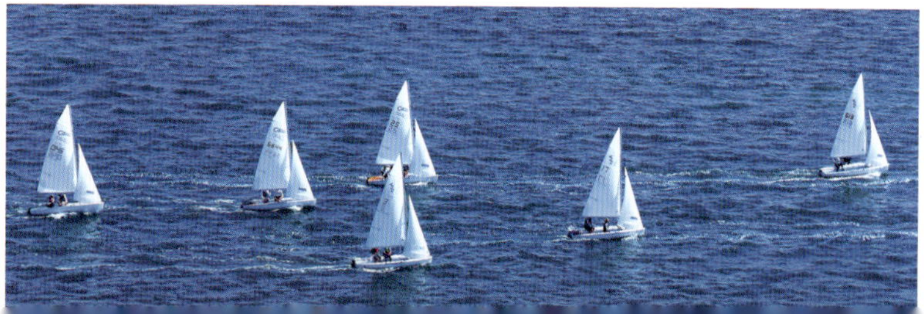

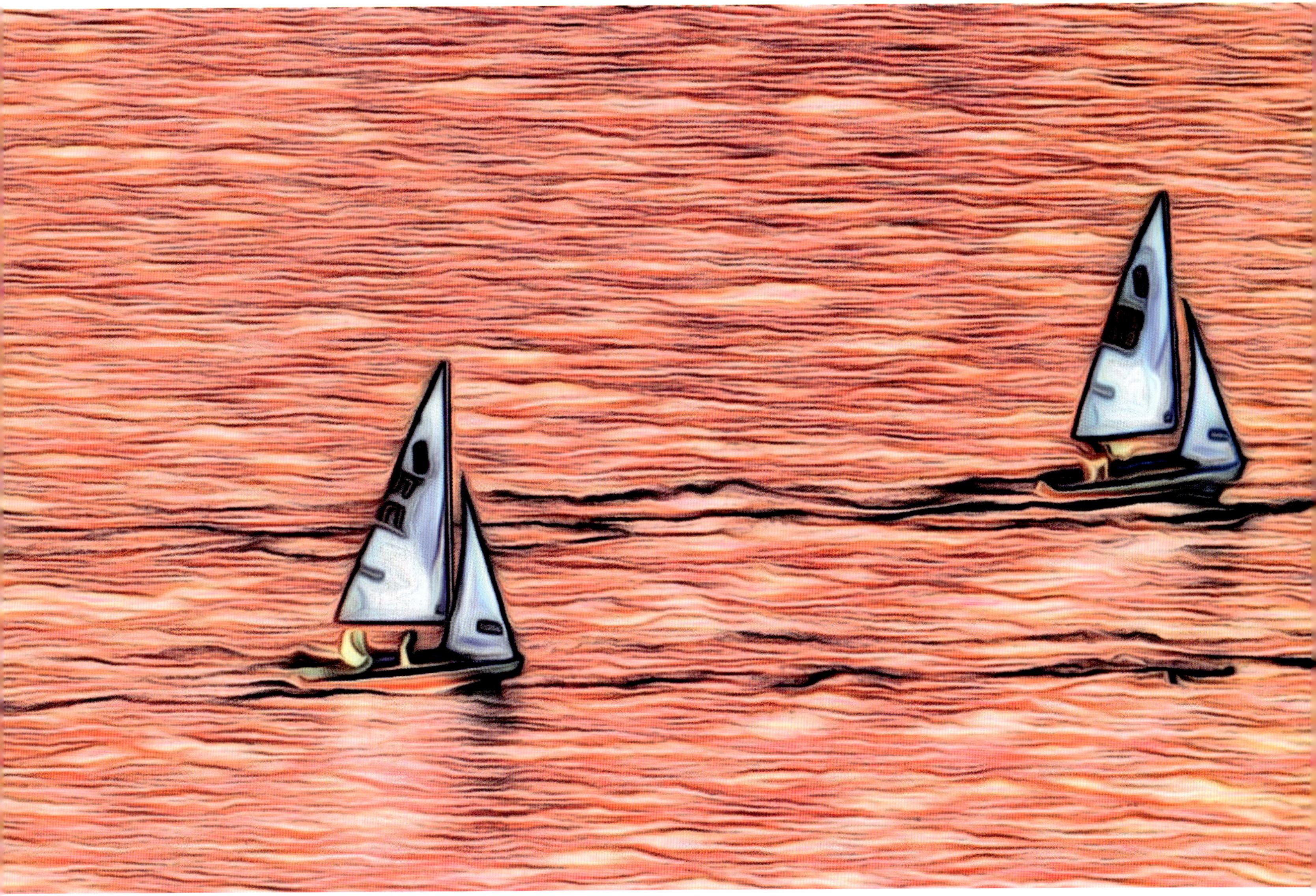

SMALL SAILBOATS

A regatta, a race
Competitive sailing
Fighting to become first
Sprint

BUD'S PAINT AND BODY SHOP

Whirring noises all around
Sanding, pounding, painting
Repaired

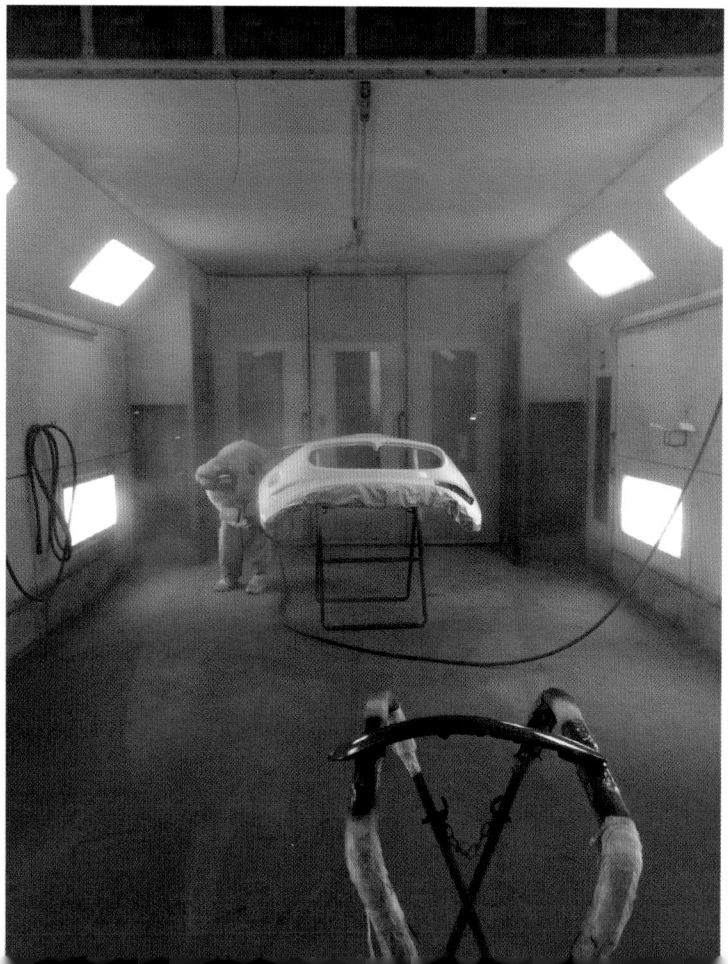

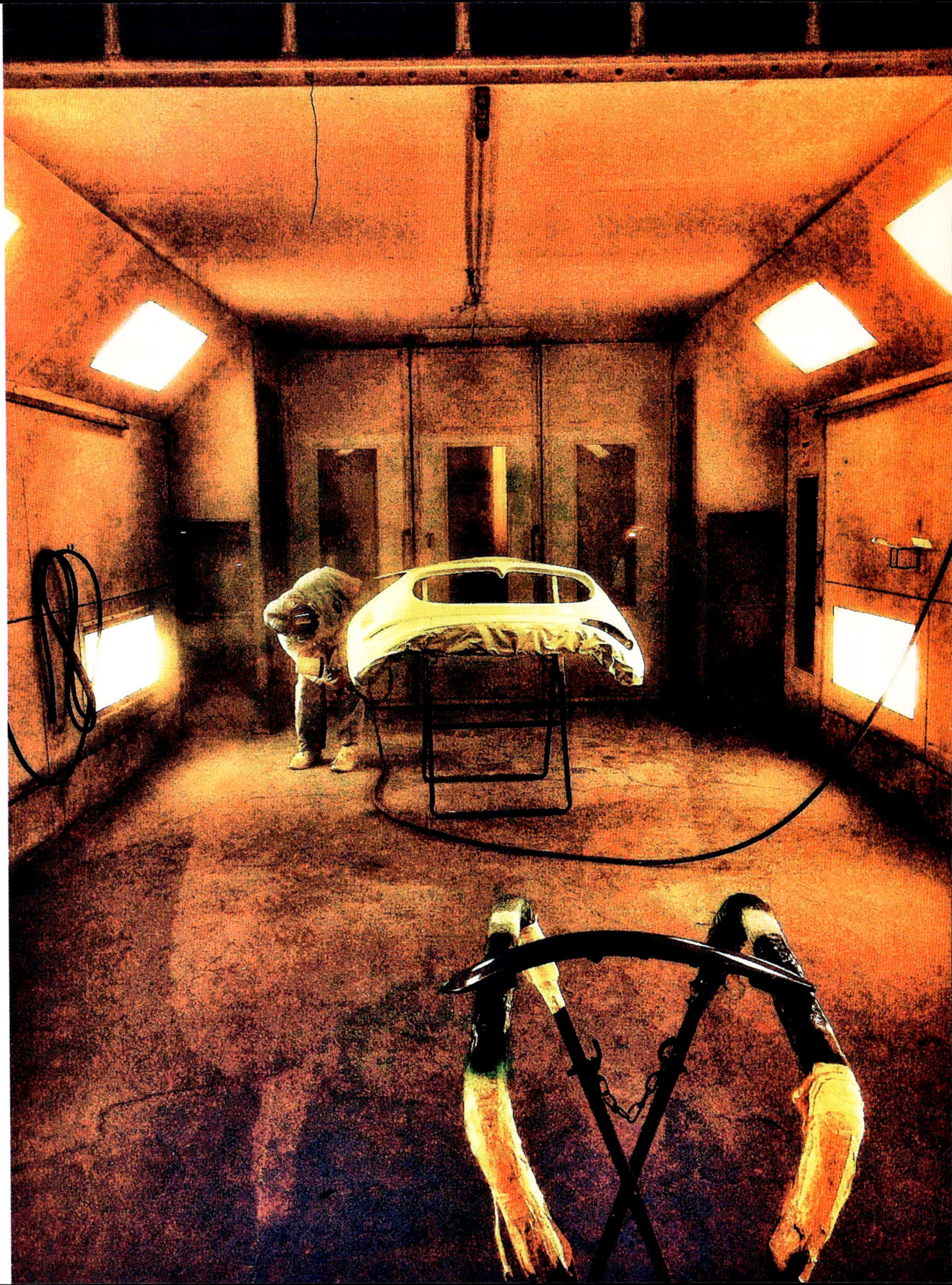

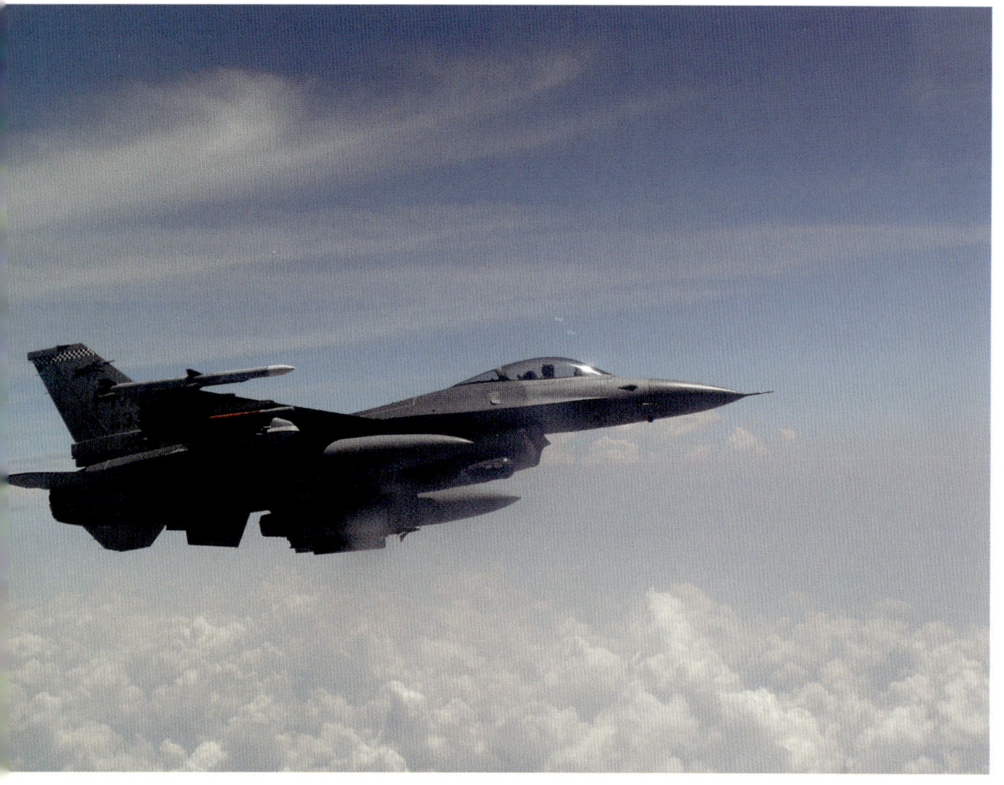

WARPLANE I

A US F-16 warplane
Coming in for fuel, fast
The mother ship is above the warplane
A fuel nozzle comes out
Tricky maneuvering

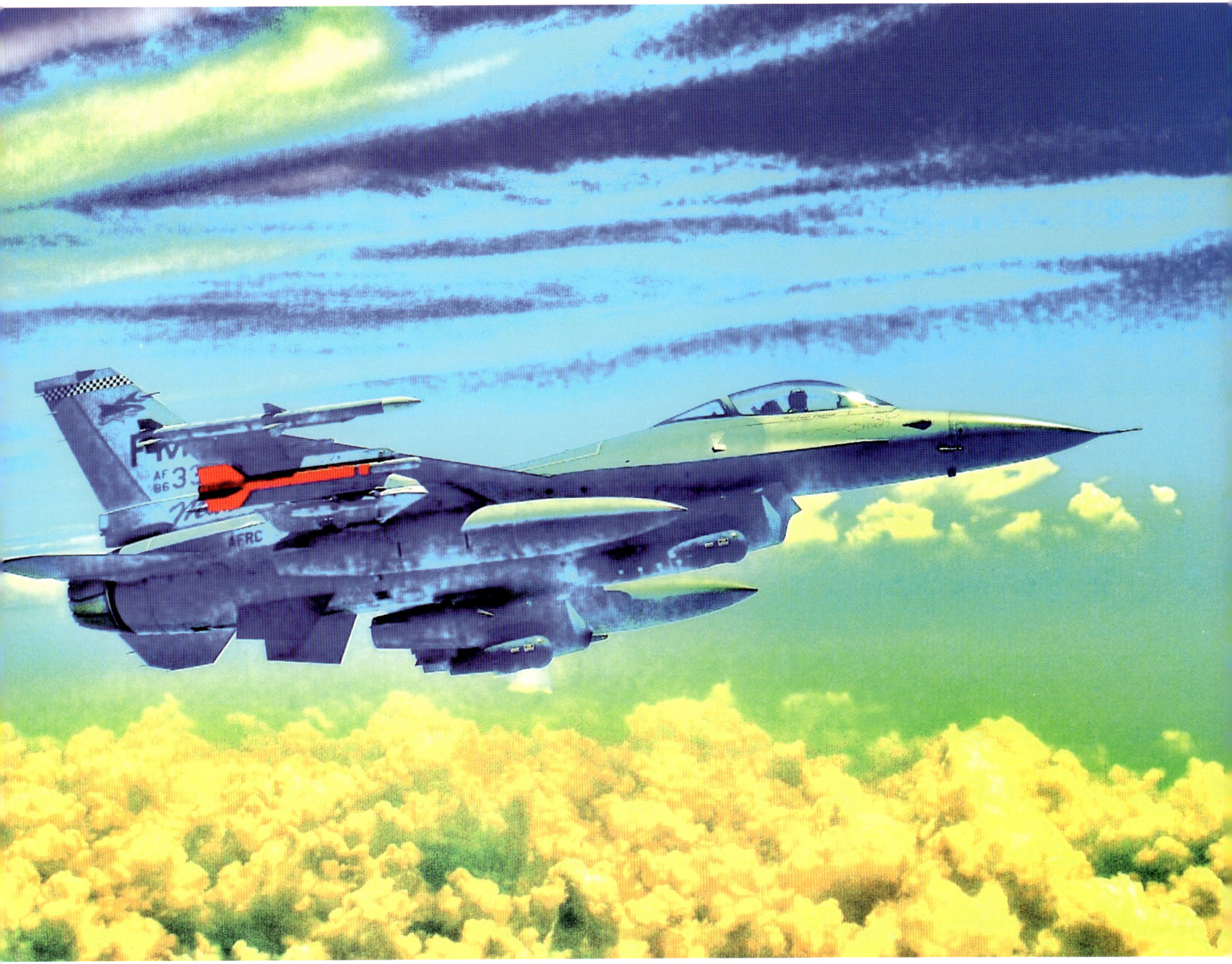
AF
86
AFRC

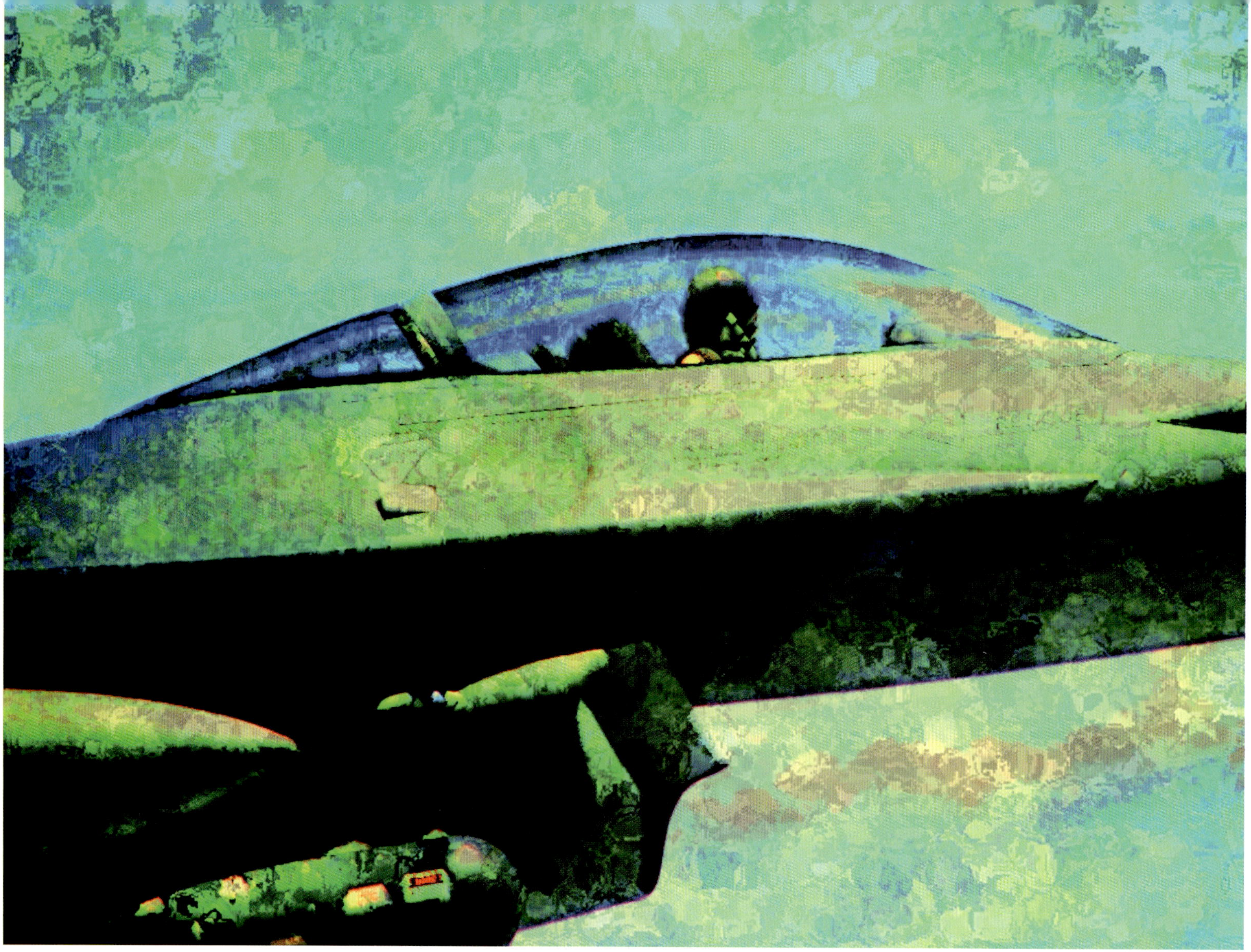

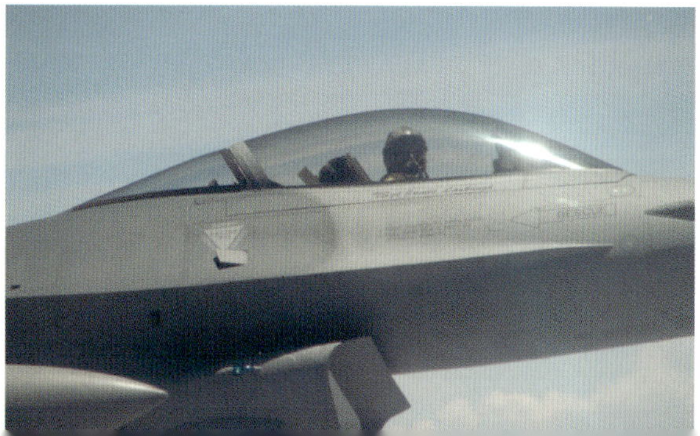

WARPLANE II

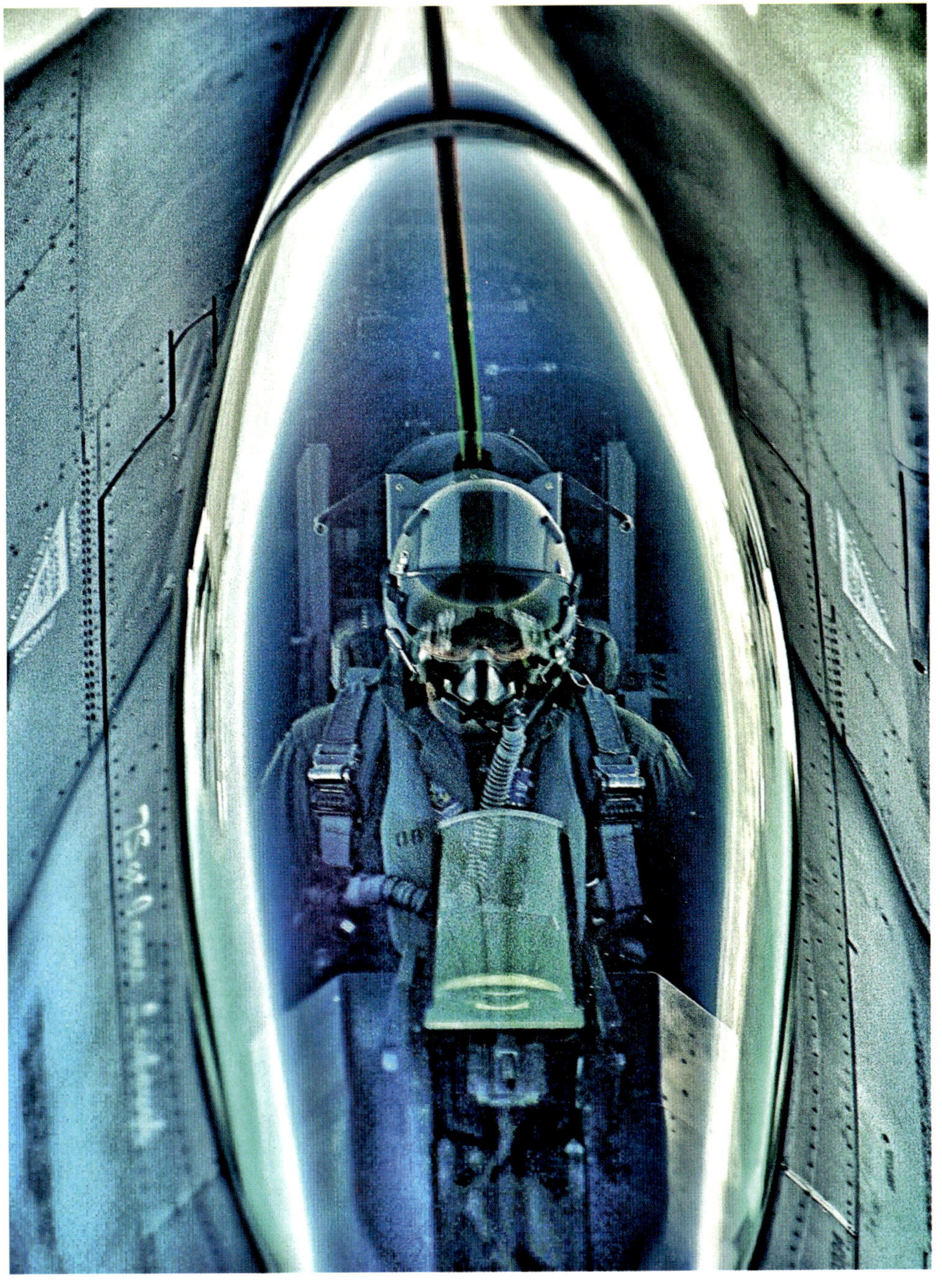

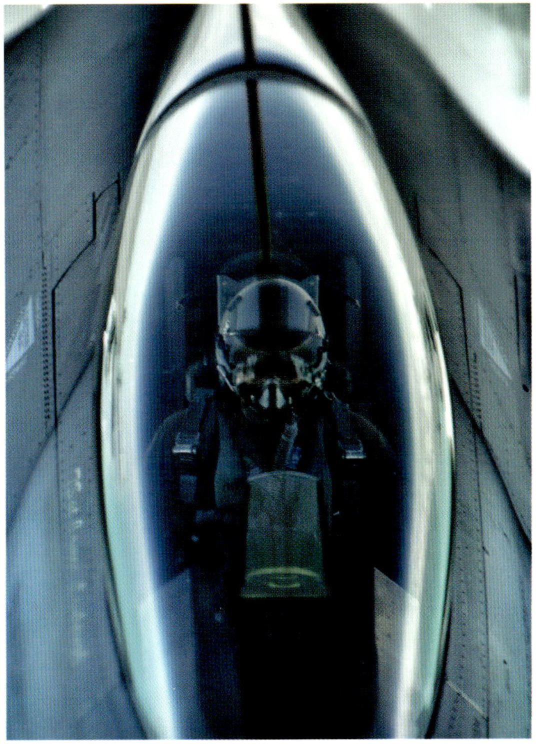

COCKPIT

REFUELING

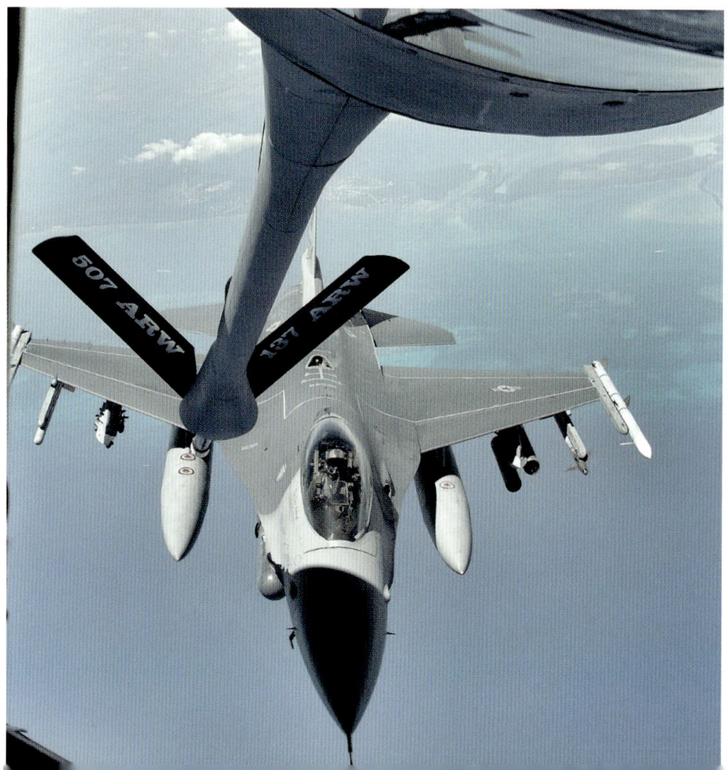

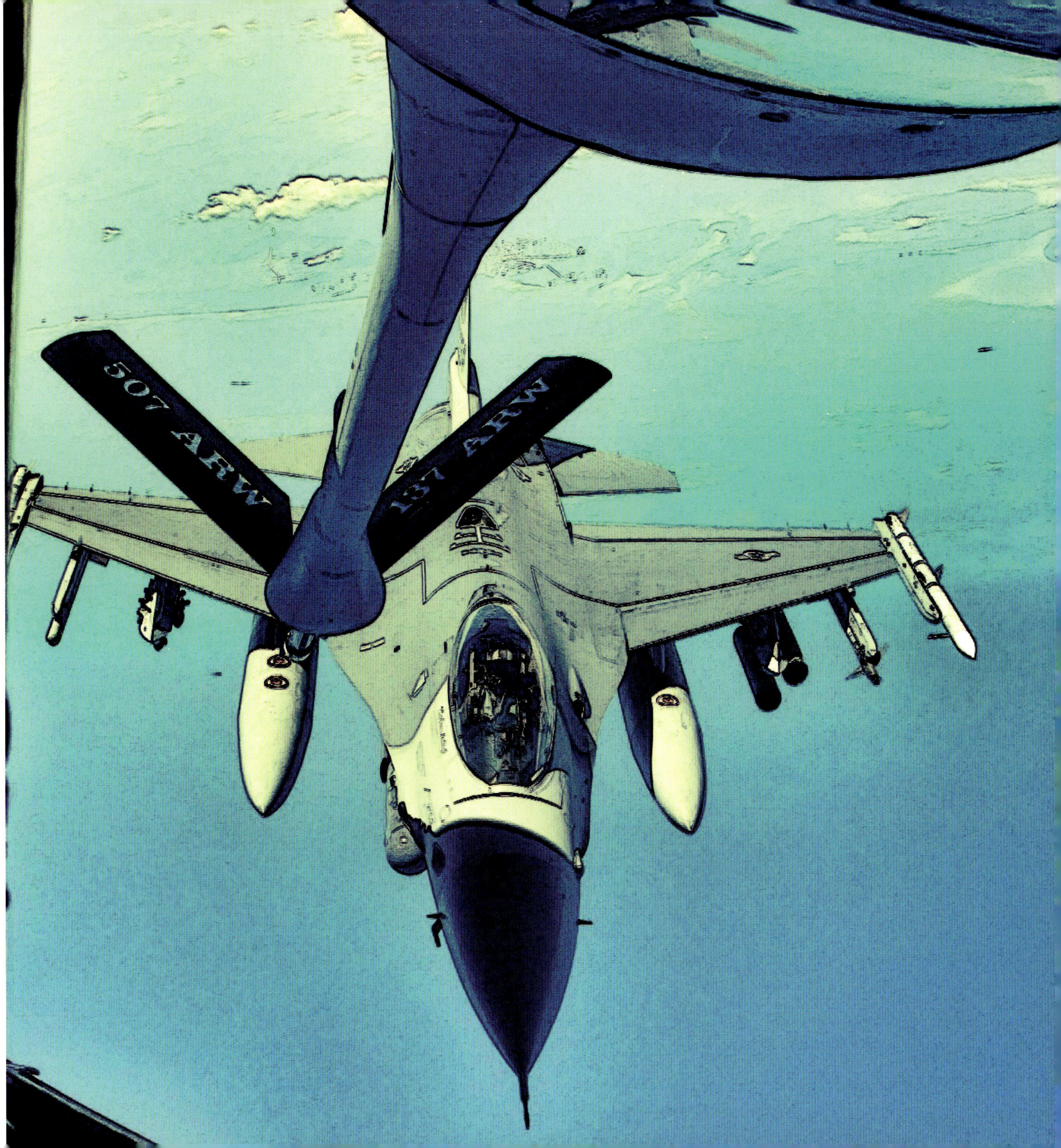

507 ARW
137 ARW

COMING IN

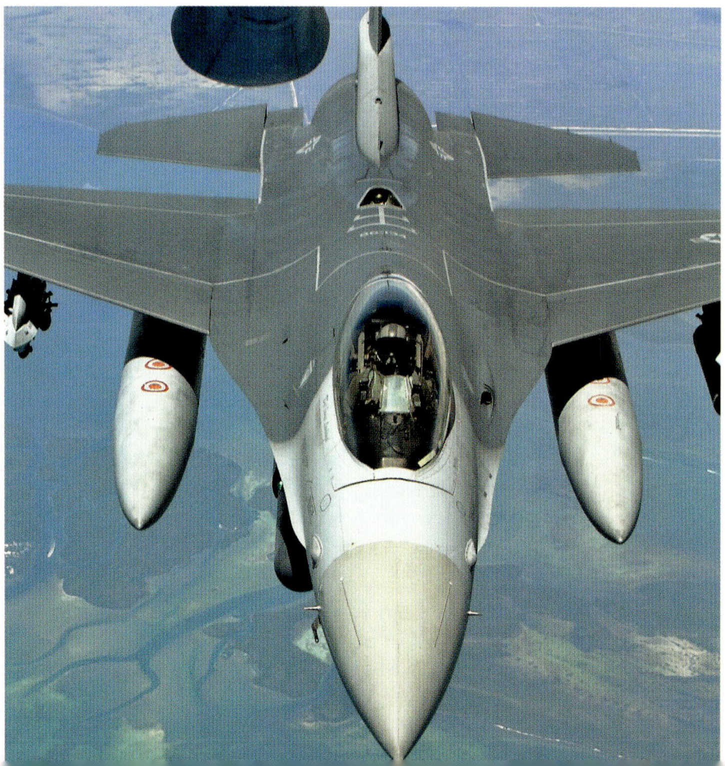

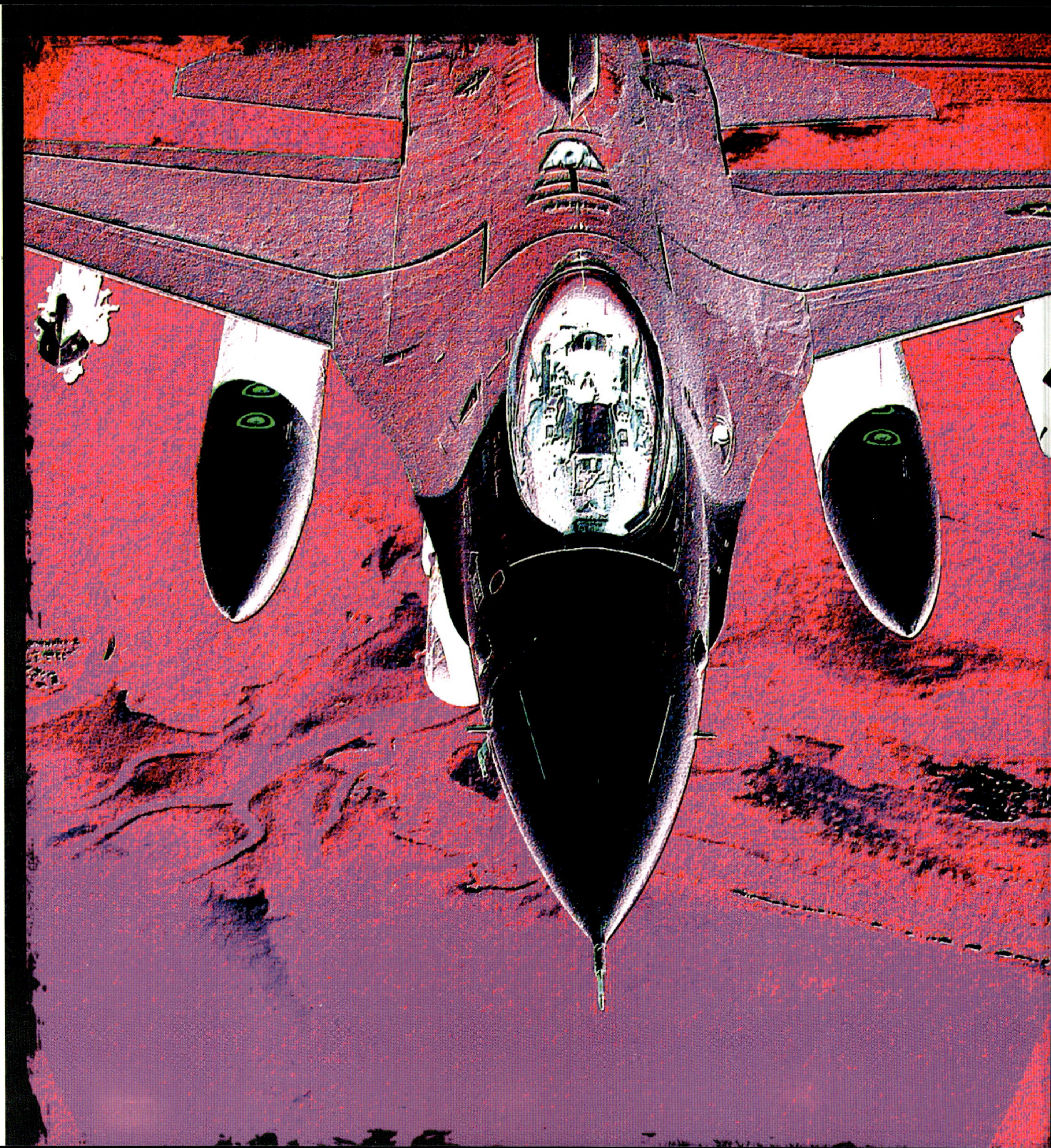

COLORFUL BIKE

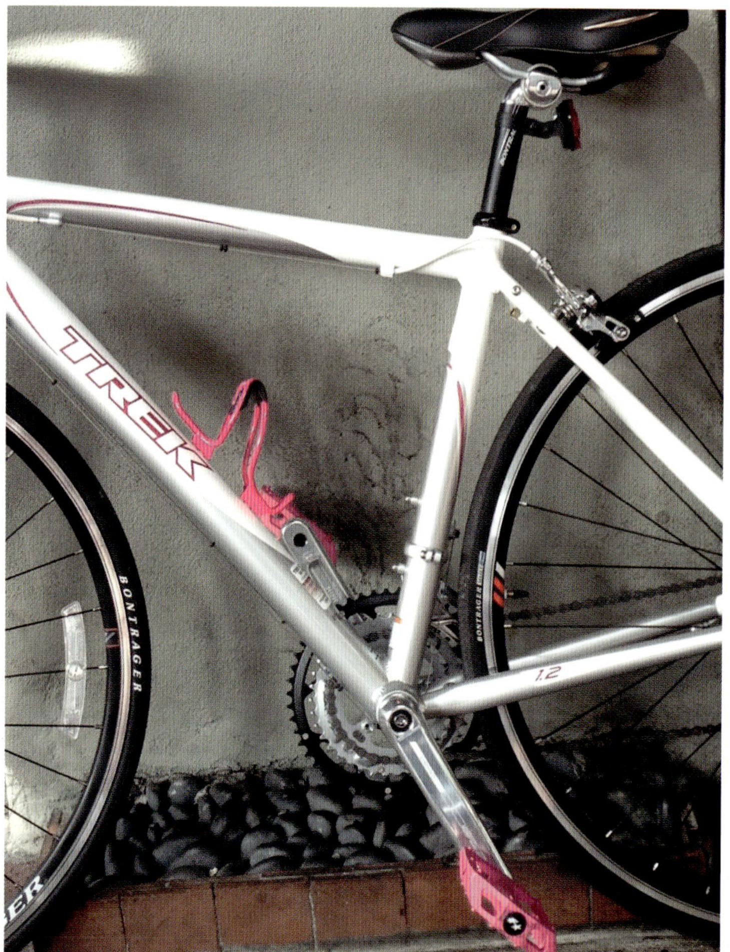

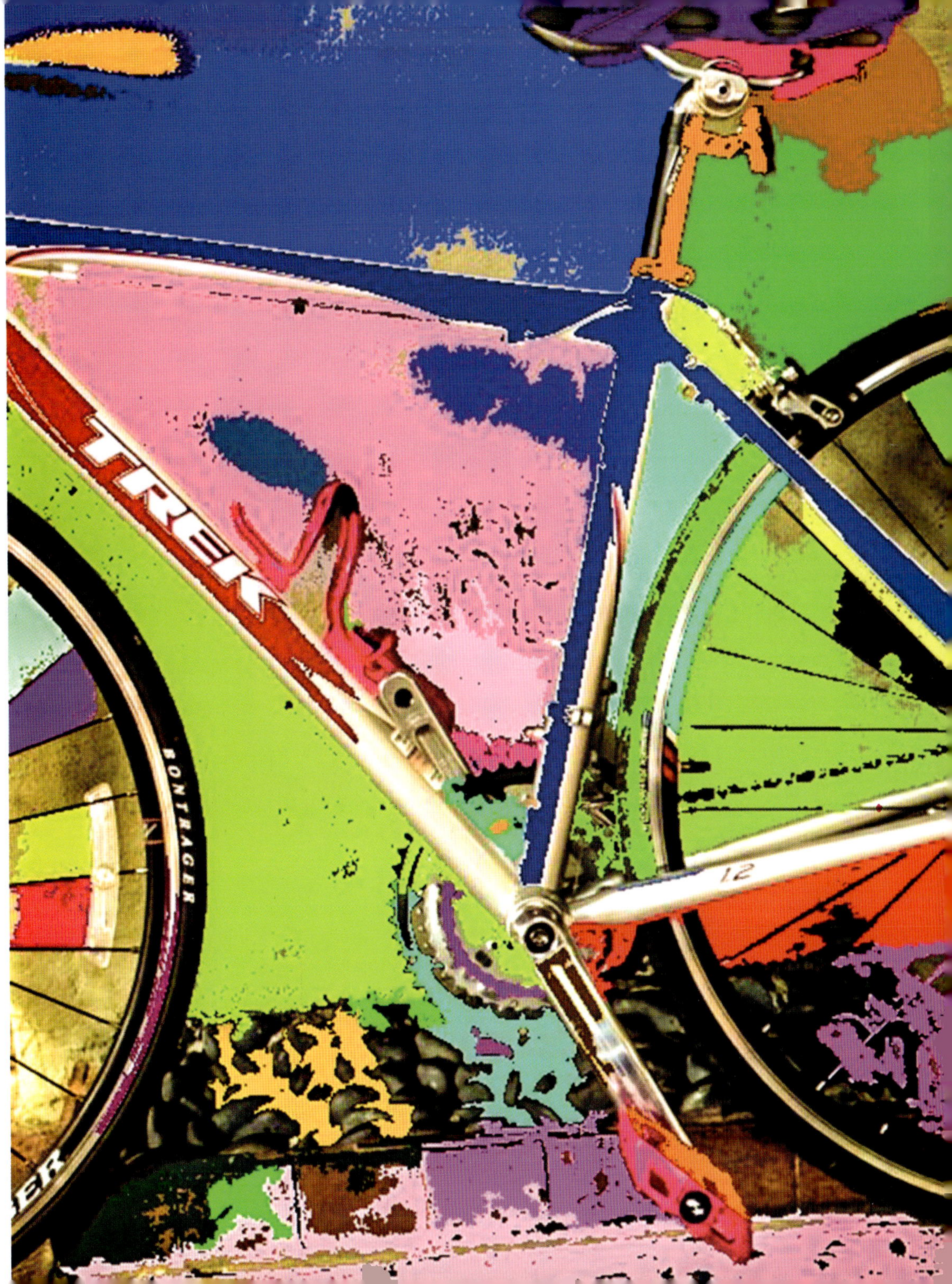
TREK
BONTRAGER

BICYCLE TIRES

A collection of bicycle tires
Goes around and around
Awaiting a bike
Popsicle colors

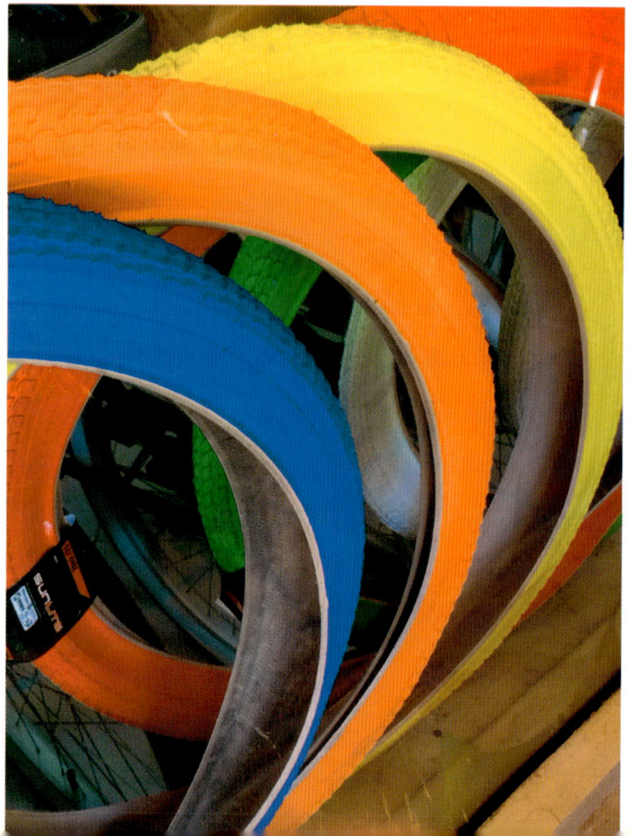

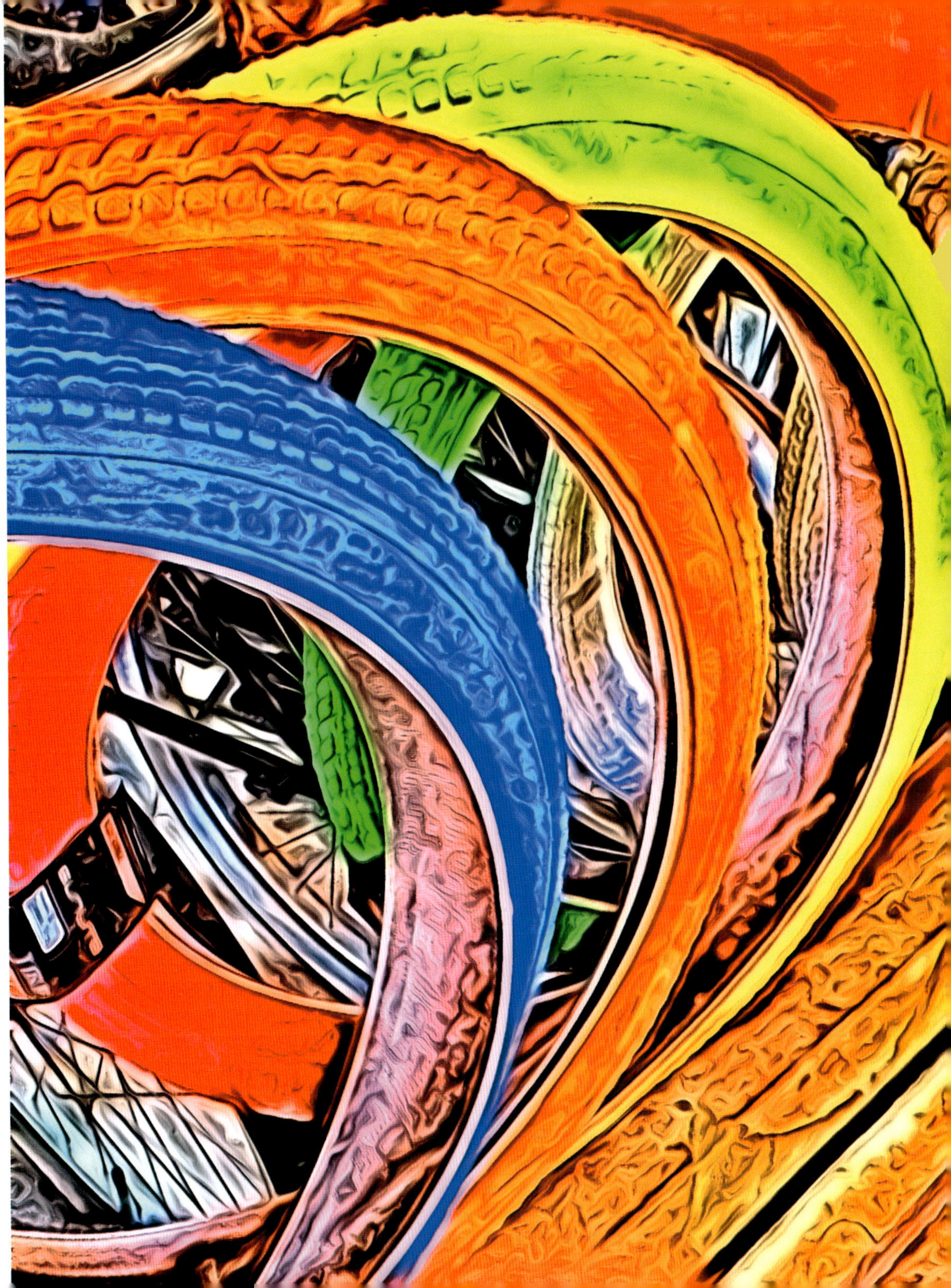

CAR IN THE GROVE

A common car in Coconut Grove
Highlights on the hood
Hot rod

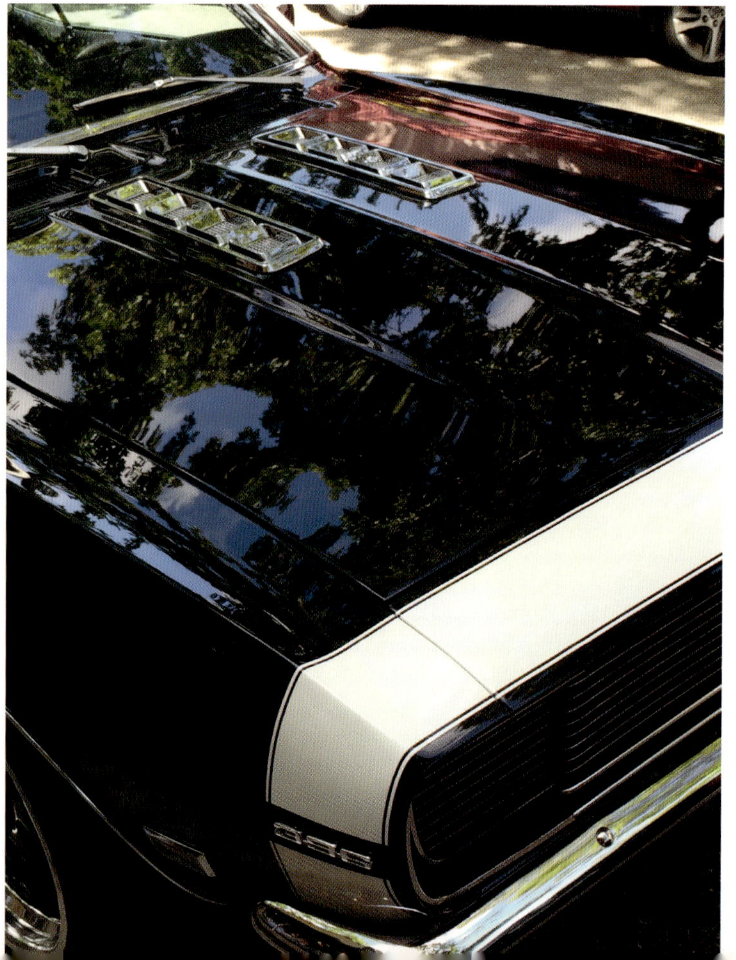

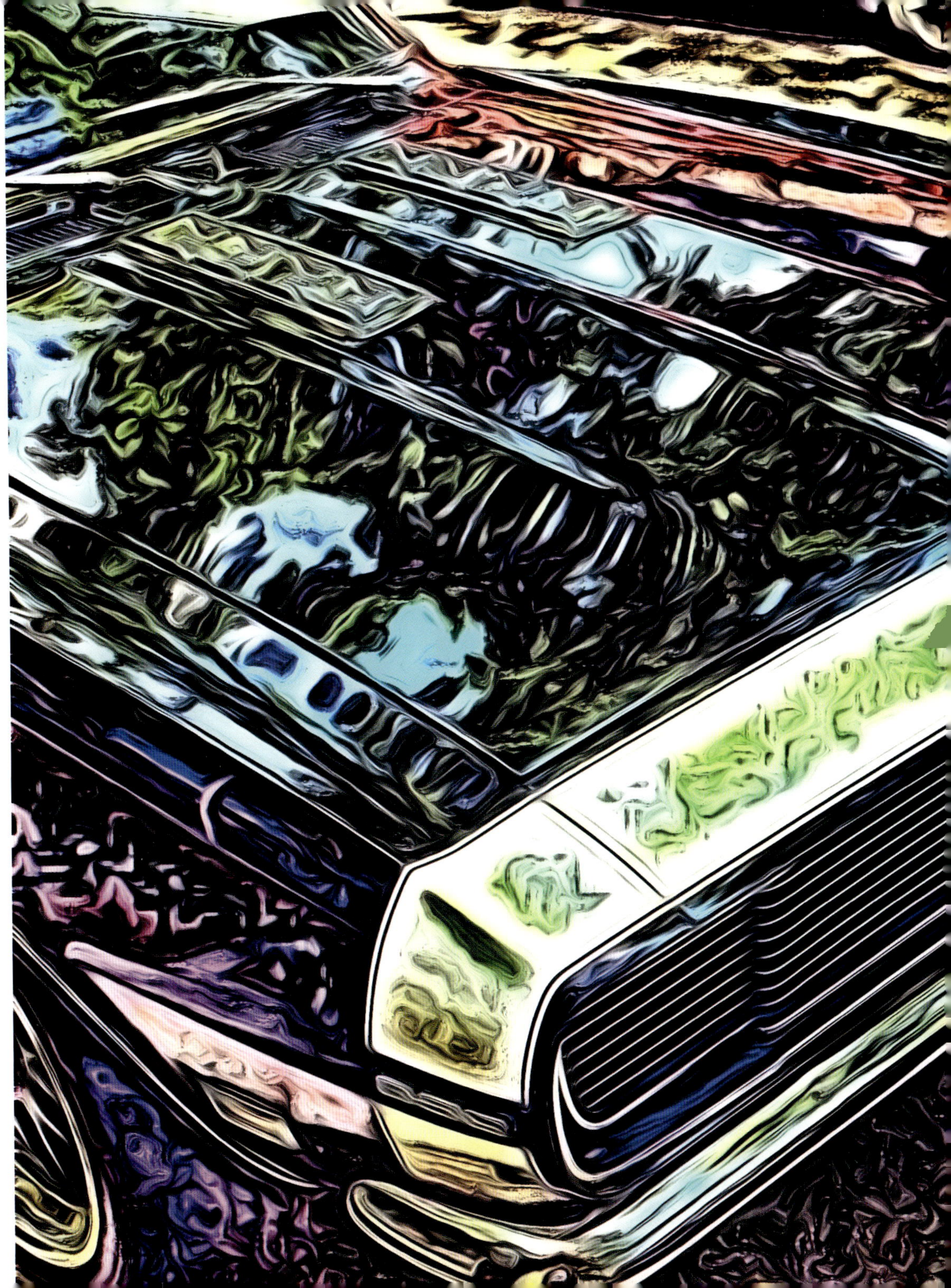

CLASSIC CAR

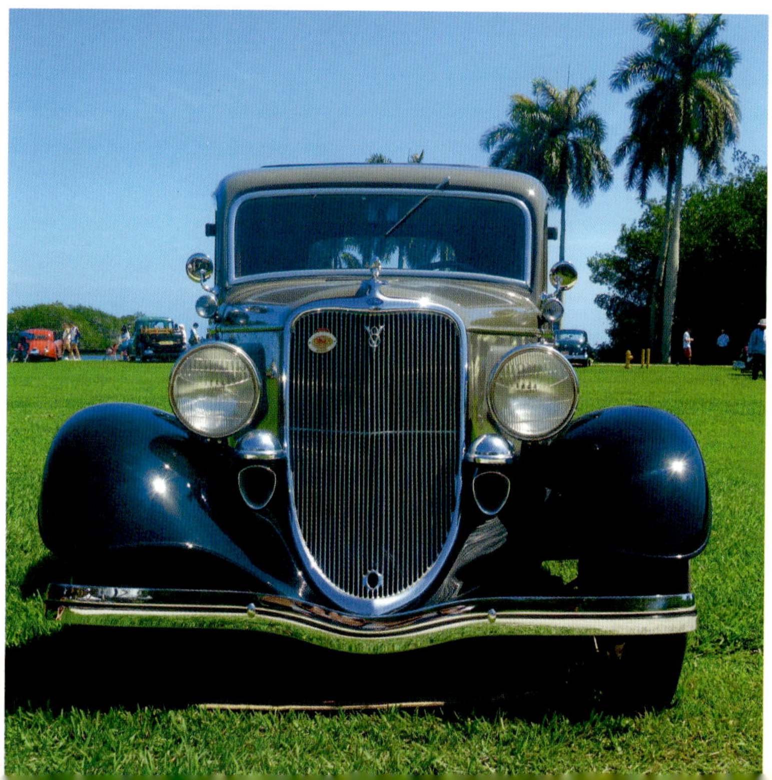

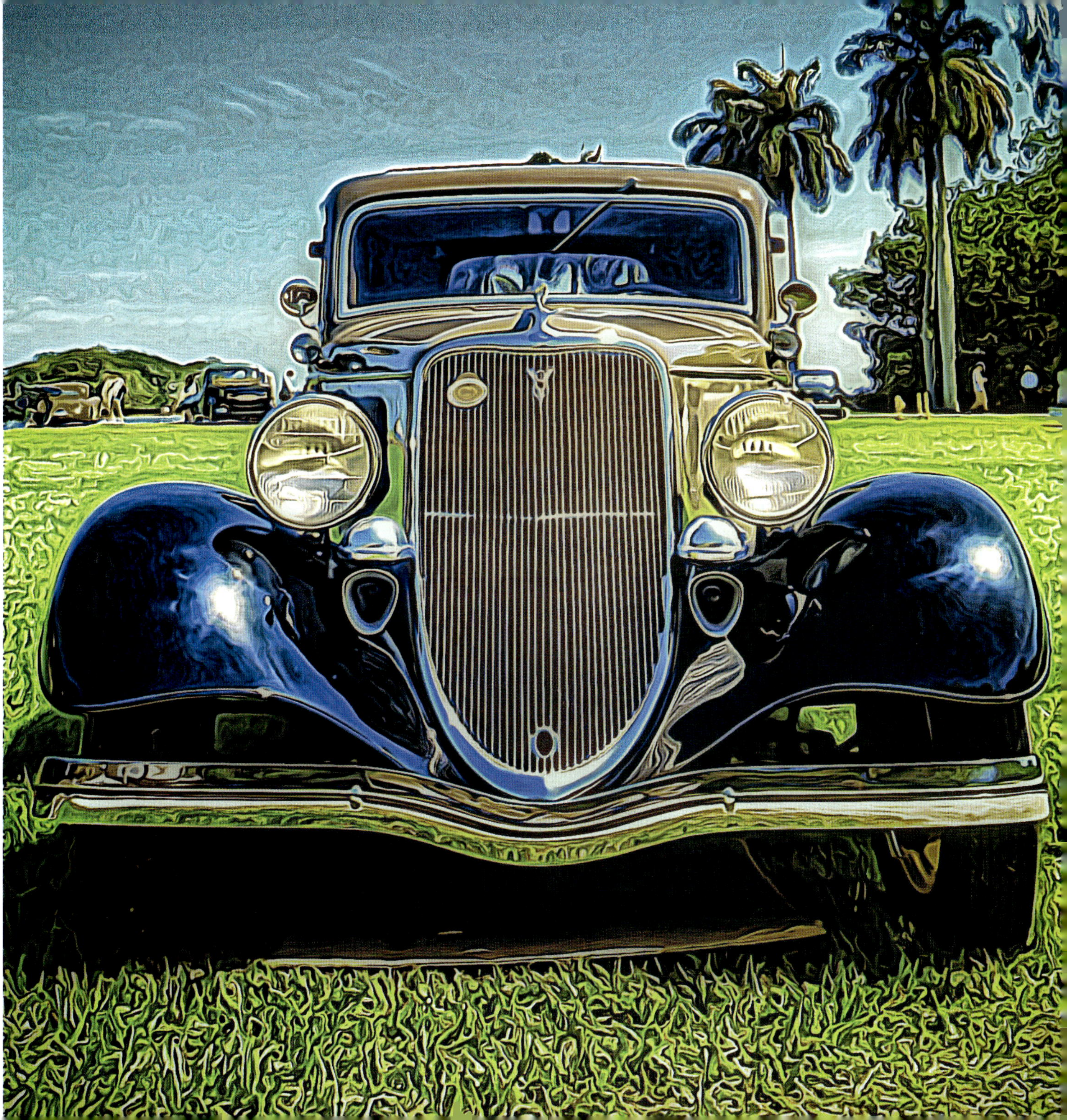

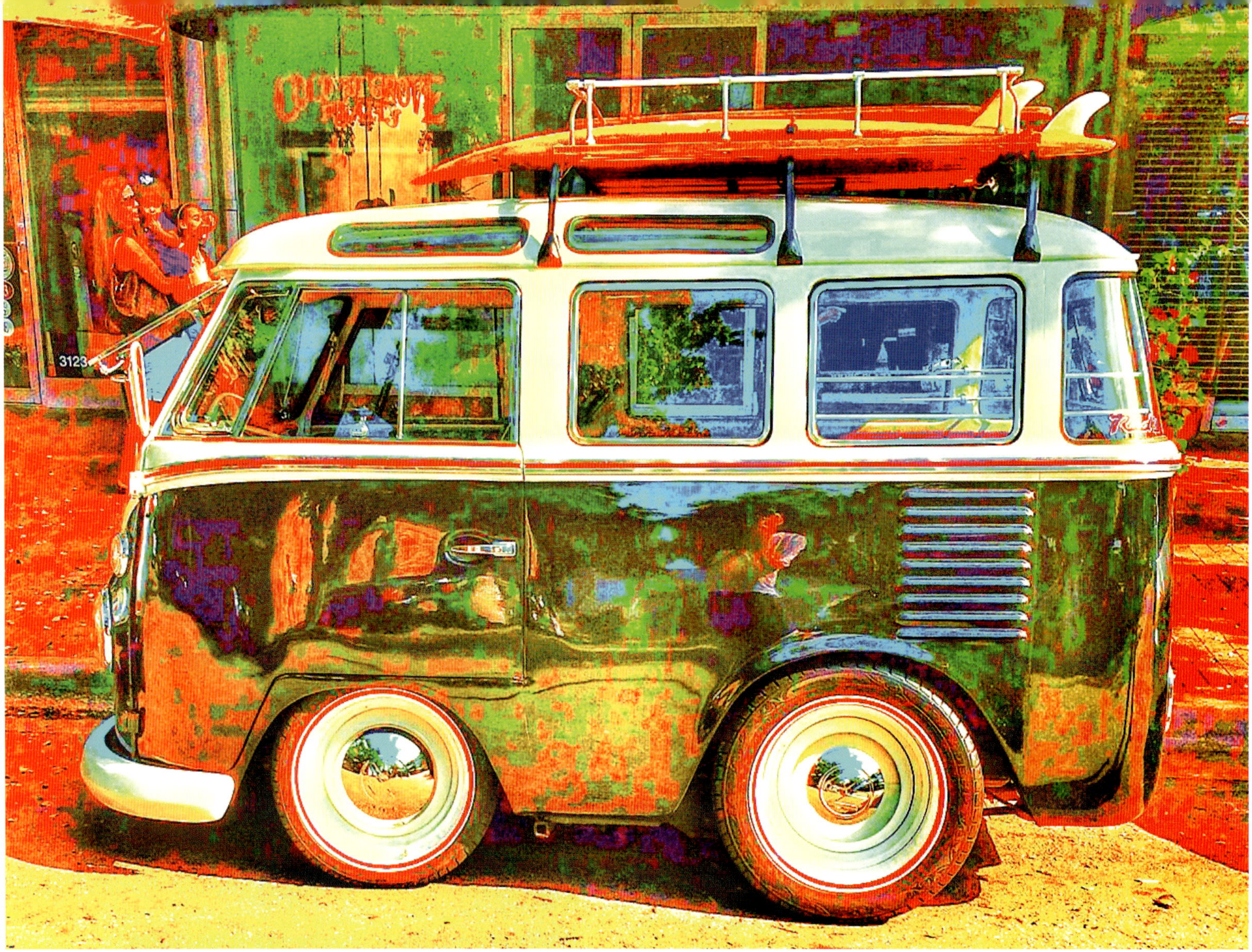

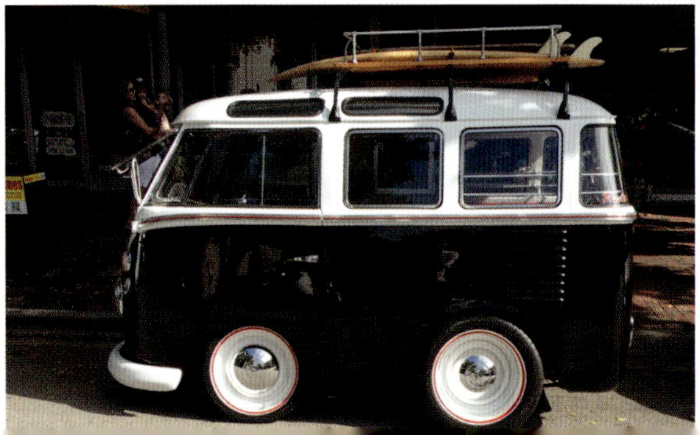

VW MICROBUS

A mini mini-microbus

Tiny and original

Ready for the road

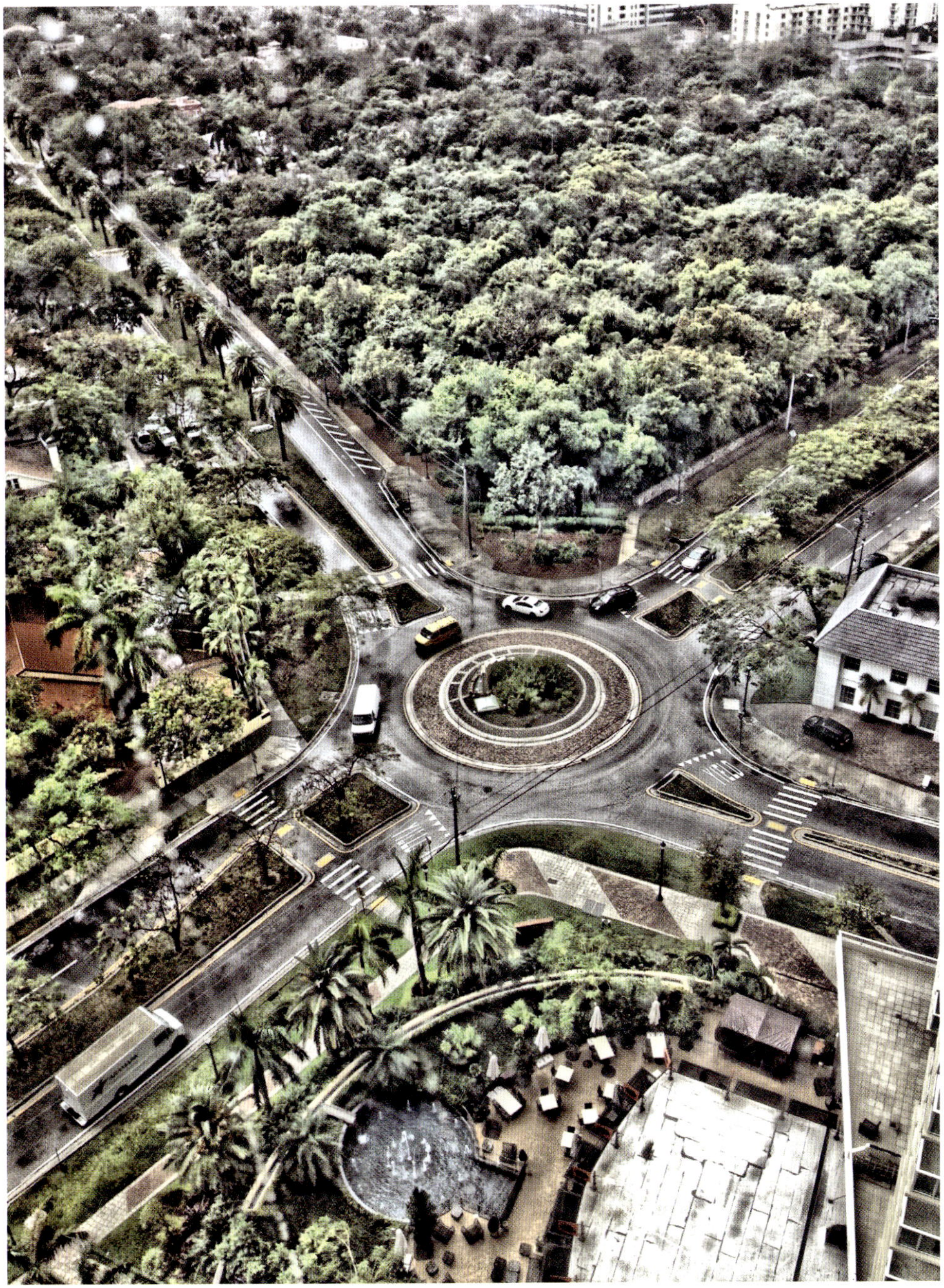

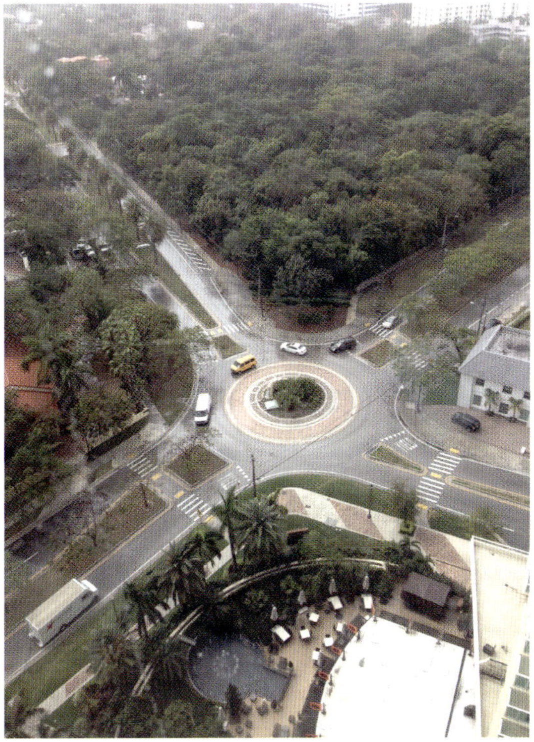

TRAFFIC CIRCLE

Bird's-eye view of a roundabout
Cars and trucks have a purpose
Somewhere to be

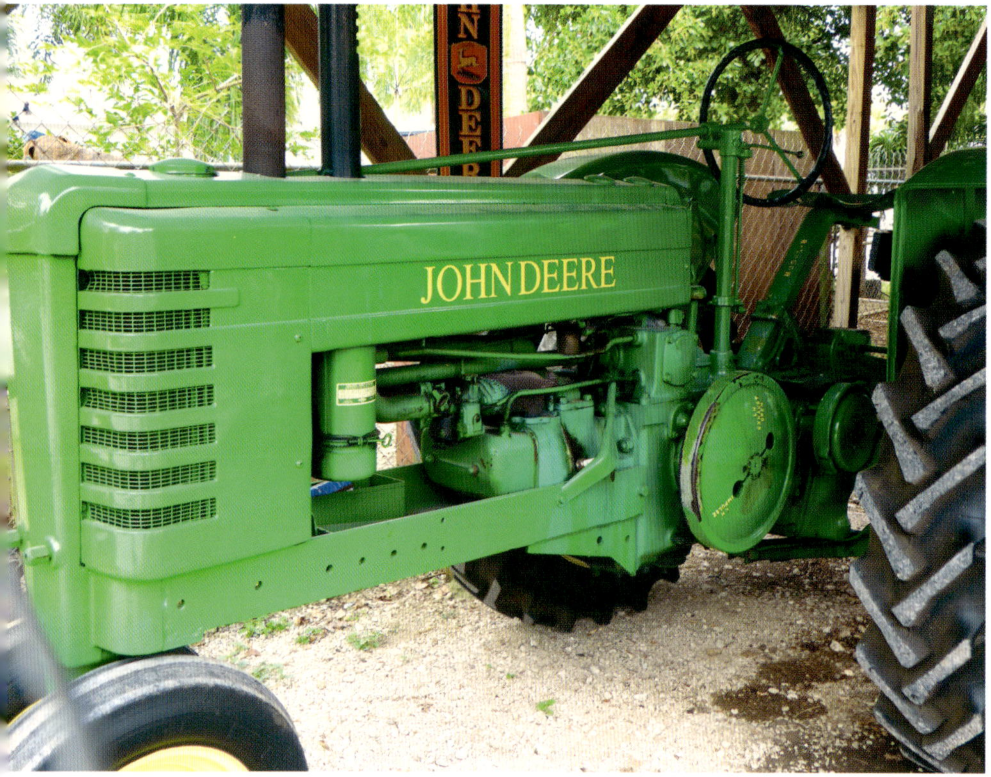

TRACTOR

A John Deere machine
Not very old
It farmed for years
Not anymore

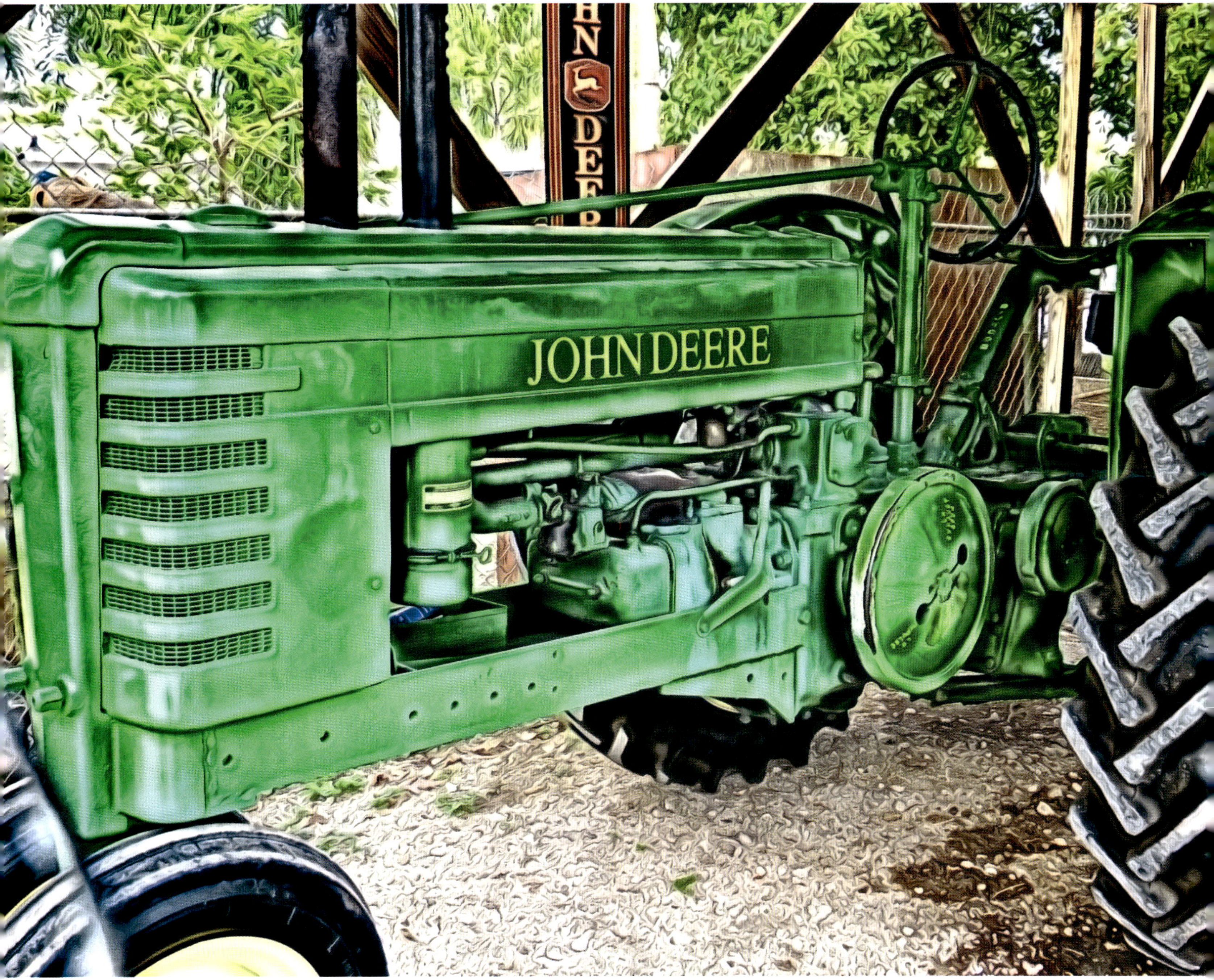
JOHN DEERE

LOCOMOTIVE I

Antique railroad engine
Massive and strong
Cow catcher on the front
Woo Woo Woo

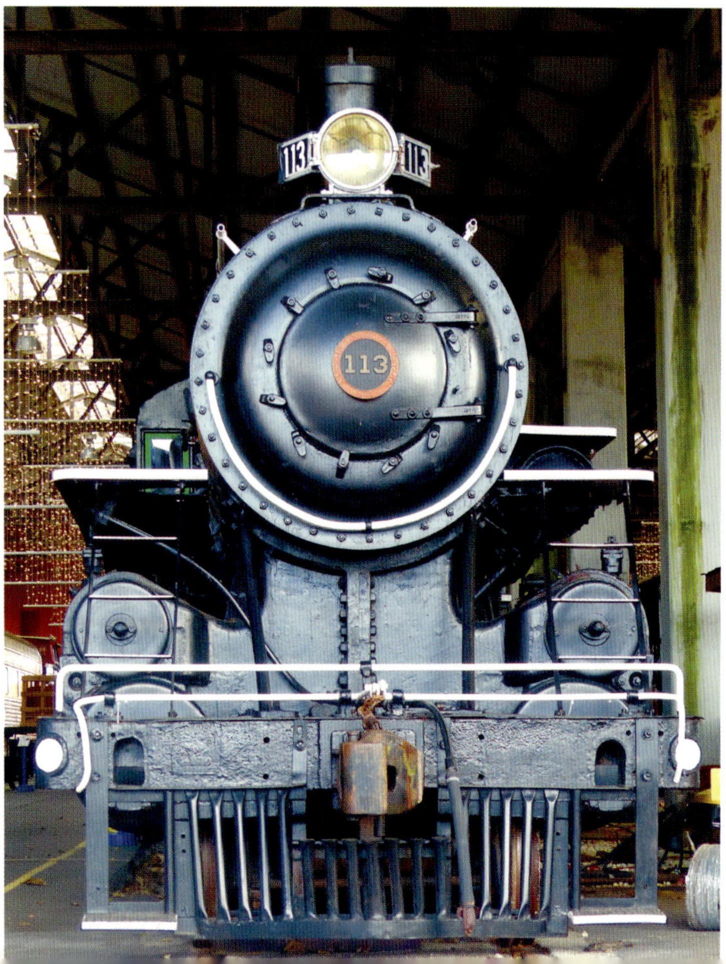

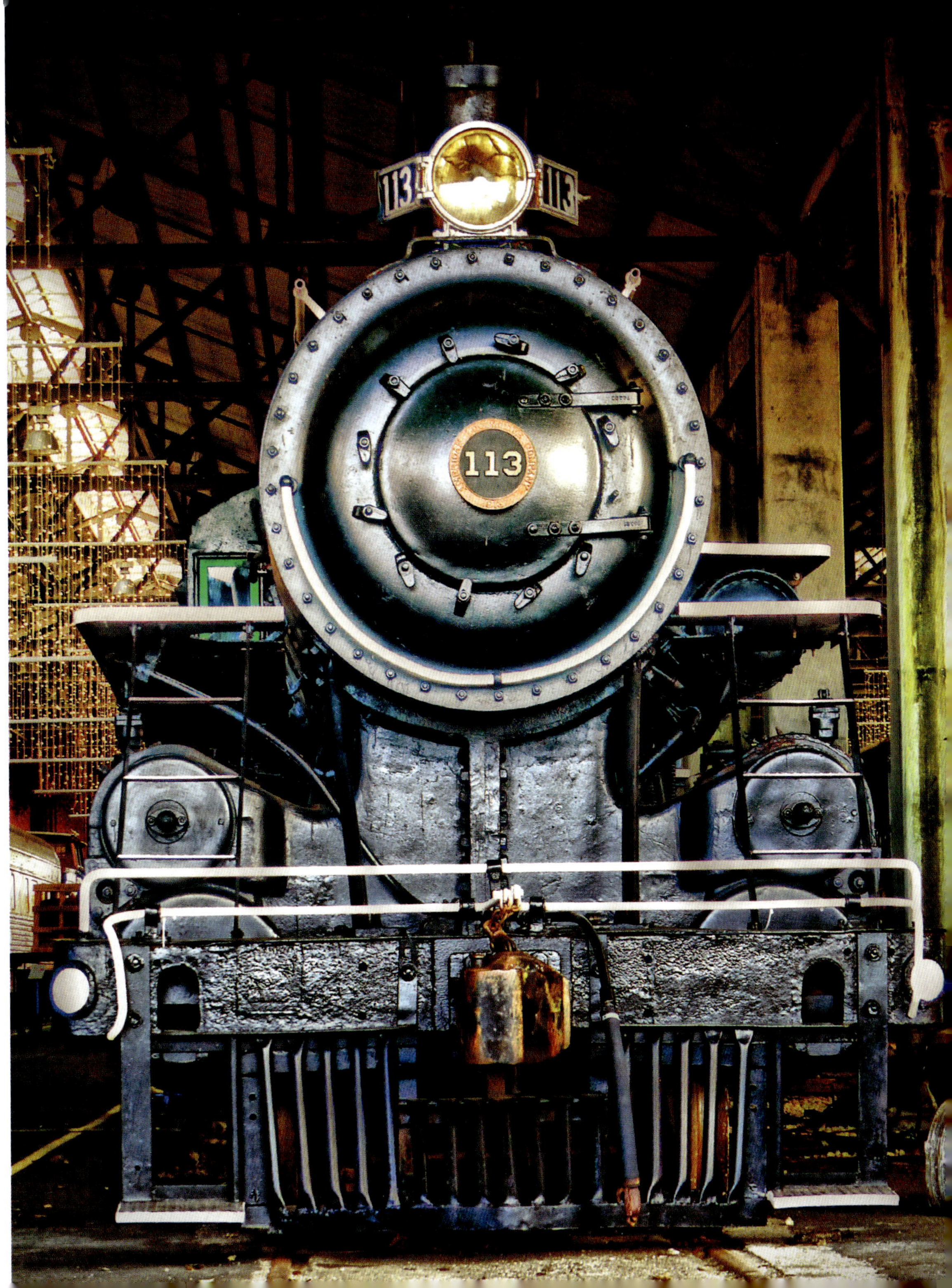
113
113
113

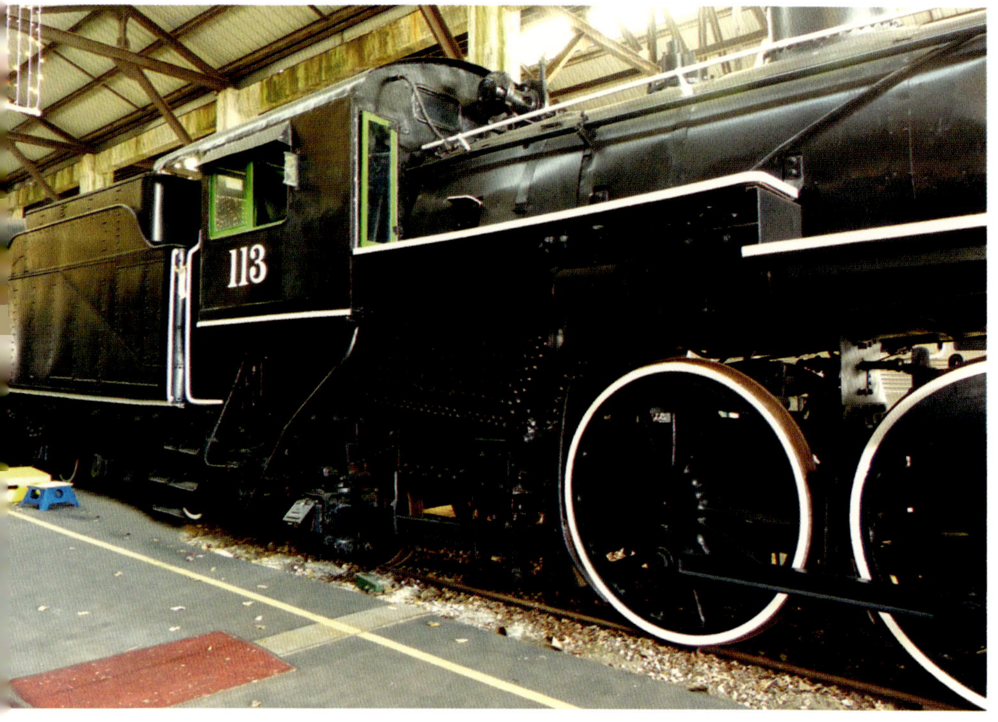

LOCOMOTIVE II

Engine 113
Eats coal
Tons and tons
On tracks

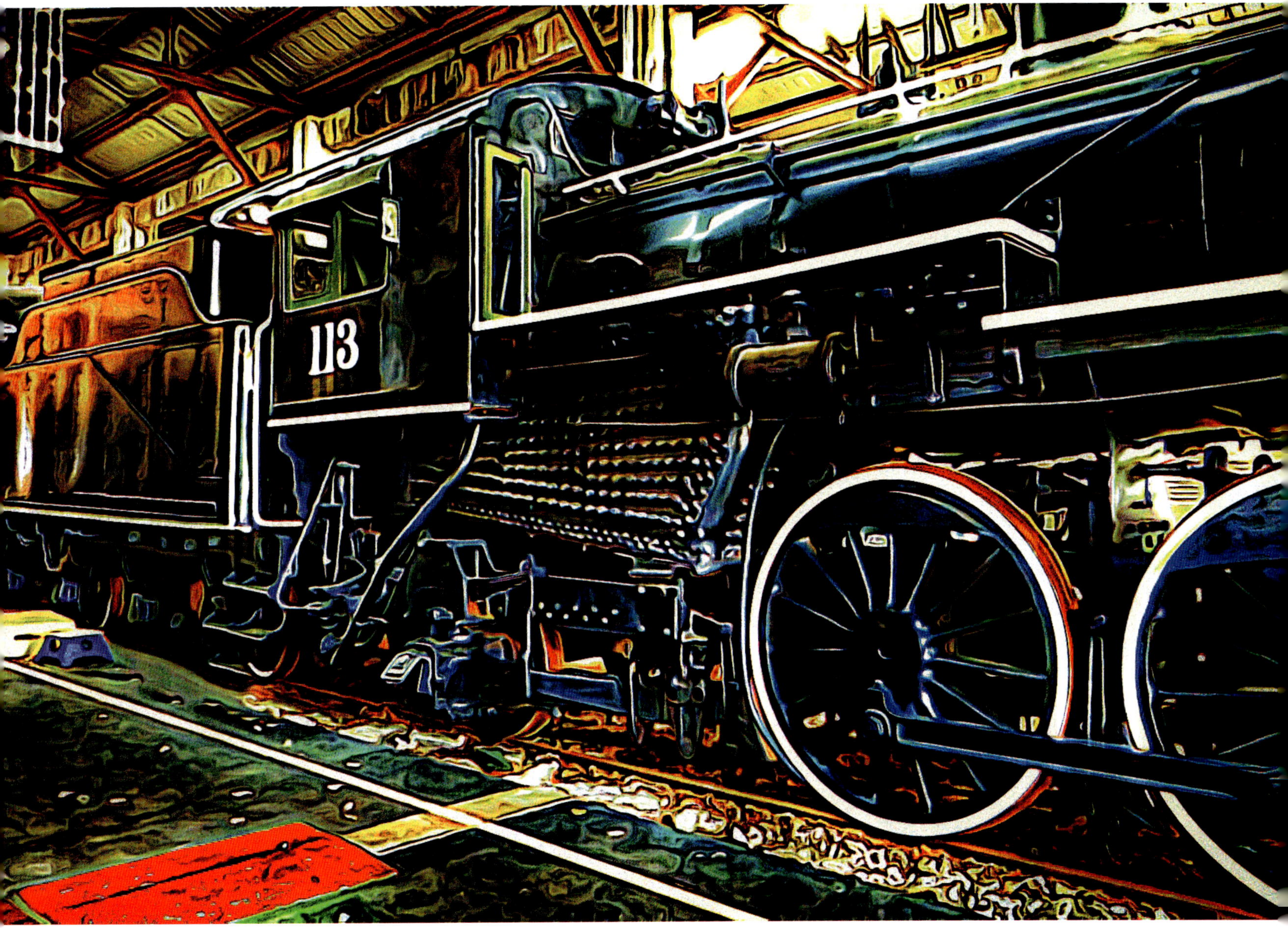
113

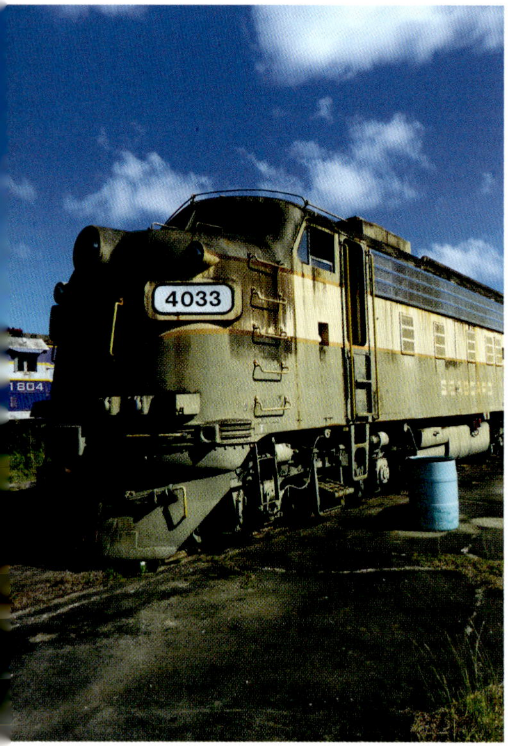

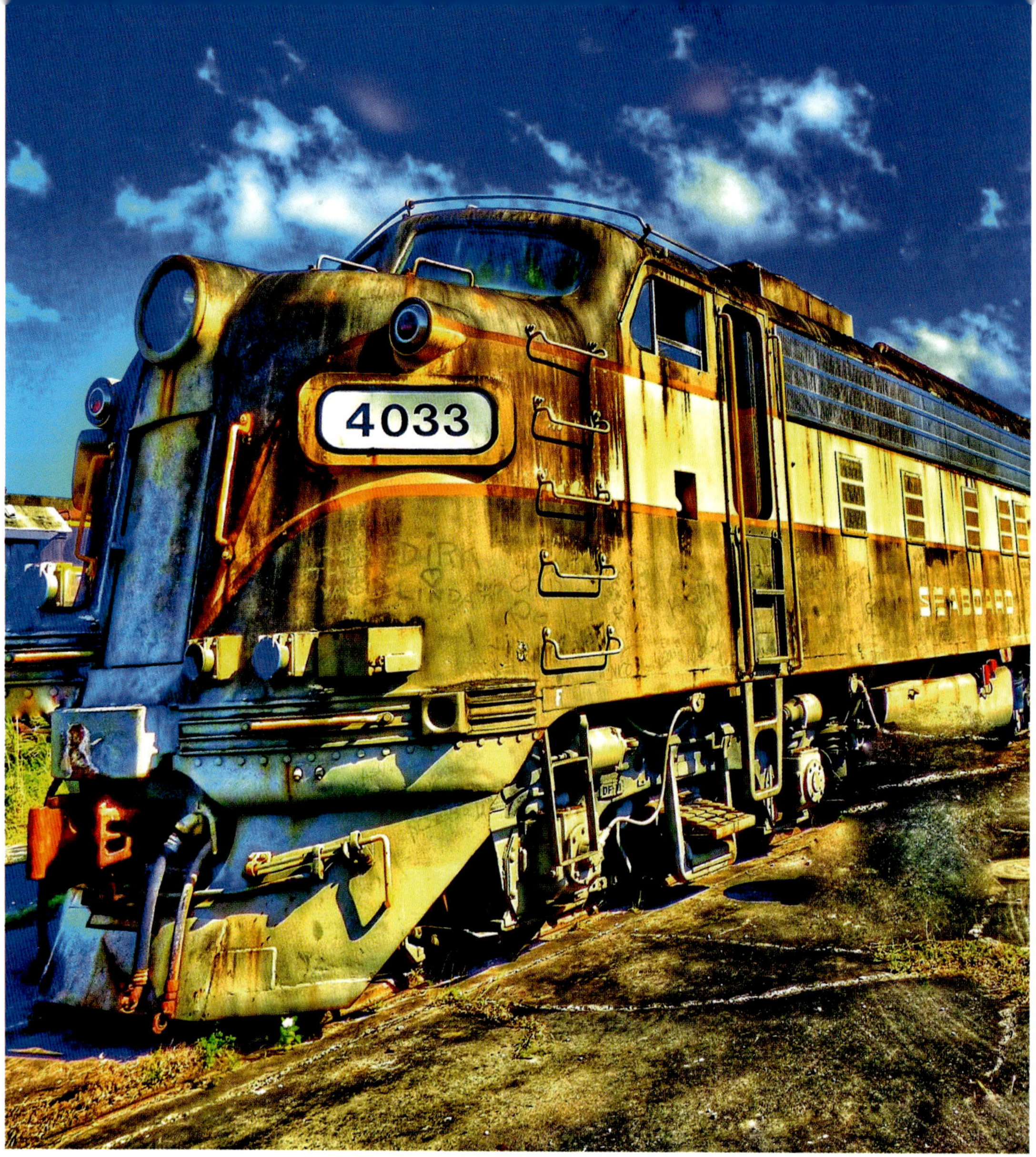

LOCOMOTIVE III

4033 was a diesel locomotive
Pulled freight with a purpose
Its working days are over
Out of service

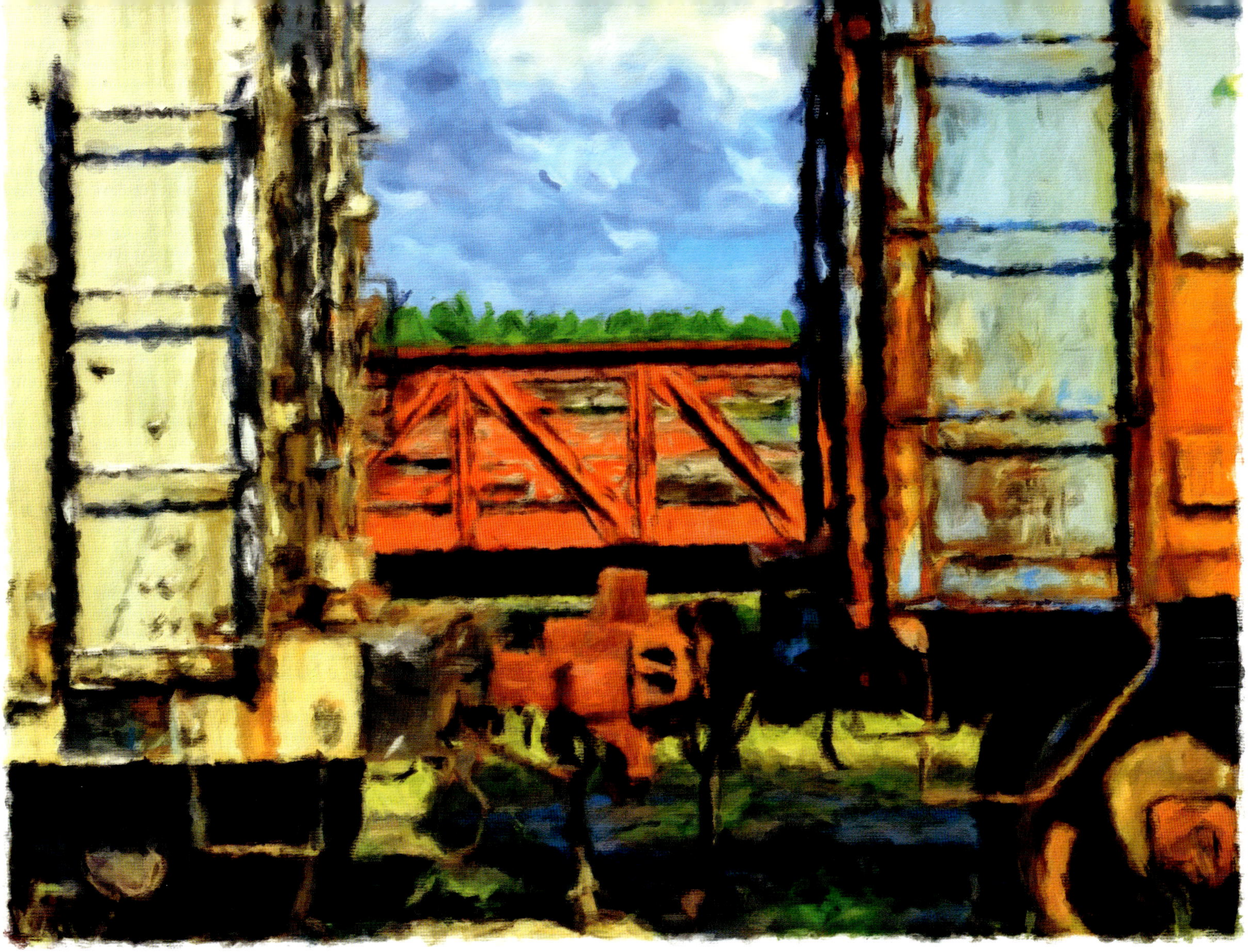

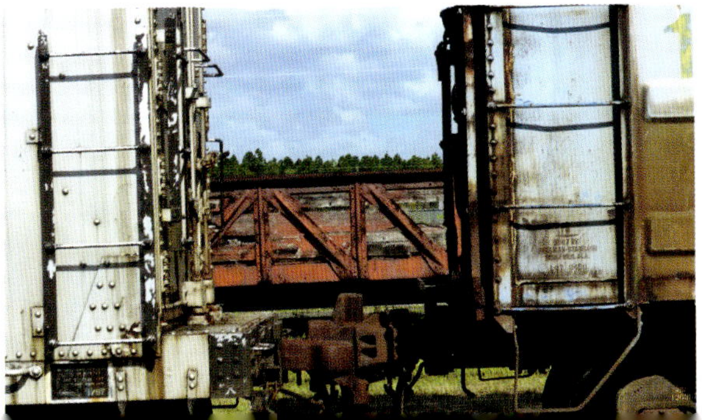

FREIGHT CARS

Chapter Five

NATURE

Nature's exuberance is on display throughout the city. Miami's warm climate, humidity, and fertile soil provide the perfect environment for some of nature's most beautiful sights. Stately palm trees, banyan tree-lined streets, and blossoming plants greet residents every day of the year. Lovely beaches and the waters of Biscayne Bay warmly welcome residents and tourists alike.

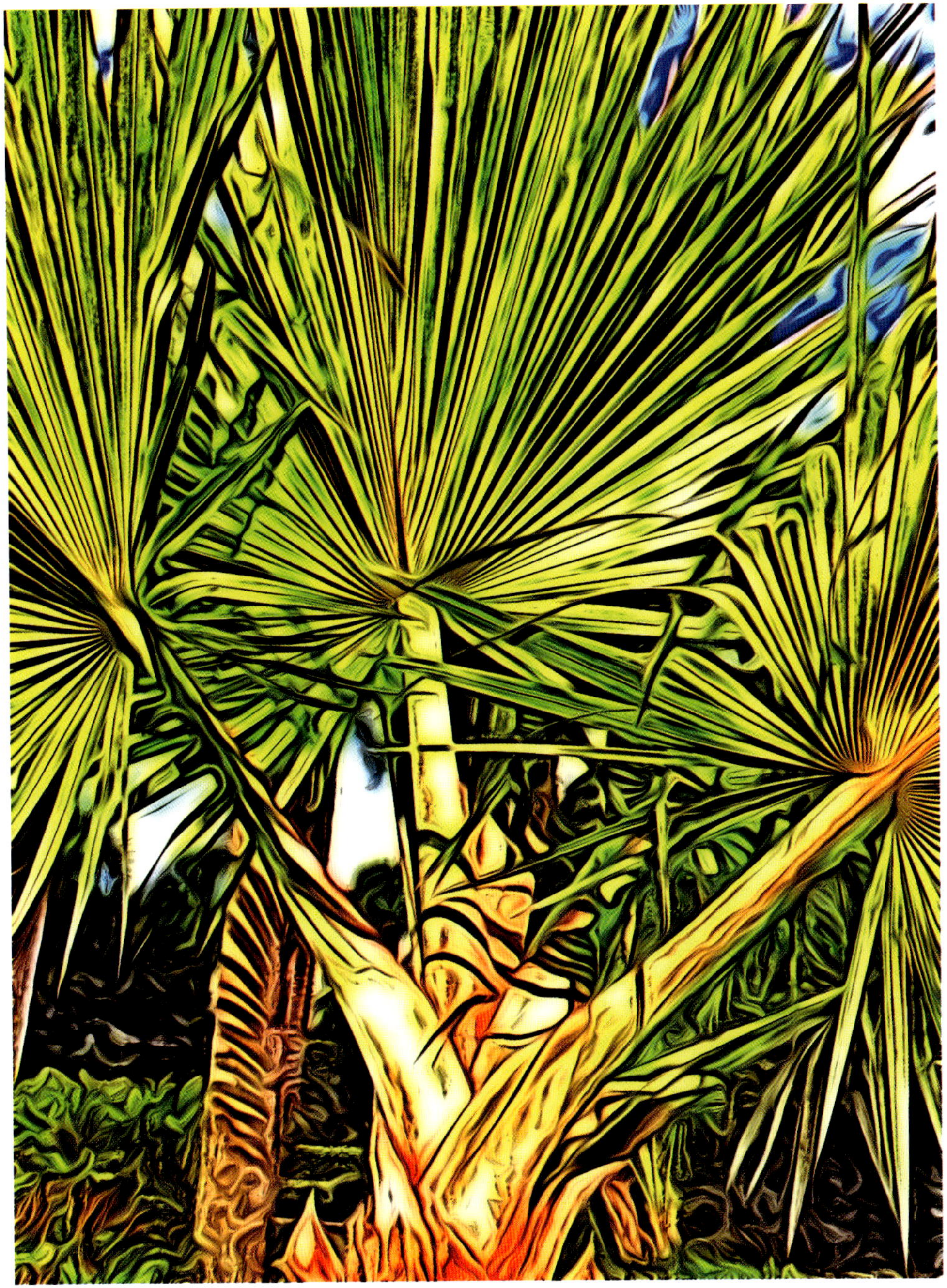

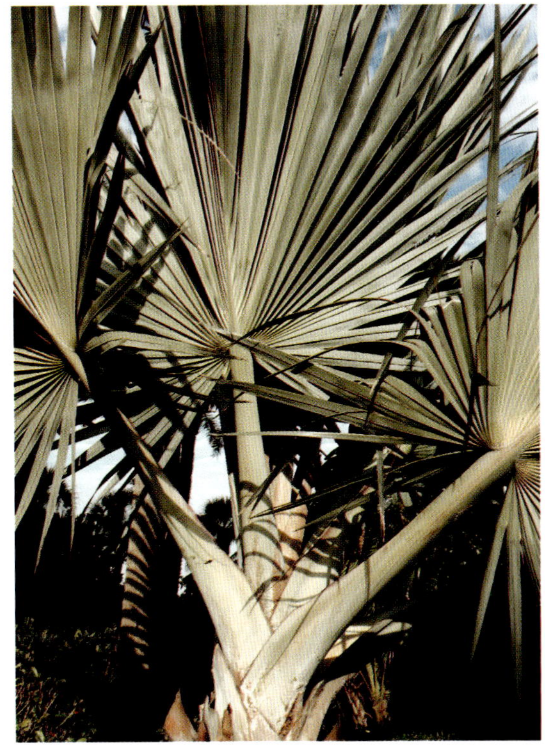

BISMARCK PALM

Greets me each day
In front of my home
Common plant or vivacious tree
Depending on how you look at it

SIMPLE ART

Art can be simple
A tree, a door, a window
Basic beauty

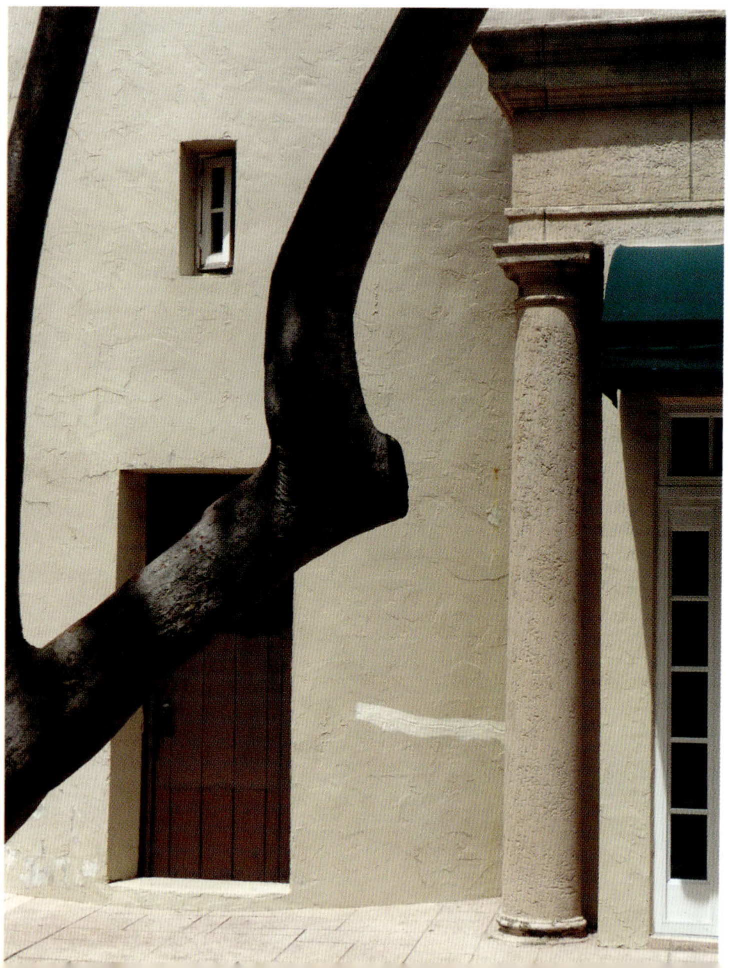

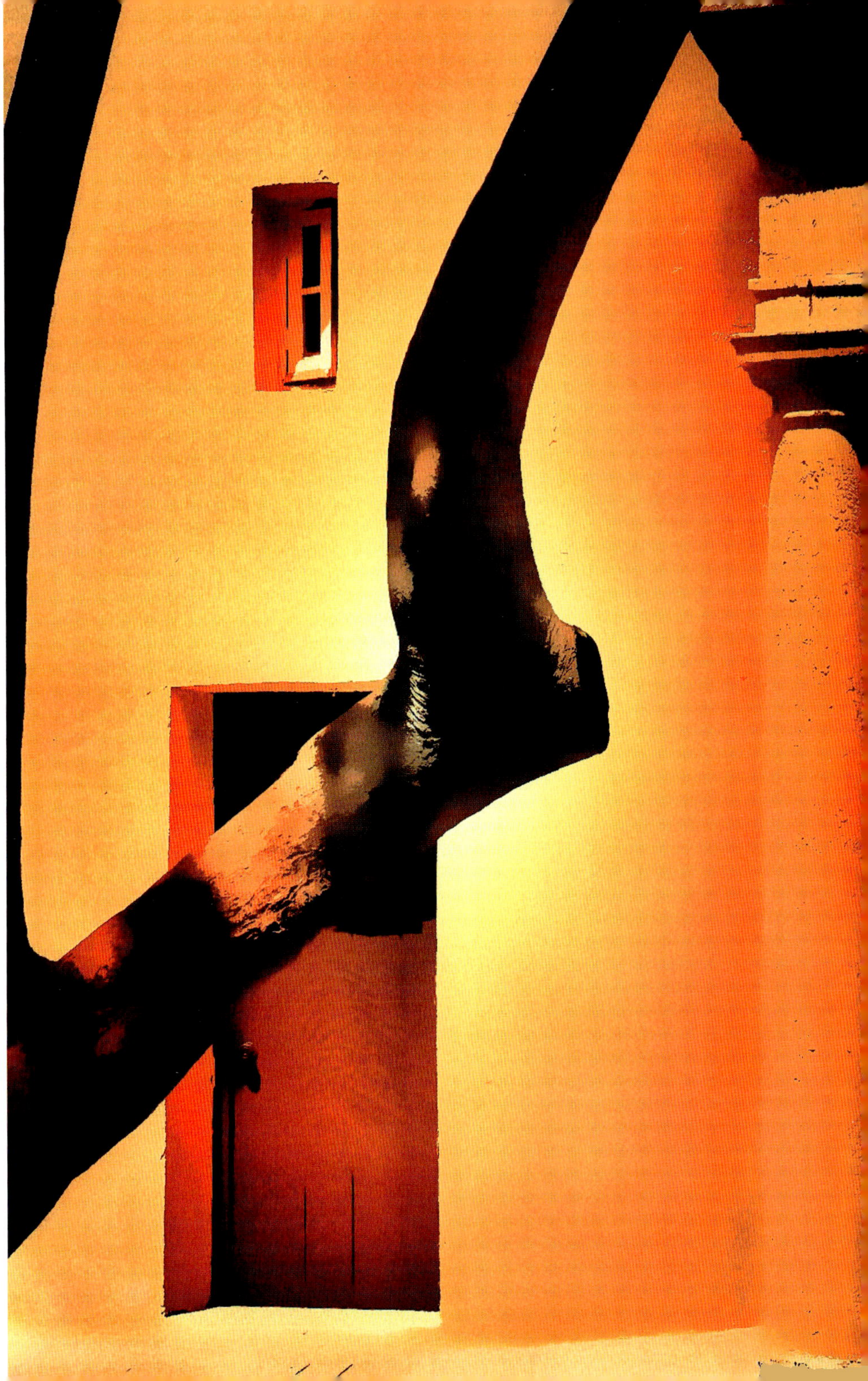

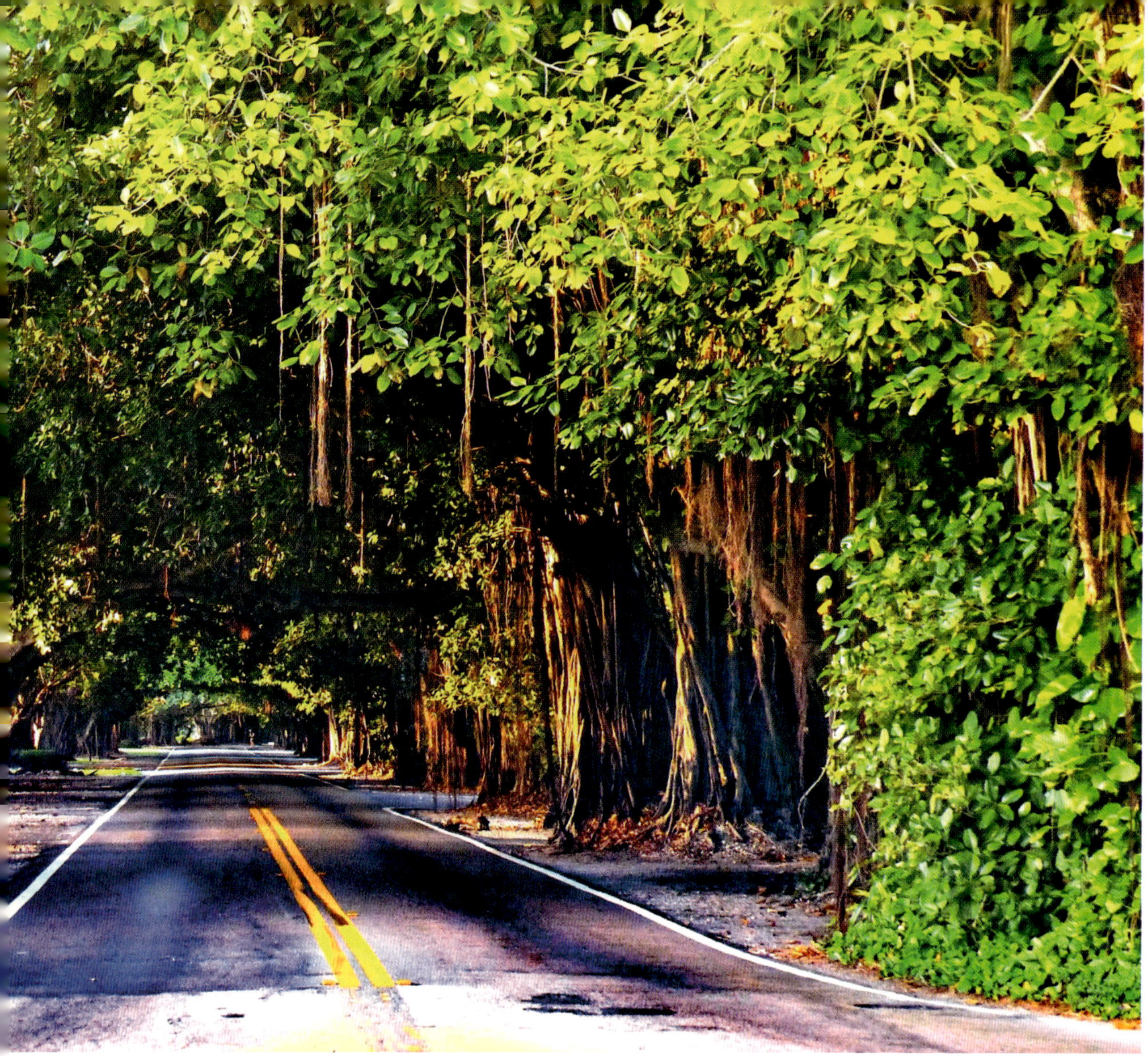

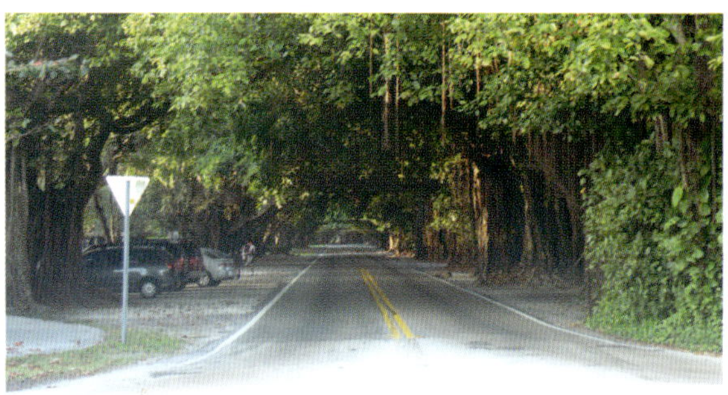

OLD CUTLER ROAD

A section of Old Cutler Road

At the traffic circle Cartagena Plaza

Gorgeous overhanging trees

Historic route

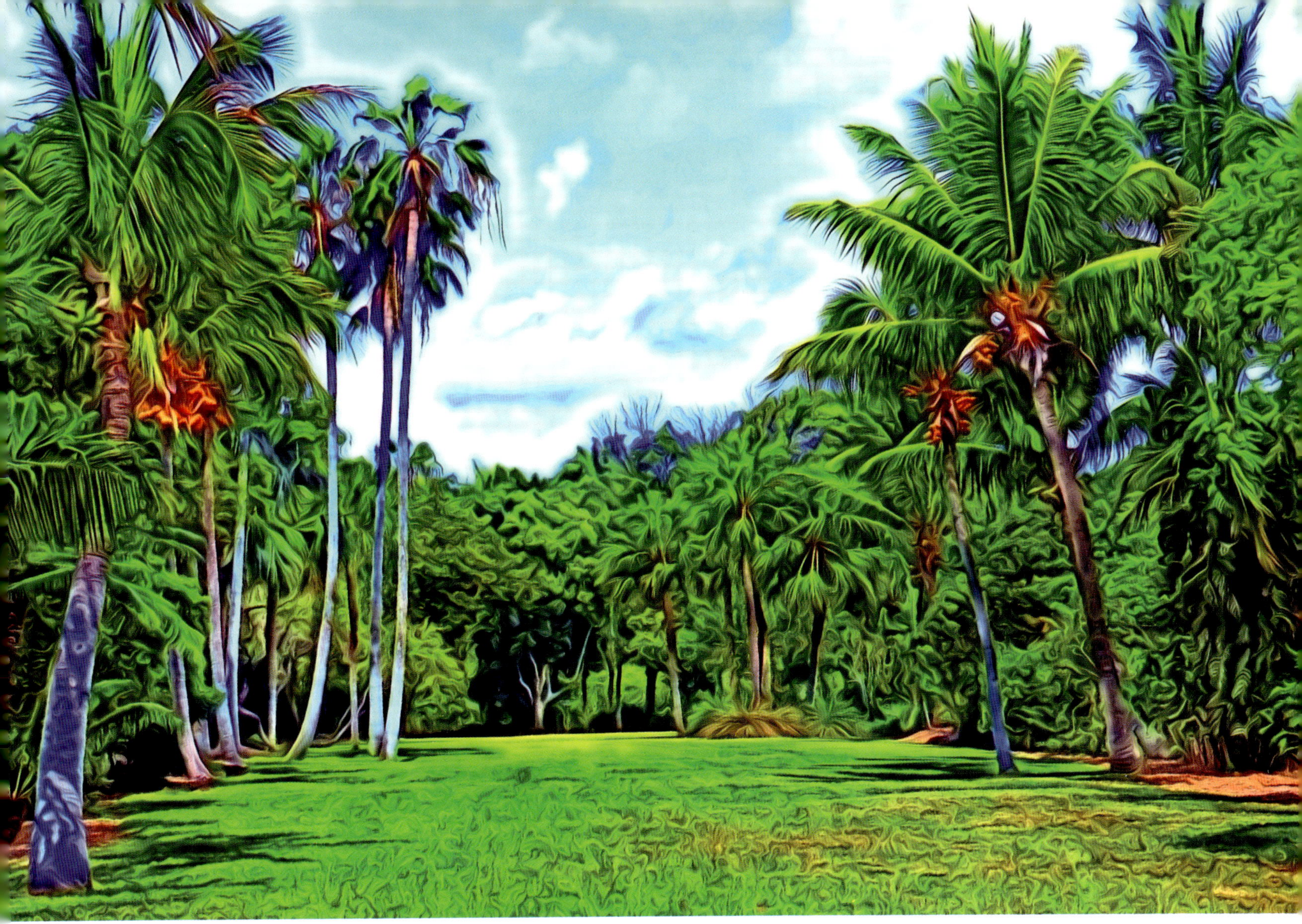

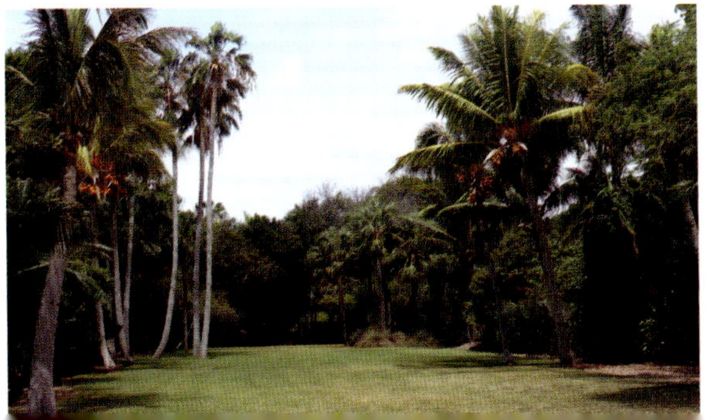

KAMPONG BOTANICAL GARDEN

Dates to the nineteenth century

Once owned by the Fairchilds

Well-known botanists

Palm tree alleé

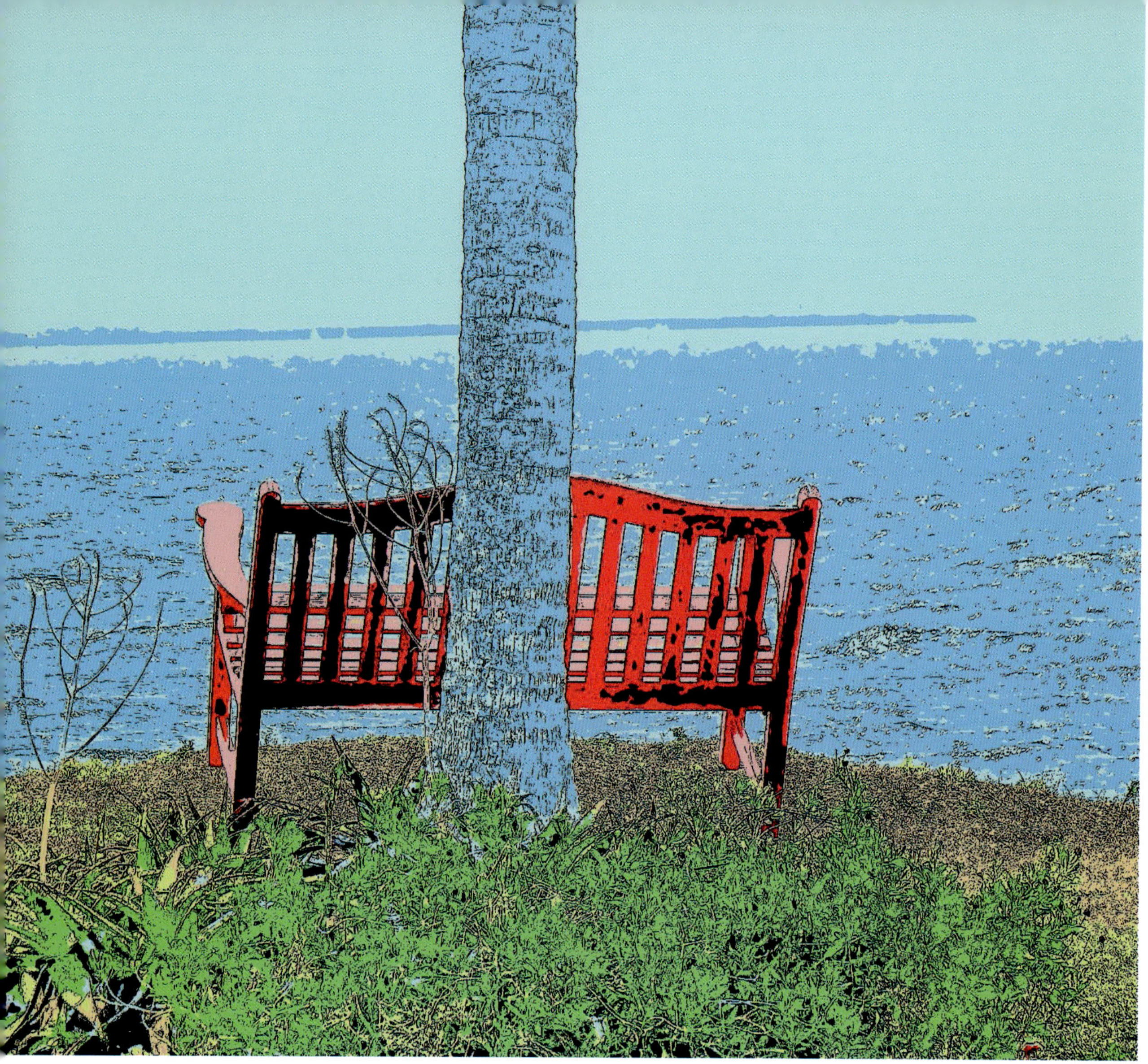

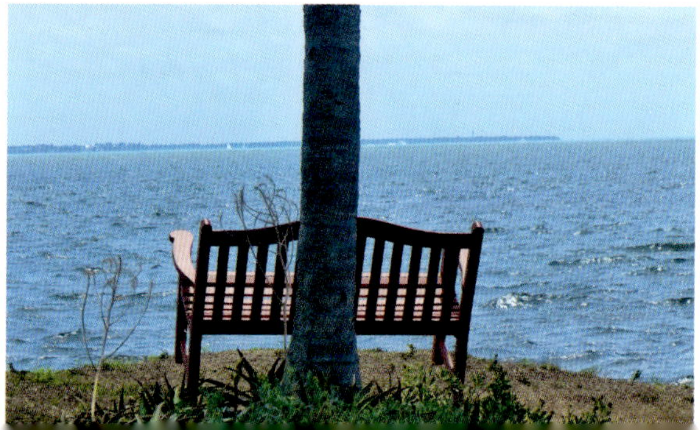

BENCH ON
BISCAYNE BAY

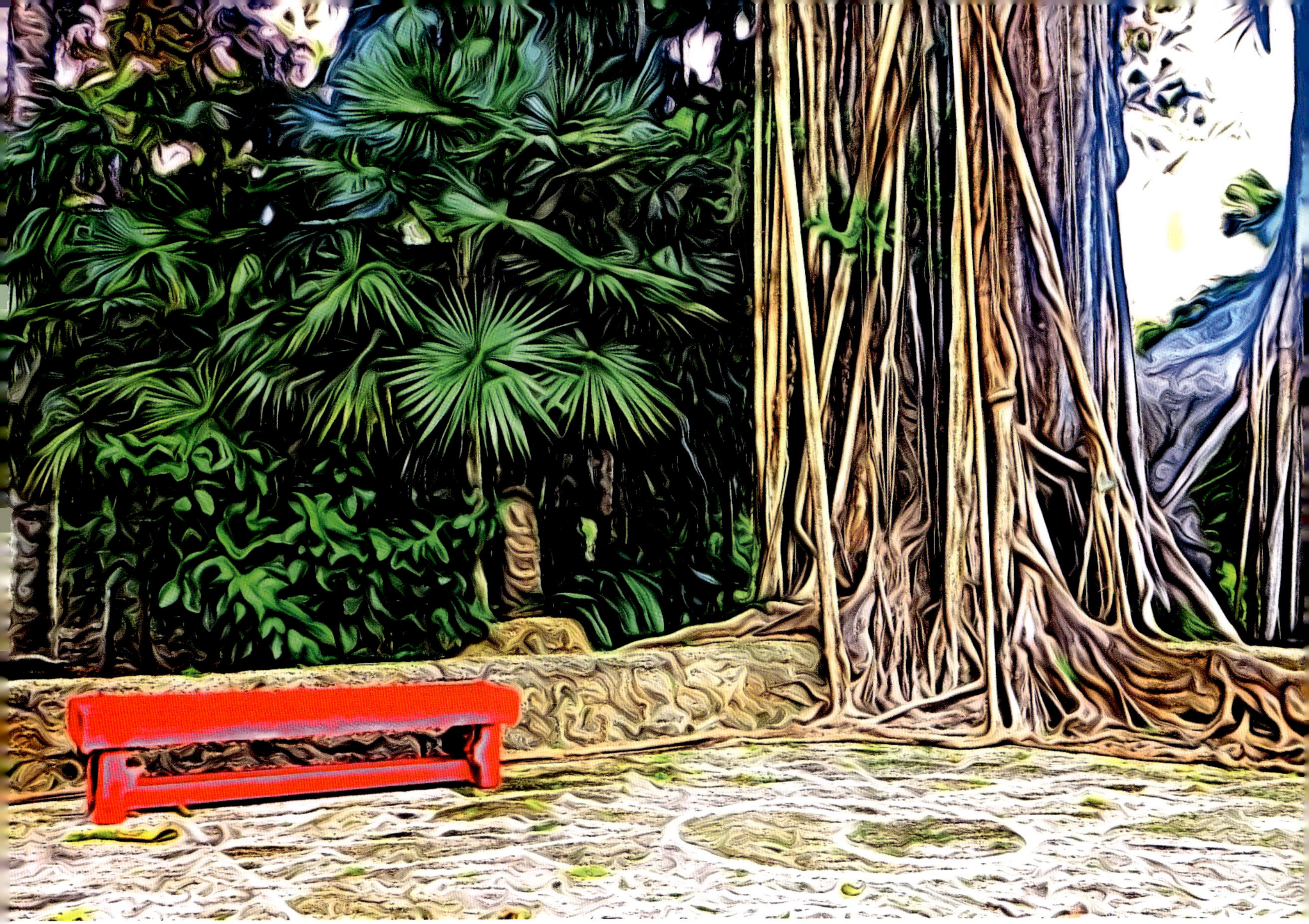

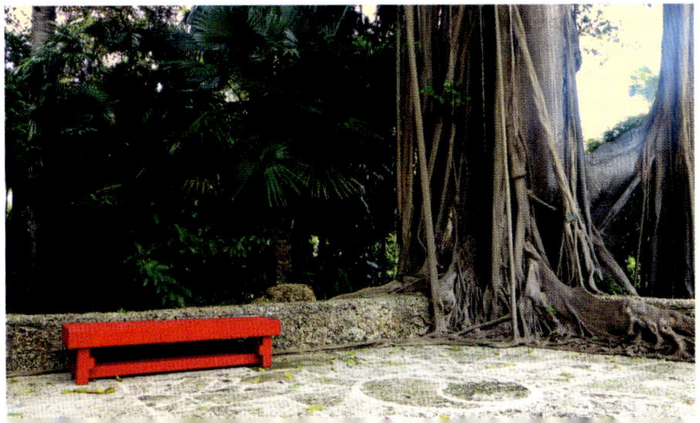

WOODEN BENCH

A red bench and banyan roots
Fan-like foliage
In Kampong Garden

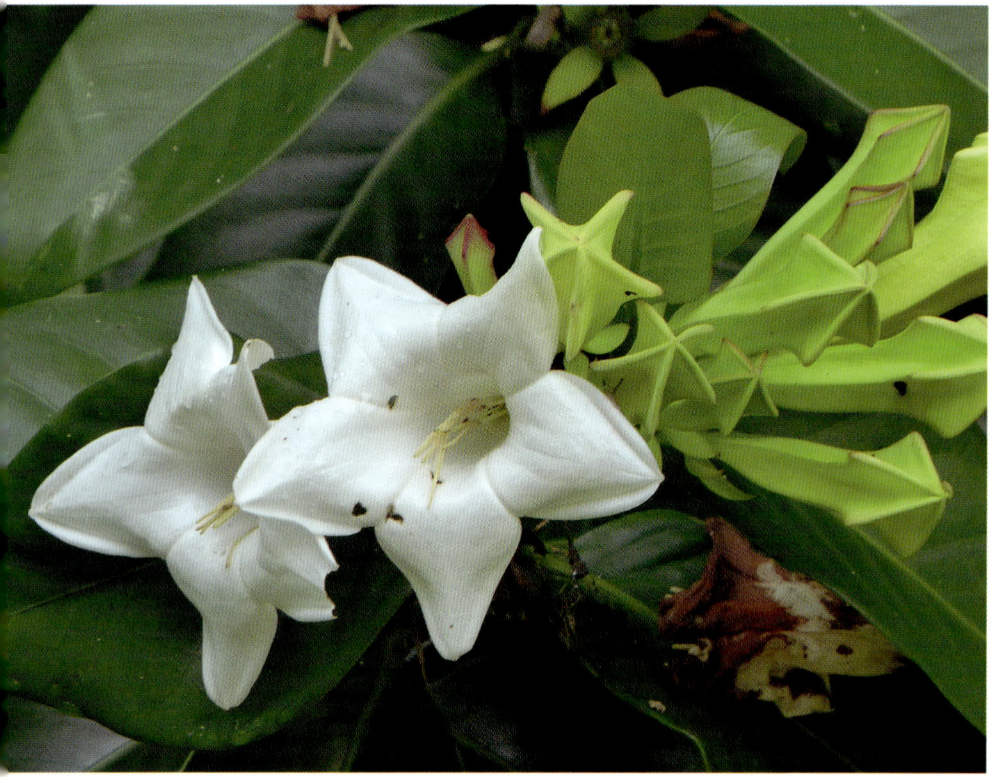

LILIES

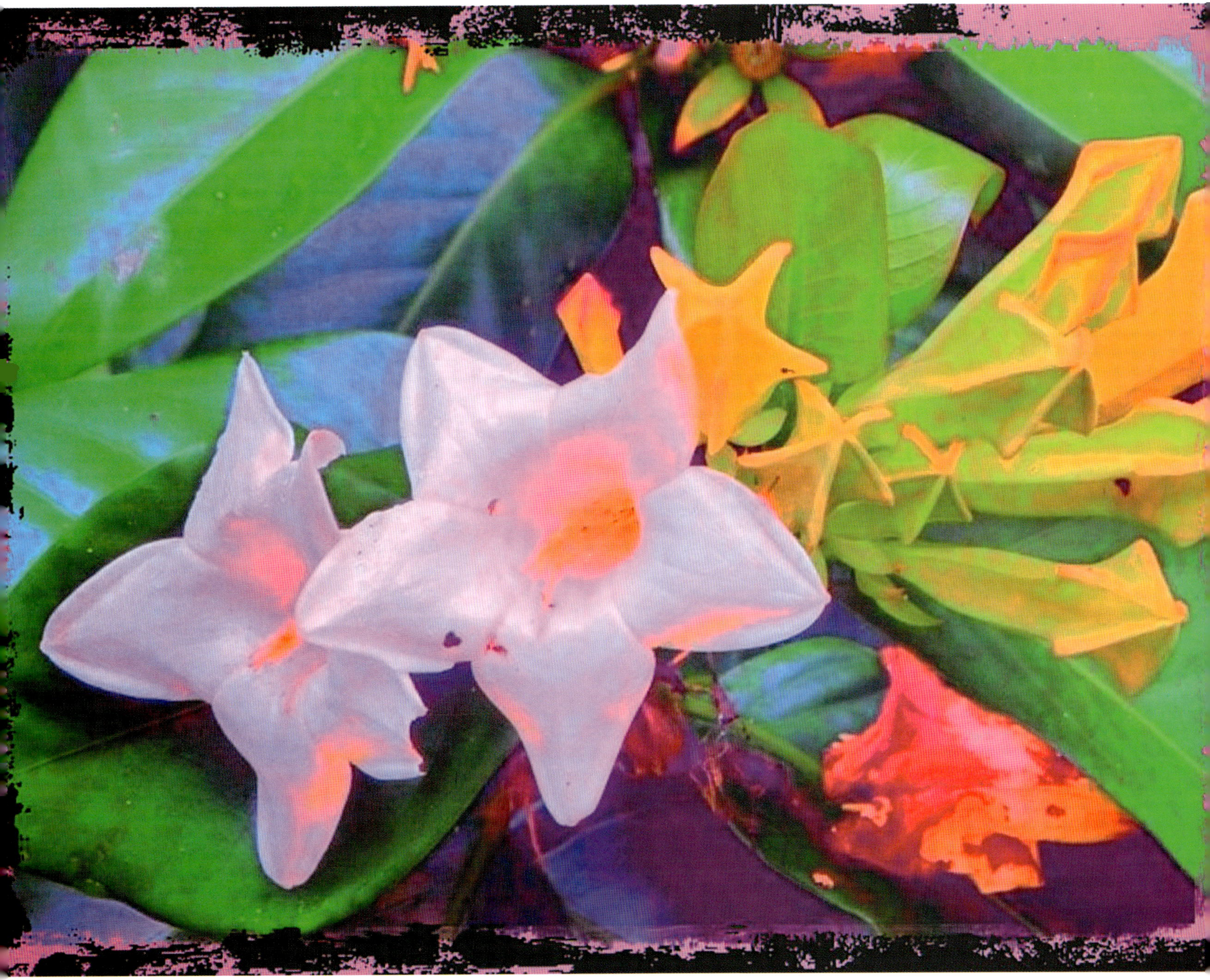

BEACH SCENE

The tip of Key Biscayne
Viewed from the lighthouse
Vibrant

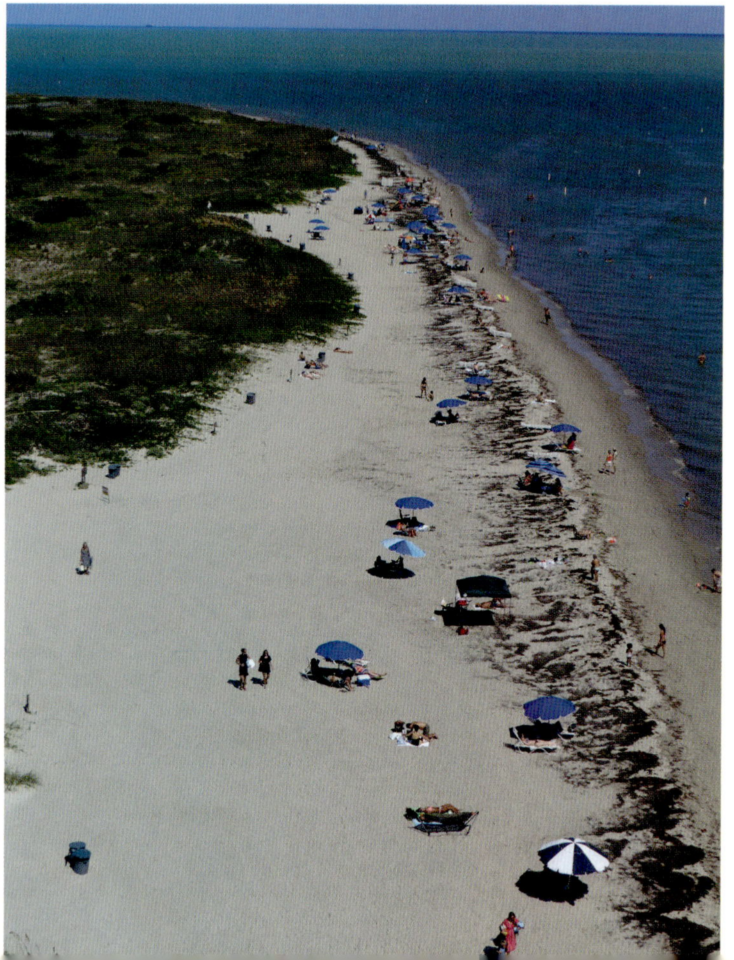

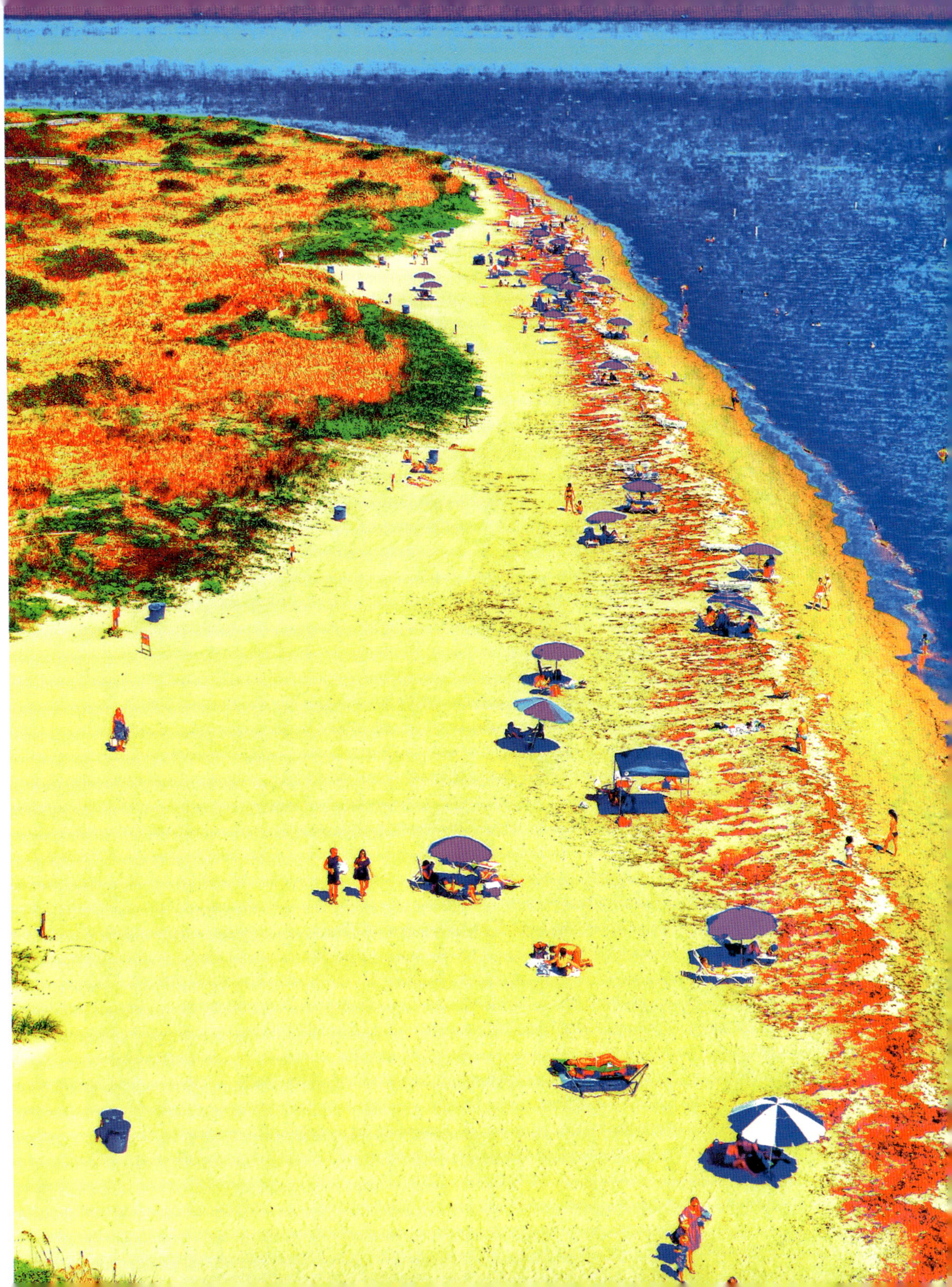

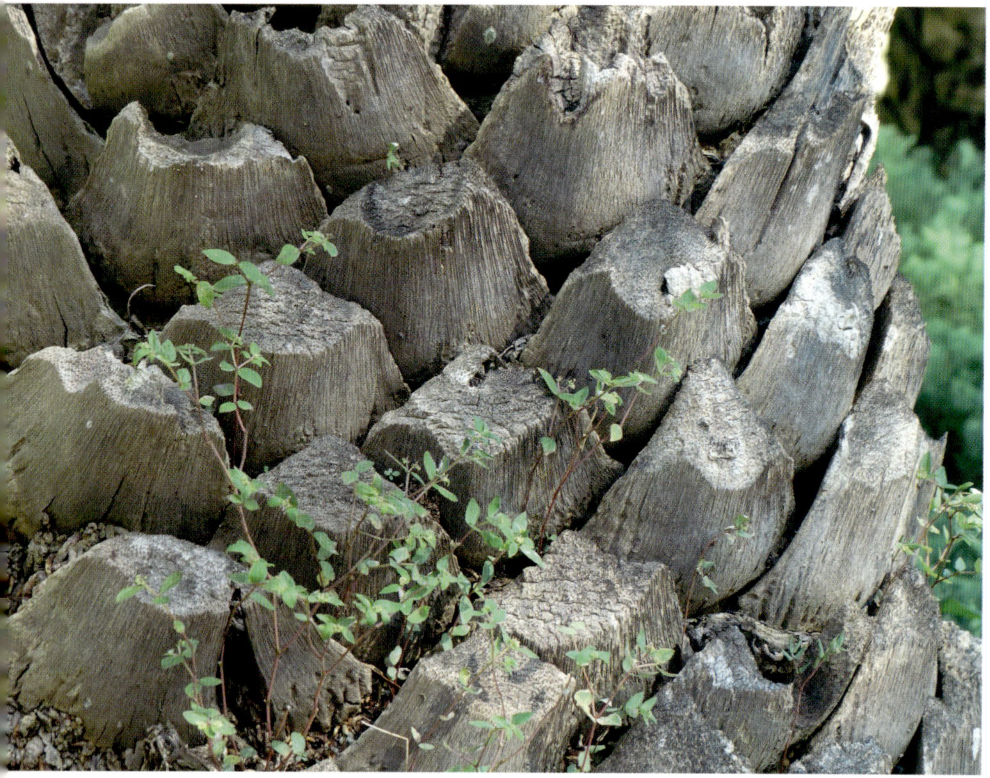

PALM BARK

The bark is rough
Yet supports small plants
A paradox

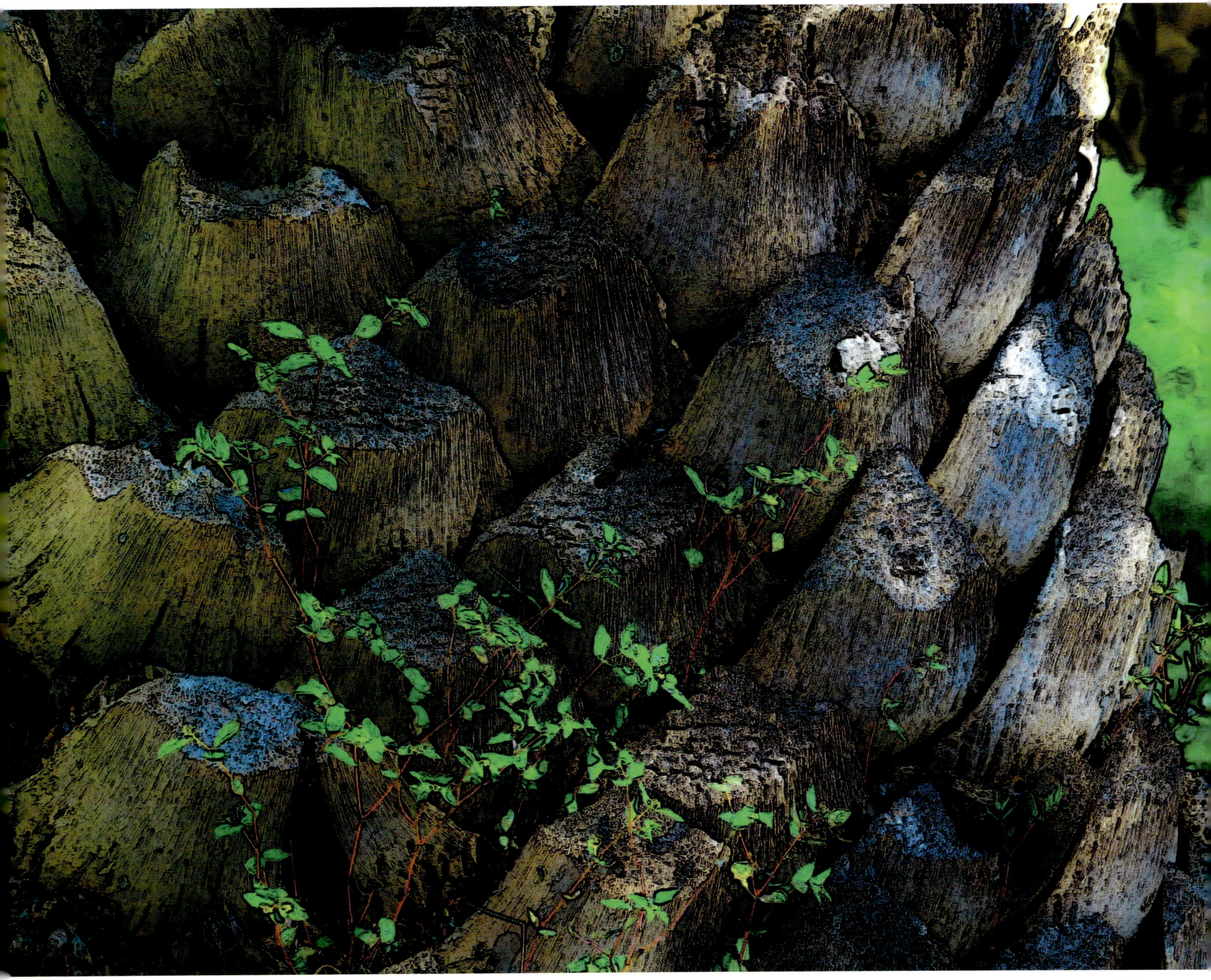

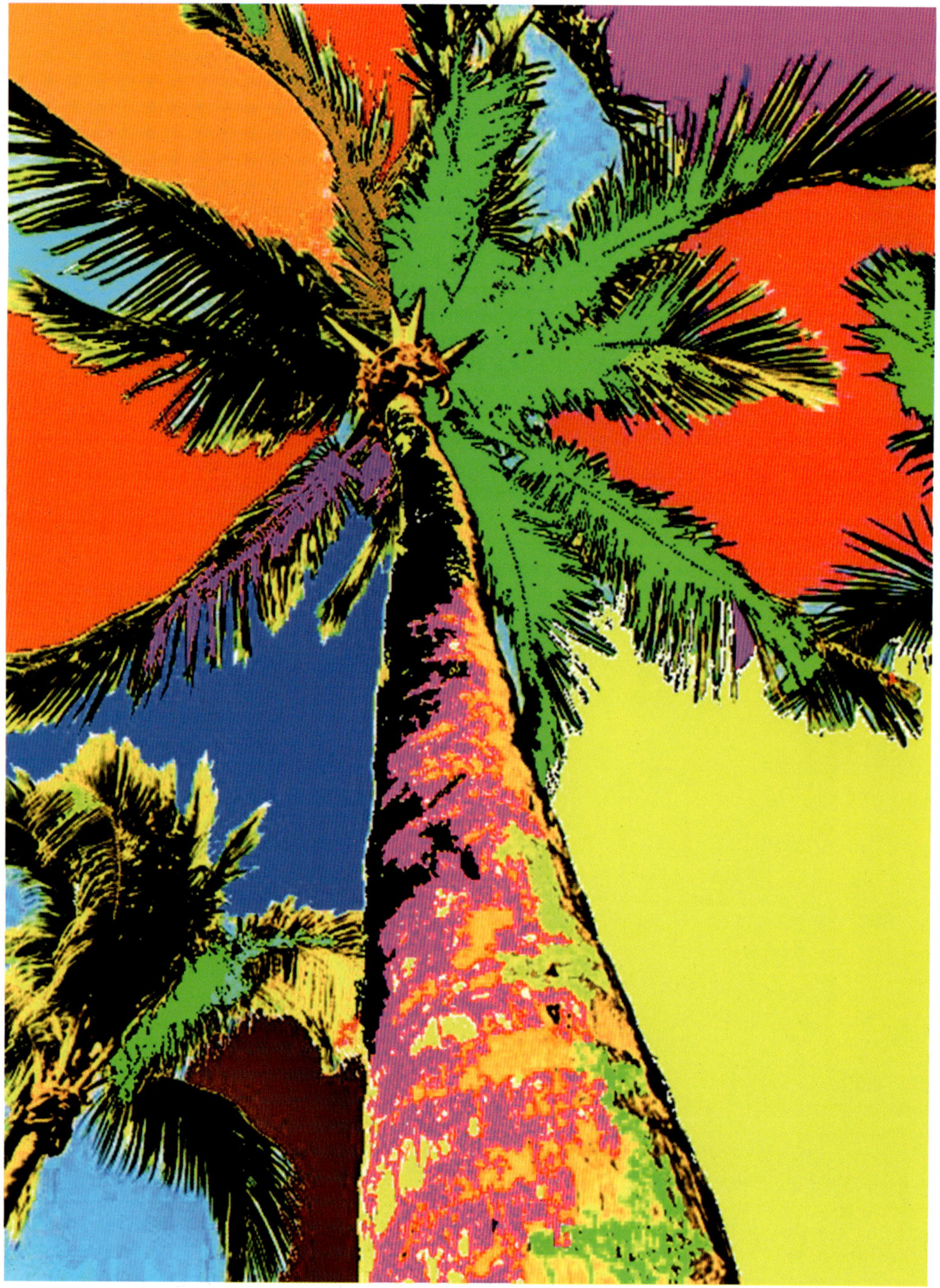

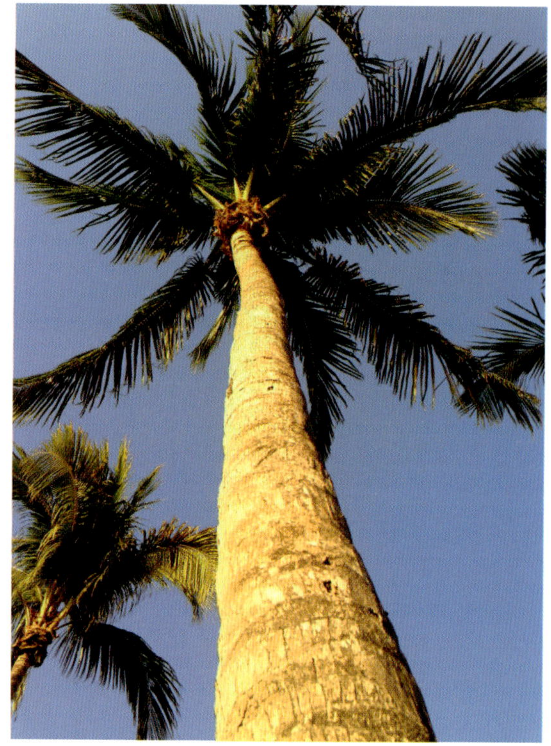

PALM TREE
PINWHEELS

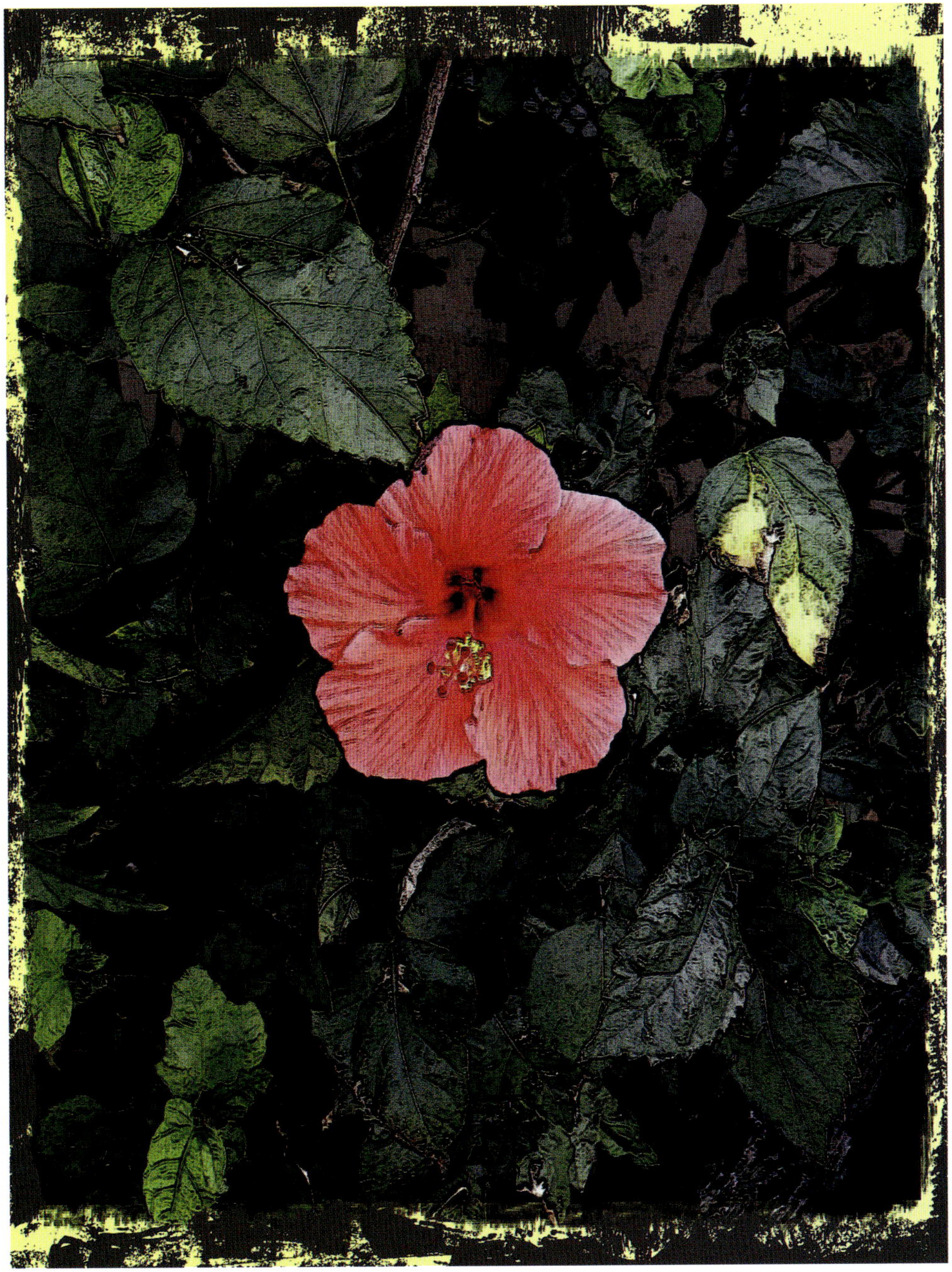

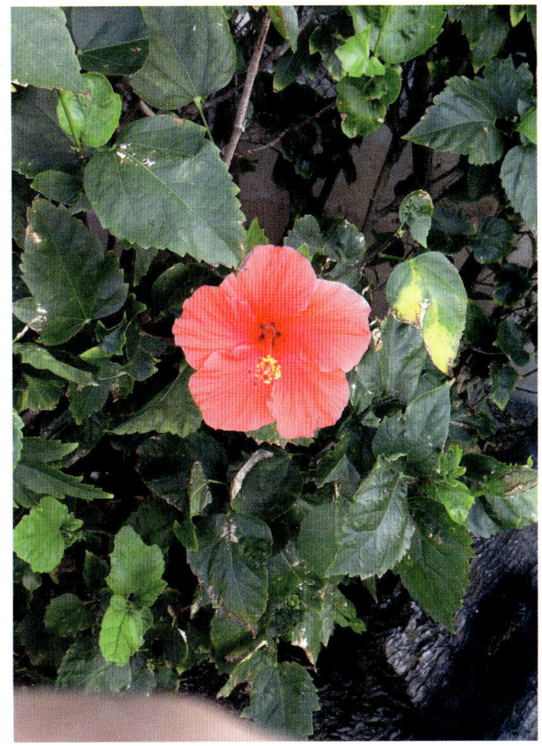

HIBISCUS

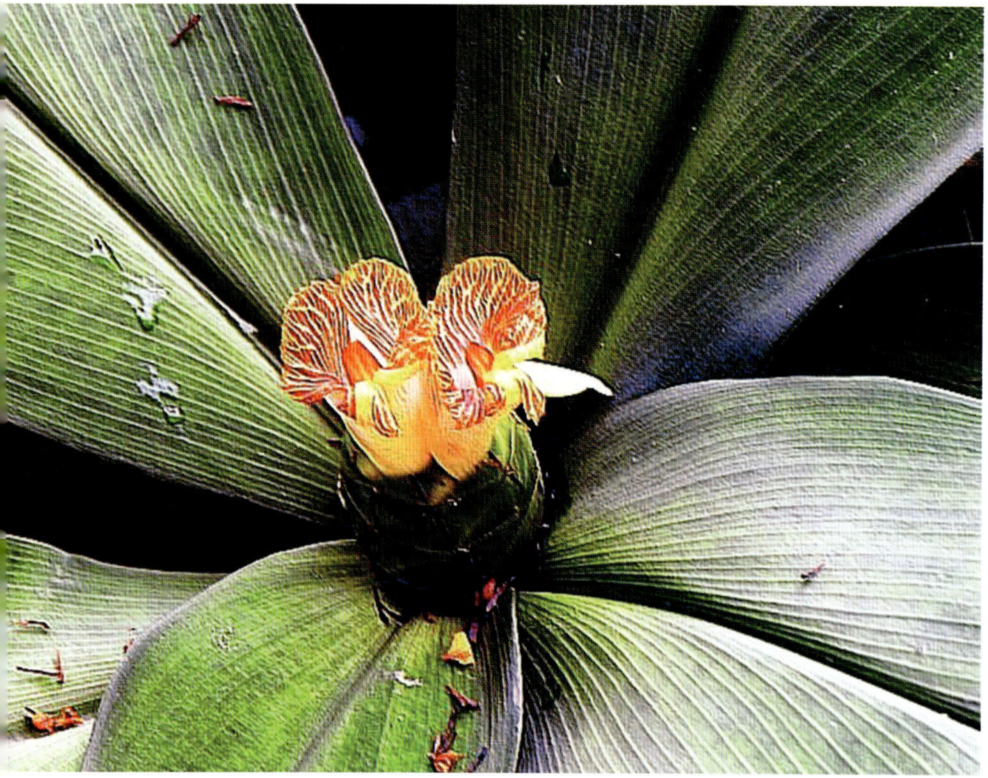

BROMELIAD

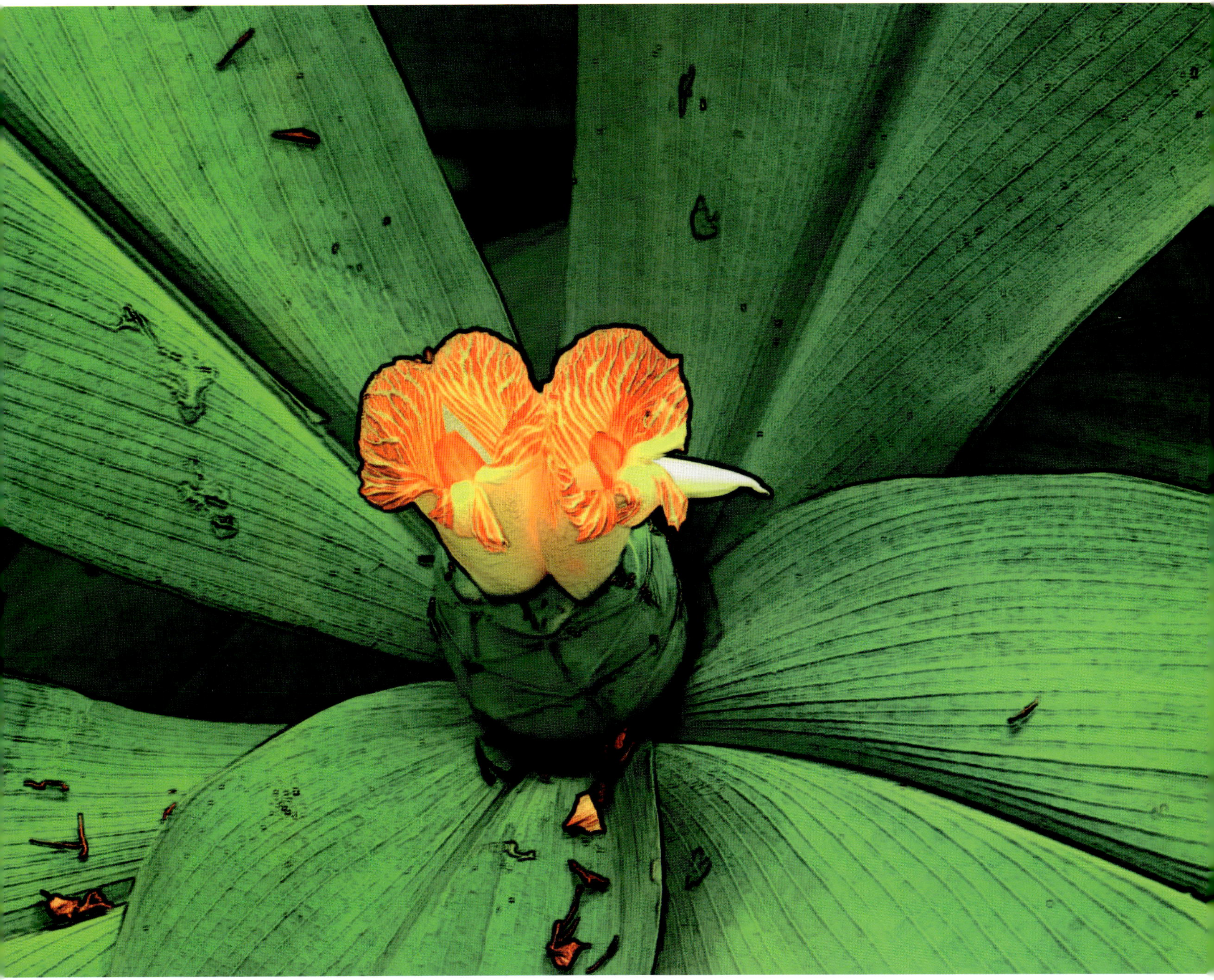

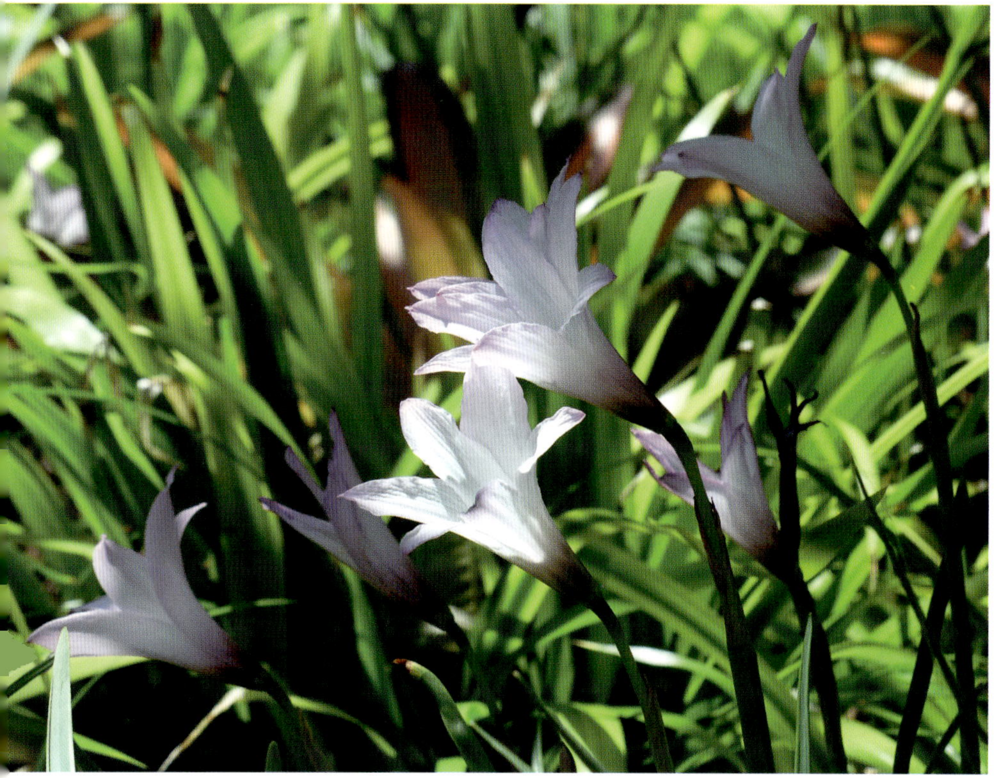

PURPLE SUNLIGHT

Reflected light
Affects the colors of flowers
Reaching out for attention
Joyful

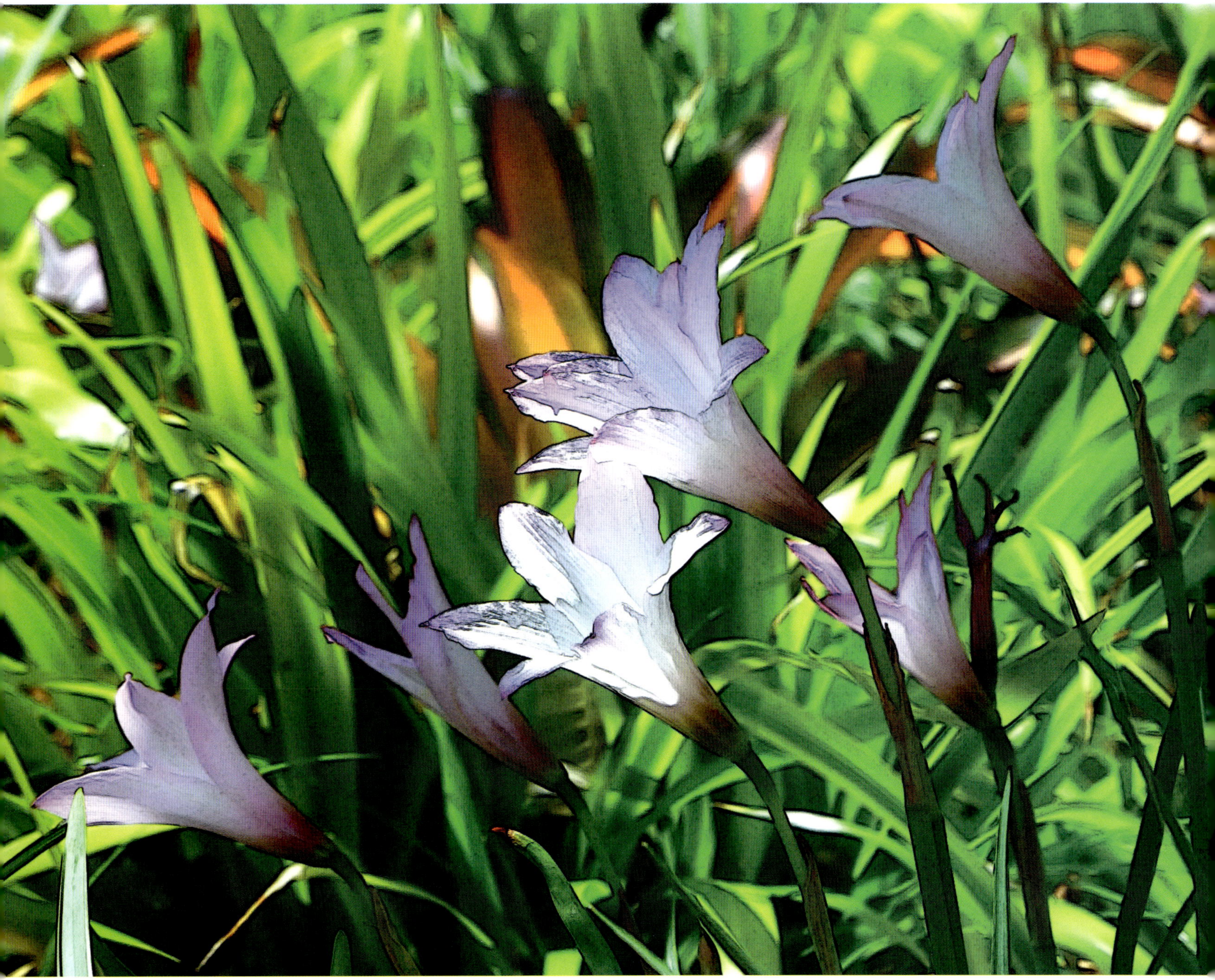

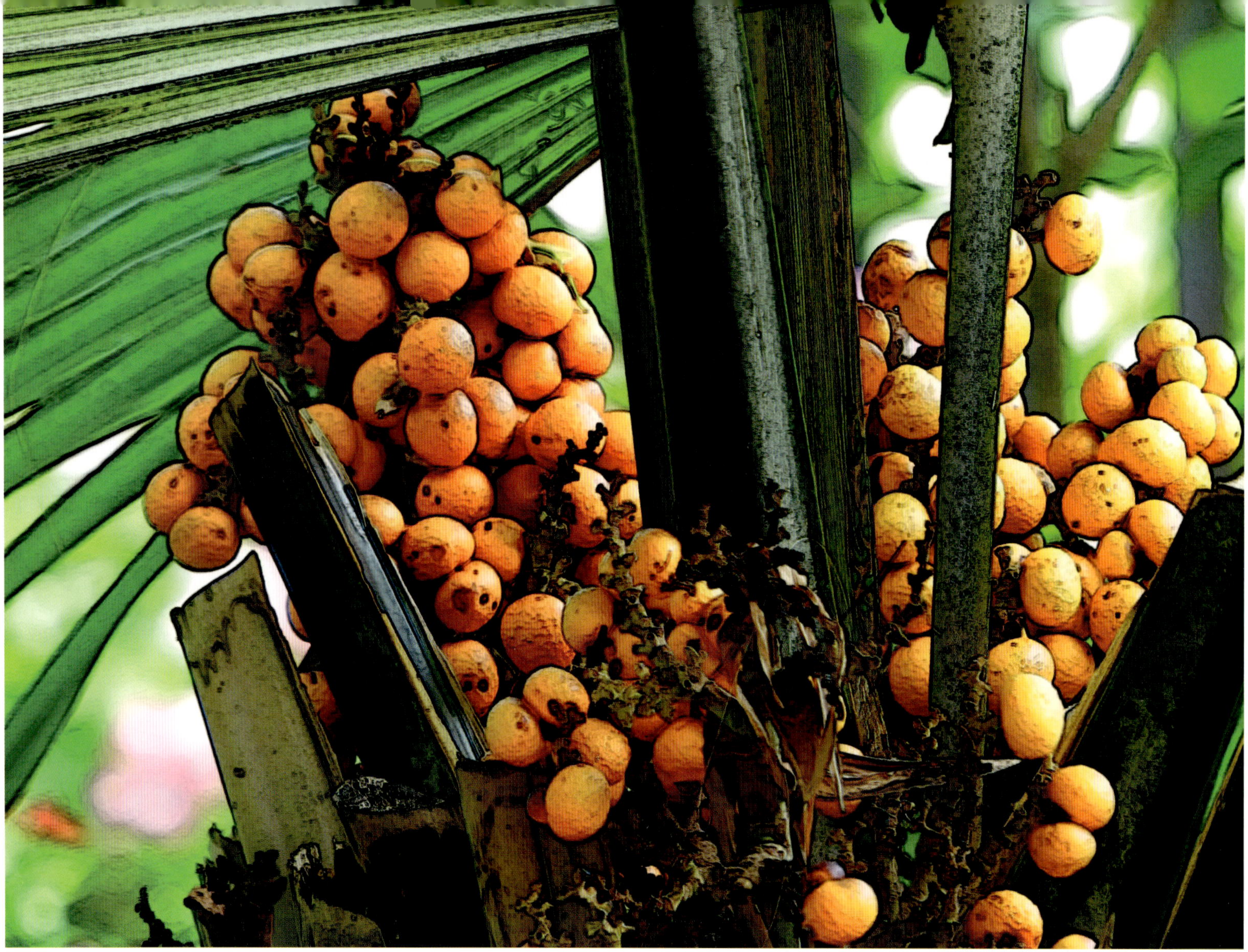

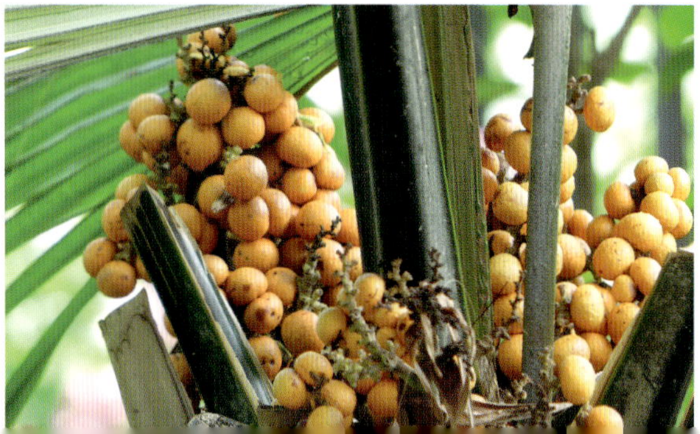

PALM TREE SEEDS

The seeds of a palm
The children of a tree
Perpetual reproduction

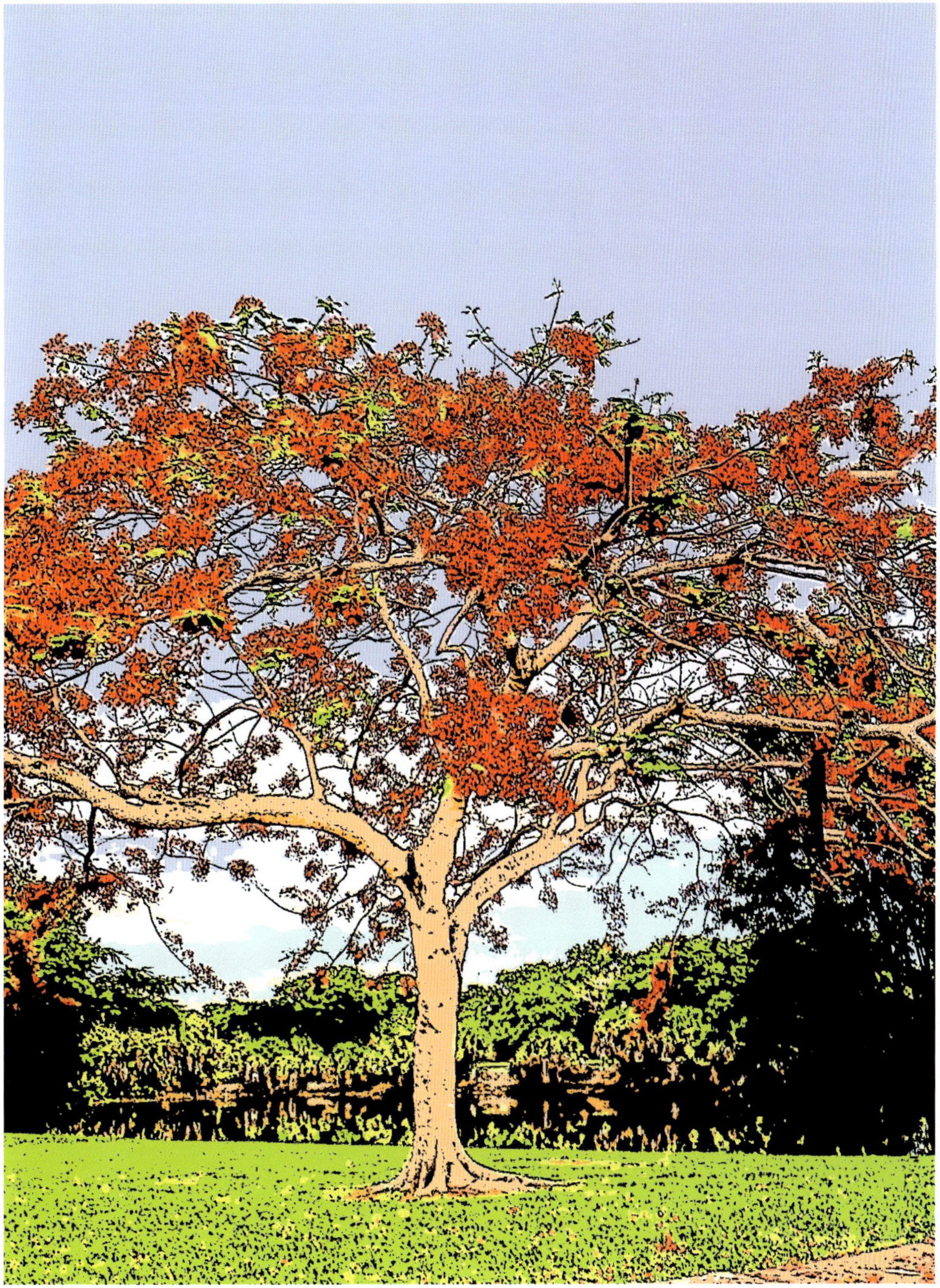

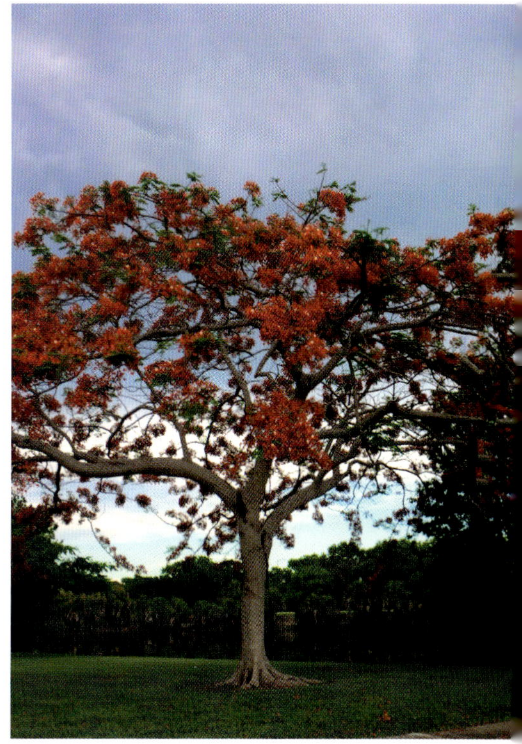

POINCIANA

A gorgeous tree

Large canopy

Red leaves

Stately

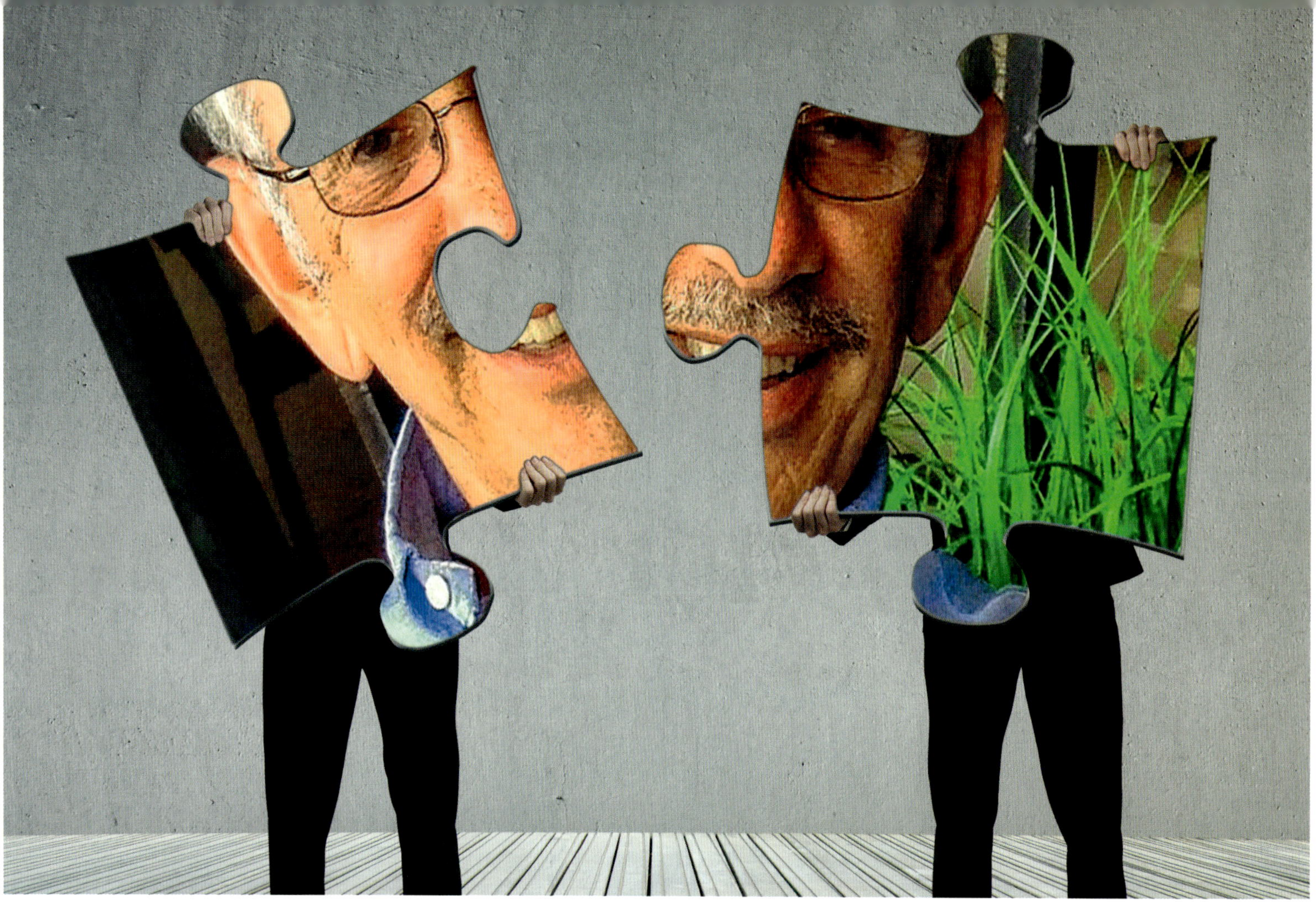

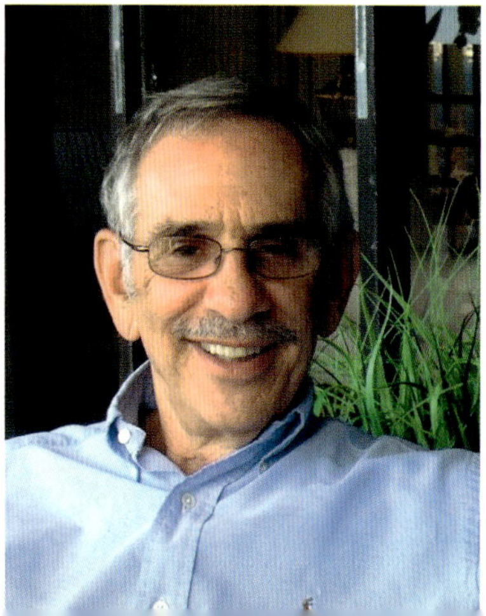

ABOUT THE AUTHOR

Early in his career, Hank Klein was a photographer for the Miami News and later became a University of Miami staff photographer under the tutelage of Wilson Hicks, the first executive editor of Life magazine. In his thirties, Klein put photography on the hobby shelf to enter the world of business, becoming a commercial real estate executive and community leader. In 2012, he suffered a devastating stroke that left him severely incapacitated. During rehabilitation, Klein rediscovered his love of photography and uses today's technology to create unique works of art. Nearly 100 percent recovered, he lives in Miami with his wife, Lisa Sloat.